SECOND EDITION

Cases in Public Policy Analysis

GEORGE M. GUESS AND PAUL G. FARNHAM

Georgetown University Press
Washington, DC

Georgetown University Press, Washington, D.C.
Printed in the United States of America

10 9 8 7 6 5 4 3 2 1   2000

Library of Congress Cataloging-in-Publication Data
Guess, George M.
    Cases in public policy analysis / George M. Guess, Paul G.
Farnham -- 2nd ed.
        p.   cm.
    Originally published: New York : Longman, c1989.
    Includes bibliographical references.
    ISBN 0-87840-767-7 (cloth : alk. paper). -- ISBN 0-87840-768-5
(paper : alk. paper)
    1. Policy sciences. I. Farnham, Paul G. II. Title.
H97.G84   2000
361.6'1--dc21
                                        99-38852
                                          CIP

"Strikes me a fellow ought to use his insight, not just a chest of tools to make discoveries. A good sailor could find his way at sea even if he didn't have instruments. Man ought to develop his brain, not depend on tools."

"Ye-uh, but if there were charts and quadrants in existence, a sailor that cruised off without 'em would be a chump."

– SINCLAIR LEWIS, *Arrowsmith*

C O N T E N T S

P R E F A C E

There are three distinguishing features in the second edition of *Cases in Public Policy Analysis* that may influence its adoption for upper division or graduate public policy courses. First, the text necessarily takes a political economy approach because it was written by a political scientist and an economist, both of whom have consulted extensively with various government agencies. This provides an important institutional and political dimension in applying economic methods to policy problems. Second, the text focuses only on the problems and tools of policy analysis rather than the entire policymaking cycle, of which the latter includes policy development, approval, implementation, and evaluation. Third, the book uses cases rather than a text/problem approach.

As William Dunn has noted, researchers and practitioners in the public policy field are still grappling with the issue of how to maximize technocratic guidance without ignoring the values and decision styles that are inherent in policy implementation (Dunn 1994, 55). Many recognize that the field needs analytic methods to ensure balance. However, excessive faith in technocratic policymaking is naïve, whereas excessive emphasis on values and decision styles may result in arbitrary decisionmaking. Policy analysts should provide useful information to decisionmakers, including the results of formal quantitative analyses, to find solutions to policy problems. However, analysts must be aware that decisionmakers will consider these results in the context of the values of the relevant stakeholders in the policy process.

We use the case method to provide decision-relevant information for the following reasons. First, cases typically provide more thorough knowledge than the text method. Robert Anthony and David Young have observed that there is better understanding when students use applied knowledge in the analysis and derivation of solutions for cases than when they read and memorize text materials (Anthony and Young 1994, 14–15). Second, cases give students insights into real-world complexity. Textbooks often use hypothetical examples or provide incomplete analyses of "messy," complex problems. Third, cases show students the importance of communicating the results of technical analyses. Many policy failures can be traced to the inability of technicians to simplify the bases for decisionmaking and communicate this to the public. Cases also demonstrate how decisions are often made under extreme time constraints and with limited information.

Some may argue that cases are ambiguous and frustrating because the reader cannot simply apply formal scientific methods to them. However, most nontrivial policy problems cannot be solved solely by the application of scientific principles and different quantitative techniques. Values are important, data are often incomplete and ambiguous, and time is usually short for obtaining results. Real-world decisionmakers must work under these constraints or be held accountable for not making decisions under pressure.

The book does not take a "pure" case approach, however. It includes background text material and basic presentations of analytic techniques useful for sorting out relevant facts and reaching conclusions on each issue. It is hoped that this combination of case information and text materials will enable students to learn more about how standard public policy topics, such as problem definition and cost-benefit analysis, are applied to real-world policy issues.

Both authors wish to acknowledge the advice and assistance of John Samples, director of Georgetown University Press, as well as one of the reviewers, William N. Dunn of the University of Pittsburgh. George Guess wishes to acknowledge collaboration during the past seven years with Mike Stevens and Malcolm Holmes of the World Bank. Their work together has expanded his horizons to include the institutional dimension of public policy. Going even further back, Dr. Guess would also like to acknowledge the efforts of his two major public policy teachers, Michael D. Reagan and Charles R. Adrian of the University of California, Riverside, to teach him policy analysis.

Paul Farnham acknowledges his many colleagues at the Centers for Disease Control and Prevention, and the public administration students he has taught at Georgia State University, who have forced him to consider how economic evaluation techniques can be applied in real-world policy settings.

The authors alone are responsible for any defects in this book.

References

Anthony, Robert and Young, David. (1994). *Management Control in Nonprofit Organizations,* 5th ed., Instructor's Guide (Homewood, Ill: Irwin).
Dunn, William N. (1994). *Public Policy Analysis: An Introduction,* 2d ed. (Englewood Cliffs, N.J.: Prentice Hall).

AUTHOR BIOGRAPHIES

George M. Guess has been a senior public administration specialist at Development Alternatives, Inc. (DAI) in Bethesda, Maryland, since 1994. Prior to that he was associate professor of public administration and political science in the Department of Public Administration and Urban Studies at Georgia State University. During his leave of absence (1991–1993), he worked for the International Monetary Fund's Fiscal Affairs Department as a headquarters-based consultant and for the World Bank as a short-term consultant on public expenditure management missions. In these capacities he worked extensively in Latin America and Eastern Europe. He has published in such journals as *Policy Sciences, Public Budgeting,* and *Finance and Public Administration Review.* He is the editor of *Public Policy and Transit System Management* (Greenwood Press, 1990). Since 1994 he has been an adjunct professor in the Graduate Public Policy Institute at Georgetown University.

Paul G. Farnham is an associate professor in the Department of Economics, School of Policy Studies, Georgia State University, Atlanta. His areas of specialization are health care economics, the economics of HIV/AIDS, public sector economics, and public policy. He has been a visiting health economist at the Centers for Disease Control and Prevention, where he analyzed the economic costs of HIV/AIDS to business and worked on the economic analysis of HIV prevention programs. His research has been published in journals such as *Public Health Reports,* the *American Journal of Preventive Medicine,* and *Inquiry.* His earlier research on local government debt and expenditure decisions has been published in the *Southern Economic Journal, Public Choice, Public Finance Quarterly, Urban Affairs Quarterly,* and *Social Science Quarterly,* among other journals. Farnham received his B.A. in economics from Union College, Schenectady, New York, and his M.A. and Ph.D. in economics from the University of California, Berkeley.

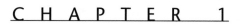

C H A P T E R 1

Overview

Policy analysis is less concerned with pure theory building than in producing information useful in political settings for resolution of defined social problems. The subject of "public" policy analysis focuses on the more profound "root" causes as well as the immediate individual behavior patterns of social problems, such as crime, that can be affected by the "admittedly limited tools government has at its disposal" (Paris and Reynolds 1983, 34). Akin to an applied public economics or political science discipline, policy analysis uses methods and tools from economics, political science, sociology and other related fields for problem solving. Policy analysis is an applied social science discipline that attempts to produce useful information for policy decisionmaking in political contexts (Dunn 1994, 4). Policy analysis is practiced by consultants to government, decisionmakers in staff government agencies, and other roles that perform analysis for decisionmaking.

Unfortunately, sound policy analysis is not always in demand by public-sector organizations. Or, if analysis is generated, the results are often not used. Given tight work schedules and scarce analytic resources, very few decisions in public-sector organizations are actually informed by thorough analysis. In addition, there is the often perverse tendency of management in large organizations to engage in protective stupidity and persistence in error despite contrary policy evidence. Once a questionable objective is established (e.g., sustaining the Diem government in Vietnam through aid policy in the 1950s), the routines of bureaucratic process can subdue intellect and encourage "wooden-headedness." In such cases, contrary advice about objectives and existing policy failures is ignored from those who were supposed to provide the major source of critical analysis in the first place (e.g., the National Security Council). Ideological commitment to fixed positions can add to bureaucratic inflexibility and shield organizations from the benefits of critical policy analysis. Decisionmaking under conditions of an overriding objective can create self-deceit and encourage "working the levers without rational expectations" (Tuchman 1984, 377).

The danger is that persistent action contrary to analytic advice will discourage both in-house production of policy analysis and serious utilization of data to change institutional behavior. The problem of unused policy analysis may be due, in part, to the apparent complexity of policy analysis itself. Analysis often appears to be an endless process, with myriad variables and overwhelming amounts of data to be considered. In some contexts analysis takes on a life of its own. Strategy meetings, multiple revisions of reports, and maximum participation of staff take up time and resources with no hard decisions reached. In some organizations, analysis may be good public relations and performed as an end in itself. In addition, even if institutional barriers to the utilization of policy analysis are minimal, policymakers are often besieged with contrary advice on seemingly sound analytical bases.

Policymakers are answerable to special interests, such as lobbies and financial contributors, and not because they are obtuse or venal. Public servants also understand the pull of populist forces and often disregard policy recommendations in final decisionmaking. For example, a $6 million, twenty-month study of the Washington, D.C., police department's structural and management problems by the firm of Booz•Allen & Hamilton produced many recommendations to improve performance: the firm recommended moving 157 administrative officers to street patrols. As of 1998, none of the Booz•Allen recommendations had been implemented (Thompson 1998). It was also found that many of the consultants' findings and recommendations were in previous reports already filed at the police department. This suggests the need for policy analysis that weighs technical solutions with political feasibility.

For such practical reasons, this book seeks to integrate economic analysis with politics. Economic analysis, in our view, needs to take account of institutional and management politics. A political economy approach teaches us that "neither markets nor governments are perfect and that one must accept compromise" (Dixit 1997, 10; Wolf 1993).

This suggests a political context into which analysis must fit or be ignored. The political context of public policy formulation and implementation underscores the need for policymakers to have field experience, as well as a good grasp of the facts, and possess sound judgment. No collections of policy techniques, such as those found in this book, can replace judgment—the ability to apply wisdom and experience to facts and analysis. Sound judgment is the product of experiences informing one or more intellectual framework. These frameworks allow the policymaker or the analyst to reject irrelevant facts and include only what is necessary for decision. Policymakers use data and techniques to narrow their range of uncertainty. A paradox is that data and techniques can rarely provide complete answers or certainty of results. Under the pressure of deadlines and crises, provision of complete answers is rarely possible. Even the most sound, most thorough analysis can rarely foresee the unintended consequences that occur during policy implementation. More important, policymakers must be able to judge for themselves which facts are important; without judgment, policymakers and managers will remain hopelessly confused and at the mercy of multiple advisors. Bureaucratic survival experts can diffuse responsibility through committees, multiple clearance processes, and the like—but ultimately they have to be accountable for processing policy advice and making a decision.

Policy analysts can help by providing information that serves the short time frames of public sector decisionmakers. For example, "windshield surveys" (Development Alternatives, Inc. 1997) were used in a USAID project in Estonia to assess civil service capacity instead of conducting skills inventories that require much more time and resources. In planning new policy areas (e.g., welfare reform), analysis can take the form of "rolling designs" that permit learning through trial and error, rather than methods that recommend linear, multiyear courses of policy action. Through such analytic shortcuts as "pilot studies," "quick feasibility studies," and "action research" surveys, marginal sacrifices in analytic accuracy can be made for the benefit of short-term decision needs. Policy analysis need not lead to abstract reports using heavy mathematics and linear programming (in some cases, the primary value of such approaches may be to scare away opponents of one's recommendations). Finally, policy analysts may anticipate complex social and institutional resistance to proposed policies and provide such alternative processes as "public deliberation" to resolve tensions between the objectives of efficiency (minimize inputs to achieve a given level of output) and effectiveness (a given level of outcome or improvements in target population for least cost) (Roberts 1997).

This book attempts to simplify policy analysis and provide useful tools to practitioners who have little time or resources to use the most advanced technical methods available in the discipline of public policy. Nevertheless, the book recognizes the need to learn basic tools for diagnosis, analysis, and evaluation of policy problems. As in the first edition of *Cases in Public Policy Analysis,* this edition will attempt to build up those skills by providing cases in "messy" problem settings to which the tools may be applied.

Public Policy and Its Formulation

"Policies" derive from legislative statutes and administrative rules. In practice, they are systems of rules and standards affecting the public interest that are established by rulemaking bodies such as parliaments, legislatures, and administrative regulatory agencies. Policies can be formulated for internal institutional governance or for provision of external programs and services. For example, fiscal policies to reform pension systems, reduce subsidies to consumers and producers, revise tax rates, or control budget expenditures are largely internal policies. "Internal" policies are reflected in nonservice or nonprogrammatic expenditures, tax expenditures (or tax breaks), and other hidden subsidies to the private sector. These have obvious "external" effects on public welfare, resource use, and other public programs. For instance, patented mineral claims on federal lands worth thousands of times their market value are sold to private miners who need only demonstrate the existence of hard-rock minerals. Despite the immense value of these claims to mining firms, the U.S. government receives no royalties. For their part, mining companies in the western United States have polluted more than 3,000 miles of streams with hard-rock mining wastes (*The Economist* 1997).

In the literature on public policy the distinction is often made among "policies," "programs," and "projects." Often the three terms are used interchangeably without great damage to understanding. Methods of applied "policy" analysis are often the same as those used for "program analysis" (Poister 1978). Nevertheless, a distinction is useful. For example, transportation policies can be broken into programs for land and air, with specific projects developed in the surface program for road and rail systems. Policies can apply internally to particular groups—a policy manual for employees of the Department of Defense (DOD) or a faculty manual for university professors—while defense policies emanating from such agencies as DOD would affect all citizens of the United States directly or indirectly. Employment policies dealing with such internal matters as recruitment, promotion, pay, retirement, severance, and grievances are formulated within DOD consistent with U.S. Civil Service requirements. Supported by internal systems, public policies and programs are aimed at external clients.

Policies are analyzed, monitored, and evaluated in regular cycles (described below and represented in Figure 1.1) that involve public inputs, partisan alliances, and coalition strategies in an effort to defeat opponents. "Analysis" refers to formal, critical examination of issues or problems in the context of incomplete facts and figures. To complete the process on time for clients, the analytic process requires application of simplifying theories, frameworks, methods, and factual assumptions. Data are normally missing. The best analysts cannot afford to wait for better data—that will result in historical analysis. The best analysts make clear and transparent assumptions that can be verified or challenged—to move the process forward and improve policy results.

The analytic process is also part of the political process. Logically, many question the ability of governments to identify high-return policies and programs and fund them through a political process. Analysis is often politicized. But the value of sound, objective analysis with clear assumptions remains. For example, many public policies such as national defense are formulated through the mechanism of "iron triangle" interaction between the U.S. president with the National Security Council, Central Intelligence Agency (CIA), State Department, policy experts in think tanks and universities, relevant defense contractors, and lobbyists. Iron triangles form between and among legislative committees/subcommittees, special interests, and parts of the executive bureaucracy with stakes in the outcome (Lowi 1979). Contrary to notions of separation of power, the iron triangle mechanism suggests that joint action can overcome opposition. These annual, and largely concerted, efforts produce a policy with a price tag that is translated into a budget request. At the same time, Congress, under heavy influence from "issue networks" of regional and weapons systems defense experts and intense lobbying from the defense industry and DOD itself, reviews and approves the request and translates it into budget authority or appropriations.

In the literature iron triangles are considered to be a stabilizing, predictable force in policymaking, but "issue networks" are considered to be the opposite. These are "shared-knowledge groups" of experts who have developed an industry on particular policies. The groups keep particular policy issues on the agenda (e.g., health care reform) and provide substantial influence to each member of the network. At the same time, the activities of issue networks complicate political calculability and decrease predictability (Heclo 1978). For example, the complex issues surrounding electric utility industry deregulation have been subject to analyses by networks and shifting coalitions of interest and advocacy groups and think tanks. In legislative terms, the complexity perpetuated by the activities of issue networks can slow reform in the sense that policy approval and implementation are delayed (Hamilton 1997). Information is generated beyond institutional processing capabilities.

Prospective or ex-ante policy analysis also needs to consider the implementation context. It may be evident that structural features will doom the policy to failure unless institutional constraints are considered beforehand. For instance, approved policies are typically implemented by drawing down budgetary funds from appropriations allocated by Congress. Obligations and outlays will be made by relevant agencies, such as DOD and Department of State in the defense area, and throughout the fiscal year crises will occur that require reprogramming and transfer of funds, emergency actions that require supplemental appropriations, and new initiatives to meet new demands. Other discretionary policy expenditures in health, education, transportation, and the environment operate similarly to those in defense.

Policies are thus "rule systems" that can be made by legislatures or administrative agencies. They are the formal rules that form part of the institutional framework of society. Viewed as a set of "rules of the game" that are then implemented by organizations, the dimensions of political debate and conflict over the meaning of these rules will vary in each case. Politics as the use of resources to exercise influence over a decision is virtually synonymous with lobbying in the case of legislative authorizations and most general fund policy appropriations by Congress or, indeed, any parliament around the world. For this reason politics is often confused with policy. For operational purposes, we consider politics a means of developing policy rule systems: political discretion is exercised at least in part on the basis of values; policy tends to change because political values change.

In the realm of policymaking, political values often boil down to partisan values. For example, criminal justice policies that advocate increases in recurrent expenditures for police and prisons may be more or less "valuable" to the public than balanced-budget policies. The reason is that public values frequently change because of cultural influences as much as from the influence of economic policy analysis. Values affect policy outcomes when they form political and analytical biases, and, as noted, values can be expressed collectively as the result of iron triangle politicking and horse trading. For instance, studies disagree on the effects of minimum wage hikes on unemployment. The issue often boils down to discretionary choices by employers who, in the face of higher required wage payments, can either continue to fill vacancies (raising employment) or find ways to economize on jobs and maintain output. For the policy analyst, this means weighing and comparing the risks of potential costs in employer profits and consumer prices against the benefits to poorer workers in increased minimum wages (Card and Krueger 1998). This is technical analysis that leads clearly to the point where decisions must be made on explicit values.

In some cases major policy "fiascoes" can be linked to just such value distortion in policymaking (Bovens and 't Hart 1996). As will be noted in chapter 2, value differences commonly arise among experts in problem definition that will affect program design and later results on the ground. For example, criminal justice strategies based on the values of deterrence and tough enforcement to change the utility preferences and cost-benefit calculations of criminals are, in principle, appealing (Paris and Reynolds 1983, 35–36). But the strategies have not been very effective in reducing the incidence of major crimes. By contrast, community policing strategies based on values of "rehabilitation" and such root causes of crime as poverty and lack of education have been more effective. This latter, more progressive approach to crime control is credited for major drops in urban crime in major U.S. cities in the late 1990s.

It could be argued that the U.S. policymaking system has evolved to the point where the ethical public norm is the reduction of undue political influences during policymaking. It was not always this way. Political machines and their party affiliates ran city councils and state legislatures for many years around the turn of the nineteenth century. In the early 1900s, local government activities were often regulated in detail to provide discretionary revenue for city treasuries from the organized, often criminal, machines that controlled and financed "paper" governments. Detailed policy rules and regulations functioned largely as a means of setting prices and negotiating exemptions (Steffens 1931).

On the other hand, attempts to "purify" policy implementation of politics or to ignore the benefits of political support for policy successes often result in an overacademic, puritanical approach to policymaking. Political will counts for policy success, and since much of this success derives from the knowledge of such local officials as mayors and governors, key groups will support them and cooperate with them. Policy analysis, therefore, needs to include political factors that affect policy implementation; otherwise such analysis risks providing recommendations that lack feasibility. In a recent book on welfare policy, for example, Rebecca Blank charged that Aid to Families with Dependent Children (AFDC) suffers from weaknesses in policy design that could have been corrected if only Americans had avoided political rhetoric and paid adequate attention to sound policy research (Blank 1997). But according to the reviewer, Theda Skocpol, "We learn little about who was purveying the rhetoric, and why it resonated so broadly. Because Blank fails to analyze what went wrong politically for welfare in the past, she cannot project feasible strategies for the future" (Skocpol 1997, 119).

In policy analysis, there is a rough consensus that political and technical factors have their separate places in the process and that they should not violate each other's territory. In the case of administrative rule systems it can be seen that politics has a much more circumscribed role. In the United States, the Administrative Procedures Act of 1946 (APA) distinguishes "formal" from "informal" rulemaking proceedings: formal rulemaking is procedurally identical to formal adjudication (Pierce, Shapiro, and Verkuil 1985, 315). Formal rulemaking effectively means a trial that bogs an agency down in formal testimony and factual issues that divert attention from important policy considerations. So, in administrative law an agency that intends to adopt a prescriptive standard of action, valid in a number of settings for a variety of parties, cannot realistically proceed by an incremental, case-by-case method. Instead, the agency must adopt informal rulemaking that replaces trial-like activities with an opportunity for affected members of the public to comment on proposed rules.

Informal rulemaking is a forum for establishing administrative rules with a minimum of political interference. Such rulemaking implies a negative role for politics beyond a certain threshold where the public interest is a technical matter. That threshold is the end of the "notice-and-comment" period (post-comment) for "interested" or "affected" parties when an agency publishes a final rule accompanied by a "statement of basis and purpose," which is subject to judicial review. The intent of the threshold is to confine the natural bargaining and lobbying to contacts of record within the structure of the rule-making process during the notice-and-comment period. Therefore, any unrecorded contact with interested parties during this notice-and-comment period is considered ex-parte contact and is assumed to contaminate the rulemaking process with politics—meaning that a resulting rule can be challenged as arbitrary and capricious. Informal rulemaking resembles the process of legislating, with all the implications of politics and lobbying.

As one example, Congress had granted the National Highway Traffic Safety Administration (NHTSA) the authority to set reasonable safety standards (i.e., policies). In 1980, after an informal rulemaking process, NHTSA rescinded a section of the Federal Motor Vehicle Safety Standards (section 208) on "passive restraints" that required either seatbelts or airbags. The premise of banning ex-parte contacts during informal rulemaking is to ensure administrative neutrality. By preventing political lobbying during the diagnostic or notice-and-comment period, the informal rulemaking process attempts to reduce external influences over the selection, weighting, and substantiation of facts (Pierce, Shapiro, and Verkuil 1985, 484). One might question the premise of this bifurcated process by which administrators can only prejudge broad policy matters but not those of specific facts. But the process illustrates nicely where politics and policy are institutionally separated to produce policy rules that at least seem to not simply reflect the preferences of powerful lobbyists (Guess 1991, 160).

In practice it may be more difficult to isolate political influences from technical processes. From what we have said so far, it would seem that we seek a "neutral" policy analysis that separates political from technical decisionmaking. But this would be a naïve quest. Much debate still focuses on what we now know to be a false dichotomy. Where discretion in judgment exists, politics intrudes because support is required for one's viewpoint, technical or not. Discretion exists for practically any technical question—from the location of a road, how to pave it, how much it will cost, and who will benefit from it.

For example, the National Railroad Passenger Corporation (Amtrak) allocates revenues and ridership across its routes on a train-by-train basis, an apparently neutral technical rule. But the allocations are "strongly influenced by analytical assumptions" (Congressional Budget Office 1982, 43). How should one allocate "split-trip" passengers or those who travel on more than one route? A passenger traveling on the "Pioneer" from Denver to Seattle also travels one-third of the way along the "Zephyr" route from Chicago to Oakland. Before April 1981 the routes were treated as separate operations with identifiable costs, revenues, and mileage; but now revenues associated with the "Zephyr" portion are attributed to the "Pioneer," and only a portion of "Zephyr" operating costs are allocated to the "Pioneer." The "Pioneer's" financial performance is thereby enhanced as measured by "passenger mile/train mile" and "Zephyr" performance is downgraded (Congressional Budget Office 1982, 44). Why? Technically, the allocation can be explained by the addition of through service from Chicago to Seattle in April 1981. Politically, it may be explained by the rise of Senator Bob Packwood (R-Oregon) to become the chair of the Senate Commerce, Science, and Transportation Committee, since the higher rate of passenger miles/train mile for the "Pioneer" saved the route through his home state of Oregon from discontinuance (Guess 1984, 388).

A Framework for Policy Analysis

Having discussed the basics of policy formulation and the role of policy analysis, we should now consider how analysis fits into the cycle of policy-making and implementation, of which conceptual frameworks are similar. Whether discussing the fields of public budgeting (Axelrod 1995), management control (Anthony and Young 1994), or public policy (Patton and Sawicki 1986), there are typically four phases with roughly the same contents: formulation, analysis, implementation, and feedback. This book focuses on the policy analysis process; therefore, we concentrate only on the first two phases.

Figure 1.1 shows that the first phase consists of problem structuring and diagnosis. The second phase concentrates on those tools and techniques that forecast both policy and institutional alternatives. Policy options will have differing social and fiscal consequences; institutional arrangements will affect the probable effects of each option. These need to be reviewed before policy approval and implementation, and failure to describe the institutional constraints at this phase can lead to official demoralization and disincentives to utilize analytic information altogether. We turn our attention to the major analytic techniques for forecasting policy options, such as public pricing, cost-effectiveness, and cost-benefit techniques. The third phase

Figure 1.1: The Policy Analysis Process

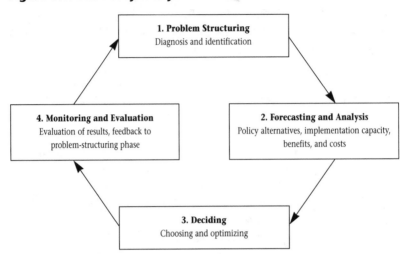

consists of deciding and approving policy proposals. The fourth phase consists of monitoring and evaluating results and feedback of information into the diagnostic and problem identification phase. The four phases constitute an analytic framework. Now, the term "framework" is commonly used to denote one or more "theories" or "models" to explain a policy problem. For example, as was said in an *Economist* article of 1998, a major problem faced by policymakers in the United States is that "no single theoretical framework explains all the unexpected changes in the current account"—that is, the sum of the country's trade surplus or deficit, income paid by or received from foreigners, and such net transfers as remittances from migrant workers (*Economist* 1998, 84)

The distinction is made between prospective or ex-ante and post-implementation analysis. Historical analysis of past policies or ongoing evaluation of new policies is called "descriptive" policy analysis (Patton and Sawicki 1986, 18). Analysis before implementation consists of prediction or projection of future states from adopting particular policy alternatives. Called "prospective" policy analysis (Patton and Sawicki 1986, 19), this requires identification of problems, comparison of alternative ways to redress problems, and generation of useful data for decisionmaking. This book will emphasize prospective or pre-implementation analysis. It focuses on useful techniques for the systematic evaluation of technical and economic feasibility, political acceptability of alternative policies, and institutional capacity to implement the selected policy.

Organization of the Book

This book will concentrate on the first, second, and fourth phases of the policy process shown in Figure 1.1: problem structuring, forecasting, and monitoring and evaluation phases. Policy analysis requires review and specification of appropriate systems, actionable problems, and feasible alternative courses of action.

In the initial problem-structuring phase, policy analysts must define problems, isolate proximate and remote causes, state objectives clearly, and specify target groups. In chapter 2 we use "Fighting Crime: The Case for Emptier Prisons" to try to define the "messy" or interdependent policy problem where existing policies contribute to new policy problems, both budgetary and ideological resources are already heavily committed, and information on policy effectiveness is lacking. Among other lessons, the case illustrates the important role of competing values or policy premises in policymaking that have little to do with technical analysis.

For example, in 1986, faced with the embarrassing task of going through the balanced budget ceiling to pay for the $1. 4 billion election year drug effort, the U.S. Senate voted within minutes to breach that ceiling. In 1986 the drug abuse problem in the United States was considered to be a "national emergency" and the idea of doing nothing was unthinkable (Greenhouse 1986). Since then, drug use and abuse has increased along with arrests for drug offenses (Treaster 1991; Schlosser 1997). But as of 1998 the drug problem is no longer the only emergency when compared with other major policy issues, even though it remains important through its links to other issues such as prison overcrowding, the problem of Mexican drug trafficking across the border, and the impact of drug use on HIV/AIDS programs. Faced with imminent failure of the balanced-budget amendment in 1997, Congress had to weigh the luxury of a balanced budget without counting Social Security trust fund revenues. This would have meant big cuts in programs such as drug enforcement to make up the difference. Placing Social Security once again off budget (as it was before the unified-budget reform in 1968) would have deprived the U.S. Treasury of substantial payroll tax revenues and forced draconian cuts to balance the budget that most political leaders were unwilling to accept. But leaving Social Security on budget to finance the balanced budget was equally open to the political charge of using a "trust fund" to pay for general revenues (Novak 1996; Blinder 1997). Studies indicate that the drug problem is probably worse now than it was in 1986, but demographics (such as the aging population) mean more pressure on elected officials to ward off threats to retirement benefits than to balance the budget or arrest drug pushers. The drug problem is "less valuable" politically than protection of Social Security benefits for those who organize strongly and vote with intense preferences for their benefits. In short, analysis of the merits of the drug issue did not drive efforts to determine the level of composition of the budget in either case—political values did.

In chapter 3 we provide guidelines and tools for the examination of institutional capacity to implement policy. It is often assumed that executing institutions matter at the margin and what really counts for effective policymaking and implementation is the amorphous quality of "political will." But institutions have a way, for better or worse, of generating momentum themselves, and if they persist long enough to develop an organizational climate or culture, can provide the necessary support to reinforce political will. Political leaders often take greater risks if they recognize solid institutional support, often translated into controls over future expenditures. Policies and executing institutions have a symbiotic relationship: the systems created by policies become the institutions that then implement the policies.

The link between policy formulation and execution becomes clearer when it is realized that not all policies are made during the formulation stage. Our framework postulates a neat division into four phases that sometimes is contradicted by reality. It will be evident from our review of financial management institutional influences that budgets and policies should not be made during implementation. Time pressures exclude analysis, and opportunities for error are increased. But such key policies as national security, particularly for sudden crises requiring Bosnia-style "peacekeeping" missions, are almost naturally "formulated" during policy execution. Banks and Straussman (1999, 136) suggest that many U.S. national security policies in the post-Korean War period have been made without authorization or appropriations and are conducted pursuant to lawful executing mechanisms to permit necessary spending. Thus, anticipation of potential constraints and opportunities filtered through executing mechanisms are critical for effective policy formulation.

Normally, institutional analysis is considered to be part of the policy implementation phase. But in this book we consider institutional analysis as part of the forecasting and monitoring and evaluation phases. To forecast policy implementation capacity, institutional analysis must proceed. Sound analysis of organizational and political variables that will affect implementation depends on data generated and analyzed as part of the regular monitoring and feedback process. The rationale for analyzing institutional contexts is that failure to anticipate control and delivery system problems will diminish the value of the overall policy analysis effort. For example, performance budget systems are frequently installed to improve the link between public expenditures and results. The easiest and most visible method is to revise the document without building underlying systems of cost-accounting and expenditure reporting that allow policymakers to actually make rational changes in allocations. Without these systems policymakers continue to rely on hunch or political influence, demoralizing civil servants who observe funds being wasted that should be serving the public interest.

As will be noted in the case included in chapter 3, "Financial Management Institutions and Public Policy," the city of Washington, D.C., is plagued by multiple dilapidated financial management systems that, through provision of distorted information and shoddy analysis, inhibit its capacity to implement basic policies, such as purchasing, road maintenance, health care, and law enforcement. These institutional systems and the skills of people who occupy institutional roles need to be reviewed, analyzed, streamlined, and managed properly through provision of professional incentives. While policy costs and benefits need to be analyzed separately, apart from related policies or other extraneous issues, factors that impede implementation cannot be ignored during the diagnostic phase.

Thus, in chapter 3 we examine the types of monitoring information necessary to forecast implementation capacity. To the extent that prospective institutional monitoring information is generated and used, institutional constraints to implementation should be reduced. In the case of implementing Washington, D.C., municipal policies, it will be evident that basic information on financial management was not available for forecasting purposes. In Washington, D.C., as elsewhere, "public policies" are systems of rules and procedures that should be taken as a given: rarely is the analyst called upon to recommend a completely new policy, so existing policies must be analyzed and revised.

There are three important questions. First, how will these rule systems work within existing organizational structures, and how will they affect policy implementation? Rule systems may discourage goal congruence between layers of the organization. Organizational roles and job descriptions may be so ill defined that, for example, senior managers may waste time in routine billing matters rather than developing programs and ensuring more effective execution of existing work. Second, how do rule systems facilitate effective management? Staff cutbacks, on the heels of civil service reforms to satisfy short-term public interest in reduced public spending, often result in management problems with remaining personnel. With insufficient personnel and resultant morale problems, senior managers are typically unable to deliver the same level and quality of services as before. Third, how effectively can organization functions be executed within existing rule systems? Very often, internal rules contribute to poor service delivery and policy results. For example, public licensing systems typically have redundant steps in the process that discourage private investment in local communities and create opportunities for bribery, kickbacks, and other forms of corruption to speed the process along.

Not uncommonly, rule systems reviews raise larger structural and functional questions. Structural issues include whether delivery should be through private contractors with public monitoring and regulation or through public institutions that set central standards and coordinate a variety of providers—private contractors, nongovernmental organizations, and public institutions. Structural questions also include management issues. What is the optimal number of layers for effective management? Should the organization be "delayered" for cost-efficiency, and at what cost in management and policy experience and potential effectiveness? How should the span of authority be defined?

Finally, functional issues must also be examined. For effective policy implementation, institutions must generate, process, and transmit useful information to managers responsible for delivery. Systems of budget allocation and allotment, personnel administration, operations and maintenance planning, program evaluation, cost and managerial accounting, payments to vendors, and cash management must all function as an integrated unit. Accurate and useful information must be available in a timely fashion. As information technology becomes more powerful, earlier problems of data scarcity have been replaced by data glut, drowning policymakers in unprocessed data and information in questionable aggregates. Failure to unclog these systems and to have them produce needed information results in the inability to plan and deliver such basic programs as transportation, education, health law enforcement, and environmental protection.

As indicated in the second phase of Figure 1.1, policy analysis requires projection of present data trends into the future so that policy alternatives can be structured with confidence. This should include analysis of both institutional and policy issues. In chapter 4 we examine how a rapid-transit agency that depends on sales tax revenues for much of its operating expenses attempts to project sales tax revenues for five years to stabilize fiscal planning. This is an extremely important area of policy analysis because recent economic uncertainties have created havoc with technical projections. Thus, more successful policy analysts have been able to creatively combine technique with judgment to satisfy clients.

In the forecasting phase, policy analysts must employ techniques to measure and compare program costs and benefits. To develop realistic trade-offs, it is essential that decisionmakers understand not only the measurement of costs and benefits but also the principles of political economy on which they are calculated. In chapter 5 we employ economic analysis to examine the issues involved with cigarette taxes. The topic of costs and prices is often erroneously viewed as the exclusive purview of accountants and of the private sector. Here we examine the question of how public pricing of cigarettes affects individual behavior and overall health care policy goals.

Health care objectives are often set in advance by government regulators as part of an effort to establish minimal quality standards. In chapter 6 we examine the issue of determining effective policy alternatives to attain a given objective, in this case HIV prevention. This technique, in which the costs of producing different levels of output to attain an agreed-upon objective are compared, is known as cost-effectiveness analysis (Axelrod 1995). Finally, in chapter 7 the strengths and weaknesses of the policy analyst's favorite (though oft misused) tool, cost-benefit analysis, are examined through an application to the case of environmental regulation.

Thus, policy analysis is a sequence of logical steps in which messy data and conflicting information are used to structure alternatives to provide a semblance of rational choice. As noted, in this book we restrict ourselves to problem definition in the diagnostic phase and institutional capacity, pricing, cost-effectiveness, and cost-benefit analysis in the forecasting phase. It is our view that the analyst who masters these techniques through case analyses will be capable of anticipating problems and resolving them during the actual policy implementation and evaluation phases.

References

Anthony, Robert and David B. Young. (1994). *Management Control in Nonprofit Organizations,* 5th ed. (Homewood, Ill.: Irwin).

Axelrod, Donald. (1995). *Budgeting For Modern Government,* 2d ed. (New York: St. Martin's).

Banks, William C. and Jeffrey D. Straussman. (1999). "Defense Contingency Budgeting in the Post-Cold-War Period," *Public Administration Review* (March/April), pp. 135–45.

Blinder, Alan S. (1997). "Constitutional Clutter," *Washington Post* (7 February).

Blank, Rebecca. (1997). *It Takes a Nation: A New Agenda for Fighting Poverty.* (Princeton, N.J.: Princeton University Press).

Bovens, Mark and Paul 't Hart. (1996). *Understanding Policy Fiascoes* (New Brunswick, N.J.: Transaction Publishers).

Card, David and Alan B. Krueger. (1998). "Unemployment Chimera," *Washington Post* (6 March).

Congressional Budget Office. (1982). *Federal Subsidies for Rail Passenger Service: An Assessment of Amtrak* (Washington, D.C.: U.S. Government Printing Office).

Development Alternatives, Inc. (1997). *USAID Public Administration Program in Estonia, Final Report* (Bethesda, Md.: Development Alternatives, Inc.) (January), p. 21.

Dixit, Avinash. (1997). "Dismal Scientists," *Economist* (20 September), p. 10.

Dunn, William N. (1994). *Public Policy Analysis: An Introduction,* 2d ed. (Englewood Cliffs, N.J.: Prentice Hall).

Economist. (1998). "Figures to Fret About" (11 July), p. 84.

———. (1997). "How Subsidies Destroy the Land" (13 December), pp. 21–22.

Greenhouse, Linda. (1986). "Drug War vs. Budget Deficit: The Senate Blinked," *New York Times* (2 October).

Guess, George M. (1991). "The Politics of Administrative Rulemaking" in Nicholas Henry. *Doing Public Administration, Exercises in Public Management,* 3d ed. (Dubuque, Iowa: William C. Brown Publishers), pp. 157–71.

———. (1984). "Profitability Guardians and Service Advocates: The Evolution of Amtrak Training," *Public Administration Review,* 44, 5 (September/October), pp. 384–93.

Hamilton, Martha M. (1997). "Power Struggle Awaits Utility Deregulation, Competing Interests Could Short-Circuit Quick Passage of Utility Reform," *Washington Post* (12 April), H1.

Heclo, Hugh. (1978). "Issue Networks and the Executive Establishment" in Anthony King (ed.) *The New Political System* (Washington, D.C.: American Enterprise Institute), pp. 87–124.

Lowi, Theodore. (1979). *The End of Liberalism* (New York: Norton).

Novak, Robert D. (1996). "What Social Security Trust Fund?" *Washington Post* (5 October).

Paris, David C. and James F. Reynolds. (1983). *The Logic of Policy Inquiry* (New York: Longman).

Patton, Carl V. and David S. Sawicki. (1986). *Basic Methods of Policy Analysis and Planning* (Englewood Cliffs, N.J.: Prentice Hall).

Pierce, Richard J., Sidney A. Shapiro, and Paul R. Verkuil. (1985). *Administrative Law and Process* (New York: Foundation Press).

Poister, Theodore H. (1978). *Applied Program Analysis* (University Park: Pennsylvania State University Press).

Roberts, Nancy. (1997). "Public Deliberation: An Alternative Approach to Crafting Policy and Setting Direction," *Public Administration Review,* 57, 2 (March/April), pp. 124–33.

Schlosser, Eric. (1997). "More Reefer Madness," *Atlantic Monthly* (April).

Skocpol, Theda. (1997). "The Next Liberalism," *Atlantic Monthly* (April), pp. 118–22.

Steffens, Lincoln. (1931). *The Autobiography of Lincoln Steffens,* Vol. 2 (New York: Harcourt Brace Jovanovich).

Thompson, Cheryl W. (1998). "Police Using Few Ideas in Report by Consultants," *Washington Post* (26 October), D1.

Treaster, Joseph B. (1991). "From the Front Lines of the War on Drugs, a Few Small Victories," *New York Times* (24 February).

Tuchman, Barbara W. (1984). *The March of Folly: From Troy to Vietnam* (New York: Ballantine).

Wolf, Charles. (1993). *Markets or Governments: Choosing Between Imperfect Alternatives* (Cambridge: Massachusetts Institute of Technology Press).

CHAPTER 2

Problem Identification and Structuring

After an hour of careful self-counseling and

analysis, and a thorough survey and

methodolocial setting-out of his problems, the

jumbled perspectives of his life slowly

reformed and sanity resumed something like

its rightful place in the order of things.

– WILLIAM BOYD

A Good Man in Africa

The first phase of the policy analysis process is problem structuring. This requires identification and diagnosis of policy problems. Bardach (1996) and others consider problem definition to be the most important part of policy analysis. Before introducing some basic techniques to structure and to define policy problems, it will be useful to indicate why it is critical to have a proper definition before committing funds. The answer seems obvious. Given lag times between policy definition and implementation effects, as well as the potential risk of committing large sums of public funds to solving the wrong problems, problems better be defined first. Good policy analysis should be able to prevent more resource misallocations in the future by focusing on the problem(s) to be solved. Obviously, better problem definition cannot reduce the lag time caused by delays in institutional processes in the fragmented and decentralized democratic system of the United States.

Major budgetary savings and improved delivery of services to policy clients can result from proper problem definition. Policy problems are sets of unrealized values that produce dissatisfaction over issues (Dunn 1981, 98). An important point often lost in discussions of this subject is that policy "problems" refer to new or ongoing ones. Failure to define problems properly is like providing incentives to the wrong group to improve program performance (e.g., to flight attendants who really have no control over passenger baggage and on-time performance that are basic to solving an airline's profitability problems). More precise definitions of the problems and specification of the levers that can be manipulated to deal with the problems beforehand can avoid wasting resources. Skillful problem definition can also lead to fiscal savings, which will increase net assistance to intended recipients in public programs and projects.

Constraints to Problem Diagnosis

It is said that at least four times as much time should be spent on problem definition and diagnosis of policy problems as on analysis of alternative courses of action (Lehan 1984, 73). This is not a reference to the tendency of experts in economics and policy analysis to disagree on conceptual and quantitative assumptions and interpretation of data. Proper definition of macroeconomic problems such as excessive levels of aggregate demand will still result in political disagreements on the scope and timing of fiscal and monetary policy applications. More precise problem definitions can reduce the scope of later political disagreements on how to share costs and benefits of alternative policy actions. By providing a useful screening methodology, this phase can also prevent definition of "nonproblems" as policy problems.

For example, Fumento (1998, 12) argues that the "road rage epidemic" problem is nothing more than old-fashioned aggressive driving hyped by the media. Mistaken creation of a problem by the media, with support from legislators in search of votes, diverts resources from real behaviors that cause road accidents and produce deaths and injuries. Although it sounds reasonable to define a problem first before committing resources, in the road rage case the administrator of the NHTSA says that "we would rather not debate the definition because we have a huge problem staring us in the face and we should focus on solutions" (Davis and Smith 1998). This would seem to be a textbook case of how not to proceed with policy formulation. Use of appropriate problem definition techniques that demand empirical evidence could eliminate overbroad classification of existing problems. Below we will cover some of the basic problem-structuring techniques that offer ample opportunity to clarify differences and proceed to the analytic phase. But, beyond the technical realm, misdefinition of policy problems can be related to three more basic causes.

First, analysts themselves can impede problem analysis by unconsciously imposing definitions that lead them astray. Conceptual straightjackets are often self-imposed. A classic example of this is called the "nine-dot problem," which allows the linear imagination to fall into a trap. Suppose a highway must link nine cities with only four highways and because of technical and budgetary reasons, all roads must be straight. No retracing is allowed. If the analyst formulates the problem by trying to stay within the implied boundaries of the problem (nine dots arranged in a square with three rows as shown in Figure 2.1), the analyst cannot do it. The familiar path followed by blindered number crunchers is to do a quantitative analysis of the distance between the points to demonstrate that the problem is insoluble (Dunn 1994, 161) and that more roads and more funding are needed. But the best solution lies in ignoring the implied boundary of the problem and connecting them as indicated below. The point is that the analyst often lacks the critical perspective needed to move beyond a traditional definition of the problem. This may account for the many "insoluble" problems that are recounted by expert analysts in fields ranging from domestic health care to foreign policy.

Second, institutional values and organizational culture may converge in procedures that contribute to misdefining a problem. Given the strength of state institutions, this convergence often creates enormous momentum in the wrong directions and can take years to reverse or reallocate funding. For instance, use of a top-down financial control decisionmaking model in

Figure 2.1: Solution for the Nine-Dot Problem

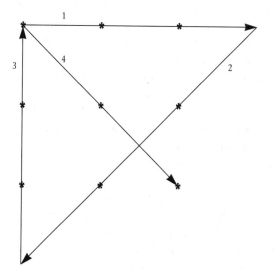

organizations is common and tends to screen out or discourage needed information from underlings, leading to partial or wrong definitions of the problem. The statist tendency to centralize decisionmaking in Latin America results in major policy implementation problems because professional managers in health and education ministries cannot redistribute personnel or transfer funds to meet contingencies. The problem of policy failures, instead, is defined as a legal problem requiring legislative change (no chance) and a bureaucratic control problem that leads incorrectly to even tighter restrictions over managers and paradoxically more wasted funds (Martner 1967, 42; Guess 1992).

In the foreign policy area, where there is a very narrow circle of policy-making responsibility, the sunk costs of enforcing a palpably bad decision are often perceived to be high: better to keep up the flow of support funds than to slow down, to reassess, and to risk falling into a ditch. The classic example here is U.S. participation in the Vietnam War. Successive definitions by core foreign policy institutions over time (State Department, CIA, DOD) led to U.S. support of a series of puppet regimes in South Vietnam and increased U.S. military participation to stop communist-threatened "dominoes" from falling. The mistake made was to move ahead, ignoring such core lessons from the past as the French debacle in Indochina, since many of them were institutionally inconvenient for justification of the expansion option (Tuchman 1984).

One of the lessons of chapter 3 of this work will be that institutions matter in both policy formulation and implementation. Given this, it can be seen that U.S. military policy actions in Vietnam were analogous to requesting budgets without considering past budgetary bases or their results. Under such irrational conditions, problems are, at best, defined and made without analytic inputs from the planning and budgeting system. At worst, sensible suggestions for redefinition of policy are ignored. The result is a series of bad decisions frozen into policy positions enforced to justify the costs of previous field failures. One can hardly imagine a surer way to waste budget and human resources.

Third, a problem may be misdefined because of ideology- or values-based treatment of the clients of existing policies and programs. That ideologies and values affect policy definitions is hardly new, but the goal should be to test such values empirically since ideological influences almost by definition are antiempirical. Even the absence of hard data to support ideologically based policies will not change minds or lead to elimination or modification of policy. In policy analysis, as anywhere, it is frustrating to argue with true believers. For example, such policymakers as U.S. Representative Tom Coburn (R-Okla) are in principle against the practice of "needle exchange" to slow HIV transmission because there are empirical arguments that needle exchange is thought to lead to increased drug use (providing needles to people that did not ever exchange them) and to undermine the goal of reducing illicit drug use. But it could also be argued that this position is "antiempirical" since there are hard data indicating that "needle exchange" is an effective means for slowing HIV transmission (Burr 1997b, 10). By this perspective, the stance closes off sensible options and prevents public health policy methods from being applied to the AIDS epidemic.

Similarly, a 1998 Clinton administration automobile safety initiative to increase seatbelt use from 68 to 85 percent by 2000 and 90 percent by 2005 was based on the estimated benefit of 10,000 lives saved per year. But the policy initiative has been opposed by several African American lawmakers and the American Civil Liberties Union (ACLU) because enforcement of the law would increase police harassment of minorities. In addition, such "white states" as Washington and Colorado also oppose the proposed law because of individualist feelings that "government has no right to tell people what to do in their cars" (Brown 1998). Ideological values are clearly an important element in both drug policy and automobile safety decisionmaking. But, as in most cases in the use of policy analysis, there must be a trade-off in values.

Before turning to this chapter's case of "Fighting Crime: The Case for Emptier Prisons," we need to review larger constraints to problem definition.

These are issues that cannot be dealt with feasibly in the short run because they deal with institutions and interest-group pressures. Following this review, we will look at basic methods for structuring policy problems and then apply them to the case.

The Concept of a Policy Problem

It will be evident that problems need to be defined not only for macropolicies (or "high" policies) such as foreign aid, health, and transportation, but also for micropolicies such as municipal animal control and police services. The only difference is the size of the population affected by public rules and procedures—the scope of the target population. Both macro- and micropolicies require formulation or implementation of public-sector rules and procedures, thus also pointing to the ambiguity of terms like "policy," "program," and "service." Since the objects of planned public expenditures are authorized by public laws and serve defined target populations, the analytic distinction between policy, service, and program typically breaks down. Analysis of program and policy problems typically involve the same kinds of techniques.

Three basic questions should be answered: (1) What is a policy problem? (2) What kinds are there? (3) Why is a precise definition important?

First, a policy problem represents a set of "unrealized values, needs or opportunities, which, however identified, may be attained through public action" (Dunn 1981, 98). A policy problem can be viewed as a "system of external conditions that produce dissatisfaction among different segments of the community" (Dunn 1981, 99). The policy problem is an event that produces dissatisfaction beyond one or two individuals. People are upset. A single complaint about the slow response by police or fire services does not amount to a policy problem—though, collectively, more complaints would be symptomatic of a policy problem. This helps in the definition. But how do we know whether it is an "actionable problem" as opposed to something simply annoying? Here it may be useful to define a policy problem by analogy—like a public question that can be settled by evidence that all rival observers have no choice but to accept (Runciman 1998, 8) (e.g., congestion measured as road density and average speed of traffic that lead to increases in measurable levels of nitrogen oxide). By contrast, the question of whether President Clinton's new seatbelt initiative is racially based because it may be used against minorities is not a public policy problem. At this stage of the policy process it is an interesting metaphysical question or an issue of political philosophy, but not a policy problem.

Policy problems should have an empirical basis. For example, arguments about the scope of the New York City "rat problem" turn on the number of reported rat complaints (dropping from 29,400 in 1994 to 18,045 for the first eight months of 1997) and reported rat bites (from 245 in 1994 to 184 in 1996) (Spurgeon 1997). "Problem truckers" caused 13 percent of 1997 traffic fatalities, which was up from 9 percent in 1996. But the National Office of Motor Carrier Safety does not keep timely or accurate statistics on problem truckers. How then do we know that this is a policy problem? Here, as in many cases, comparative data from a similar jurisdiction are useful in establishing a norm. Virginia State Police keep numbers that reveal that 22 percent of the trucks inspected have defects so serious that they must be taken off the road. Based on such numbers, Congress has called for an investigation of the national office by the U.S. Department of Transportation inspector general and the General Accounting Office (Reid 1998).

What we are after is a practical or "actionable" statement of a public issue from which expenditures can be made, personnel deployed, and procedures developed that will reduce or eliminate the undesirable state of affairs without undue harmful consequences to related activities. In principle, policies can be defined and actions taken that do not cause unintended consequences. In practice, unintended consequences need to be anticipated, if possible, through prior analysis of comparative lessons from policy implementation under similar conditions, and review of similar administrative mechanisms that redeploy resources quickly and efficiently. This refers to the institutional issue in policy analysis: management needs flexibility to change course if a problem has been misdefined.

Policy problems are not conceptual constructs like atoms or cells, but expressed as parts per million cells of sulfur dioxide in the air, constructs can serve as measures for design and enforcement of policy for dealing with air pollution. The constructs are "problematic situations" that are the product of thought acting on the environment and are artificial in the sense that someone subjectively judges these conditions to be problematic. The constructs' inherent artificiality makes it easier for policymakers to misconstrue the real problem. One way around such misconstrual is to disaggregate problems—but disaggregating policy problems into smaller, more manageable ones runs the risk of providing the right solution to the wrong problem. For example, the past worry of what government should do (if anything) about the declining economic international competitiveness of the United States was frequently boiled down to an issue of excessive foreign access to American technology. But Robert Reich (1987, 63) argued that this misinterpreted the real problem. "The underlying predicament is not that the Japanese are exploiting our discoveries but that we can't turn basic inventions into new products as fast or as well as they can." Defining the problem in this way precludes the policy alternative of holding back basic inventions from foreigners through more regulation and points toward more flexible solutions that give American workers and engineers experience in quickly turning basic inventions into products.

Second, it is important to distinguish among levels of problem complexity. It should be made clear to clients of policy analysis that more complex problems should be harder to solve and take longer. Policymakers often ignore this distinction between simple and complex problems in the rush to gain public approbation. Former House Speaker Newt Gingrich recently argued that Clinton's ten-year drug policy strategy was too pessimistic, saying "The Civil War took just four years to save the union and abolish slavery. Why can't we solve the drug problem, another form of slavery, in just a few years?" Changing the intractable behavioral foundations of policy problems requires time, resources, and continuity of effort. Declines in drug use are gradual; demanding quick solutions to complex problems can be frustrating, leading to more severe penalties, the making of minorities into scapegoats, and, finally, discouragement (Musto 1998).

For such reasons, policy problems can be broken broadly into "messy" (complex) and "not messy" (simple) categories. Here the issue is how one defines and distinguishes the problems for decisionmaking in order to resolve present problems and prevent future policy crises. The not messy problems are rare in public-sector work and usually involve routine support matters such as personnel and internal management. However, routine matters can get out of hand and turn into messy "high"-policy problems. The breakup of Yugoslavia, a solid example of interrepublic ethnonationalistic policy conflict in the Balkans, can be traced back to either remote, messier causes or to more discrete, proximate causes. The remote causes are not directly actionable but are required for comprehensive understanding of policy conflicts in this region. The more remote causes refer to President Slobodan Milošević's use of the state-dominated press to whip up Serbian nationalist fervor against what he portrayed as an evil conspiracy in Kosovo to secede from the Yugoslav federation. In 1991 Milošević skillfully used nationalism against Kosovo Albanians to turn Serbian public opinion against growing secessionist movements in Slovenia and Croatia. But his overzealous efforts to secure his own power led to the breakup of the entire Yugoslav federal system into independent countries and its replacement by Serbian military-based power in a smaller rump republic (Silber and Little 1995, 82). These are remote causes of the breakup of Yugoslavia.

The more immediate, perhaps actionable cause of the Yugoslav breakup and subsequent quest for ethnic partition might be reduced to an issue of classroom space at the University of Pristina in Kosovo—even though this sounds pretty far-fetched and reductionist. How can the breakup of an entire country be blamed on a university's administration or lack thereof? In 1981 riots had broken out over poor conditions at that university. Originally designed for 15,000 students, by 1982 it had 47,000. Indifference by administrators to student protests soon led to wider demands that Kosovo become the seventh Yugoslav republic or that the region be integrated into Albania. Local factory workers soon joined the ranks of students. The official response by the police was harsh, leading to the arrest and beating of students and the summary replacement of local party leaders. Milošević was able to inflame the situation in 1989 and after by using the secession issue as fuel for Serbian nationalism and to fortify his personal political power (Joffe 1996, 92–93).

Had a courageous university dean stepped forward to defuse the immediate problem of classroom space, degeneration of the conflict into wider issues (such as the alleged conspiracy to secede and take the Serbian "holy" land—the Field of Blackbirds, *Kosovo polje*) might have been delayed or resolved altogether without civil war. Had Yugoslav policymakers, with a minimum of foresight, defined the issue as a matter of providing sufficient municipal capacity and administrative authority to resolve regional problems, the unfortunate outcome for the former Yugoslavia might well have been different. But Yugoslav policymaking was dominated by Serbian definitions of the problem, and under such conditions an actionable problem definition that could have resolved wider issues was not likely. This is an extreme case of foreign policy. Given that this and other international problems typically have a large number of variables and intervening factors, most of them remain very messy and ill-structured problems.

Third, and finally, precise definition of a problem is confounded by the reality that the same information can be differently interpreted. Different problem definitions derive from the fact that different constituencies or stakeholders are doing the defining. This in turn can lead to policies (and usually their reward in mandated expenditures) that disproportionately distribute costs and benefits among affected interest groups. For example, definition of the "elderly poor" where the distribution of poverty and density are not congruent will affect service delivery and its cost. Prolonged economic expansion in the United States has generated widely different intepretations of its effects on reducing the poverty problem. The Census Bureau, for example, indicates that the number of "very poor" Americans increased from 13.9 million in 1995 to 14.4 million in 1996. This would point to a major policy problem for poverty advocates. But the Census Bureau uses a narrow, cash-income definition of poverty, excluding such noncash benefits as food stamps and Medicaid. Using a broader income measure leads to the different interpretation that only 10.2 percent of Americans were below the poverty line in 1996, and Latinos, women, and residents of the South were the largest gainers in household income growth from economic expansion (*Economist* 1997c).

Thus the incidence of the poverty problem was changed, creating a different composition of stakeholders. What is needed is a problem definition that recognizes geographic and sociological differences as a prelude to policy development. Failure to include all reasonable constituencies and options in defining policy problems amounts to a major economic and political mistake—that is, failure to deal with all dimensions of the problem at hand permits underlying social conflicts to fester and leads to wasted public expenditures. For this reason, policy development should include safeguards for public notice and comment, active participation, and a transparent appeal process.

In general, the stakeholder with the greatest number of political resources (technical sophistication, rewards/punishment, charisma, and intense supporters) will have the most influence on problem definition and ultimate selection of alternatives. For example, suppose that the number of complaints in a community about roaming dogs has been increasing annually. Suppose also that the number of impoundments has been decreasing at a similar rate. Based on this limited information, what is the "animal control problem?" In contrast with a "regulatory" definition that focuses on licensing, leashes, fines, and animal contraception (i.e., owner-controlled solutions), a "capital investment" definition would focus on the need for a larger and more accessible dog pound. Community critics of the capital investment approach can argue that a new pound would not necessarily eliminate strays (the real objective) and would merely shift the costs to the non-dog-owning public for services required by improper behavior by dog owners. Hence, from this perspective a more appropriate solution would be to require some combination of steeper fines, higher service charges or license fees for dog owners, and animal contraception (a regulatory package) (Lehan 1984, 66–67). Since policy alternatives must ultimately be traded in institutionalized settings (usually committees), "politics" will affect both initiation of the regulatory solution and its priority in relation to the capital investment (pound) solution. Often, capital construction solutions to complex policy problems are driven by the political pressures of construction firms that donate campaign money and underscore the political benefits of leaving tangible results to local constituencies.

Structuring a Policy Problem

Given the difficulty of defining real-world problems objectively and finally, and the necessity of moving fast to a policy solution, simplifying techniques must be used. To produce information on the nature and solution of a problem, one must apply the "policy-analytic procedure of problem structuring," which Dunn calls the "most important but least understood aspect of policy analysis" (1981, 98).

In general, selection of an appropriate technique for problem definition depends first on a preliminary assessment of data trends, causation among variables, and relevant stakeholder positions. New information that can change our assumptions about these subjects will probably emerge during the process of problem structuring. In this event, the definition will change but the techniques for definition will not. Of initial importance to defining a policy problem is how likely it is, based on the information we have, that the problem can be structured for institutional action in the short or medium term? Dunn (1981, 103–04) suggests that policy problems fall into three classes:

- Well-structured
- Moderately structured
- Ill-structured problems, based on their degree of complexity and interdependence

Brewer and deLeon (1983, 51) also recognize that a problem may remain complex, because once the problem is defined by the analyst, it becomes subject to competing individual, organizational, and external environmental (client) preferences.

WELL-STRUCTURED PROBLEMS

William Dunn (1981, 104) defines these as "those which involve one or a few decision-makers and a small set of policy alternatives." Low-level agency operational problems, such as the optimal point of replacing agency vehicles, given age, repair, and depreciation costs, are "well structured" because all consequences of all policy alternatives can be programmed in advance. Life cycle, maintenance planning and budgeting, and condition assessment systems can provide needed data to make decisions in this relatively simple policy context. For example, the city of Milwaukee uses database systems for condition-based project planning for many of its municipal services, thus enabling officials to anticipate and define problems before they become serious. For surface transportation, the city uses a "pavement management system" (PMS) to plan more cost-effective paving budgets. This inventory and condition assessment system contains records of more than forty street-condition inventory elements, including type of pavement, age of pavement, and maintenance history. Streets are rated according to the "possible pavement condition index" from very good to very poor, depending on scores received. The city began using the PMS in 1988; 20 percent of its database is updated annually, allowing the city to survey its entire system within five years. For health services, Milwaukee uses the following condition criteria to determine capital needs: (1) age and condition of facilities, (2) use patterns of facilities, and (3) safety needs of clients (city of Milwaukee 1996, 84).

Throughout the nation, by and large, city garbage problems can be classified as "well structured" because of the greater number of decision-makers and policy options. Recycling is becoming more costly because of greater supplies and falling raw materials prices, and this will affect sanitation policy results. With political commitments to recycle 50 percent or more of garbage, U.S. cities and counties have moved aggressively and cost-effectively and now recycle on average only about 40 percent. The annual costs/household for moving from 40 to 50 percent are calculated and well known. In Montgomery County, Maryland, which recycles 38 percent of its garbage, it is $64.66 per year (Day 1997). But the question is whether it is appropriate to charge residents more to reach 50 percent or, alternatively, use the money for schools, public safety, recreation, and other recurrent expenditure needs?

Is the municipal garbage problem to be seen in terms of one or a combination of the following?

1. Excessive cost of recycling, meaning a focus on such means of reducing costs as newly designed garbage trucks that separate paper, glass, and plastic and thus reduce the number of trips required.
2. Excessive quantities of garbage, meaning a focus on such revised policies as refusal to accept lawn clippings or charging by the number of bags of refuse thrown out each week.
3. Overcapacity in the recycling industry where too many firms may be competing for recyclables whose prices no longer cover costs, such as newspapers. In other cases, it may now be cheaper to make single-use containers than recycling. This affects the market price for recyclables and requires higher charges to cities that must pass them along to households.

4. A problem that may be the result of law, such as the growing number of state laws that mandate minimum thresholds of recycling.
   Such laws ignore local costs of recycling and constrain use of policy alternatives such as dumping and incineration (*Economist*
   1997d, 63).

Not infrequently, policy problems can be caused by laws from another
level of government, laws that mandate supply without demand, and that
ignore alternative means of achieving the same public purposes. An issue
then is how to change the law? In any case, this problem is well structured
and amenable to problem definition techniques. Whether policymakers
and budgetary institutions will use them in policy formulation is a different
question.

The New York City rat problem, noted above, is an example of a well-
structured problem. Mayor Rudolf Giuliani declared war on the city's estimated 28 million rats (4:1 rat-resident ratio, double that of Washington,
D.C.) by establishing an interagency Rodent Extermination Task Force with
an annual budget of $8 million (Spurgeon 1997). As usual, resolution
requires reconciliation of competing problem definitions. The scope of the
problem can be estimated, as noted, first by data on reported rats and rat
bites: in other words, rats are a public safety issue. But if the problem is
defined as a health issue, solution lies in more competent building inspections and steeper fines for owners and those who leave food for rats to continue breeding and infesting more neighborhoods. The World Health Organization works with this definition, noting the past links of bubonic plague
with rats and their fleas, and by this definition, the problem is owner
behavior that can be changed with such disincentives as fines and regulation enforcement. But given the immediacy of the problem, the preferred
choice among many groups is one of extermination for public safety: that
is, how to poison and kill the existing rats that bite and cause disease. The
two definitions of the problem, as in the case of other well-structured problems such as stray dogs, lead in different implementation directions.

MODERATELY STRUCTURED PROBLEMS

By contrast, moderately structured problems are "those involving one or a
few decision-makers and a relatively limited number of alternatives" (Dunn
1981, 104). Unlike the well-structured problem, the outcomes are not cal-
culable within acceptable margins of error or risk. For example, the "social
insurance" problem is described as a "demographic time-bomb": populations in industrial countries are aging fast and birth rates are declining.

Honoring current commitments means that spending on state pensions will rise steeply, which means a sharp rise in taxes for baby boomers, children, and grandchildren who must pay for the elderly. The problem is clear in that social insurance tax and expenditure forecasts can be reasonably made on existing demographic data (*Economist* 1998b): contingent government liabilities to future budgets can be precisely forecast. This part of the problem is well structured in that the need for cash transfers derived from population dynamics and social insurance claims can be forecast within acceptable margins of risk. But given the enormous increase in forecast spending to cover these claims (it will double by 2007), the important problems are how to ration health care: how to decide how much is enough and who should get it and on what basis. These problems involve the uncertainties of regulation, managed care organizational behavior, and the effects of privatization options on health care costs and service coverage. The solutions to these subproblems are less predictable and make the overall social insurance problem "moderately well structured."

ILL-STRUCTURED PROBLEMS

The more typical and potentially dangerous problems are "ill structured," meaning that they involve "many different decision-makers whose utilities (values) are either unknown or impossible to rank in a consistent fashion" (Dunn 1981, 105). Many of the most important policy problems are ill structured. A good example of such a problem is that of tobacco smoking. Should it be regulated? How should it be regulated? This is a multidimensional problem involving major health effects, producer needs, restaurant interests, potential links to more dangerous drugs, and attendant social effects. The problem can also be broken down functionally into overlapping and potentially contradictory organizational responsibilities for each of the component parts of the problem.

One of the lessons of political science, public administration, and other related disciplines is that well-structured and moderately structured problems are rarely present in complex governmental settings. One of the main tasks of policy analysis, therefore, is the resolution of ill-structured problems (Dunn 1981, 105). Ill-structured problems are not simply those caused by such difficulties as the inability to forecast demand for program services. Many programs, like hospital care, for example, must respond to a volume of often uncontrolled demand. This has been a problem with Britain's National Health Service, which provides most medical care at little or no cost. Such a program differs from those with controlled demand, where response is based on programmed resources, such as miles of roads to be maintained (though a harsh winter that destroys roads can change the demand from controlled and forecast to uncontrolled).

Similarly, such programs as mass transit face both types of demand. Exposure to the subproblem of excess traffic congestion (measured by average road density and speed of traffic) often generates uncontrolled demand for transit in some cities. Municipal bus and rail authorities must try to deliver fixed levels of service, often with varying fare structures, to passengers whose demand schedules can also vary (or produce high price elasticities of demand).

While ill-structured problems create difficulties for budget programming, they are technically no different from known and structured problems. Development of accurate forecasting methodologies, as will be explained in chapter 4, can render these problems manageable from a resource efficiency perspective. An additional variable in dealing with ill-structured problems is that they usually cut across institutional lines. The problems themselves may be technically simple but institutionally messy. Multiple institutional responsibility, in such areas as mine safety, can result in different problem definitions that for policy execution dilutes accountability and responsibility through various forms of buck passing. In other areas, regulatory agencies such as the Federal Aviation Agency may have multiple conflicting responsibilities (air traffic promotion versus air safety regulation) that can compromise policy results. In many cases, because of opposing client pressures on responsible institutions, there are major disincentives for these actors to define the problem clearly.

For example, the Anti-Drug Abuse Act of 1986 (then-President Reagan's new drug policy) attempted to define and resolve a major ill-structured problem, drug abuse. First, in the drug abuse area there are really few agreed-upon societal values, only those of conflicting individuals and groups. All would like to see drug use reduced (except suppliers), but consensus largely ends there. For example, even consensus on an understanding of addiction is elusive. Do drugs give addicts a habit or do addicts make a habit of drugs? Research indicates that addiction is related to a damaging mix of biochemistry and bad social conditions.

Despite the difficulty of neatly structuring the drug abuse problem and lack of consensus on basic concepts, the bulk of the proposed $1.7 billion (65 percent or $1.04 billion) budget for fiscal year (FY) 1986 flowed to enforcement and only 27.5 percent (or $441 million) was allocated to educational and drug-treatment activities (Brinkley 1986). For comparative purposes, the $17. 1 billion FY 1999 request for the overall federal drug control policy allocated $11.1 billion (66 percent) for enforcement or "supply reduction" and only $6.5 billion or 34 percent for "demand reduction" (Office of National Drug Control Policy 1998, 16). While the categories are somewhat confusing ("supply reduction" via the threat of law enforcement also reduces demand), the resultant allocation of funds in both years (ten years apart) suggests continuing major differences in both perspective and power resources among actors involved in drug policy. Since 1996, the major goal of the national drug control strategy has focused on prevention efforts among youths. Policy analysts advocate rebalancing the national drug budget. Antidrug war "doves," for example, cite the Rand Corporation study that concluded that treatment is seven times more effective than enforcement in reducing cocaine consumption, and twenty-three times more effective than destroying foreign drug sources (*Economist* 1999a, 73–74).

Second, in general, policymakers tend to maximize their own values along with key client groups and are not motivated to act on the basis of societal preferences. The prospect of substantial antidrug enforcement money quickly turned the chance for a coordinated policy into a gold rush and resulted in a predictable turf battle between the U.S. Customs Service and the Coast Guard, both of which then wanted new radar planes from the Senate (Brinkley 1986b). Thus, any technical difficulties of defining the drug policy problem were overwhelmed by bureaucratic infighting related to available funding. Failure to control the institutional environment through strong policy leadership resulted in misdefinition of the problem that predictably led to continued enforcement failures.

Third, commitment of resources to existing policies and programs prevents policymakers from considering new alternatives. This is partly a fixed-cost budget problem exacerbated by an incremental budget process the bulk of whose base (often around 70–80 percent of the annual budget) is already committed. Failure to analyze programs and policies from a "zero" base is partly a technical problem, but mostly a problem of scarce time resources and lack of political will owing to intense political pressures by clients to continue the programs. This normal context provides real little incentive for analysis of policies that can absorb the remaining 20–30 percent of funds for them and for new initiatives. More powerful stakeholders in the annual budget process are able to lock in expenditure preferences (legally through earmarks, permanent appropriations, or entitlements). These provisions cannot be easily changed because they are permanent law. In Latin American countries and many U.S. states, sectoral expenditure shares are actually mandated by laws and constitutions. This is especially common for health and education services. These are longer-term policy drivers that work against institutional change and redefiniton of policy problems. Try and change them by next fiscal year! The same expenditure mandate pattern recurs in federal, state, and local government policy processes and removes the bulk of items from policymaker discretion. In this fashion the politics of the budget process determines much of the content of public policy.

Related to budget mandates is the problem of perceived political mandates. Policymakers make laws and policies (rationally) on the basis of perceived constituent demands, thus driving out policy analysis. As will be discussed further in this chapter's case study, paradoxically enforcement of marijuana laws may be driving people to use cocaine and more harmful drugs. "Zero tolerance" laws and harsh sentencing for possession of marijuana have increased the risks of cultivation, and this has encouraged growers to produce more potent strains of the drug that bring a higher price with a lower volume of sales (Schlosser 1997, 99). Consistent with basic market economy principles, price increases can lead to producer efficiency gains. Producers respond to higher prices with investment in more modern equipment for cultivation and transport of drugs, leading to increased competitiveness and greater profitability for the illegal enterprise. Moreover, suppliers prefer cocaine because it is easy to conceal and transport, and its prices are much higher than marijuana, which is bulky and harder to transport. By contrast, enforcers prefer marijuana because its bulk looks impressive before the cameras and seizure of a few tons increases productivity measures at lower risk than for cocaine. Thus, according to law enforcement experts, enforcement of marijuana laws contributes to higher marijuana prices and lower supplies, which drive people to harder drugs (Lindsey 1986). In this context, the 1986 recommendation of Georgia's attorney general to make possession of marijuana a felony instead of a misdemeanor (Hopkins 1986) can be viewed as either selection of an inappropriate solution contrary to valid and reliable data on policy impact or simply part of the rush by elected officials racing to "get tough on criminals." Based on available evidence, such a law would increase the incidence of hard drug users and make enforcement even more difficult.

These institutional features, together with inability of policymakers to collect enough information on all possible alternatives or predict the range of consequences associated with each alternative, render the ill-structured problem largely immune from conventional definitional techniques. Dealing with the most common types of policy problems, we are faced with the difficult choice of both methods and facts to maintain our credibility as policy analysts. The wrong method or model can select the wrong facts and give us the right solution to the wrong problem (e.g., the crop eradication or "technical fix" model as a solution to the problem of cultivating cocaine in

Bolivia when definition of the problem must include the dimensions of local elite power and high demand for cocaine in the United States). Despite these obstacles, let us turn to a "best available" methodology for defining an ill-structured problem.

Methodologies for Problem Definition

> "I mentioned to you that a grand vision has certain components. . . . One of them is scale. Don't send me dross. No grapeshot. Not 'Here, Scottie, take this bag of bones and see what your analysts make of it.' Do you follow me?"
>
> "Not quite sir."
>
> "The analysts here are idiots. They don't make connections. They don't see shapes forming in the sky. A man reaps as he sows. Do you understand me? A great intelligencer catches history in the act. We can't expect some nine-to-five fellow on the third floor who's worried about his mortgage to catch history in the act. Can we? It takes a man of vision to catch history in the act. Does it not?" (Le Carré 1996, 249)

Dunn (1994, 165) discusses six techniques that may be helpful in problem structuring to avoid sending "grapeshot" to one's superiors. Like other policy analytic procedures they tend to yield results that are plausible and uncertain. Policy analysts will select from them based typically on time available for reaching a solution and analytic capacity for problem definition. These techniques will be useful as the basis for our next step in the process: forecasting policy options (see chapter 4). Let us now review these methods and see how they can be applied to our case in this chapter.

BOUNDARY ANALYSIS

To be certain that one is defining the whole problem, methods are needed to establish boundaries. To define the scope of the problem, the analyst should employ broad survey techniques, review pertinent data, conduct field inspections, and master the special nomenclature associated with that particular policy area. Like a good journalist checking alternative sources to ensure that nothing major has been left out of the story, the policy analyst may employ three procedures.

First, there should be "saturation sampling," which consists of contacting stakeholders by telephone or personal interview and asking them to name additional stakeholders. Stakeholders should include dissident groups

of administrators that are often excluded from defining problems. Saturation sampling is continued until no new stakeholders are named. This
method also provides a list of the key influences in policymaking and can
be used to estimate their influence in actual problem definition.

Second, analysts can elicit problem representations from sampled
stakeholders, whose perspectives will vary widely. In my use of this technique to define the forest policy problem in Costa Rica, it was noted that
there were major definitional differences among stakeholders. These included the dimensions of rural population growth, absence of logging regulation to ensure sustained yields, absence of a national policy to protect tropical forest resources, absence of fiscal incentives to the forest-based industry,
the high U.S. beef import quota that encouraged pasture expansion and
burning of forests, and forestry department corruption or incompetence
(Guess 1979). Problem definition was dominated then as now by the powerful beef-cattle industry that defined tropical forest elimination in self-serv-
ing fashion as the inevitable effect of normal expansion of the agricultural
frontier. This definition, carried over into a "nonpolicy" on several fronts,
was leading at that time to major loss of tropical forest resources and associated jobs and income opportunities for the rural poor of Costa Rica. In
eliciting problem representations, the analyst should avoid "positive hearing" where "words are put into people's mouths that they would have said
if they'd thought of them at the time" (Le Carré 1996, 277). Despite the Le
Carré character's assurance that "everybody does it anyway," the analyst
must guard against the use of positive hearing in interviews.

Third, the analyst can engage in boundary estimation by constructing
a frequency distribution with cumulative new concepts and problem representations elicited from stakeholders on a vertical axis arrayed against the
number of policy stakeholders on a horizontal axis. When the number of
new representations tapers off the curve will flatten, indicating the probable
boundary of the problem (Dunn 1994, 165).

CLASSIFICATION ANALYSIS

In the use of this technique, the analyst tries to divide up the apparent
problem into components to facilitate analysis and design of remedial
actions. Based on straightforward data classification principles from statistics, analysts break down problems into logically component parts and classify persons or objects into larger groups or classes. The rules for both procedures are well known. There are no absolute guidelines on correct

perception of policy problems, but classifications should be relevant and logically consistent (Dunn 1994, 167).

First, the classification should be relevant. The categories should be designed with action and performance in mind. To this end, in chapter 6 we employ "decision analysis" to structure a cost-effectiveness problem. Often, major classification efforts are engineered that are not relevant to improved decisionmaking. A common problem with many "program budgeting" exercises to improve policy results, for example, has been the emphasis on rigid accounting classification of linkages between agency workloads and expected results. The purposes of the exercises are accounting and control rather than reprogramming of funds for solution of policy problems for which the agency was created (e.g., health, education). The emphasis has so far been on research linking levels of expenditure to policy results through yield coefficients or other mathematical relations that are, at best, theoretical in the real world of budget changes. The classifications often yield knowledge for its own sake rather than decisive action. Given the action-oriented and time-deadline nature of the agency environment, the results of program classification exercises are rarely used in practice, while the exercise itself is often deemed to be a waste of time by practitioners.

Even though classifications need to be relevant, there are no firm guidelines for relevance. One important caution is that the classification should clearly flow from the analyst's views of the causes of the problem. This will allow for transparency of assumptions and avoid narrow definitions of problems. For example, classifications of poverty problems can be derived from causal assumptions that it is a problem of inadequate income, cultural deprivation, or psychological motivation. Should the analyst focus on only one type of classification, contrary assumptions are ignored, and that can lead to policy misformulation. Ignoring relevant data may also lead to faulty explanations of poverty rates (e.g., among elderly and disabled versus families with children) and a corresponding inability to explain the differential access of groups to program benefits with cuts in federal Medicaid expenditures (Johnson 1997, 15). Failure to classify data relevantly and to make underlying assumptions explicit can produce erroneous policies.

Second, categories in the classification system should be "exhaustive." That is, all subjects should fit into one category or another. If they do not, one must create new categories. They should be "mutually exclusive," that is, with subjects assigned to only one category to avoid double-counting. Finally, the subjects should be "consistent": each category and subcategory should be based on a single classification principle. If this is not done, subclasses will overlap—as in classifying a family according to whether it is above the poverty line or receiving welfare payments (Dunn 1994, 167). Since the same family could be in both categories, the categories are inconsistent. Classification analysis is aided by use of diagrams and classification schemes to present categories in visual form. Pictures often lead to questions and linkages that can be hidden by language. Diagrams reveal hidden assumptions and facilitate problem definition.

CAUSAL ANALYSIS

The rules guiding causal analysis are the same as those used for classification analysis: relevance, exhaustiveness, mutual exclusiveness, and consistency. The basic purpose here is to identify the controlling variables (Lehan 1984, 74) or those factors that if significantly altered would decisively affect such problems as jail overcrowding, nutrition status of the elderly, or poverty. From controlling variables it is more feasible to establish objectives and specify performance criteria. Causal or "hierarchy" analysis (Dunn 1994, 170) allows the analyst to distinguish causes from symptoms and to organize data in categories that indicate the difference among the major three kinds of causes, as follows.

First, "possible" causes are those that are remote but contribute to problem occurrence. Studies linking elite power structures and official conspiracies to the persistence of poverty are self-satisfying and make riveting tales, but are actionable only on the macrorevolutionary level. In most societies this means either a long-term solution—or a very short one! In other cases, persistent political influences of certain interest groups lead to consistent policy definitions and solutions (e.g., builders and contractors and capital expenditure solutions for roaming dogs). Revision of policy and budget formulation processes to include wider public participation is a medium-term solution to deal with more remote or "possible" problems like this.

Second, "plausible" causes are those that are proximate and have been empirically linked. These are the "controlling variables" that should be actionable in the short run. For example, studies have linked resistance to work with poverty. If the causation is valid, one policy solution would be to use workfare incentive programs with tight monitoring standards and controls: the presumed incentives would be both monetary and nonmonetary (self-esteem). Other studies have found that health coverage for the elderly and access to Medicaid assistance was often provided at the expense of another class of poor people: families with children. A policy solution might be to expand Medicaid coverage to women with children. The results could be improvements in health care equity but at the price of higher program costs (Johnson 1997, 20). Similarly, data indicate that the increased incidence of roaming dogs can be linked to the logistical problem of inefficient impoundment and absence of pound space—or to weak regulatory enforcement, for instance, the absence of owner incentives to license and control dogs (Lehan 1984, 74). In the health care area, studies have linked higher fees for hospital and clinic services to reduced demand (a 1 percent increase in fees reduces demand by 0.3 percent—roughly the same price elasticity of demand as in urban transit) (*Economist* 1997e, 84). But studies also link higher fees (plausible causes) to higher rates of certain diseases and the possible spread of contagious diseases. The problem should be defined to include plausible effects on both system cost recovery and the impact of fees on poorer groups.

In their quest for plausible causes, analysts have had difficulty distinguishing causality from correlation. To deal with this problem, policy analysts have searched for an "instrumental variable." This variable acts as a proxy for one variable in statistical analysis but is unrelated to the others. For example, in examining the relationship between imprisonment and reduced crime, it is difficult to find much of an effect due to increased incarceration. Increased incarceration could even lead to increased crime through the unintended effect of a convict absorbing collegial training during his or her sentence. But suppose there is another variable related to incarceration that is unrelated to crime rates? Use of an instrumental variable, in this case litigation over prison overcrowding, might clarify the causal relationship between incarceration and crime rates. Using data from 1973–1997, researchers found that where litigation is filed and prison populations fall, crime rates increase (*Economist* 1998d). Finding an instrumental variable in such litigation over prison crowding can strengthen the relationship between the other variables. This technique illustrated the need for the creative use of empirical analysis and for use of multidisciplinary approaches to problem definition.

Third, "actionable" causes are those that are subject to manipulation by policymakers in the short or medium term. Both "plausible" and "actionable" causes are those that the policymakers want to hear about. The purpose of causal analysis is to make decisions based on identification of plausible and actionable causes. Both construction of a dog pound and improved regulations covering dogs are short-term solutions based on actionable causal analysis. Setting alternative rates of health care fees or bus fares are similarly plausible and actionable causes of changes in patient and bus rider behavior. The stray-dog options are favored by different stakeholders but differ politically in that the regulatory solution is longer term with potential risks of failure, whereas the pound solution is short term and leads to a brand-new building that can provide photo opportunities for leaders. Similarly, with establishment of plausible causes in health fees, policies can focus on avoiding harm to sick people who are also poor, thus making hospitals more cost-efficient and pushing doctors to consider costs when prescribing tests and treatments.

Causal analysis also requires analysis of the unintended consequences of otherwise logical policy choices. This is easier said than done—the consequences are often unpredictable. Federal prison reforms of 1976 that allowed inmates to write to each other created the structures that later evolved into organized prison gangs (*Economist* 1998a). As an example, suppose a policy objective is to reduce the number of stray dogs. The option of reducing them through the construction of a pound could result in more stray or itinerant dogs unless owner behavior is also sanctioned, meaning that regulation and construction should not be viewed as singular causes leading to either-or policies. All relevant policy assumptions and causes need to be reviewed to properly define the problem. Dunn (1994, 171) provides the example of pretrial release as a favored policy to reduce jail overcrowding in the United States (citing Nagel and Neef 1976). But this causal explanation overlooks the possible effect of plea bargaining on jail overcrowding. If pretrial release leads to reduced plea bargains, the waiting time for trials may increase, which leads to more overcrowding. Failure to include an additional plausible cause in the matrix leads to a policy with major unintended negative consequences.

USE OF ANALOGIES

This tool draws on comparative experience to structure policy problems. Studies repeatedly show that policymakers tend to ignore both past similar problems that could contain lessons for present ones or current similar problems experienced by neighboring jurisdictions. Many sound policies are developed through comparative analysis of the experiences of other similar jurisdictions: recentralization of the Washington, D.C., homicide unit through the use of this technique was noted in the previous chapter; the United States has looked to California to determine the impact of managed care in the health arena. Tendencies to think that problems are new or must be solved alone ignore the contribution of past thought and efforts to grapple with similar issues. For example, over several decades many cities and states have stumbled forward to reform budget systems, converting them from input to output "program" measurement tools for management control and policy planning. Most jurisdictions made the same mistakes, overemphasizing technical measurement and fixed definitions of programs and subprograms. They ignored lack of line management incentives or authority to manage most programs. They also ignored legislative interest in line-item formats. Many failures have resulted. In this case, the availability of nonthreatening institutional advice from such professional associations as the Government Finance Officer's Association and International City Management Association have helped penetrate the thicket of isolated policymaking among self-sealing organizations and have allowed city officials to draw upon technical experience of their associates in neighboring jurisdictions.

Similarly, recent experience with civil service reform policies at the state and local level reveals that they have often been designed and implemented in isolation. Unintended negative consequences of downsizing on staff morale, downstream budgetary costs, performance of private contractors, and service delivery quality were often ignored despite the availability of substantial comparative information on the dimensions of the problem. In this case, journalists and news media intervened to serve as transmission links with information that helped policymakers reformulate definitions of such local policy problems as these: How to cut the size of government? How to privatize? How to stimulate public productivity? How to measure service delivery effectiveness and develop incentives to improve delivery of certain services?

Finally, many cities have reduced crime rates by restructuring and reorganizing their police departments. In contrast, the Washington, D.C., police department has ignored most of these lessons for problem structuring. With problems similar to those of Washington, New York City decentralized accountability and authority to its 76 precinct commanders and now holds them accountable for results. Boston targets gang crime by including unarmed probation officers on police patrols—this is significant because the officers need no "probable cause" to stop juvenile offenders suspected of violating their terms of probation. And, as part of its community policing program, Chicago uses computerized mapping to generate maps of crime to allow police to share information with communities (Harlan 1997).

As suggested by Dunn (1994, 173), policymakers may produce at least three types of analogies to aid in structuring policy problems. First, one can use "personal" analogies by putting oneself in the position of stakeholder or client in order to uncover political dimensions. Being in the position of a public-transportation-dependent bus rider, for example, can reveal the intensity of political opposition to major cuts in bus-rail service and elimination of routes. These were dilemmas faced by policymakers in Miami and Washington, D.C. Miami (Metro-Dade County) wanted to eliminate at least ten of seventy-eight routes and reduce service on fifty-six others as well as reduce rail service as part of its FY 98 budget plan (Vigliucci and Epstein 1997). Despite any technical arguments for fiscal savings, poorer riders are trapped by distance and time constraints and cannot afford cars. By failing to use personal analogies to reveal the unintended consequence of cutting such bus lines, policymakers risk reduction of overall ridership and increased incentives for car ownership that will further clog already overcrowded roads. In fiscal terms, the short-term savings can lead to longer term transit system losses because public funds will have to be spent for more roads and additional subsidies to cover operating losses of transit systems

Second, one can use "direct" analogies by finding similar relationships between two or more problem situations. In structuring problems of drug addiction, for example, analysts may construct direct analogies from experiences with control of contagious diseases (Dunn 1994, 173). Third, policy analysts like to employ "symbolic" analogies, using such mechanisms as temperature thermostats, electrical circuits, hydraulic systems, ecological systems, and automatic pilots. As indicated in chapter 1, the policy process itself is frequently characterized as an ecological system, with issues in problem formulation and analysis, or policy implementation, control, and evaluation. The integrated financial management system described in chapter 3 is based on a systems analogy. As noted, the systems analogy is flawed in the minds of some who argue that all components are not equal and that the budgetary allocation in real political systems is the most important function in the system. But use of the analogy allows one to clarify these arguments and narrow the range of disagreement among specialists.

BRAINSTORMING

This technique is widely used to identify and conceptualize problems. It is one of many types of techniques that attempt to use conflict creatively in structuring policy problems. It is used as much in analysis of film scripts and other artistic endeavors as in the formulation of technical policy solutions. Note that previously discussed techniques rely more on more rational, empirical-technical foundations. This technique focuses on group dynamics and seeks the creative dimensions of problem definition to forge more innovative and effective policies. It will be noted in chapter 4 that a similar group approach (called the Delphi Technique) can be used to critique policy solutions, such as alternate revenue forecasts and scenarios, as well as to initially define problems. There are several major guidelines in conducting successful brainstorming. First, groups should be composed of experts from various professions that are knowledgeable about the sources of public dissatisfaction on an issue. Second, it is very important that the idea generation, or free-form phase, and the idea evaluation, or critical phase, should be kept separate (Dunn 1994, 175). This is a common caveat in script writing that is used to avoid eliminating potentially useful insights and sound ideas that more timid analysts might be afraid to express for fear of criticism. It should be used in technical policy analysis to define problems as well. The generation versus evaluation structure is designed to avoid premature criticism and debate that can exclude dimensions of policy problems, such as the potential effects of plea bargaining on jail overcrowding.

ASSUMPTIONAL ANALYSIS

Assumptional analysis is a technique that is useful for ill-structured problems, where multiple self-contained organizations are involved in sequential policymaking over time and where the analyst must include other public policies that may affect problem definition. Other policies include mandatory minimum sentencing laws for hard drug abuse that discriminate against African Americans and tend to fill up prisons (*Washington Post* 1997). In such cases, the analyst enters the actual fray with the necessity of learning about how assumptions have changed, along with problem definition actors, acronyms, and the real limits that any policy will face no matter how the problem is defined. For this, the policy analyst must have a good sense of historical linkage, be a good storyteller, and perhaps have an absurdist, Kafkaesque sense of humor to guard against being overwhelmed by petty detail.

As with brainstorming, the creative use of conflict is used to ferret out and challenge assumptions. But unlike previous techniques, assumptional analysis begins with the policies recommended. The analyst reviews identified stakeholders and works backward from recommended solutions to supporting data and assumptions. The assumptions when coupled with the data should allow stakeholders to deduce the policies recommended. Explicit specification of problems and assumptions with the same data set allows one to test the reliability of problem definitions and policy recommendations. This technique encourages participants to systematically compare assumptions and counter assumptions (e.g., poverty caused by lack of income or psychological deprivation). With synthesis of assumptions either the problem definition is verified in its original form or revised.

Table 2.1 summarizes the methods covered in this chapter for problem definition and provides a brief checklist of factors to consider.

Table 2.1 Problem Definition Methods

METHODS	FACTORS TO CONSIDER
Boundary Analysis	Saturation sampling
	Elicit representations from competing stakeholders
	Construct frequency distribution of new representations
Classification Analysis	Categories relevant to decisionmaking
	Categories exhaustive and mutually exclusive
Causal Analysis	Identify controlling variables
	Distinguish possible (remote) from plausible (proximate) causes
	Focus on actionable causes
	Distinguish short-, medium-, and long-term effects
	Consider unintended consequences of multiple causes
Use of Analogies	Personal impact (bus service cuts)
	Direct comparison of how related programs treat causes (contagious diseases)
	Symbolic (use of systems, circuits for policy process; triangles for organizational structures)
Brainstorming	Recruit knowledgeable experts on issue
	In group process, separate idea generation from idea evaluation phase
Assumptional Analysis	Start with recommended policies
	Work backward from solutions to stakeholders, data, and supporting assumptions
	For lack of congruence, critically review linkage between policies, data, and assumptions

CHAPTER 2 CASE STUDY

Fighting Crime: The Case for Emptier Prisons

America now imprisons more people than Russia. According to statistics released on December 3rd, 565 out of every 100,000 Americans are behind bars. And although blacks comprise only 13% of the population, they account for almost half the country's 1.4m inmates.

It is true that America has more crime than other places, and that black Americans commit too much of it. But these two facts do not explain everything. Black Americans commit about the same share of violent crime as they did in 1976, and the total crime rate has actually fallen since 1980. Over the same period, the number of inmates has tripled, and the proportion of black prisoners has increased.

Why, then, do Americans continue to vote for those who vow to lock yet more people away? One reason is that fear of crime does not diminish, even when the incidence of crime falls. Another is that although total crime rates have fallen since 1980, violent crime has increased by about a third. Law-abiding people naturally want murderers, rapists and muggers caged. But this does not explain why the prison population has risen almost ten times faster than the rate of violent crime.

It is not crime that has changed, but punishment. A study of why the prison population has grown attributed about a third of the growth to demographics, the increase in violent crime, more arrests and longer sentences. The other two-thirds came from jailing people for offences that did not require prison sentences in the past. In particular, the war on drugs has crammed America's prisons with non-violent petty criminals. In all, the number imprisoned for drug offences tripled between 1986 and 1991, and has grown since; in Washington state, the number of prisoners in for drugs crimes has risen almost 1,000% since 1980.

As a result, violent criminals are a decreasing share of the prison population. In 1991, according to the Cato Institute, only one out of five drug offenders in state prisons, and one out of three in federal ones, had a violent history. And the increase in the number of drug offenders in prison comes at a time when usage of all illegal drugs is lower than it has been for years, although it remains high in the inner cities.

Black Americans have been disproportionately hit by the war on drugs because they tend to commit the wrong kinds of drug crime. For example, under federal law the possession of five grammes of cocaine powder is a misdemeanour that carries a maximum prison sentence of a year. Possession of five grammes of crack cocaine, though, is a felony that carries a mandatory five-year sentence. Blacks are much likelier to smoke crack: the result is a large increase in the number of blacks in prison.

Such mandatory minimum sentences, at both federal and state level, are filling up prisons faster than new ones can be built; more than a dozen states also have "three-strikes" rules, which require long prison stretches for a third felony. Mandatory sentences, in either form, are crude. In particular, they do not distinguish between levels of seriousness of different types of crime; the federal minimum sentence for possession of a small amount of LSD is ten years, much more than for kidnapping, rape or attempted murder.

The basic aim of the war on drugs has been to remove anyone involved in the drug trade from the street to the cells. Yet demand for drugs remains high in the inner cities, and the history of the trade demonstrates that supply always meets demand. Locking up a drug courier does not mean there is one courier the less at large: only that an aspiring, often under-age, one gets his chance.

Mandatory minimums thus do not inhibit the operations of the drug trade; but they ensure that lots of non-violent, low-level drug offenders sit in prison for a long time. In 1990, almost 90% of first-time drug offenders in federal courts went to prison, with an average sentence of more than five years. First-time violent offenders went to jail less often and for shorter periods. No wonder that the proportion of drug prisoners in federal prisons goes on rising.

Much of this rampant incarceration is pointless. Drug-users do not need to spend five years in jail to know they have offended: like most petty criminals, most grow out of their bad habits quickly enough. Besides, most give up crime, and hardly anyone starts, after the age of 30. But mandatory sentences mean that more minor villains will stay in prison well past their criminal prime. At a cost of $21,000 a year for each increasingly creaky inmate that is a waste of money that could be better spent on deterring the dangerous young.

America is good, and getting better, at locking up the worst and most incorrigible criminals. But it casts too wide a net. The 1995 crime bill, with its proposed $12.2 billion in prison construction and extension of mandatory sentences, is very much in this mould. There are better and more creative ways of dealing with many criminal misfits.

One would be to try to cut the demand for drugs rather than the supply. The latter has never worked, as the stable or falling street price of drugs makes clear. A Rand Corporation study found, however, that a dollar of drug treatment lowers consumption as much as $7-worth of law enforcement does. Treatment lowers the volume of drugs consumed; the less the consumption, the fewer the drug-related crimes.

There is also a case for insisting on prison for violent first offenders and tougher treatment for violent juveniles. A study by the National Bureau of Economic Research found that the cost of locking up a violent criminal was much less than the cost of the mayhem he would probably have committed. The great majority of violent criminals in state prisons have at least one violent conviction in their pasts.

And there is a case for developing forms of punishment that stop short of prison. Technical parole or probation violations, such as being caught drinking or in the wrong district, are the most common reasons why people go to prison. That can be an over-harsh—and hugely expensive—punishment for people considered non-threatening enough to be on the streets.

It is not just criminals who are paying an exaggerated price for America's addiction to incarceration. The criminal minority, in effect, consumes an increasingly disproportionate share of the public purse. State spending on prisons has increased more than sixfold in real terms since 1979, using money that could have been spent on education, parks and hospitals. Getting tough on crime is punishing not just the bad guys, but law-abiding citizens as well.

Analysis of Chapter 2 Case Study

This provides an excellent opportunity to use many of the problem definition methods noted earlier in this chapter. For example, first it appears that past policies seem to have been limited by assumptions introduced by analysts themselves (e.g., the nine-dot problem). Policymakers have literally imprisoned themselves by linear thinking, but the intellectual vacuum should encourage creative thinking and the use of assumptional analysis of past problem definitions in order, for instance, to try and reduce prison populations without increasing crime rates. Second, what are the boundaries of this problem? Have all stakeholders been approached and surveyed? Are current policies based on inadequate boundary analysis? Third, does reclassification of convicts lead to new problem definitions? That is, are current policies based on superficial classification of data? Fourth, what are the causes of jail overcrowding? It was noted that earlier analyses revealed missing causal factors, such as plea bargaining (Nagel and Neef 1976). Fifth, what analogies could be used to contribute to a more comprehensive definition of the problem? Is prison overcrowding analogous to other policy problems? Sixth, would brainstorming help? Here, we can propose ideas for discussion and follow with suggestions for their constructive critique and evaluation.

THE BOUNDARY PROBLEM AND LINEAR THINKING

In many states in this country, governors proudly proclaim more annual public expenditure for prison construction to deal with "the problem" of overcrowded prisons. For example, to the existing thirty-two prisons holding 148,244 prisoners, California will add six more. It is estimated that eleven more will be required to keep up with demand (*Economist* 1997b). This is a solution similar to "the lack of lane space" as a definition of the traffic problem given by highway engineers, leading to policies that must build ahead of demand. It may also remind one of the practice from earlier centuries of locking up debtors until they could pay their debts. Thus, characterized by narrow, self-imposed boundaries, the erroneous definition of the jail problem as somehow separate from the drug control problem is useful to highlight flaws in problem definition and in the failure or misuse of problem structuring techniques by policy analysts and decisionmakers.

One should first approach the issue from the general to the specific. What are some background factors of the political environment that can condition problem structuring? Perhaps as important as the composition of expert teams participating in policy analysis (e.g., are they all prison construction engineers?) is the locus of their activity. For example, is the analysis to be done in a think tank with a political reputation? Is it a study from the state's department of prisons? Will it be a gubernatorial office analytic unit? Will it be a legislative policy analysis unit? The conclusions, for example, from a legislative unit may carry more weight with legislators who ulti-mately write the laws that guide court decisions or judicial policymaking.

Another general consideration is the question of who participates in the stakeholder analysis. How broad should the definition be? There are many experts on crime and criminal justice policy in universities and con-sulting firms, and there are others working out of their converted garage offices. They know about the habits of different types of criminals, what deters them, what could cure them, how demographics affects criminal behavior over time, and so on. As stakeholders, these professional views are essential to forging a comprehensive definition of the problem and a work-able and effective public policy. In principle, their ideas carry equal weight and stand or fall on their merits. In practice, in the debate over prison pol-icy, because of predominance of the narrower definition, prison officers have become a political force in the land. Their powerful and outspoken support for continued prison construction and "three strikes" mandatory sentencing is well-recorded (*Economist* 1997b). Think also of possible links between public works contractor lobbies and the prison construction policy option. Many governors, such as Pete Wilson of California, also support both approaches to crime control. But it is also clear that other stakehold-ers, relying on technical studies and differing assumptions about current policies, are harshly critical of this approach. It is important to maintain a broader definition of stakeholders, including members of the public, correc-tional facilities, and administrators.

CLASSIFICATION ANALYSIS

Generation and use of data in the crime area is extremely important in that much of policy often turns on conflicting interpretations of the data. As in many ill-structured policy areas, the facts do not speak for themselves. For this reason, before the interpretation war begins the analyst needs to get the facts straight. In the case of prison crowding, there are several significant data trends and data categories that need to be considered to analyze poli-cy, perhaps forcing redefinition of the problem.

First, as indicated in this chapter's case study, since 1980 the prison pop-ulation has grown 10 times faster than the rate of violent crime. While the overall rate of crime has fallen, the rate of violent crime has risen by about 33 percent. But also since 1980, although the number of inmates has tripled, the number of violent criminals as a share of the total prison population has decreased, according to the Cato Institute. The data lead to the obvious ques-tion of causation. Some argue that the increased rate of incarceration has led to reduced crime rates. But in New York crime has fallen along with the incarceration rate (*Economist* 1999b, 30). Thus, causal relationships need to be examined further.

Second, a useful distinction could be made between categories of prisoners and drug users to get a clearer picture of the problem. What is the profile of prison offenders? One study explains that 67 percent of the increase in prison population after 1980 is the result of jailing drug offenders (the mandatory drug sentencing statutes did not exist in 1980). Thus, the bulk of prisoners are drug offenders, with nondrug offenders accounting for only about 33 percent of the prison population increase. The number imprisoned for drug offenses tripled from 1986 to 1991. In Washington state the number of prisoners for drug crimes has risen 1,000 percent since 1980.

To clarify the data further, one might ask, What is the change in reported use of cocaine and other hard drugs since 1986? Note in chapter 4 that use of a moving average technique results in an expected increase in use of 2.75 percent. Has it continued to increase? Could actual use be declining despitĕ an increase in arrests and incarceration of drug offenders? Drug use among the household population (past month, or current use of any illicit drug) is down from its peak of 25,399 (14.1 percent) to 13,035 (6.1 percent). Although adolescent drug use increased from 1992 to 1996, it leveled off in 1997. Some suggest that law enforcement has caused it to go down. Further, what is the racial composition of offenders and their socioeconomic status? Is there anything distinctive about these data that could point to a need to reexamine problem definitions? In fact, the case suggests that African Americans have been hit disproportionately by the war on drugs. What is the proportion of African Americans in the 67 percent increase in prison population caused mostly by drug offenders? According to 1998 figures, the incarceration rate for them is eight times that for Caucasians (*Economist* 1999b, 31), and a large proportion of African Americans are in prison for drug offenses. The case is not clear on this, and this issue would be a useful piece of missing information for the analyst.

Finally, is there anything distinctive about the racial component of drug consumption? African Americans consume about 95 percent of crack cocaine in this country, Caucasians and Latinos predominate among powder cocaine users (*Washington Post* 1997). Why is the racial component of drug consumption important to a definition of the prison crowding issue? One answer is that under federal law possession of 5 grams of cocaine powder is a misdemeanor and carries a maximum sentence of only 1 year. By contrast, possession of 5 grams of crack cocaine is a felony and carries a maximum sentence of 5 years. If more than 50 grams of crack is found, the mandatory sentence goes to 10 years. A difficulty in resolving policy problems is that separation of powers and partisan politics intervenes in classification analysis. While Congress is proposing even greater penalties for cocaine use, the Clinton administration has proposed reduction of the disparity between crack and powder cocaine sentencing.

CAUSES OF PRISON CROWDING

What kind of problem are we dealing with? As in most public policy issues, this is an ill-structured or messy problem. It is more than a prison problem and requires examination of larger related problems such as drug control. Why is this a messy problem? One could classify the problem as such because it involves many decisionmakers (e.g., executive, judicial) and it is the product of many policy alternatives rejected. Messy and ill-structured problems are complex and contain many interdependencies. The statistics point to these interdependencies but do not point to simple solutions—most such solutions would have major unintended consquences.

Despite reduced rates of reported crime for the period 1993–1999, the prison population continures to grow. The rate of increase in the prison population is now 4.4 percent (down from 6.2 percent in 1990) but still enough to generate 1.8 million inmates. This amounts to an incarceration rate of 668 inmates per 100,000 inhabitants of the United States, which is five to ten times the rates of Western European countries (*Economist* 1999a, 30). Since 1980, the number of people behind bars in the nation for drug offenses has increased eight times to 400,000 in 1995. Drug arrests also doubled from 1980 to 1.1 million in 1995. Despite spending $30 billion at all levels of government for drug control and two-thirds of the federal drug budget for enforcement, drug prices continue to fall. The price of cocaine is now half as much as in 1980 and heroin sells for 40 percent less than in 1989. Purity has also increased—despite enforcement efforts—as supplier efficiency has increased (*Economist* 1999a, 71).

The prison crowding issue is complex because even after definition it is subject to competing institutional preferences. For example, in the drug control/prison crowding area, Congress generally supports interdiction and prison construction. The boom in prison construction is now supported by a network of powerful political interests called the "prison-industrial complex." This multibillion-dollar industry is akin to the military-industrial complex that fuels defense policy (Schlosser 1998, 63). The federal government executive often supports softer treatment and testing programs, however. But recent legislation such as the Drug Free Communities Act points to a new direction—shifting funds to state and local governments. As in the federal government, the bulk of funds goes to enforcement efforts that are perceived to reflect local preferences. Thus, with a view toward redefinition of the problem and policy reform, it is critical that all forms of causation, including institutional, be established.

The analyst should begin with "remote" causes. Remote causes are evident in the drug policy of interdiction and enforcement that in the process of vice control also creates a strong black market for drug production and sale around the world. This raises the price and encourages new entrants into the market, thus ensuring sustained supplies of crack and powder cocaine, heroin, and related drugs to consumers in the United States. Analysis of remote causes must also include "demand" as well as supply. Demand for drugs is a function of a number of factors, including the the risk of being caught (which is related to the efficacy of enforcement programs). From the "supply" perspective, the chance is slim that U.S. drug policies can reduce supplies of drugs around the world, making the price so high for drug consumers that they revert to alcohol and cigarettes. In addition, despite political support among several influential circles, the chances for legalization of drugs are slim. Legalization of drugs in the minds of legislators and their perceived base of supporters would be a defeat for the traditional culture of personal responsibility and self-control: it would be an admission of defeat for crime control advocates who dominate policy debates. These are remote causes and consequences that cannot be changed in the short run.

More "plausible" and "actionable" causes can be found as noted in the relationship between crowding, pretrial release, and plea bargaining. Note that the 1976 study of Nagel and Neef dealt with prison crowding before the advent of new mandatory antidrug statutes. Thus, an additional cause is the effect of antidrug statutes on plea bargaining. If this diminishes plea bargaining and pretrial release, the courts would be even more clogged, leading to an increase in jail overcrowding. Three-strikes legislation has resulted in more jury trials in efforts by defendants to avoid prison. While only 3 percent of the 26,237 Los Angeles Superior Court cases in 1996 were three-strikes cases, they accounted for 24 percent of the jury trials. The three-strikes law will require an extra 17,000 jury trials at an expense of $27 million (*Economist* 1997b).

Thus, the major controlling policy variable for prison overcrowding currently seems to be three-strikes type of mandatory sentencing for drug use that is in effect in more than twelve states. It could be that drug policy is working against both sensible prison policy and justice administration. As indicated, a major—perhaps unintended—consequence of the mandatory sentencing laws has been to fill prisons with petty, nonviolent, frequently first-time offenders. Almost 90 percent of first-time offenders in federal courts went to prison in 1990 with an average sentence of more than five years; first-time violent offenders went to jail less often and for shorter periods. In California, twice as many people have been imprisoned for marijuana offenses as for murder, rape, and kidnapping combined (Schlosser 1997, 92). Under the mandatory sentencing law, a district attorney decides the rank of the crime: misdemeanor or felony. If one is convicted of three felonies, he or she receives the five-year maximum sentence. The third offense may be a misdemeanor (e.g., theft of a piece of pizza) but classed as a felony by the district attorney. If the defendant has committed two violent felonies before, this would be sufficient for imposition of the five-year sentence. Clearly, this is a crude form of legislative action (something like mandating budgetary balance at the federal level) that does not distinguish between levels of seriousness of different kinds of crime. The result is widespread disparities in crime classification and uneven sentencing, which violate the basic legal precept that sanctions should be clear and predictable to avoid violation of due process.

The question is, what can be done about changing the controlling legal variable? Here it is important for the analyst to distinguish and measure the costs of bad effects of drug use and the bad effects of drug abuse control through enforcement (Kleiman 1992, 17). A recent California Supreme Court ruling held that presiding judges may now exercise their own judgment in deciding whether the third crime or the two committed previously are actually misdemeanors rather than felonies (*Economist* 1997b). By returning discretion to the judiciary, some of the harsher impacts of the laws may be mitigated in the future. It could also replace the confusion caused by the actions of district attorneys with new confusion caused by judges, increasing the overall uncertainty of sentencing and legal process.

BRAINSTORMING

Here is our opportunity to move out of the nine dots and provide creative policy problem definitions that will lead to like solutions. Given the propensity for policy experimentation at the state and local levels of government in the United States, such analysis is useful and often successful in influencing change. Let us propose several ideas that should be constructively assessed, followed by separate criticism and evaluation. Current drug policy is based largely on an enforcement problem definition: How do we remove anyone involved in the drug trade from the street to the cell? It has been billed as "supply side" drug policy. As noted previously, 66 percent of the $17.1 billion FY 99 budget for drug control is for enforcement and only 34 percent is for demand reduction through education and treatment programs (Office of National Drug Control Policy 1998, 16). Is this an appropriate definition? Brainstorming can help by providing alternative definitions.

First, one must think counterintuitively. Can one suppose that the overcrowding is functional? Can one suppose that the mandatory sentence laws operate exactly as intended and that the appropriate response now is to construct more prisons and add more juries? Similar to the effects of congestion costs on highways, according to economic theorists, drivers often react rationally and behave differently, taking mass transit or driving at different hours. Following this analogy, at least one thesis is that fear of prison conditions will cause potential drug offenders to think twice before consuming and ending up in the criminal justice system. In short, suppose that the consequences are not unintentional but exactly as predicted? California officials make this argument in citing the 4.2 percent drop in violent crime and the 12 percent drop in the overall crime rate in a six-month period. The rate of violent crime in the United States has fallen each year from 1991, dropped 7 percent in 1996, and is now at its lowest level in ten years (*Economist* 1997b).

Studies do suggest that existing successes in combating crime reflect a more innovative and aggressive criminal justice system, such as in its use of community policing. Other studies suggest that the drop is due not to policy but to other factors over which policy has no control: the aging of the population and the crack cocaine market (Thomas 1997). Following this line of thinking, one should consider that existing policy could remove substantial numbers of actors from the drug trade and streets to cells, thereby substantially weakening the drug trade and reducing consumption. Accepting this proposition, the question then is how to minimize the damage to first-time offenders and other nonviolent offenders and focus on the dealers, distributors, and upper level drug traders? Suggestions here might include, for example, increased judicial discretion in classifying crimes as misdemeanors and increased targeting of hard-core drug traffickers and their allies by more flexible and community-based policing strategies.

Second, suppose that we propose the opposite and recommend legalization of drugs—that the policy problem is one of excess control (analogous to poorly designed internal control systems that attempt to micromanage all expenditures, merely creating opportunities for corruption and incentives for mismanagement). Swiss authorities have demonstrated the success of legalizing drugs through a "partial legalization" program that gives program participants (1,000) who are hard-drug dependent injections of pure heroin at nominal prices in exchange for psychological counseling. In recent years, major gains have been achieved in finding permanent jobs, reducing unemployment, reducing drug abusers' participation in drug and theft crimes, and increasing the health of participants. The program is complemented by increased police regulation and enforcement against public use of drugs. Voters in Zurich acknowledged the success of this program by approving it in a referendum in 1996 (Frey 1997). Buoyed by the success of earlier drug programs, in 1998 Swiss voters were asked to approve a referendum to legalize the use and sale of marijuana, heroin, and cocaine through the *Drogleg* program (*Economist* 1998c).

In short, it may be argued that following the comparative example of Switzerland and the analogy of alcohol regulation in the United States, enforcement should be tempered by legalization of drugs and regulation of sales, with strong "demand side" enforcement sanctions for misuse by certain classes such as minors. The following idea could be examined: Since prohibition approaches (e.g., enforcement, three-strikes laws) have not stemmed the flow of drugs, policies should be changed to include legalization accompanied by suitable regulations. First, successful legalization could reduce the prison population; reduce capital expenditures for prisons; cut future operations and maintenance commitments from current budgets; and reduce the price of drugs and associated violence among drug lords. (The annual cost per prison inmate in the United States is roughly $21,000.) From this perspective of at least partial legalization, the proposed FY 1995 crime bill with its recommended $12.2 billion in prison construction and extension of mandatory sentences was largely a waste of money.

Second, legalization would generate public-sector revenues, similar to the 80 percent levy for a pack of cigarettes and 60 percent for whiskey. Third, to legalize narcotics pragmatically and incrementally the established regulatory regimes for alcohol and tobacco could be replicated with licensed sales outlets and minimum ages for purchase. In many cases, such as with the drug "ecstasy," purity and quality could be ensured by licensing manufacturers (*Economist* 1997a).

Fourth, as an alternative to prison sentencing we could recommend drug treatment programs. But how effective is this in controlling drug use and abuse? Program evaluation studies have been conducted since the early 1970s, and the success of the Swiss example after two years was cited above. All the forms of treatment have been shown to succeed in reducing drug use and other antisocial behavior that are outgrowths of drug use. The reduction in costs to society of drug-related crime is much greater than the cost of treatment programs. Drug treatment is cost-effective in that it can minimize jail overcrowding in existing prisons and reduce the capital outlays for new ones (Mieczkowski et al. 1992, 347).

Fifth, suppose we recommend enhanced drug testing for prisoners and integrate testing with both prison construction and release programs? In the 1970s President Nixon focused on the demand side of drug use based on an innovative pilot drug treatment program in Washington, D.C. In the 1960s this city, like so many others, was gripped by a heroin epidemic. So, it set up a network of clinics offering the synthetic narcotic methadone and other treatments to get addicts off heroin. Impressed by Washington, D.C.'s 5.2 percent decrease in crime rate (the first decline in years), President Nixon created the Narcotics Treatment Administration in 1970 modeled on the Washington, D.C., treatment program. By 1973 the heroin epidemic in that city and the United States as a whole was ebbing, and many attribute its decline to this treatment program (Massing 1998). Subsequent U.S. presidents opted for enforcement, as noted, and more than two-thirds of federal drug progams are devoted to enforcement or supply-side activities.

Nevertheless, in 1998 President Clinton directed the U.S. attorney general through the Office of Justice Programs to amend guidelines for prison construction grants and require state grantees to establish and maintain a system of reporting on their prison drug abuse problem. The president has also instructed the attorney general to draft and transmit to Congress legislation allowing states to use federal prison construction funds to provide a full range of drug-testing, sanctions, and treatment programs. A pilot drug-testing program is now underway in twenty-five of the ninety-four federal judicial districts; its intent is to allow federal judges to determine appropriate release conditions for defendants.

Subsequently, as part of brainstorming, the well-known critiques of these propositions should be presented. First, unreasonably harsh drug policies alone have not produced lower crime rates. (It should also be noted that crime rates nationally have declined irrespective of any states' three-strikes laws. There are other factors, too, including the design of enforcement programs themselves, that affect demand.) Second, the social costs of legalization could be higher than at present: it would be harder to stop the spate of available drugs after its having flooded the country with legal drugs than to continue the existing policy. The Swiss did fail earlier with their famous "needle park" experiment that turned Zurich into the drug magnet for Europe. Third, even with the generally positive evaluation of treatment programs, the return to drug use is common. In most programs, better outcomes are associated with such factors as intact marriage, jobs, short histories of drug use, low levels of psychiatric problems, and little or no criminality (Mieczkowski et al. 1992, 347). Both sets of propositions should be developed and critiqued, then synthesized into a concise set of policy recommendations based on a revised definition of the problem.

PROBLEM ANALOGIES

Analogies can also be useful in attacking the problem of overcrowded prisons. Analysts can think of many types of personal and direct analogies for dealing with this issue. Two that may be used are (1) the regulatory and construction alternatives proposed for the control of stray dogs and other animals in many cities, and (2) disease control and treatment programs that focus on similar target populations.

First, for the stray dog analogy data are needed to compare the cost benefits of regulatory and construction alternatives. To reach a satisfactory definition of the problem, the analyst needs to correlate the animal control problem (stray dogs) with each alternative. For example, if data support a correlation between licensing and animal owner responsibility, the case can be made that the problem is regulatory. If most nuisances are caused by unlicensed animals, a direct attack on delinquent owners through a census, steep fines, and other such measures might be a worthy alternative to constructing a shelter or increasing staff hours to cope with increasing complaints (Lehan 1984, 76). That is, as in drug use and abuse, if owner motivation can be positively influenced, the animal nuisance situation may be altered at its roots, reducing dog impoundments and the need for a new pound (reducing jail overcrowding and the need for new jail construction) (Lehan 1984, 74). Using the analogy of licensing as a controlling variable for the animal problem, the benefits of drug user behavior modification through treatment and fines and/or penalties for failure to adhere to regulations could be explored.

Second, since addiction is analogous to a disease, one could use the analogy of disease control to explore problem definitions for drug policy. In the case of AIDS control and treatment, for example, lessons have been learned that may be applicable to drug policy. One significant lesson cited above is that political and ideological constraints impede an appropriate definition of many policy problems. AIDS is a health policy problem but has been treated as a civil rights issue. It is both. The absence of a database of those infected, because of fear of retaliation against those infected, has hindered public health efforts to test and monitor the spread of the disease (Burr 1997a).

In the case of drug use, the mere mention of drug liberalization or scaling back enforcement seems to cause insanity not among users but, seemingly, in those who define the drug problem and are charged with development of new policies. During the Reagan administration, a public health approach to drug control was replaced with emphasis on law enforcement. Why? According to Schlosser (1997), drug use was no longer considered an illness; all drug use was deemed immoral, a symbol of the weakness of a liberal and permissive society. It caused the slovenly appearance of youths and accounted for their lack of motivation. Given the current political conservatism of both major parties, drug enforcement has become a bipartisan effort with nothing to be politically gained by defending drug abusers from excessive punishment (Schlosser 1997, 94). Despite the recent redefinition of drug use as a form of immorality, the analogy of addiction and use as an illness is still valid. As already emphasized, the effect of failure to use this analogy is jail overcrowding and administrative stress on the criminal justice system. In short, it is more reasonable to define the drug problem as being in the public health sphere rather than more narrowly as a matter of criminal justice.

ASSUMPTIONAL ANALYSIS

To test our efforts to critique and redefine the problem of prison crowding, the analyst should link existing policies and supporting data with underlying policy assumptions. First, it is recognized that drug and prison policies may be working against each other. Prisons are filling up with low-level, nonviolent drug users, while the perceived availability of drugs seems to remain constant, and violent crime is still a major problem in most cities (despite drops in crime rates). The database used to generate a definition of the problem as one of moving all drug traders and users into cells consisted largely of patterns of drug consumption. But after years of draconian legislation and tough law enforcement, the flow of drugs into the United States seems to be continuing at about the same rate. Data since 1980 indicate that the prison composition has changed and that continuation of existing policies will continue to fill jails without substantially reducing drug use. Based on changed data on prison composition that strongly indicates major unintended consequences of drug policies (revealed also by California Supreme Court ruling returning discretion to judges, from district attorneys, to classify the gravity of offenses), the assumptions of current definitions of the drug use problem need to be reexamined. What are the assumptions? First, tough law enforcement will stem drug use and reduce supplies. Second, more prison construction will provide space for the new supply of offenders. Given the data and results, the assumptions are questionable and the analyst should challenge them logically with available data.

CONCLUSION

This chapter's case study provides the analyst with a good opportunity to employ basic tools to assess the effects of competing definitions of the prison overcrowding problem. Based on a new definition of the problem, one should now try and compose a goal statement and performance criteria for a new program based on a revised problem statement. For example, the goal statement might be to "reduce the number of repeat drug offenders by 10 percent in six months" or "reduce the prison population by 10 percent in one year by legalizing drugs." Using a target population (drug users going to prison), one could outline performance criteria for a proposed program that may be used for monitoring and postevaluation of the program later. Included are assumptions, standards, and causal relationships that affect the target population and that will affect the scope and direction of the program. One would also want to develop standards that allow existing policies to work more effectively by hitting intended targets (i.e., hard-core offenders) and using treatment programs for many now sent to jail; or conversely that may allow changed policies (i.e., legalization and treatment) to function without generating excessive short-term social costs.

The authors gratefully acknowledge the assistance of Ms. Sumona Guha for her critical comments and suggestions on this chapter. Ms. Guha received her master's degree in public policy from the Georgetown University Graduate Public Policy Institute in 1996. Until 1998 she was an economist at the Office of National Drug Control Policy in Washington, D.C. She is currently a Foreign Service officer with the U.S. Department of State and will soon move to her first post in Ukraine.

References

Bardach, Eugene. (1996). *The 8-Step Path of Policy Analysis (A Handbook for Practice)* (Berkeley, Calif.: Academic Press).

Brewer, Garry D. and Peter deLeon. (1983). *The Foundations of Policy Analysis.* (Homewood,Ill.: Dorsey Press).

Brinkley, Joel. (1986). "Drug Law Raises More Than Hope, The Turf Battles Are Likely to Reach New Heights," *New York Times* (2 November).

Brown, Warren. (1998). "Seat Belt Push Raises Race Issue," *Washington Post* (3 April), A1.

Burr, Chandler. (1997a). "The AIDS Exception: Privacy v. Public Health," *Atlantic Monthly,* June, pp. 57–67.

————. (1997b). "Letters," *Atlantic Monthly,* September, p. 10.

Carter, F. W. and H. T. Norris. (1996). *The Changing Shape of the Balkans* (London: University College London Press).

Davis, Patricia and Leef Smith. (1998). "A Crisis That May Not Exist is All the Rage," *Washington Post* (10 November).

Day, Katherine. (1997). "Recycling: Higher Price, Lower Priority? City Governments Debating Cost Effectiveness of Programs," *Washington Post* (30 March), A1.

Dunn, William N. (1994). *Public Policy Analysis: An Introduction,* 2d ed. (Englewood Cliffs, N.J.: Prentice Hall).

————. (1981). *Public Policy Analysis: An Introduction* (Englewood Cliffs, N.J.: Prentice Hall).

Economist (1999a). "Ending the War on Drugs" (2 January), pp. 71–74

————. (1999b). "Prisoners: More Than Any Other Democracy" (20 March), pp. 30–31.

————. (1998a). "Out of Jail and Onto the Street" (5 December), pp. 29–30.

————. (1998b). "Survey of Health Insurance" (24 October), p. 26.

————. (1998c). "On Prescription: Drugs in Switzerland" (28 November), pp. 51–52.

————. (1998d). "Journey Beyond the Stars" (19 December), pp. 107–12.

————. (1997a). "Shopping for a Drugs Policy" (16 August), pp. 43–44.

————. (1997b). "Three-Strikes Legislation: It Needed a Bit of Tidying Up" (12 April), p. 27.

————. (1997c). "Better Off, But Not Much" (4 October), p. 35.

————. (1997d). "A Funny Sort of Market" (18 October), pp. 63–64.

————. (1997e). "Coughing Up" (24 October), p. 84

————. (1995). "Fighting Crime: The Case for Emptier Prisons" (9 December), p. 25.

Frey, Bruno. (1997). "Legalizing Drugs," *Economist* (6 September), p. 6.

Fumento, Michael. (1998). "Road Rage Versus Reality," *Atlantic Monthly* (August), pp. 12–17.

Guess, George M. (1992). "Centralization of Expenditure Control in Latin America," *Public Administration Quarterly* 16, 3, pp. 376–94.

————. (1979). "Pasture Expansion, Forestry and Development Contradictions: The Case of Costa Rica," *Studies in Comparative International Development* 14, 1 (spring), pp. 42–55.

Harlan, Stephen. (1997). "We Can Cut Crime," *Washington Post* (27 April), C7.

Hopkins, Sam. (1986). "Bowers Suggests Making Possession of Small Amount of Pot a Felony," *Atlanta Constitution* (1 November).

Joffe, George. (1996). "Muslims in the Balkans" in F. W. Carter and H. T. Norris. *The Changing Shape of the Balkans* (London: University College London Press).

Johnson, Jocelyn M. (1997). "The Medicaid Mandates of the 1980s: An Intergovernmental Perspective," *Public Budgeting and Finance* 17, 1 (spring), pp. 3–34.

Kleiman, Mark. (1992). *Against Excess: Drug Policy for Results* (New York: Basic Books).

Le Carré, John. (1996). *The Tailor of Panama* (London: Hodder and Stoughton).

Lehan, Edward. (1984). *Budgetmaking: A Workbook of Public Budgeting Theory and Practice* (New York: St. Martin's).

Lindsey, Robert. (1986). "Marijuana Drive Reduces Supplies and Raises Prices," *New York Times* (4 October).

Massing, Michael. (1998). "Nixon Had It Right: A 70s Project Showed Drug Treatment Works," *Washington Post* (8 November), C1.

Martner, Gonzalo. (1967). *Planificacion y Presupuesto por Programas* (Mexico City: Editoriales Siglo Veintiuno).

Mieczkowski, Tom, Douglas Anglin, Shirley Coletti, Bruce Johnson, Ethan Nadelmann, and Eric Wish. (1992). "Responding to America's Drug Problems: Strategies for the 1980s," *Journal of Urban Areas* 14, 3–4, pp. 337–57.

Milwaukee, City of. (1996). *Capital Improvements Program 1996–2001* (Wisconsin: City of Milwaukee).

Musto, David F. (1998). "This 10-Year War Can Be Won," *Washington Post* (14 June), C7.

Nagel, Stuart and Marian G. Neef. (1976). "Two Examples From the Legal Process," *Policy Analysis* 2, 2, pp. 356–57.

Office of National Drug Control Policy. (1998). *National Drug Control Strategy* (Washington, D.C.: Office of National Drug Control Policy).

Reich, Robert B. (1987). "The Rise of Techno-Nationalism," *Atlantic Monthly* (May), pp. 62–69.

Reid, Alice. (1998). "Majority of Truckers Fail Virginia Inspections," *Washington Post* (22 October), D1.

Runciman, W. G. (1998). "Debatable," *Economist* (10 January).

Schlosser, Eric. (1998). "The Prison-Industrial Complex," *Atlantic Monthly* (December), pp. 51–77.

———. (1997). "More Reefer Madness," *Atlantic Monthly* (April), pp. 90–102.

Silber, Laura and Allan Little. (1995). *The Death of Yugoslavia* (London: Penguin-BBC).

Spurgeon, Devon. (1997). "Guiliani, New York City Declare War on Rats—All 28 Million of Them," *Washington Post* (4 October) A3.

Thomas, Pierre. (1997). "Violent Crime Rate Drops 7% Nationwide," *Washington Post* (2 June), A1.

Tuchman, Barbara W. (1984). *The March of Folly: From Troy to Vietnam* (New York: Ballantine).

Vigliucci, Andres and Gail Epstein. (1997). "Quien Pierde, Quien Gana en Presupuesto de Penelas," *El Nuevo Herald* (16 September), 1A.

Washington Post. (1997). "Crack and Cocaine Penalties" (16 April), A14.

CHAPTER 3

Forecasting Institutional Impacts on Public Policy Performance

In the diagnostic or problem-structuring phase of policy analysis (Figure 1.1 in chapter 1), we seek a correct assessment of the problem to be addressed by allocation of public funds. In chapters 5 through 7 we will present analytic techniques to allow estimation of policy benefits and costs. But in an initial problem diagnostic phase, the aim should be to avoid dwelling on symptoms or erroneous questions that lead to misallocation of budgetary resources. This is the stage in which policy analysts should loosen up their thinking, explore different hypotheses, and develop alternative problem definitions. Lehan (1984, 73) suggests that the ratio of diagnostic to analytic time should be about 4 to 1. One should cast a wide net here—employing broad survey techniques, reviewing files and documents, surveying formal literature, consulting with experts in countervailing roles who have different perspectives (like good journalists writing a story). These steps will help define the problem and assess the relative significance of the data.

As noted in chapter 2, problem definition and diagnosis should lead to an attempt to forecast the effects of policy alternatives and institutional effects on implementation. Defining "actionable" problems means remedial action by institutions that will implement the solutions recommended to solve the problems. Information for such analysis can be derived from periodic consultant reports or the results of management and performance audits of budget and policy implementation. In both types of analysis, policy analysts will examine information gleaned from monitoring and evaluation. The effects of institutions on policies that are designed in response to a problem are critical. The question of where institutional effects on policy should be analyzed is not so critical: their potential effects should be reviewed beforehand based on either feedback or information from monitoring policy performance. For new policy initiatives, institutional analysis at the problem-structuring and options-forecasting stages would be appropriate. The important point is that it be done!

A major set of institutions affecting the implementation of options derived from initial problem definitions are budgetary and financial. These are the institutions and processes that develop plans and allocate resources for programs and policies, and they will affect any definition of the problem and affect policy results. It was noted in chapter 2 that the U.S. Justice Department's interest in spending most of its funds for drug law enforcement rather than drug abuse treatment is a major determinant of the problem of jail overcrowding. Also, dilapidated financial management systems contribute to more than one policy failure. The absence of road maintenance, for example, linked to weak controls over non-wage-budgeting that permits funds to be reprogrammed into salaries, allows roads to deteriorate prematurely, diminishes the value of public assets, and harms the transportation of goods and passengers. Road policies in many countries have failed for these and related institutional reasons and have wasted public resources.

Often small financial management components of institutions are defective and can predictably derail policy implementation. Why analyze the costs and benefits of, for example, the options for U.S. Indian trusteeship policy (dating from the Dawes Act of 1887) if the accounting and payments systems contribute to contravention of both the goals and objectives of that policy? The U.S. Department of the Interior (which oversees the Bureau of Indian Affairs [BIA]) is responsible for the payment of oil, timber, and gas fees from leases to the BIA, which is charged with transferring the funds to American Indians. About $500 million passes through the Individual Indian Money trust accounts each year to the U.S. Treasury, which is the custodian of the accounts, for payment to the Indians. But the accounting and payments systems are in such disarray that it is estimated that up to $10 billion may still be owed to Indians. For example, the Indians have no idea which companies (lessees) are working their lands, how much is being taken from the lands, or how much these lands have earned (*Economist* 1999, 34–35). The accounting and treasury payments need to be analyzed as part of the policy problem of how to improve the quality of life for Native Americans through transfer payments from leases consistent with policy objectives. Failure to do so risks approving a nice paper policy that will not work. Thus, the institutional dimension needs to be examined during the policy design and diagnosis phase, not merely during policy implementation when for all practical purposes it is too late. In the above instance, the evidence for utilization of institutional evaluation data during implementation is very weak.

For these reasons, this chapter focuses on the institutional and organizational context of public policymaking. Institutions matter to public policymaking and implementation. Just as neglect of organizational requirements of policy reform is usually lethal for implementation of reform (Schiavo-Campo 1994, 5), so also is it lethal for policy diagnosis and design. For example, policy proposals to decentralize health care administration to local governments implicitly assume that such organizational capacity exists. Some proposals explicitly include institution building based on analysis of capacities to ensure that implementation proceeds smoothly. So, the Clean Air Act of 1970 includes grants (section 105) for institutional technical assistance to local governments to monitor and enforce ambient air quality standards. Thus, the policy analyst needs to know the "institutional" context (regulations and procedures) as well as the "organizational" context (those units that will implement and enforce the rules and procedures). Douglass North (1990) distinguishes the institutional framework of formal and informal rules from the organizational units that will enforce them. Policy analysts need to know how to advise on both policy design (the rules) as well as the policy administration (via organizational development).

Institutional Context and Public Policy

This chapter provides an introductory analysis of the organizational context. Obviously, there is some overlap between the two concepts of policy design and policy administration. Implementing organizations may make rules too (administrative regulations), and institutional actions may affect enforcement (such as congressional earmarks in foreign aid policy). In some policy areas, implementation is charged to several organizations (environmental protection) across several levels of government. These organizations make rules and regulations, the combined effect of which is to create an institutional policy network or the kind of "issue network" discussed in chapter 1 (Heclo 1978). This network creation further blurs the distinction between organizational implementation and institutional policymaking that, boiled down further, begins to sound like administration versus politics and policy. Nevertheless, the distinction between institution and organization should be kept in mind to avoid misspecification of the policy problem that can lead to the waste of resources and frustration with the reform process itself. Even though only some of the principles, methods, and tools presented in this chapter are applicable to the case studies used, ample opportunities exist for their use in preventing policy failures in both design and implementation!

Further, it should not be thought that public policy issues and analysis refer only to "high" policy issues such as international relations, national transportation, defense, and national health care. Even state and local governments now make "foreign" policies: California counties and cities pass resolutions regularly on such matters as sanctions against Burma for human rights violations (Blustein 1997). National policies, such as highway transportation, have their state and local counterparts. These statutes and ordinances have been passed with some attention to costs and benefits, or with policy analytic inputs. For our purposes, public policies should be viewed as any program, project, regulation, or law that costs public money and will provide a potential stream of benefits. The proposals need analysis before budgets begin to finance them.

Policy analysis needs to go beyond mere rule- and lawmaking into the very strengths and weaknesses of public-sector institutions themselves. More traditional perspectives on public policy reserve this analysis for the implementation phase on the theory that course corrections will be made during the evaluation phase. But in the real world, the practical constraints to feeding back evaluation data and producing institutional changes mean that policy analysts must face these issues early in the diagnostic phase. This conclusion is bolstered by the current movement to contract out public services to improve efficiency and save money. In particular, social policies (food stamps, Medicaid, income support, and nutrition supplements for the poor) are increasingly contracted out to private firms that are held accountable by state and local government units for effective service provision.

Analytically, this means that the costs and benefits of the institutional delivery arrangements need to be figured into the policy-planning phase. Empirical estimates of potential savings to be generated by contracting out can be added to expenditures to increase policy coverage of beneficiaries and strengthen social safety nets. There are weaknesses in the estimates of contracting out services that policy analysts and their clients need to be aware of (Boyne 1998). Because of the decentralized nature of program and service delivery in the United States, experiments and pilot programs to improve service efficiency are commonplace. But often such innovative programs (e.g., "community policing") are not supported by deeper changes in policies and administrative systems. Existing programs are often housed in hierarchical bureaucracies featuring command-and-control management systems. Development of new programs frequently does not affect existing policies, procedures, and organizational structures. These existent systems continue to reinforce a process of control rather than supporting a results-driven orientation (Gianakis and Davis 1998). Part of the problem, finally, is that analytic capacities for administrative and financial management systems are weak, and improvements in analytic tools and capacities to apply them to institutions are critical to linking operational changes to policy reforms.

For example, in Ohio the state contracts with and oversees nonprofit health providers. Contracts (or transfers) are allocated on the basis of data reported on performance. Providers report on and are assessed for "efficiency" (in this instance, given levels of services at least cost such as diagnosis, counseling and treatment) and "effectiveness" (here, level of outcome or client improvement for least cost such as reduction of alcoholism attributable to treatment). Efficiency measures unit cost of service (e.g., operating cost per passenger mile of transit service); effectiveness measures how well a service or policy is performed (e.g., decreases in fire department response times).[1] In Ohio the state negotiates service contracts with providers based on maximum allowable unit costs for each service (Byrnes, Freeman, and Kauffman 1997). This system of transfers from the state budget provides a hard budget constraint on outlays and a set of institutional incentives for efficient and effective service provision. Policy evaluation is fed into the planning phase via the budget process for health program expenditures. (A similar system of performance-based transfers is used to finance part of urban mass transit operations in the United States.) Thus, policy analysis in such cases includes not only costs and benefits of eligibility requirements for particular groups but also the institutional delivery arrangement itself. Again, the institutional context should be included in the diagnostic phase.

Since budgetary institutions and processes in particular affect the calculus of costs and benefits in practice, the more obvious issues of institutional performance must be anticipated by policy analysts. Public policy analysts need to pay attention, as well, to the structure and capacities of those institutions that will actually implement the policies in the design stage. A predictable danger of moving institutional analysis to the diagnostic phase is that sound policies may be delayed by opponents who charge that weak implementing institutions will waste resources. It needs to be recognized that weak institutions also increase failure risk and drive up the costs of present policies. To avoid the subterfuge of false delay, it is important to have data on institutions' performance that specify how the institutions will affect policy performance. Much of this analysis will have to be done, in fact, during and after implementation—but it should be considered during the diagnostic stage. This chapter will present tools and procedures that have been used to analyze structural and functional components of public financial management systems as part of the institutional context.

In practice, most policies are partial and incomplete systems of rules and procedures that must be analyzed and likely revised. The policy analyst must function effectively in this environment of informational uncertainty, with frequently missing facts and figures and regular conflicts between laws and regulations. There are three critical questions that should be asked by a policy analyst. First, how do these rule systems operate within the existing organizational structure? Second, does the structure imposed by these rules impede effective management? (Is there a better way to organize the work? Are there too many reporting layers? Is management discretion too narrowly prescribed?)

Third, how effectively can core financial management and other organizational functions be performed within these structures? Specifically, do dilapidated systems distort information and increase transaction costs for service clients? For effective policy implementation, responsibility must be assigned to generate and process the right amounts of useful information to department managers. Otherwise, managers can be literally drowned in information that is useless for making quick decisions. This means that the core systems of budget allocation and allotment, personnel administration, operations and maintenance planning, program evaluation, cost and managerial accounting, payments to vendors, and cash management must all function as an integrated unit. This chapter focuses on methods useful for diagnosing problems—for "root-and-branch" reviews of organizational structures and financial management processes.

Organizational Structures and Policy Management

Over the past decade, all levels of government in the United States have been under mandate from voters and political leaders to cut costs and deliver services more efficiently. An important issue is what methods can be used to improve efficiencies without damaging program or policy effectiveness (allocative efficiency). To conduct performance audits and management reviews, governments in this country typically use in-house departments (e.g., Dade County, Florida, Office of Management and Budget), special teams (e.g., Organizational Review Team, Dade County), or private consultants (e.g., PricewaterhouseCoopers). There are other alternatives for the public sector. Montgomery County, Maryland, uses a customer service department to determine how well the county delivers social services to the poorest residents, conducts training, and provides public education on county services. The information generated and authority exercised by such institutions are critical in designing and revising social policies: rather than simply examining whether regulations are met or paperwork is completed, county workers are held accountable for the outcomes of their efforts toward policy results. Such an innovative approach recognizes that institutions matter as much to public policy planning as to implementation.

Whereas many evaluations focus only on institutional processes, the Montgomery County analysis focuses on its own service processes as an outcome and designs incentives accordingly. Unfortunately, the political payoffs to elected officials from such insights may be few. Montgomery County has proposed a 5 percent cut in its proposed current budget, meaning that nine of twenty positions could be cut (Levine and Perez-Rivas 1997). Whatever the political context, the purpose of institutional review should be to determine (1) whether existing functions are being effectively carried out by existing units and (2) whether the units' resources are being managed economically and efficiently. As noted, the formal name for policy reviews in the United States is a "management" or "operations" audit. The broader "value-for-money" purpose of such an audit should be kept in mind: it is not to solve all problems, but only those that can become economically significant.

As noted in chapter 1, emphasis on policy reform refers to rationalization of institutional structures, organizational functions, budget processes, and personnel systems. The policy analyst needs to have a broad portfolio of tools to work on these institutional and management issues. In the field, the analyst discovers rapidly that public-sector organizations responsible for policy implementation develop cumbersome structures that impede management authority and make it difficult to achieve program targets. A "structure" can be defined as an interlocking set of systems, roles, and responsibilities with authority to perform a function. There are four basic structural issues that should be examined during policy diagnosis:

1. Number of management layers
2. Span of task control
3. Reporting systems
4. Scope and method of service delivery

First, in regard to the number of management layers, organizational reform efforts often focus on such well-known techniques as decentralizing operational authority, consolidating functions, and reducing the number of management layers as efficiency moves. Not surprisingly, organizations grow into ill-designed shapes as they expand into new mission areas and occasionally need pruning. For example, organizations may become top-heavy and concentrate excess authority at the upper levels. Organizations may also be heavy around the waistline with too many midlevel officials, thus stymying performance with too many layers of management between the line officials and the senior staff members.

Accordingly, organizations need to know when to apply the right reform techniques. In some cases, reform efforts use hybrid policies, such as decentralization and the improvement of service response times. For example, after an organizational review to improve the performance of the Washington, D.C., police department, Booz•Allen & Hamilton recommended decentralization of the homicide unit into district stations. This resulted in frustration for detectives that missed important information by being iso-lated in the districts. So, following a study of homicide unit structures in six major U.S. cities by its own detectives, the department is moving to recen-tralize homicide unit functions (Thompson 1998).

Policy reformers also need to know when to add layers—to get control of fragmented activities—and when to eliminate them. Elimination of too many midlevel managers, for example, could save response time in the short run but create long-term costs by eliminating vital and often informal communication links between senior staff members, line managers, and people on the shop floor. The modern public-sector reform trend is to devolve authority to line managers to achieve centrally set performance tar-gets. But communications links to senior personnel need to be maintained without intruding on line manager autonomy. Organizations often employ staffing ratios to compare their operations with, for example, transit agen-cies, housing authorities, and personnel departments in other jurisdictions. A 1993 analysis of the California state government concluded that it was suffering from an institutional paralysis that had produced a budget deficit of $11 billion. California's "ill-functioning structure of government" was linked to multiple layers that served as a complicated channel for the buck to be passed among federal, state, and local authorities (*Economist* 1993, 22). As with such discrete organizations as departments, governments must also examine themselves for problems of excessive layering and the lack of clear lines of authority.

Second, effective task performance depends on apportioning the right amounts of task "span of control." This is the authority and capacity of managers to supervise particular types of tasks. Organization designers can misspecify the span of control by setting up tall multilayered, hierarchical structures for complex tasks that reduce professional autonomy. Such pro-fessionals as engineers, architects, and doctors working in government typ-ically need freedom to exercise their skills in nonroutine tasks not subject to detailed regulations. Narrower spans of control may be useful for rou-tinized tasks, such as the issuing of permits and licenses. Spans of control should be wider and layers of management fewer for more complex and nonroutine tasks such as the planning of new policies projects or research and development.

Organizational structures should permit exploration and innovation, meaning a broader span of control with flat structures and few, if any, lay-ers of management between tasks and staff members. It is important that organizations periodically determine whether they have too many layers or ill-defined spans of controls—again, by comparing their structures with the costs and outputs of organizations with similar policy missions in other jurisdictions or levels of government. For this task, the organizations can use in-house policy analysis units or outside management consultants. The danger of using outside consultants is that the review and reform experience is not made internal and instead becomes an expensive one-shot deal.

Third, organizations often suffer from ill-designed reporting systems. If reporting chains are unclear, employees may end up serving several masters, and accountability and performance suffer. This is a common problem in government where "messy" policy problems exist that cross geographic and organizational boundaries. The simplistic solution is tighter reporting and control systems that ultimately ignore staff morale problems created by excessive reporting requirements—often leading to excessive data generation and inordinate operational time in developing reports when that time should be spent in allocating resources to improve policy delivery.[2]

Where organizations share reporting responsibility to regulators (e.g., for mine safety), incentives are created to pass the buck and avoid taking politically difficult decisions (i.e., repairing or closing the mine). On the fiscal side, excessive layering without clear lines of authority can lead to "intergovernmental cannibalism" and regulatory failure with a high probability of major disasters. As noted, the state of California suffered from this problem in 1993. Conversely, certain fiduciary tasks may actually require unified command authority with shared information, such as authorizing checks, checking vouchers, and performing internal control operations. For such cash management type of functions, it is important to provide checks and balances through the division of responsibilities and duties. Definitions of reporting roles and responsibilities should be clear. For example, the duties and responsibilities of department heads and supervisory employees should be defined and their relationships set forth in organization charts and written instructions contained in administrative codes and policy ordinances.

Fourth, in considering the scope and method of service delivery, basic structural issues are often critical for effective policy results. Systems may be clogged by internal problems that have major implications for policy results. The organization of fiscal management systems, for example, can affect the planning and implementation of macroeconomic policies. Weak costing and expenditure planning systems can lead to the underestimation of multiyear investment programs that often leads to major fiscal deficit problems. Budget systems need to be informed by cost-accounting systems that reveal the full costs of programs to allow for rational cuts and additions to competing programs—for example, primary versus higher education, primary health care versus preventive medicine, or roads versus education. Only through the operation of such support systems can policy costs be measured to allow analysis of the relationship between costs and benefits and costs and program effectiveness.

Improvements in cost-accounting are not cheap or easy to make, and they take time. For political reasons, it is often easier to ignore institutional constraints that impede the administration of policy and simply paper them over with shiny new computer systems. In the past decade, the U.S. Internal Revenue Service (IRS) has spent more than $4 billion on new computer systems to permit management control over the tax code. The proper policy would have been to perform a root-and-branch review to simplify the tax code itself and deal with IRS structural and management problems before automation. Note that, unintentionally, emphasis on the institutional context may be distracting focus from problems with the policy rules and procedures themselves. Automation of the IRS cannot change the tax code.

In short, an exclusive focus on the institutional and organizational context here without prior change of the policies themselves can delay reform. In other policy areas as well, emphasis on expensive computerization of inefficient and opaque institutional systems may not make much difference. Many government reform efforts are misguided to automation of bad systems that diminish policy results.

By contrast, where fiscal management systems support sound fiscal policymaking, the results can be both rapid and quite spectacular. For roughly the past decade, political will at the national level of U.S. government has been strong enough to force down inflation, unemployment, and growth in fiscal deficits to their lowest levels in several decades. Including revenues from the Social Security trust fund, at the time of this writing the U.S. budget has had a surplus for two years and is projected to continue in the black well into the early part of the twenty-first century. Appropriate fiscal policies have created the right environment for economic growth. Effective fiscal policies in the 1980s and 1990s have produced "virtuous circles" in which resultant economic growth increased private earnings and public revenues. Assuming some causality, economic growth has lowered the fiscal deficit, in turn reducing inflationary pressures on interest rates. Lower interest rates on loans encourage borrowing and investment, which, as multiplied through the economy, produce further economic growth and so on (Pearlstein 1997). Improved growth benefits certain policies, such as income and poverty policies, which require less budgetary funding as median household incomes rise. At the same time, the ability of policymakers to concentrate public resources on the poor depends largely on knowing fiscal balances and making proper projections on expenditure commitments and available revenues.

Similarly, a lesson for service performance is that often more funds and more personnel are needed. This is a lesson that needed relearning after years of downsizing and cutbacks that often achieved worse service, albeit at lower short-run costs. Cuts in the Washington, D.C., Public Works Department in the 1990s, for instance, produced declines in street sweeping, paving, and construction. Since 1996, budget increases have produced progress in on-time trash collection, response to litter complaints, time needed to register motor vehicles, miles of roads resurfaced, and such fleet management measures as snow-removal vehicle readiness (Lipton 1998). While the performance falls short of planned improvements, the link between funding and performance is also clear.

This is not to say that institutional context can make up for poorly designed policies. Structural issues, specifically definitions of institutional roles and management systems, are important to policy results, but they are not as important as having technically sound policies in the first place. Policy rules and procedures may be inappropriate to good policy results: organizations may follow these rules with precision but achieve poor results. For instance, child protection systems that implement social service policies face this problem. Children are often abused, or even killed, by "dysfunctional adults" even after social service agencies follow all their rules "to a T"—investigating complaints, tallying reasonable explanations for child injuries, visiting families, and even paying utility bills to keep families together. But in many cases, children are often returned to the dangerous, dysfunctional "families" and continue to be abused by adults. Such situations lead to another round of public complaints and calls for clarification of agency policies and standardization of routines (Jeter and Levine 1997). The question is raised about whether these policies unrealistically assume that implementing agencies can completely control their environment (e.g., families, dysfunctional adults, laws requiring confidentiality and restricting information sharing with police). The policies themselves, perhaps, may be technically deficient and need to be reviewed.

There are two contemporary questions pertaining to organizational structure: What should be the optimal size of the organization implementing policy or delivering the service? Are there cheaper, more effective means of policy implementation than in the public sector?

First, what should be the size of the staff needed to deliver a service? A common problem with modern government agencies is "mission overload," in which the growth of workloads results in multiple and conflicting activities that are hard to manage and to control. The budget of the U.S. Immigration and Naturalization Service (INS) doubled to $3.1 billion in FY 97 from only four years earlier. It is one of the fastest growing agencies in the federal government, being charged with the conflicting missions of controlling the nation's borders, expelling illegal immigrants, processing citizenship applications, and hiring foreign workers. A recent proposal has recommended the reorganization of INS duties along functional lines. The agency itself would retain border control functions, but citizenship applications and administration of hiring foreign workers would be transferred to the U.S. State and Labor Departments, respectively (Schmitt 1997).

Under such conditions of growing agency workload and conflicting missions, policy analysis can link, through management audits, activities and tasks to specific roles organized as cost centers. This would allow management to link costs and results and to measure costs per unit of outputs (either directly or by proxy). Around the world contemporary civil service reforms are concentrating on determining the appropriate size of policy delivery organizations. Such determination is often difficult because the size of organizations may not have been measured correctly. Position control requires that job descriptions relate clearly to pay and grade scales and that the latter should be linked to the payroll system—eliminating the "ghost" worker problem and establishing a base for determining policy by the optimal size of an organization. A common way to determine optimal size of the civil service by policy area is to use comparative staffing ratios (e.g., staff members per line personnel, employees per capita, teachers to students, and administrators to teachers).

Second, should the policy be delivered by a private contractor instead of a public-sector agency? Should the structure of the public-sector agency be modified to exclude particular functions altogether? These are the "what" questions that should be asked early on to streamline policy institutions. Failure to do so can result in such common flaws as performing inappropriate tasks more efficiently and computerizing bad systems. To minimize waste in policy implementation, it is critical that management have sufficient authority and responsibility to allocate necessary funds. Many now believe that improved service effectiveness and efficiency can be achieved by a new linkage: public funding and private delivery. State and local governments in the United States have experimented with privatization (also known as commercialization or contracting out) in such areas as sanitation, ambulance services, transit, prison operation, car towing, and tree trimming. Many years of experience with this coordinating mechanism suggests that there are at least five rules that should be followed if privatization is to function properly (Raimondo 1992, 42).

* The goods or services should be precisely defined.
* Selection must be by a truly competitive process.

* Private-contractor performance must be regularly evaluated.
* The public sector must be able to replace inept private contractors.
* Government must be concerned about end results, not the means by which the goods or services are provided.

Administrative Functions

ORGANIZATIONAL FUNCTIONS

Inadequate functional performance (the "how" questions) can also stymie policy results. To perform a "functional review," the organization should first be subdivided into responsibility centers that relate to core functions. Related functions should then be combined into single managerial units. Over time organizations will face the latest ideas of new chief executive officers and consultants. Repeated reorganization may occur that will disrupt the workflow and weaken performance in the process of trying to install a new system based on the latest management fad. Recall the example of the decentralized and recentralized homicide unit of the Washington, D.C., police department following two functional reviews that reached different conclusions (Thompson 1998). For example, functions may be added to strengthen the political influence of an organization as much as to improve its performance. Unrelated functions are often added without improving performance that instead create later management coordination problems. Hence it is wise to periodically determine which functions should be eliminated or consolidated, and this should be done by an institutionalized review process. If no such process exists, it can be done in house through the management audit process. Outside consultants can serve this function, but ideally an organization should gain the capacity to review its own operations.

Examples abound of misplaced or redundant functions. For example, in many countries the business-licensing function is spread through several levels of government, vertically, and across several departments, horizontally, within a city administration. Conducting a revenue survey may determine constraints to fee and tax yields caused by ill-placed revenue functions. Here it may be useful to consolidate licensing and revenue functions in one tax office serving a particular area and then review the efficiency of operations. Failure to do this may impede economic growth and service efficiency. In Ukraine, for instance, establishing a business requires contending with forty sets of rules, licenses, and tax requirements administered by several agencies. This is obviously more than an institutional efficiency issue—

the very existence of the rules serves as a roadblock to entrepreneurs and benefits crony capitalism (*Economist* 1997b, 45).

Comparative analysis of other governments can suggest which functions should be included in an organization and how they should perform. For example, most finance departments in state and local governments in this country include tax, budget, accounting, payroll, and debt management, with purchasing often a separate department and function. Similarly, functional processes may reveal major inefficiencies. Managers may have immersed themselves in the details of a system and never examine the process systematically with an eye toward elimination of unnecessary steps. The "unnecessary" step may also be bribery points and serve the function of a supplementary pay system in poor countries. Since this is the abuse of public position for private gain, it is called "corruption." As an example, federally funded municipal road construction and repair projects in Washington, D.C., required approvals from twenty-seven different city officials. This complicated approval process delayed road projects and increased budgetary costs (through inflated contractor bids to cover for time lost and through payments to officials to move paperwork along). Following a review of process workflows in 1996, the approval process takes only twelve officials: this should cut the time required for contracts approval by up to six months (*Washington Post*, 1996).

FINANCIAL MANAGEMENT FUNCTIONS

The key functions and systems that should be examined by policy analysts are financial. "Following the money" to determine what is happening is important in public policy as in any other field. While structural issues and matters of redefining management authority often take longer than plugging fiscal management holes and straightening out accounts, fiscal management issues are in the more immediate term. This means that budgetary and policy outcomes are affected by institutional arrangements that can be broken down into functional financial management components. To the extent that planning, policymaking, and budgeting are linked by good financial management policy results are likely to be improved. For example, recommendations for major policy changes could be misdirected when the problem is internal fiscal management. The first formal audit of the Medicare program revealed annual losses of up to $23 billion in overpayments to hospitals, doctors, and other health care providers. (*Economist* 1997a, 25). This suggests that improvements in internal controls and financial management systems may be as much of a cause of high health care expenditures as poor health care policy design. In short, there may be high payoffs in improved policy results from strengthened fiscal management systems.

Financial management typically refers to a series of functions, including budgeting, accounting and reporting, cash management, debt management, payroll systems, procurement, treasury disbursement, internal control and audit (Coe 1989). The problem for policymaking and policy implementation is that these functions are rarely integrated into a system and they typically function well or badly in isolation. Under these circumstances, fixing one function normally makes little difference to overall policy implementation and there is the erroneous conclusion that fiscal management makes little difference for policy results.

For governments in the United States and overseas efforts are needed to integrate financial management systems. This by itself will not solve all organizational and institutional problems and magically lead to policy nirvana. But efforts to integrate financial management often unearth major problems in both policy design and organization performance that need to be fixed. The very process of installing an "integrated financial management system" (IFMS) is itself a form of policy and institutional analysis. In essence, an IFMS means that all financial and physical transactions are recorded in one main account and shared across financial functions and organizational levels for policymaking. The purpose of an IFMS is to set central standards that allow information to be aggregated and compared across operational units, but not to control these units directly. The IFMS concept presupposes that implementation authority to combine resources and achieve these standards will be delegated to lower operational units. Rigorous fiscal management through the IFMS is combined with operational freedom to manage services without intrusive central controls.

IFMS reform efforts also recognize that different levels of institutional decisionmaking require different levels of information aggregation. This is a systems design issue that directly affects policy performance, and the correct level of data aggregation must be available at each managerial level for different institutional units. Design must encompass both institutional units (central versus local) and organizational levels (strategic planning versus daily task control). For example, central health officials will want information to compare program costs and benefits (vaccination versus treatment of childhood diseases). Regional managers may need information to compare regional clinic operating costs: they need both physical and fiscal data. Managers at individual clinics may need data on line-item expenditures to compare budgeted with actual figures and other data to measure the clinic's effectiveness (Bartel 1996, 7). At the same time, senior managers at regional health centers do not want to be engaged in routine operational issues, such as billing or fee collections, at the expense of their responsibilities for strategic planning and revenue generation.

A major organizational problem is that fragmentation of fiscal functions within and across policy institutions prevents obtaining timely and accurate data for decisionmaking. An IFMS is one means to develop a system to share information and allow tracking of policy and program costs. The core functions of the financial management system are typically budgeting, accounting, and cash and debt management. Budgeting lays out the financial plan to achieve organizational objectives and allots funds to agencies for such purposes as expenditure control and program management. Cash management forecasts supplies of fiscal resources needed to complete the plan. Accounting records the fiscal effects of implementing policies and provides budget and cash management functions with feedback on what resources have been received and expended and still need to be secured to fulfill the financial plan. Debt management arranges financing for longer-term investment projects. Information provided by budget, cash management, and accounting allows the debt or public credit function to arrange timely financing that does not exceed the capacity of the budget to cover debt service payments (Bartel 1996, 13). Ancillary functions that may be added later to the system are asset management, procurement, and personnel management. It is not easy to foresee policy problems if information from these functions is not available and is not used for policy management. For example, failure to link payroll disbursements to the personnel roster can result in overbudgeting for personnel costs. Fixed personnel costs for particular policies become inflated, resulting in superficially high cost policies that could then be discontinued for the wrong reasons.

If these functions deteriorate, the financial management system can become discredited as a means of planning and allocating resources and as a means of implementing policy. Cycles of mutually reinforcing skepticism will diminish incentives of officials to take policy analysis seriously. Under these conditions, where it is perceived that the existing system has little to do with fiscal resources needed to attain effective policy results, officials have every incentive to sidestep existing regulations and seek as much "rent" as possible for their ministry, policy area, or even their own pockets.

How can improved financial management systems and institutions lead to better public policy? Suppose, for example, that analysis is needed on the costs and consequences of water and sewer systems privatization. First, analysis would be needed on whether delegation of authority should proceed to private firms. This requires cost and result information on present systems operations. Second, information is needed to establish the policy framework, the system of rules in which action should take place (e.g., policies in many countries are needed to guarantee that concessionaires can cut off service for nonpayment of tariffs by consumers and firms). Third, information is needed on current system problems. In the water and sanitation sector, major problems are overstaffed public water authorities, underpricing, leakage or lost water (unaccounted for water), and fee collections and billing: all contribute to poor service coverage and quality and undermaintained and antiquated systems.

Note that information to perform the analysis is highly specialized, and in some cases may not even be available to a government. Yet required information falls within the purview of several components of the financial management system. The budget should record obligations and outlays to private contractors on water/sanitation concessions, and there should be activity statistics in the budget, whether zero-based or performance formats are used, and the statistics should indicate costs per unit and costs per result on a multiyear basis. But budgeted costs and resultant outlays need to be linked by a cost-accounting system that analyzes costs of production. A government may not know what it actually costs to deliver sanitation services and, hence, what it should pay in a concession agreement. That is, the government unit knows only what it has been "spending" from the budget and not really "costing" on a procurement basis. To perform cost-benefit and cost-effectiveness analysis (see chapters 5–7), public-sector organizations must have either cost-accounting or cost-finding systems that allow costs to be measured and distinguished simply from appropriations expenditures.

As a point of entry on cost-of-services measurement the procurement system can contribute. Competitive bidding can help discover information on fees, performance targets, and qualified operators that governments may use to design fee policies and set performance targets (Haarmeyer and Mody 1997, 37). The revenue system will provide information on rates of fee collection, and the accounting system will provide information on obligations and outlays to allow budget officials to monitor expenditure progress and avoid deficit spending. The budget system will also provide information on maintenance needs of existing facilities and operating costs of future capital investments. Together the functions will provide policymakers with a composite picture of the fiscal implications of policy decisions.

Thus, each function should be evaluated regularly to guard against breakdown and deterioration. Let us review the relevant areas for each function and suggest ways to strengthen them.

PUBLIC BUDGETING

Budgeting matches needs with resources in a process that results in an approved spending plan. The budget process contains four sequential phases: formulation, approval, implementation, and evaluation.

Budget Formulation and Approval

Budget formulation is critical because it is in this phase that ministries can make their case to the central budget office for new programs and continuation of existing ones. Budget formulation is the translation of government policies and programs into their financial implications. The central budget office (Office of Management and Budget, OMB in the United States, or ministry of finance—MOF—abroad) has the job of reviewing the macroeconomic situation and translating aggregate fiscal balance and debt sustainability limits into budget ceilings for departments. It is important that budget policies be legally and financially transparent, and policies should proceed from representative institutions. In 1981, for example, New York state voters defeated a $500 million bond issue for new prison construction. Governor Cuomo then used the Urban Development Corporation (a public agency charged with building housing for the poor) to issue revenue bonds. And so, state prison policy was decided against voter wishes and used an opaque financing instrument that required higher interest payments than general-obligation, voter-approved bonds (Schlosser 1998, 56). Since interest costs on debt are an opportunity cost for other recurrent programs in the budget, budget policy analysis needs to examine the costs and benefits of such policies as well as the effect on future financial conditions. Naturally, where policies will be decided at higher levels regardless of technical analysis, policy analysts have few incentives to proceed, but it is important to go on record in any case.

To prepare budgets that are transparent to planners and useful to managers, a number of ingredients are essential. First, budget codes should not contain excessive classifications. Too much detail can hide essential information and overload the system. Classifications should also cover all sources of revenue and expenditure destinations, including extrabudgetary funds, such as public enterprises and such off-budget items as trust funds. The chart of accounts should be consistent with budget codes to avoid loss of control over outlays, such as maintenance that might be classified as a capital expense and financed instead of paid for on a current basis with fees and taxes. Budget structures should also be reorganized periodically to reflect changes in government policies and programs. Otherwise they become outmoded and hinder effective management.

Second, budget ceilings should be communicated in instructions from the central budget office before sectoral submissions by departments. Procedures for budget formulation and expected data for submissions need to be transparent. Failure to make the budget "call" instructions clear severs the link between planning and budgeting, and "real" budgeting starts to occur during the execution phase rather than the expenditure planning and formulation phase. The result is short-term budgeting that drives out planning. To encourage proper expenditure planning, ceilings should apply to both current and capital expenditures and be based on a public investment program with inputs from each sector (e.g., health, education).

Third, capital and current budget items should be clearly defined and distinguished to avoid capitalization of operating funds and misallocation of resources. Current budget items should not be normally financed by the capital budget because this can hide major operating deficits. At the same time, expenditure planning for both should be an integrated annual process. In many countries current and capital budgets are planned separately. This encourages construction of many projects that likely will be undermaintained and prematurely replaced by more debt financing. The resource implications of capital budgets on operating budgets, especially future operating and maintenance requirements, should be displayed clearly for effective policy choice. The relationship between a capital plan and capital budget is illustrated by the following table. This describes a three-project capital budget and six-year capital improvement plan (CIP) that illustrates several points:

- The capital budget is the first year of the capital plan. As the plan changes each year, the first year "slice" will be modified ("rolled" forward) or annually updated.
- The relation between time and funding requirements is important. Funds must be available at each point or projects will stall. If progress on any one project slips, this affects the viability of the entire CIP. The question then becomes what methods should be used to allocate funds among unfinished projects of varying urgency?
- Capital expenditures are "lumpy," especially construction contracts. Expenditures occur at different times for such necessities as site purchases, architectural and engineering contracts, construction contracts, and furnishings and equipment.
- Inputs from the operating units should enable the central budget office to develop performance measures (physical and fiscal) to assess efficiency and effectiveness. Budgets should be presented in

multiyear formats (past, current, planned) with both fiscal expenditure data and unit cost of activity data. Measures should be selected with incentives in mind. For example, use of a cost per mile of new road-paving measure would encourage managers to skimp on construction quality, thus increasing downstream budget costs for maintenance in future years. To prevent this kind of gaming with activity statistics, departments could use measures that combine the level and cost of road maintenance. Finally, budgets must be realistically finalized. The central budget office must be able to assess whether submitted requests are based on realistic costs. For this cost and policy analysts are critical. Conversely, the office must be able to appeal arbitrary cuts that ignore analysis and need.

In Table 3.1 below, note that almost 50 percent of total CIP funds are needed in year 4. This suggests that the financing plan should be evened out. In terms familiar in the United States, municipal bonds should be issued, for example, with maturities so that the annual debt service payments in the operating budget for interest and amortization remain the same over the life of the bond issue. The length of the bond issue should mirror the useful life of the facility to be constructed.

Budget Administration and Expenditure Control

Just as Figure 1.1 in chapter 1 postulated a neat division between policy formulation/analysis and implementation, so also does the literature divide budget preparation and implementation. Budget analysis is performed during preparation because once the budget is approved there is little time to rethink basics during the pressures of day-to-day operations. Systems that exclude analysis because capacities are lacking or because cynics recognize that revenues will not materialize anyway tend to produce budgets that are

Table 3.1 Example of Capital Budget and Five-Year Program

YEAR	CAPITAL BUDGET 1	CAPITAL PROGRAM 2	3	4	5	6
Sewer Project	$500,000	$150,000		$3,000,000		$500,000
Water Project		$100,000	$50,000	$1,000,000		$200,000
Road Project			$75,000		$2,000,000	
Total	$500,000	$250,000	$125,000	$4,000,000	$2,000,000	$700,000

relatively meaningless as guides to policy progress. But some policies are normally planned and analyzed during execution! Since the post-Korean War period in the United States, national security policies have been increasingly made during the execution phase. Lacking authorization or appropriations, operations begin and continue pursuant to such lawful mechanisms as transfers, reprogramming, and rescissions to finance policies, either with other program funds or budget savings through reestimation of inflation or fluctuations in foreign exchange rates (Banks and Straussman 1999, 136).

Nevertheless, budget administration or implementation is important to public policy because it is often at this stage that major control problems arise. Implementation is often called the Achilles heel of public policy and budgeting: during this phase, the central budget office pulls various levers to try and control the budget in action, such as in allotments, preaudit and internal control, and cash management (Axelrod 1995). (Note that cash management is considered a budget function by Donald Axelrod, but one of many financial management functions by Margaret Bartel and Charles Coe.) Constrictions in budget "plumbing" are a major cause of poor service delivery and project implementation and thus need to be anticipated during policy formulation. Ideally, funds released match needs proposed by spending units. To the extent that funding shortfall occurs, line managers have sufficient authority to reprogram funds to keep policies on track. In practice, a top-down financial control model pervades most of government that is based on distrust and that largely encourages more distrust.

The allotment system should allocate funds to programs and projects on a timely basis. Systemic and procedural bottlenecks delay release of funds; for example, procurement procedures for purchasing may delay fund releases to departments for needed supplies, materials, and capital equipment. The bottlenecks generate arrears to suppliers that are carried forward in higher future bids. Both arrears from the system and inflationary bids by suppliers can drive up the costs of policy implementation. Rigid procedures include those covering managers who need flexibility to transfer and reprogram funds to keep services delivered. When revenues do not materialize and funds are not forthcoming from an OMB, MOF, or central budget office to spending units, these controls so often discourage management from doing anything other than following the expenditure plan made at the beginning of the fiscal year.

At the same time, budget departments must act when revenues collapse or expenditure overruns become evident from monthly reports and often have to impose "cash limits" on departmental spending (i.e., emergency measures that convert what was an annual budget into twelve monthly allotments). If such actions are combined with procedures that prevent allotments for accounting and reporting irregularities by spending departments, the finance department creates a quarterly or monthly budgeting system, with all that this implies for fiscal uncertainty, planning problems, and "repetitive budgeting" (Caiden and Wildavsky 1975). Under these conditions, budgets must be constantly remade and will "disappear," for all practical purposes, while the ink is still wet. They do not guide management or policy decisions. Although they turn off the flow of funds at the source and preserve fiscal balance for macroeconomic reasons, cash limits are very difficult to design so that they do not disrupt policies and programs. They create microeconomic difficulties in exchange for apparent macroeconomic benefits.

Flexible controls during budget implementation are needed to encourage managers to allocate resources creatively to get the most results from the least funds. Line managers need transaction approval authority and budget flexibility. Failure to provide line managers with expenditure approval authority can actually result in transactions being approved by those who have no authority or experience to do so (Bartel 1996, 22).

Similarly, because most policies face unforeseen difficulties during the year, budget administration needs to be flexible. Flexibility is hindered in the name of control by (1) line-item controls over expenditures, (2) narrow limits on transfers and reprogramming during the fiscal year, and (3) preaudit or precontrol by internal control accounting personnel. First, controls over line-item expenditures for contracts, personnel positions, and other specific transactions like travel or supplies are usually counterproductive. The controls consume staff time, delay approval requests, restrict managerial flexibility, and discourage optimal approaches in policy implementation (Hayes et al. 1982, 65). Control can be exercised by quarterly allotments processes without the need for line-item control of specific transactions. Such control usually generates a large volume of budget modifications, most of which have little significance for policy or budgeting. Efforts to prevent noncompliance cost more than they are worth. The more cost-effective approach is through ex-post audit (Hayes et al. 1982, 66).

Budget transfer authority is not an easy area in which to design controls, and some countries simply prohibit all modification. In the centrally planned economies, such as the former Soviet system, the budget passively executed the "plan," and few modifications were necessary for implementation of what were conceived of as near-perfect material investment concepts. Rigid controls over modification ensured that managers would not engage in efficient or innovative behavior. In many cases, budget controls resulted in policy failures.

On the other hand, failure to control reprogramming and transfers eliminates the budget as a guideline for expenditures and as an instrument of policy. (Funds that were budgeted for poor people may end up as public-sector salaries.) But excessively rigid controls prevent managers from implementing policy—discouraging risk taking, that is, innovative behavior by empowered personnel, which is the current rage in the "reinventing" government movement. Since few policies are self-executing, this means waste and inefficiencies.

An option is the one that Australian managers, for example, have: almost complete authority to reprogram funds during the year (including between personnel and nonwage categories) in exchange for tight responsibilities in attaining policy targets set by the central finance department. Because this policy combines management incentives for performance with results-oriented budgeting and decentralization of operational responsibilities, the Australian (and New Zealand) models of financial management reform are currently in vogue around the world. In Australia, the Department of Finance provides "forward estimates" that combine budget ceilings and policy output targets. The "running cost" system provides funding releases in single lump sums to departments whose managers may then transfer between line items and even across fiscal years with Department of Finance approval (Keating and Rosalky 1990). Reprogramming that requires higher level approval has to be limited to major line-item shifts (e.g., personnel to nonpersonnel costs). Managers are held accountable for policy performance targets and permitted maximum flexibility in the use of resources to attain them; controls are largely ex-post audit rather than pre-control or preaudit.

Finally, as will be dealt with later in this chapter, budget administration can be hampered by excessively rigid internal controls. Rather than verify the sufficiency of funds and the legality of the expenditure consistent with approved appropriations, internal control personnel can be overzealous and begin second-guessing program and policy staff members on technical matters. This is a major problem now with U.S. federal budget foreign-aid contracts.

One example is found in how and why program and technical people in the U.S. Agency for International Development (USAID) approve project proposals from contractors for work overseas (e.g., in reforming local governments in Macedonia). The technical people are agents of contract officials and are "contracting officers technical representatives." This means that the technical people have the last say on what decisions will be approved in the field. In the context of almost totally unsettled conditions in some foreign countries, USAID contract people often exercise narrow line-item controls over minor transfers and second-guess technical field people on qualified personnel. (For example, is "county" government employment really "local" government employment? Since the technical contract position states that local experience is required, USAID contract people often fail to exercise judgment and demand another employee!). As already indicated, the way to avoid cost-ineffective control is to use ex-post control, which encourages innovative action and allows for retribution where decisions have been illegal. Ex-post control serves as a better deterrent to official malfeasance than costly attempts to prevent noncompliance.

Monitoring implementation results requires a good reporting system. Line managers need incentives to take time from the uncertainties and frustrations of actual implementation to report ongoing work. One good incentive is to not delay funding releases for failure to submit timely reports: this delay penalizes policy clients and service users and creates further backlogs to budget releases. And under the resulting conditions, the annual budget is sliced into monthly and weekly allotments that impede smooth policy implementation. Excessive reliance on central control results in massive reporting requirements that paralyze implementation and weaken policy results. Nevertheless, managers can be expected to provide feedback to the central budget office on the status of revenues and expenditures. More important, if managers can be induced to buy into policy evaluation through incentives, they will report on physical performance as well. For example, managers in many state and local governments in this country report on unit costs and physical results of current services and capital investment projects. Incentives include actually approving next year's budget or making policy changes consistent with reported performance data; provision for additional personnel; and exemption from controls on budget reprogramming, expenditure approvals, and purchasing.

Central budget office officials often view delegation of approval authority (for reprogramming funds and reporting uses) as a loss of oversight control. This is a mistaken view because maintaining authority at the center often results in real loss of budget control in a blizzard of small transactions. The control system intrudes into management discretion but leads to ineffective policy results. What can be done to delegate authority without giving up oversight control? There are three standard techniques that are widely used in state and local governments in the United States (Bartel 1996, 23). First, budget managers use "exception reporting." Instead of reviewing all transactions, only those with major planned versus actual variances beyond a preset standard are flagged and examined in more detail. Second, managers can review only major financial differences in operating performance between like units (e.g., variations in expenditures by two clinics for medicine). Third, managers can decide to review approvals for transactions only above a certain threshold. These three techniques preserve substantive control at higher levels and allow delegation of operating authority to line units. The goal should be to shift expenditure controls to after-the-fact reviews, analogous to postpublication sanctions for libel rather than imposition of prior constraints. Reduction of intrusive precontrols over expenditures should be part of a package to reform public management in order to improve policy results.

ACCOUNTING SYSTEMS

Public budgeting can be no better than its supporting information systems. The two most critical systems are accounting and performance measurement. In particular, accounting systems are considered the "bedrock of budgeting" (Axelrod 1995). To assess the capability of the accounting system to implement policy, it is important to know (1) the fund structure, (2) the rules for measuring revenues and expenditures, and (3) the system's capacity to relate "costs" to volume of policy outputs. Note that budgeting usually refers to public "expenditures," accounting often refers to "costs." What is the link? Frequently, the link is not made and both are assumed to be the same, with unfortunate consequences for policy analysis.

Current policy issues can be seen in the debate on how to expand university systems and increase access to higher education. A policy of reducing "expenditures" per student typically results in a lowering of educational standards, which can be measured in declining faculty-student ratios, classroom overcrowding, uneven quality of teaching/learning, or increases in administrator-faculty ratios. Analysis of expenditures can avoid reduction of standards where the analysis indicates that most outlays are absorbed by salaries instead of supplies, books, and teaching materials. This kind of analysis is useful in policymaking. But a focus on expenditures can only go so far in institutional reform. The policy objective should be to reduce the "cost" per student through analysis of resource consumption by school organizations and comparison with similar units elsewhere. Cost-accounting systems can feed cost information on the pattern of fixed and variable costs, thus permitting analysis of prices for orders, payments for services, inflationary effects, and so on. A modified accrual system can track commitments and orders before cash payments, leading to improved analysis of costs and decisions that can improve organizational performance.

By providing data on cost per unit of production, the accounting system provides budget and policy analysts with essential data on the cost of attaining policy results. Data on marginal changes in cost per result (e.g., cost per passenger mile of transit system) can then be compared with the cost per result of other programs and policies (e.g., cost per graduate of school system). Examination of such data, along with projected changes in demand for services and the rates of increase or decrease in costs per result, can narrow the basis for allocating resources. Policy analysis, fortified by strong cost-accounting, can rationalize budgetary allocations for policies and programs.

Governments should account for commitments (that is, obligations for purchase orders or contracts where funds will be spent later), outlays, and revenues by fund. Funds are divisible into "general" and "special." General funds cover most transactions of general government, including civil service payments, and intragovernment revolving funds for support operations within the government (e.g., printing, purchasing, stores, operations). Special funds record dedicated transactions for such specific purposes as service for principal and interest on long-term debt, enterprise funds for business-type activities like utilities, toll bridges and roads, and trust funds for retirement systems. Cash flows between these funds and particularly general and special funds need to be carefully recorded under "interfund transfers" and monitored to avoid hidden subsidies. For example, budgeting a state enterprise through the general fund could mask heavy subsidies paid from general revenues to cover its operating losses. This distorted picture will cause policymakers to misallocate resources unknowingly that could have been used for more worthy policy causes.

Accounting rules for recording transactions must be made clear. The purpose of accounting rules should be to give policymakers a complete picture of funds available for expenditure. Otherwise, the policymakers can overspend or fail to commit funds that may then revert to the treasury and not be used to benefit program clients. As noted, the U.S. government policy on American Indian trusteeship has been largely a failure, not from miscalculation of known costs and benefits but from the exclusion of the costs of defective financial management systems. In particular, the failure by the Bureau of Indian Affairs (BIA) of the Interior Department to keep records of income earned on leases inhibited the tracking of collections, investment, and distribution of monies from the Individual Indian Money trust accounting system. (*Economist* 1999, 34–35) Whether a government uses cash or modified accrual systems, it must be consistent and enforce reporting rules. Otherwise, defects in the existing financial management systems, coupled with frequent indifference over such mundane matters by oversight organizations (here the Interior Department and BIA), will diminish policy results.

The two major rules in the United States are cash and modified accrual. Cash accounting is based on flow of funds in and out of the budgetary account. Finance directors also need daily information on cash position—disbursements, receipts, and statements of operations on line to plan debt service obligations and to ensure that deficit targets are not exceeded. It is a simple rule, and most budgets are based on estimated cash outlays for the fiscal year. Cash limits, used as a control device by finance departments to deal with revenue shortfalls or unanticipated outlays, are based largely on flow of funds analysis. But the cash rule has several problems.

First, the rule can ignore accumulated debt to vendors and result in a floating debt. This complicates cash management efforts by finance departments and can lead to increases in unfunded liabilities. Second, by estimating budgets on an annual cash basis, multiyear policy benefits tend to be ignored as well, resulting in poor planning and a policymaking system that is driven by a cash-accounting mentality. But the use of a modified accrual rule takes account of obligations and allows encumbrances of money to pay vendor purchase orders and other contracts. Unlike the cash rule, modified accrual takes account of net liabilities and payables. On the expenditure side, funds are locked up (e.g., by issuance of a purchase order to a vendor) to reveal available balances and to prevent overexpenditures. On the revenue side, revenues are recorded only when available and measurable. If revenues are recorded when due (accrued), budget planners could artificially increase the size of budgets by overestimating future collections. Accrual is modified to record revenues on a cash basis. Whatever rule is used, there is no guarantee that actual costs will be reflected in the accounts.

For policy formulation costs of production and delivery are needed: policymakers need to know how efficiently services are being delivered. Expenditures for similar policies may help. But often outlays and expenditures may not be the same as expenses; the latter require measurement of resources consumed for delivery. The cost of public production ("force account") may differ from market production of most services. To assess the feasibility of such policies as contracting out education, health, and transportation, costs of programs and policies must be determined. To do this, two steps must be followed: (1) expenditures must be converted to expenses by use of cost accounting, and (2) expenses must be allocated to organizational responsibility centers for proper policy management (Kory and Rosenberg 1984, 51). Cost or managerial accounting are systems that measure fixed, variable, direct, and indirect costs. They also allow development of costs of service, and accumulation of data on a job basis (e.g., construction) or process basis (e.g., licensing). In practice, such systems are expensive and rare even in such wealthy countries as the United States. For this reason, "cost-finding" systems are used that rely on existing budget data and simply recast the data periodically to derive the estimates or costs needed (Kory and Rosenberg 1984, 52). The important point is that the jurisdiction use some reasonable method of ascertaining program costs—almost anything in this area is better than nothing. Many jurisdictions use no method and imply falsely to legislatures and taxpayers that expenditures are the same thing as expenses.

Whether a full-fledged cost-accounting or activity-based costing system or a partial cost-finding system is used, the accounting system needs to keep budget people informed so that properly costed policies can be developed. The vehicle for this is the cost-accounting report that regularly provides a record of costs incurred against programs and projects (World Bank 1997, 60).

CASH MANAGEMENT

A common systemic problem is that funds are unavailable to finance public policies. As implied here, this is often less a problem of poverty than misallocation and waste due to ill-designed fiscal management systems. The cash management system should prevent cash deficits or excesses from occurring. It is more than a system of disbursing funds and should be used to plan and manage flow of resources to public policies to minimize costs and maximize effectiveness (Bartel 1996, 34). Whether a cash or accrual accounting system is used, the cash management function should prepare cash flow projections based on the approved budget. Failure to do this can result in a build-up of idle balances. Excess cash on hand should be invested or used to pay down short-term lines of credit. Conversely, approved budgets may suffer from lack of liquidity, resulting in loans from vendors in the form of unpaid bills or arrears. This costs a government for its ineffective policies: vendors increase prices to cover costs tied up in receivables (leading to inflationary pressures) or provide a lower level of service (lowering efficiency) (Bartel 1996, 34).

There are three methods of dealing with cash management problems: (1) basing budget allotments on solid projections of policy implementation activity, (2) providing flexibility for line managers to transfer and reprogram funds to meet policy targets, and (3) integrating budgeting and cash management. First, the allotments process is one of the major levers in budget control that is exercised by a finance department (OMB in the United States). An OMB allots funds from approved budgets in quarterly payments, but the timing and amounts should be based on inputs from the line agencies. Arbitrarily dividing budgets into twelve equal branches ignores demand and seasonal variations. Policies and programs during the cycle will be starved for cash or have excess spending authority at critical points in the service year. Hence, the cash flow budget developed by line agencies as part of the budget formulation process should reflect cash requirements for the year (or multi-years if such authority is available). This avoids short-term cash flow problems that lead to repetitive remaking of the budget, which can destroy both agency and client confidence in annual budgets (Caiden and Wildavsky 1975).

Second, budgets should be implemented as planned to avoid shifting the actual budgeting stage to implementation from formulation. At the same time measures need to be built in for unplanned occurrences, such as learning how to do the job better while managing resources. Authority to transfer and reprogram funds during the year should be available and transparent. Overly rigid and time-consuming processes frustrate management, reduce efficiency, and maximize incentives for making end-runs around the system. For this reason, such countries as New Zealand and Australia delegate maximum discretion to line managers for budget implementation within the framework of set fiscal and policy performance targets. This policy maximizes management incentives to learn how to deliver services better and to cut costs—and prevents gaming to make deficits superficially disappear.

For example, faced with political pressure to minimize fiscal deficits and preserve solvency of the Hospital Insurance Trust Fund, the Clinton administration transferred $55 billion in home health care expenses from that fund to another Medicare fund (Part B). The trust fund is payroll-tax financed and nearly bankrupt, but the Part B fund is covered by U.S. Treasury appropriations. The transfer allows the administration to avoid asking for an increase in Medicare premiums—resulting in a political benefit. But given the availability of general fund financing, the overall effect of the transfer will be to send medical expenditures soaring. There is no explicit budget constraint, such as the payroll tax base. Home health care costs are currently rising at 10 percent a year (Chandler 1997). And the transfer will simply shift costs without resulting in improved policy effectiveness, thus draining the general budget. It is clear, then, that transfers need to be approved by a quick and "transparent" or openly understandable process to avoid inefficiencies. But at the same time, the line between transfers for efficiency reasons and a policy change that may effectively change approved budget priorities needs to be clarified. Failure to do so allows administrators the discretion to make and change policy during the fiscal year (unacceptable) rather than during budget formulation (acceptable).

Third, budgeting should be linked to cash management to avoid cash flow problems. Cash flow projections should be constantly updated and revised by operating units and passed to an OMB. Properly alerted to the need for cash during the year, the treasury can plan ahead by investing idle balances and protecting principal from losses. This function (often called treasury management) converts the office from a passive disbursement agency into an active fiscal planner in behalf of budget priorities.

PERSONNEL ADMINISTRATION

Since personnel and staffing resources are usually the largest item in policy budgets, it is important to plan them out and to control them. (Ample evidence exists that they are often not controlled.) In many developing countries, and occasionally in the U.S. government, officials have no idea of how many people work for the government. For example, USAID's New Management System (NMS) was designed to integrate fiscal and program information systems, including personnel. Previously, there had been eighty databases supporting three different accounting systems, but because of underlying organization and management deficiencies, the NMS has not been able to reveal USAID staffing levels (Barr 1997). Efforts to streamline government often turn on the reduction of personnel costs and increasing the productivity of the remaining workers. But to perform the necessary streamlining steps, which include developing a typical worker salary profile, calculating gross cost per job abolished (including a comparison of payouts, pensions, and other benefits that must be paid to those severed from employment), and assessing net benefits (including the flow of new hires and retirees) after one year, personnel administrators must have basic data on staffing and wages. Without these data from financial management systems, civil service reform cannot go forward and policies may be more expensive than they should be.

Wage budget planning means estimation of workloads, staffing ratios, and necessary overheads. Calculation of time and staffing allows comparison with other jurisdictions but gives no indication about the quality of output or how much labor is actually needed for a given workload. Analysis of staffing and workloads can flag areas of possible over- or understaffing and raise questions about labor use. For example, in civil service reform efforts it is important to measure whether average costs are increasing or decreasing. Since a major component of costs is labor, policy analysts need to know whether revenues per employee are increasing faster or slower than costs per employee. Revenues per employee should be converted to hours and tasks per hour to allow an assessment of productivity (output per hour).

Using the work programming technique, labor-hours can be converted into positions. Multiplying the number of positions by pay grades and scales gives the total personnel budget (Axelrod 1995). Actual personnel costs include not only fringe, pension, Social Security, and health costs, but also related costs in supplies, travel, and equipment. It is easy to see why personnel is the largest item in the budget.

Controlling personnel costs requires more than analysis of workloads and action on them. To deal with the tough questions of administrative reform, policymakers have to make unpopular choices that can cost community support and votes. Policy analysis has an obligation to deal with institutional issues if improved results are the goal. In this vein, civil service reforms should focus on the "what" issues before the "how" issues (e.g., whether government should be involved in delivering tourism services before workload efficiency is approved). Reversing the order runs the risk, as noted above, of computerizing bad systems that should not be functioning in the first place. Perhaps the most basic "how" issue is measurement of the level of staffing in the first place. In many jurisdictions, slippage can occur between the personnel roster, the payroll system, and the personnel budget: people are paid who do not work for the government ("ghost workers"), and others are not paid who do (a cash management problem linked to overpayments caused by weak internal controls on personnel administration). Hence position controls are needed. The most basic control device is "position control" (Government Finance Officers Association 1978, 88), a system that ensures that people in approved positions (based on job descriptions) are paid at approved standard rates of pay. Making this basic linkage prevents personnel fraud and can help ensure that scarce budget funds for public policy implementation are not wasted on unproductive wages.

PROCUREMENT

Policymakers should be aware of the capabilities of existing systems of procuring goods and services. Much of public policy boils down to civil servants' salaries and items purchased from vendors. To the extent that purchasing systems are faulty, planned policies will deviate from actual results. There are a number of key elements of a procurement system that should be in place to facilitate efficient purchasing and to prevent fraud and/or conflict of interest.

First, purchasing should be centralized in a single department rather than allowing each department to purchase independently. This allows for lower cost bulk purchases and greater financial control, with more timely payment of bills, resulting in vendor discounts for prompt payment.

Second, such core matters as the duties of purchasing agents, threshold amounts for competitive bidding, how to prequalify bidders and maintain a bid list should be dealt with by legislative statutes. These basic purchasing policies are the regulations for purchasing that should then be spelled out in more detail in administrative procedure manuals for operational personnel.

Third, purchasing agents need to know when and how to standardize materials for bulk purchases of products (e.g., gasoline, office supplies) and facilities (e.g., design specification for public works construction).

Fourth, purchasing commitments must be duly registered by the accounting system and transmitted to the budgetary accounts as an encumbrance (recorded purchase order) to prevent overexpenditures of available appropriations (Coe 1989, 90–100). Purchase orders should be traceable to requisitions and invoices paid for control purposes.

INTERNAL CONTROL

A lot of what goes wrong with public-sector performance and policy results falls in the categories of corruption and mismanagement. Public policies fail for a variety of reasons, but a major reason is often corruption and leakage of scarce public funds into the wrong hands. Where an official violates public laws, such as by transferring funds into an unauthorized account and spending them to improve policy results, is this corruption? One could argue that this is a failure of internal control (perhaps failure of design of internal control procedures) and a violation of law. But it could reasonably be argued that it is not corruption. Some of the best managers and policy-makers knowingly violate rules to get the job done, and for this they are often—unjustly, it seems—punished (McAllister 1996). Assuming policies have been properly assessed, resources are still not managed properly to achieve planned results. In reality, of course, the institutional environment impinges on policy results and needs to be taken into account during the process of allocating resources. This often does not happen.

Corruption and mismanagement often signal a failure of internal control systems, which are organizational plans and methods to safeguard assets, check reliability of accounting, and promote operational efficiency (Hayes et al. 1982, 82). Internal control systems ensure that procedures are followed for receipt and disbursement of funds. Those who exercise internal control are typically accounting personnel within ministries or departments.

Internal control systems focus on two major themes: (1) procedures for recording receipts and expenditures, and (2) separation of organizational duties to prevent fraud and misappropriation of funds. First, procedures need to be in place for competitive bidding, certification of new civil service hires, authorization of obligations or disbursements, and coverage of obligations by appropriations. Integrated financial management systems are set up to control errors. For example, an accounting system can reject obligations for which unencumbered balances are not available or vouchers for which approved purchase orders or contracts have not been entered (Hayes et al. 1982, 133). Procedures must be enforced by personnel who check source documents (requisitions, purchase orders, external vouchers and invoices) for payroll, contracts, leases, and requests for payment to suppliers. Just as important for internal control is that the accounting review does not interfere with substantive program matters and legitimate management discretion. Accounting control should focus on proper authorization and documentation. But going beyond ensurance of procedural compliance becomes intrusive. In many government systems, obsession with accounting approvals and line-item controls over budget matters delays action and can drive up the costs of purchases from vendors that suffer from late payments or arrears. The internal controls themselves in such as case contradict the goal of operational efficiency. Known as preaudit in the United States or precontrol in Latin America, such permissive internal controls lead to unproductive second-guessing of agency decisions, at best (Hayes et al. 1982, 84), and open season for bribery or corruption of internal control officials, at worst.

Procedures should exist that prevent multistage transactions from being handled by one person. For example, one should not be able to select vendors and authorize payment. Transaction authority should be separated from asset custody (Coe 1989, 30). Failure to divide responsibilities to prevent conflict of interest can derail public policies fast. In such cases fiscal officials would be like foxes guarding chicken coops. Procedural changes rather than enforcement of existing policies are necessary to prevent recurrence of waste or fraud.

Summary and Conclusion

In sum, this chapter suggests that the institutional failures likely to affect policy results often relate to fiscal management and budgeting. Any rule or procedure that unreasonably raises transaction costs for clients should be subject to review. Intrusive administrative procedures for receipt of prenatal care, for instance, may discourage treatment by prospective clients. Because fewer units of service would be provided for the same fixed costs, such procedures would raise unit costs of the program. This negative trend should be picked up by the accounting system and transmitted to the budget function for analysis. Often data on administrative contributions to transaction costs, derived from workflow or service planning analyses, are not available to policymakers. This is a failure of several components of the fiscal management system. Other common problems include the following:

- Lack of professional civil service capacity that permits decisionmaking based on weak or nonexistent data
- Budget administration that is constrained by tight preaudit and complex reprogramming requirements that hamstring management and waste resources
- Financial functions that are handled independently—budget and accounting data not being shared and linked to organizational responsibility centers for management control of operations
- Budget formulation that proceeds without solid accounting data on commitments and outlays from the previous year
- Studies of physical policy performance that are not factored into budget development for the next year

How can institutional factors be considered objectively during policy formulation? Again, the goal is not to hamstring policy development with evidence of possible institutional failure. As will be discussed in chapters 5–7, application of policy analysis methodologies focus on estimation of costs and benefits of alternative policies. Through the use of well-known policy analysis techniques, risks and uncertainty created by institutional factors can be factored into sensitivity and decision analysis to reduce benefits or increase costs of the proposed policy.

Let us now turn to a case study of institutional constraints to policymaking and implementation. The study illustrates how financial management institutions affect policymaking in a large U.S. city. It also illustrates why structural and management changes are necessary (i.e., imposition of a federal financial control board to oversee local finances) and why the generation and use of policy analysis needs to be made systematic rather than ad hoc or produced to cover immediate crises. The District of Columbia represents an almost classic case of institutional breakdown and ineffective policies across the board. To some extent this is a structural problem of unitary government: the District lacks the authority and tax base of a state but is saddled with many state-type policy responsibilities that cost more than it can afford. For example, Washington, D.C., must pay Medicare and pension costs that other cities do not have to pay but it collects no tax on 41 percent of its property that is occupied by the federal government and other tax-exempt institutions. The annual payment from the United States government of $660 million does not allow even a semblance of balancing the budget. The unfunded pension liability for the District alone is now $4.3 billion (*Economist* 1997d).

CHAPTER 3 CASE STUDIES

Services Suffer as District Cuts Corners, Report Says

U.S. Study Says Public Works Understaffed

By Alice Reid
Washington Post *Staff Writer*

The District department responsible for city services from road maintenance to trash collection is so short-staffed it operates in a crisis mode, scrambling only to fix what is broken and forsaking the monitoring of contracts and contractors, according to a federal study.

The study by the Federal Highway Administration portrays a Department of Public Works virtually coming apart at the seams—struggling to keep traffic lights working and to fill potholes but unable to keep proper tabs on multimillion-dollar road projects or spending with contractors.

The department has lost hundreds of staff positions in the last five years, yet still must answer to a layered city government bureaucracy that reviews road projects, delaying crucial work by as much as six months and adding considerable expense, says a draft of the report obtained by *The Washington Post*.

Despite the report's criticism, Public Works Director Larry King said he welcomes it and its recommendation for more manpower and tools, such as computers, to help manage the department. "It gives me ammunition, helps me make the case for my budget in fiscal '97," King said yesterday.

Public Works is responsible for trash collection, water and sewer service, snow removal and maintaining 1,040 miles of city streets. Like most city departments, it has been forced to lay off personnel and has seen its budget cut.

Particularly hard-hit has been the division that looks after traffic signals, maintains the city's 237 bridges and several tunnels, lines the traffic lanes and keeps road signs in place. Five years ago, 25 engineers worked in the Bureau of Traffic Services; now there are nine. The bureau is only half as large as similar divisions in cities the size of Washington, according to the report.

The consequences of the layoffs are many. Maintenance on the fans that vent the refurbished Interstate 395 tunnel beneath the Mall is not being done. Although virtually every cushion barrier at exits on roads including the Anacostia and Southwest freeways is damaged, there is no one to repair them. When traffic signals get out of synchronization, causing traffic buildups on major roads, there's not enough manpower to fix them.

Although the report does not make a direct connection, it does point out that traffic fatalities on city streets have been increasing.

The grim study coincides with equally grim news about ongoing budget pressures. Thursday's passage of the federal budget, and the District's along with it, continues the squeeze on department expenditures. Although officials are still scrutinizing the details of this year's approved spending plan of about $153 million, they say it will be virtually impossible to fill any of about 200 vacant positions in public works.

"Over the past years, we have lost about 600 people, through buyouts and early retirement, and, of course, they have been our most knowledgeable and experienced people," Deputy Director Cell Bernardino said.

The report suggests using consultants to replace some of that lost expertise and suggests finding ways to pay them with federal highway funds, rather than city dollars.

According to the report, the department's construction management staff is stretched so thin and financial data are so sketchy that in the Construction Management Division the staff has to resort to asking contractors what they have been paid in order to track expenditures.

The time-consuming reviews of road work have held up dozens of major projects worth millions, including, most recently, work on the M Street bridge over Rock Creek and construction on the Whitehurst Freeway.

The effect on road contractors can be devastating, according to Kent Starwalt, president of the Metropolitan Washington Road and Transportation Builders Association.

"The delays can mean that you're open or shut as far as a business is concerned," because while reviews go on endlessly, a contractor's limited bond is held by the city, Starwalt said. "They're holding your bond for months, sometimes years...so you're hostage to this bureaucracy."

Failure to Compute Adds to D.C.'s Bills

Disparate Systems Fall Short of Needs

Second of two articles

By Mary Pat Flaherty
Washington Post *Staff Writer*

When it counts, the District government has a problem.

One computer system couldn't count how old foster care children were. So, $165,000 was spent on recipients who had turned 21 and should have been off the program.

Another couldn't count how many checks it sent to the same foster care provider for the same bill. So, $431,000 in over-payments went out.

A third system couldn't count how many $93 checks intended to cover monthly utility bills were going out to people living in fully subsidized shelters for the homeless, so, according to a sample taken by city auditors, about one in 20 checks went to someone who didn't have a utility bill.

Since 1989, the D.C. government has spent $130 million to $150 million a year on information equipment and services, including data terminals, personal computers, software and telecommunications charges for data lines, according to an estimate in a report released early this year by Mayor Marion Barry's transition team. The buying showered automated systems on some departments, left others with few and was disjointed overall.

The islands of information have led to more than a techno-Tower of Babel. As the city wobbles on the brink of financial collapse, it struggles with computer systems that often are incapable of monitoring the flow of red ink, let alone stemming it. As burdensome as that is in the day-to-day running of government, the problem looms as an even larger hurdle for the incoming federal financial control board, especially since the systems that count the city's money and count its workers are two of the most archaic.

Quick fixes on some systems have been made, such as a reprogramming of the foster care computer to alert workers when children are about to become too old for the program. But the city's two biggest counting systems, financial management and payroll-personnel, still fall short of government's needs, according to interviews by *The Washington Post* with nearly 20 current and former managers of city departments and a host of studies since 1990 for the D.C. administration.

In some aspects, those big systems are so unwieldy that they inadvertently encourage workers to avoid them altogether—thereby also sometimes avoiding bidding requirements designed to ensure fair competition and good prices for city purchases.

The personnel and payroll system currently is not designed with a safeguard that would prevent agencies from hiring and paying more employees than their budgets allow. Managers cannot get running tallies of their department's overtime because of the delay in converting paper records of time worked into a computer report. The lag in entering information also explains why managers find out monthly—but not more frequenty—where they stand in relation to their budgets.

"Mind you, I was near the front of the line when I wanted something done for me, but even with that, if I asked how much overtime the city had paid as of March 1, it would be March 15 before I got the printout, and by then, the information already was two weeks out of date," said former city administrator Robert L. Mallett. "You can't be a tight manager with that system, no matter how hard you try."

As the city's budget gets tighter and workers are trimmed, the handicaps show more starkly, said former city controller N. Anthony Calhoun. "When we had more bodies doing things, the weaknesses in our systems were covered. Now, with fewer bodies, the weaknesses are magnified."

An example is the number of technicians who operate and maintain the thousands of computers in the city.

Wrestling With a 'Dinosaur'

Because the District government bought so many kinds of machines and programs, there is little consistency in operating systems, computer languages or software programs. That created a need to hire an assortment of technicians, some of whom could deal with one machine, some with another. Four years ago, there were about 630 technicians handling the various systems. As of January, there were about 500, which means that when something goes wrong, it can be difficult finding someone readily who knows exactly how to fix it.

The financial management system that monitors the District's income and spending is "a real dinosaur," as D.C. Controller Robert Reid describes it, because of its age and its programming limits. "We've got some old hands who do a great job keeping that system up and running, but if they walked out the door one day, I don't know what we'd do."

City managers got a glimpse of how fragile their system is during this fiscal year's budget preparations, when, right before the central financial system became overloaded with data and crashed, the technician most familiar with how to fix it took an early retirement. No one else could quickly get the dinosaur back on its feet. With information from every city department flooding in, budget officials hastily pieced together a network of personal computers that enabled departments to enter information into a central site. But then that network became infected with a computer virus and crashed, too.

By that time, the budget deadline was only days away, forcing staff members to run from one department to another carrying computer disks of information as they patched together the budget.

The city has 80 agencies whose budgets are fed by six streams of funds. That would be a burden on any financial tracking system. But it further taxes the District's system, which is five generations old in terms of computer development and has been aging even as the city has wanted—or been required—to add layers of detail about its funds.

So severe are the ledger's shortcomings, Reid said, that city departments can't quickly or easily pull out what they need to do their jobs."

Ironically, even when it was spanking new, the financial management system was chronically underutilized. When the District bought the system, it "got a gold-plated Cadillac that never was put to its full use. They probably could have done with a used Chevrolet, if they'd really thought through how they would match the capabilities of their work force with the requirements of the system," said Bert Edwards, a retired partner with Arthur Andersen & Co. accountants. Edwards conducted five audits of the city books and does consulting work with governments throughout the Washington area.

Had the city better trained more employees in the use of the financial system, Edwards said, it would be able to use "all of the bells and whistles in there. But you have to remember, every system has three parts: hardware, software and people-wear. If you wear the people out trying to get them to use your system, you're going to fail. It's just that simple."

Inside D.C. government there is a "type of technological resistance [that] is very real," said the transition team report to Barry. The mix of workplace technologies frustrates both users and technicians, especially given that virtually no training is made available to keep personnel skills up-to-date," the report said. A side effect, it said, is that city agencies often become "captives of the vendors," who give free training on the equipment they sell—and in doing that, build brand loyalty.

To get the most value out of the financial system, Edwards said, the city should demand that managers be disciplined in its use.

In just the last few weeks, the Barry administration has acknowledged that some departments have been holding back bills—by not entering them into the financial system to be paid—to make it appear as though they're running within budget: "No computer system is going to cure that sort of problem," Edwards said. "Putting in discipline, so that managers understand it's a far worse crime hiding a bill than it is 'fessing up, is what's needed."

But others say that the weaknesses of the financial management system encourage managers to bypass it. To start the process that leads to a purchase or a payment on a contract, city departments are required to commit funds—in essence, debit their accounts—through the financial management system. But to do that, they must be able to access the financial computer, which can be difficult.

Each evening and for a few entire days at the end of every month, the financial management system closes down so it can process updates or monthly reports. During those times, nothing can be entered into the system. If holidays also fall during the down cycle, the system may be inaccessible to a department for as long as a week.

A department manager then faces a choice: wait for the system to reopen or proceed with an order or a contract and square up the bookkeeping later, using mechanisms that are supposed to be reserved for emergencies or to correct mistakes. Squaring up would be the household equivalent of writing a check but waiting to record it in the check registry. It's a practice that makes for loose bookkeeping and that makes it appear there is more money than is available. At the level of $4.3 billion in annual spending, the problem is graver, because higher amounts are involved and because several people within a department may be drawing on the same account.

An internal auditor for the city, who asked not to be identified, said the corrections allow too much wiggle room for managers trying to manipulate the budget: "As an operating manager who may not have much incentive to live within your budget, it's to your advantage that the system is awkward and doesn't work very well."

Auditors both inside and outside the city government have criticized resorting to emergency and no-bid procedures to overcome the complexity and lag in the financial management computer system. The criticism has been a standing feature in the annual report on procurement by the District's inspector general, and it was noted by the city's independent auditor, Coopers & Lybrand.

As the Barry transition team report stated, the financial management system "cannot meet modern management information needs for operations or policy-making, and it is not a particularly good implementation of an accounting system either."

The problems hobbling payroll and personnel illustrate the larger story about the price taxpayers pay when a government enterprise relies on outmoded information systems.

From its introduction, the Unified Personnel and Payroll System was misnamed. It was never unified.

As planned, it was to capture and store personnel information about each employee at the time of hiring, then mesh that with workweek information and feed it to the system that cuts paychecks.

Amid some early programming difficulties, the accountants in payroll and the personnel specialists battled over who would control the system, said a current payroll manager, who did not want to be identified. Expediency resolved the turf battle: Paychecks had to go out, so the system shifted toward that function.

Improvements over the years served payroll needs, with upgraded mechanisms to track retirement, insurance and pension information. Improvements than would have aided personnel were not done.

Except for one automated form, every personnel record on each of the city's 46,000 full-and part-time workers remains on paper. That manual system limits the city's ability to profile its work force and answer such basic questions as what skills do workers have, which workers can "bump" others out of jobs if their positions are eliminated, or who is now in a job other than the one for which they were hired—all important issues for managers faced with cutting the work force.

The payroll-personnel system is clumsy for even the most basic tasks, such as adjusting salaries when raises are negotiated. The payroll system is hard-coded, meaning any change to information must be made through the computer's programming code, which is a complex mathematical formula. Modern payroll systems are table-driven, meaning that information is changed through easily used tables that appear as columns of information on a computer screen.

Cleaning Out the Drawers

To understand the difference, picture a big chest of drawers. In a table-driven computer system, information is separated and sorted into drawers. Changing information is the same as dumping out a single drawer and replacing the contents. So, if all workers covered by a certain contract are scheduled for a 2 percent raise, the computer is told to search for the drawer that holds those workers, dump each one's old salary information and insert the new figure. The other drawers in the chest needn't be touched.

Doing the same change in a hard-coded system, such as the city's, entails sifting through every drawer, first to find the right workers and then to change each one's salary line by line. Making the changes that way demands the technical skills of a programmer and has required that the entire city payroll system be shut down for as long as a week while the work is being done.

Because the personnel system separates hiring information from pay information, there also is no quick way to determine whether a budgeted job slot exists for every employee entered into the payroll system. So, extra employees can be entered into the system and have a check cut before it becomes clear a department has exceeded its personnel costs.

Congress twice appropriated $2 million to pay for a new personnel system, but the city delayed soliciting contracts for it. The money will be spent this coming fiscal year on the start-up costs of a system scheduled to be operating in October, followed in January by the first phase of a new payroll system. The integrated personnel-payroll system also will hook into the main financial ledger in a way that guarantees absolute control over job positions. If a manager attempts to enter a new employee into the computer system when his department has no openings, the main ledger will prevent money from being debited to cover the paycheck.

The city hasn't yet found an alternative to the paper time-and-attendance cards processed every two weeks. They are filled out as part of the jobs of 4,000 timekeeping clerks, reviewed by hundreds of supervisors and then manually scanned and key-punched into the payroll system. But, said D.C. Personnel Director Larry A. King, the changes planned for October we finally have a team of good strong horses pulling together."

It's that push toward improvement that the District needs, said Edwards, the retired Arthur Andersen partner. "The District lags in lots of technology that would make things easier, better, smarter," he said, "and if the District doesn't bring that in, you can bet the financial control board will."

City Diverts Money from Job Training

By Hamil R. Harris
Washington Post *Staff Writer*

The District government has budgeted nearly $7.3 million over the last three years for job-training programs, but not a single person has received training because city officials used the money to pay for salaries, benefits and outside contracts.

The failure of the job-training effort reflects a broader breakdown as Mayor Marion Barry, the D.C. Council and the D.C. financial control board struggle to reorder the city's priorities in the face of shrinking revenue, according to city officials.

Barry administration officials say money routinely has been shifted within and between government agencies to cover shortfalls, often to the confusion of those responsible for keeping track of the city's finances.

The matter came to a head this week when the D.C. Department of Employment Services asked the council for an additional $3 million for job training in the coming fiscal year. Although the mayor long has given high priority to job training, council members noticed that no one had been enrolled in the training program since fiscal 1994, despite allocations totaling $7.3 million.

"We need to know where the dollars went," said D.C. Council member Kathy Patterson (D-Ward 3), head of the council's Government Operations Committee. "There is clearly a problem with accountability for money in our government. One of the reasons we have a financial control board is because there is a lack of oversight in where the dollars go."

F. Alexis Roberson, director of the Employment Services Department, said that in fiscal 1996, the $1.1 million job-training allocation was used to cover budget shortfalls elsewhere in her agency. In two other years, fiscal 1995 and 1997, the money was shifted to other city agencies, she said.

The confused trail created by perpetual budget revisions was underscored yesterday when four budget specialists in the office of Chief Financial Officer Anthony A. Williams tried to account for the money.

It took them much of the afternoon to reach conclusions that differed from some of those presented by Roberson. They said that in fiscal 1995, the agency's job-training allocation of $3.3 million was reduced to $2.5 million and that only $1.22 million of it was spent. The following year's allocation of $1.1 million was diverted within the agency to replace money lost in budget cuts. Thus far in the current fiscal year, $350,000 of a $2.9 million training allocation has been spent on salaries and one outside contract.

Laura Triggs, the city's associate chief financial officer, said uncertainty about budgets has had a paralyzing effect on some city departments.

"Various agency budgets . . . have changed or were at risk of changing so many times [that] managers managed programs by not implementing them [for] fear that their budgets would be eliminated," Triggs said.

Before Congress created the control board to oversee the city's troubled finances, the mayor was required by law to get council approval any time more than $50,000 was reallocated.

Congress eliminated council approval as a requirement, however, because the financial crisis required constant tinkering with spending levels. Now the control board has the authority to review and approve changes proposed by the mayor.

The city's contribution to Employment Services, which also receives a hefty federal allocation, declined from $18 million in fiscal 1995 to $9 million in 1996. For this fiscal year, the agency received $14.3 million in city dollars.

"Each year, training dollars are very vulnerable," Roberson said. "It is very frustrating because I think job training should be a priority. We should not have to cut job-training money."

She said unemployment within the city is triple that of the surrounding suburbs and that the city has the fifth-highest jobless rate among the nation's 26 largest cities. "It is not that jobs do not exist in the area," she said. "District residents do not compete as effectively as their suburban counterparts."

Job training has been a crusade central to Barry's political career. Thirty years ago, he headed Youth Pride Inc., a nonprofit organization that put 1,400 young people to work. His defense of summer youth jobs programs has become legendary. And his return from political ruin after a 1990 drug conviction was built on a campaign promise of full employment.

In last night's State of the District speech, Barry said, "Over 13,000 young people had summer jobs last year because I fought to preserve these for our youth."

Roberson said her agency's plans include a $3 million job-training program for people east of the Anacostia River.

But Patterson said, "We are not going to budget dollars anymore for programs that either don't exist or are not working."

Staff writer David A. Vise contributed to this report.

A Well-Financed Failure

System Protects Jobs While Shortchanging Classrooms

By Sari Horwitz and Valerie Strauss
Washington Post *Staff Writers*

At Tyler Elementary School in Southeast Washington, water poured in from a leaking roof, sending hundreds of children to classes in nearby schools and churches for the last two weeks.

At Wilson Senior High School in Northwest, 10th-graders went 11 weeks without an English teacher because bureaucrats downtown would not hire a replacement for an instructor on sick leave.

Inside Patricia Roberts Harris Education Center in Southeast, ninth-graders work with private reading tutors on vocabulary and grammar they should have learned years ago.

What does a school system that has some of the lowest test scores in the nation do with $594 million a year? How do D.C. schools allot $7,389 per student—among the nation's highest spending rates—and still wind up short of books, crayons, toilet paper and, in some schools, even teachers?

Interviews with dozens of former and current city and school officials and an examination of hundreds of school documents and memos reveal some answers:

- School officials violated federal law by continuing to pay tens of millions of dollars to administrators who had been ordered laid off by the D.C. Council. Two years ago, school officials announced that they had abolished nearly 180 bureaucratic positions—but school records reveal the cuts included almost 100 teaching slots instead.
- School authorities spent $21 million annually to send 1,079 special education students to private schools because the District fails to provide services in its own schools. Their spending rate is five times the national average.
- The federal government revoked grants worth $20 million because the system so badly mismanaged grant funds. In one instance, officials spent $1.6 million on unrelated employee salaries, rather than on extra instruction for underprivileged students as required by law.

School officials accomplished all of the spending maneuvers largely through a budgeting and accounting system that employed two sets of books—one hidden from public inspection. Rung Pham, the former schools controller, acknowledged in an interview last week that senior officials knew they were breaking city laws regulating how public money is spent—but did it anyway.

"It makes me so mad, because you really feel sorry for the children of D.C.," said Abdusalam Omer, the school system's chief financial officer, hired last summer to clean up the chaotic finances. "There is a lack of passion for children, particularly those who are disadvantaged. . . . There are children in Anacostia who have never been in the Smithsonian [Institution] because there is not enough money for field trips."

Now, Julius W. Becton Jr., a retired Army general, has come to embody the hopes of children and parents across a struggling city desperate for quality education in the District's 152 public schools. The D.C. financial control board hired him as chief executive and superintendent Nov. 15 after firing Superintendent Franklin L. Smith. Smith assumed control of a badly failing system 5 1/2 years ago, and by most analyses, produced little in the way of management reform or improvement of student performance.

It is up to Becton and his staff to figure out where their predecessors went wrong and to make fixes for the future. But it is no small task they take on as they face an entrenched bureaucracy and a budgeting system that Omer said was created to obfuscate.

"Did they really set it up this way on purpose? I think so," he said. "It's very clever."

'Ample Resources'

Anyone who first learns about the District's dilapidated public school buildings and the persistent shortages of basic materials might quickly assume the D.C. system has been starved for money. Wrong.

"The school system has ample resources to educate children. It's the management of resources and the lack of any plan or guide on how to use those resources that is the problem," said Jim Ford, the former staff director of the D.C. Council's Education and Libraries Committee.

Every year, the D.C. school system, an independent city agency, receives about $475 million from city funds and more than $100 million from federal grants and private donations.

"Where does the money go?" Omer asked. "The money goes to create a middle-class community. It goes to salaries."

Year after year, the schools employed more people than authorized in annual budgets approved by the D.C. Council and Congress. The extra personnel, according to Omer, cost $50 million from 1990 to 1995, money that should have been spent on textbooks, field trips, athletics, facilities and other student items.

Even former superintendent Smith's harshest critics agree that when he was hired as superintendent in 1991 to reform the system, he confronted an intransigent bureaucracy that valued one thing above all else: jobs.

But Smith didn't stop overspending for personnel. In fact, the practice worsened during his tenure.

In the 1992 school year, Congress approved $429.3 million in local funds for salaries and benefits. Smith's administration spent $9.52 million more on personnel—taking money away from, among other things, school supplies, student programs and textbooks to make up the difference. The next school year, Smith's administration spent $9 million more than allocated for payroll and benefits, again by taking money from classrooms.

For the 1994 school year, Smith spent $12.5 million more for salaries and benefits than his budget allowed.

The next year, Smith's administration did it again, overspending on excess personnel by $11 million—and pulling money from other accounts to cover it.

Two Sets of Books

School officials were able to "re-program" the money to pay unauthorized workers by keeping two sets of books.

One is in the giant Financial Management System, a computerized system used by the entire District government to track budgets department by department. It is controlled by the city's treasurer and chief financial officer.

The second system is controlled solely by the school district's administration. Known as the Resource Management Control and Information System, or REMCIS, it was set up many years ago to help the school system track its spending in detail at its own headquarters.

Omer discovered "there is no relationship" between the congressionally approved budget that is entered into the Financial Management System and the spending recorded in the school district's own computer system. There have been disparities since the 1980s, and they have increased, Omer said.

Just two weeks ago, newly hired school authorities brought in D.C. Inspector General Angela L. Avant to investigate $250,000 missing from a 1995 school fund, according to a school source.

"The public budget was essentially a fiction," said Mary Levy, the counsel and budget analyst for an education advocacy group, Parents United. The school system had so many funds, and Smith reorganized the administration so often that it was "impossible for any outside organization or person to keep track of everything," Levy said.

A 1993 report by then-city Auditor Otis H. Troupe identified eight funds on the school district's private books that were not authorized by the D.C. Council when it passed the system's budget. The accounts included some $26 million in 1991 and $21 million in 1992—money that was being used to pay personnel but had been shifted from other categories in the published school budget.

Troupe's report—which went to Smith, the school board, the mayor and the council—strongly objected to "appropriated funds being shifted into areas which are essentially hidden and for which disclosure is non-existent." The number of full-time employees being paid "has been drastically understated to the point of an absolute lie told to the City Council and Congress. . . . The statutes say it is illegal to defraud and waste the District's money."

The federal Anti-Deficiency Act states that no D.C. employee may make or authorize an expenditure or obligation exceeding an amount available in an appropriation or fund for the expenditure or obligation. The Home Rule Act states that no amount may be obligated or spent by any officer or employee of the D.C. government unless Congress has approved the amount.

"Any time you overspend your budget allocated by Congress, you are definitely violating the Anti-Deficiency Act, and that was the case for 1994, 1995 and 1996," Omer said.

"Yes, they did violate the Anti-Deficiency Act," said Rung Pham, the longtime controller who was fired in December by D.C. Chief Financial Officer Anthony A. Williams.

Pham said that in one year—1994-95—he initially refused to pay a $500,000 bill because it would create a deficit and violate the law. "I wouldn't do it until I got a clear message from the top to do it," he said.

Smith canceled an appointment to discuss this and other issues with *The Washington Post* and did not reschedule or return repeated phone calls seeking comment. He also did not respond to a letter delivered to his home that requested an interview.

By law, the Board of Education also was required to give Congress, the mayor and the D.C. Council "an accurate and verifiable report" every year on the positions and employees in the public school system, including information on salaries and precise job descriptions. School authorities did not file any of the required reports, and the council and Congress did not force them to comply.

The former longtime chairman of the council's Education Committee, 81-year-old Hilda H.M. Mason (Statehood-At Large), had years ago taken a back seat to staff director Ford, an expert number cruncher and analyst on school finance. Mason had lost credibility with many in the education community who were concerned about her sometimes intemperate and unpredictable behavior and her inability to push school reform.

Like Troupe's reports, Ford's annual committee reports—which foreshadowed the conclusions reached in fall 1996 by the financial control board—had little impact. Some school board members angrily denounced the reports; others ignored them. And Ford's immediate supervisors, the D.C. Council, did nothing.

"The tendency over the years has been to say, 'Oh, education, that's the school board's responsibility," said Kevin P. Chavous (D-Ward 7), the new chairman of the council's Education Committee. "While we have mouthed the words that education is a priority, we have not acted like it's a priority."

Instead, he said, politics prevailed.

Each city ward has a council member and a school board member. School board members traditionally have used their positions as a stepping stone to council seats. So, council members, in an attempt to reduce the chance of creating political rivals in their own wards, have allowed school board members to take the lead on school matters.

"There was that unspoken agreement," Chavous said.

For Ford, it was "extremely frustrating" to have his reports unheeded—and at times criticized for unequivocal language.

"The council still had oversight responsibility," Ford said. "And year after year, the excess personnel, the overspending, the misinformation and the pattern of lying was brought to the attention of the council."

No Basis in Reality

The District spends about 85 percent of its funds on personnel, close to what many school districts spend. What is unusual is the proportion spent on central office administrators. According to the non-profit Council of Great City Schools, D.C. schools in recent years had an average of 16 teachers per central administrator, compared with Los Angeles's 60 to 1.

In 1979, the school system had 113,000 students and 511 central office positions, including clerical workers, administrative assistants, deputy superintendents, assistant superintendents, coordinators, directors, assistant directors and other downtown office workers who had little or no contact with children.

By 1992, the school system had lost 33,000 students, but the number of central office positions had climbed to 967. Former superintendent Smith cut several hundred administrators toward the end of his tenure and didn't replace other central office workers who left.

But critics said he didn't trim fast enough.

The financial control board, in a report in the fall that coincided with Smith's firing, said that in the last year of his tenure, the system still employed 900 to 1,400 more people than were authorized.

During each of the last five years, Smith and school board members testified before the D.C. Council during budget hearings and asked for an increase of $40 million to $100 million in the school budget.

But those budget requests weren't based on realistic numbers. In 1996, for example, the board requested $75,000 for garbage pick-up even though the actual costs in several previous years had exceeded $1 million annually. Other numbers, the D.C. Council believed, were exaggerated.

Each year the council denied the request, gave the school system even *less* money than it had the previous year and ordered the superintendent and board to make specific cuts in the central office staff and reallocate the savings to classrooms.

But school officials ignored those orders, Ford said, and acted as if they'd been given the tens of millions they'd sought. The elected school board, as chief policy-maker, was supposed to determine how money was spent, but it ceded that power to Smith and his predecessors.

"Don't forget, the board doesn't run the school system," said Erika Landberg, who represented Ward 3 on the school board from 1988 to 1996. "A board is supposed to do oversight, not micro-manage."

Pham, who is looking for a new job after being fired as controller, said he was made a scapegoat for his bosses.

"I was a team player," he said. "I did whatever I had to do," including over-spending on personnel and underspending on other items.

Questions About Priorities

In a system facing hard financial choices, Levy and others for years have questioned school officials' priorities, big and small.

For five years starting in 1991, for example, the system spent nearly $2 million on a Values Education Office, which was supposed to promote education that raised "the consciousness level of social issues." Yet even some school board members said it was useless, and it was killed in 1996.

At the same time, programs that seemed to benefit students suffered.

Eugene Williams, a 13-year D.C. school employee, directed a program to give prospective National Merit scholars extra classes and tutoring. National education journals lauded his work. As part of his budget cuts in 1996, Smith abolished Williams's position, ending the program.

Meanwhile, the Board of Education spent well on itself. It allocated $1.4 million for its own use in 1996—more than five times the amount Fairfax County's board spent and more than twice what Montgomery County's spent. Until last year, when their $30,000 salaries were halved by the control board, the 11 members—who work part time—were paid more than members of any other school board in the country.

Former school board president Karen Shook countered criticism of the board's own funding and oversight of the system, saying year after year that the school sys-tem needed more money and had laid off everyone it possibly could, arguments that Smith also made often.

The trouble was that neither Shook nor the rest of the board knew how many stu-dents truly were enrolled or how many people the schools employed at any given time or where they worked.

The confusion existed despite an identification system that should have safe-guarded against it. Every school system employee is supposed to receive a personnel number that puts the worker on the payroll.

Uncounted Numbers

Yet when Omer arrived to review the school budget and personnel records, he found 1,734 people on the payroll who had no number but were paid nevertheless. Nearly 200 other people—all of whom were paid—shared personnel numbers with one or two other people. Personnel number 0058043, for example, was held by people at Webb, Clark and Petworth elementary schools—and was the basis on which each of the three drew a paycheck.

The system left Omer stunned. "It was totally messed up," he said.

Landberg said recently that the board knew all about the confused personnel numbers. "Dr. Smith told us they were making progress. But we knew the numbers weren't cleaned up yet," Landberg said. Last fall, payroll data showed some adminis-trators classified as teachers, some teachers as administrators and some employees as working at schools that had closed. There also were personnel numbers on the pay-roll for eight people who were dead.

A memo written nearly two years ago by school budget director George Letsa—whom Becton fired last fall—foreshadowed what Omer and the control board would find. The memo was attached to a computerized list of 130 employees who were not authorized to be employed. It said: "The individuals listed . . . appear on the payroll file but are not on personnel and budget files. In other words, although these individuals are being paid, there are no audit trails in our budget and personnel files to document their existence."

Things were so chaotic when Becton took over that his staff found boxes stuffed with overdue vouchers payable to more than 250 vendors who had done business with the system, ranging from a single teacher to the largest book seller in the country. One of the bills alone was for $600,000. "They didn't know how much they owed," Omer said. "Nobody kept track."

Budget and employee staffing matters certainly are not the only problems facing the general. But, according to Omer, the knotted personnel list must be untangled before Becton can begin genuine reform.

During Smith's first year as superintendent, he was asked how many employees he had. He said he couldn't say. Five years later, he still couldn't answer."

Becton said in a recent interview that, based on payroll and an audit, he's come up with an answer: "About 10,461."

"But," he quickly added, "I can't tell you how many of those are dead."

For More Information

For a statistical analysis from the D.C. financial control board showing how the District's public school system mismanages its money, go to the front page of *The Post*'s Web site at *http://www.washington-post.com.*

In an Ailing City, Vital Services Cease to Function
Dozens of Departments Failing D.C. Residents

By Vernon Loeb
Washington Post *Staff Writer*

If Bill and Hillary Clinton ever pull the fire alarm at the White House, the D.C. Fire Department's rule book calls for Tower 10—a glistening ladder truck with a massive hydraulic arm and mounted platform—to speed through the back gate and rescue them.

Luckily for the Clintons, fire hasn't been one of the calamities to befall 1600 Pennsylvania Avenue recently: Tower 10 has been in the shop for two months. Last week, it sat parked outside a garage in Beltsville, waiting for D.C. bureaucrats to conduct a rescue mission of their own and pay the repair bill.

Tower 10—ready to roll but hemmed in by hobbled school buses and garbage trucks—serves as a powerful symbol for the vast government of the District of Columbia, a $3.2 billion, 42,000-worker maze of agencies and departments that is not only broke, but broken.

For months, the District has hovered so near insolvency that it has become the region's most notorious deadbeat, refusing to pay hundreds of contractors large and small for jobs they already have done. But many who deal with city government say that that problem masks an even more deep-seated crisis: Dozens of D.C. departments aren't even coming close to providing the basic services they were created to deliver.

Complaints about the delivery of city services already were widespread when Mayor Marion Barry left office four years ago, and they accelerated under his successor, Sharon Pratt Kelly. She inherited a deficit of as much as $300 million. This month, after Barry was sworn in for another term, the shortfall was estimated at more than $500 million.

By numerous accounts, the District's government is in free fall, failing to meet daily obligations that range from carting away trash to caring for abused children. Exasperated judges have seized control of several municipal programs, and even the District's auditor, Russell A. Smith, said recently that "a lot of our systems—personnel, procurement, accounting—have broken down, and they need to be fixed."

But if you want to hear from the real experts, listen to the people who deal with city government on a regular basis—D.C. residents.

Listen to Frank S. Chalmers, whose condominium association in Northwest Washington has been waiting six years for a $600 tax refund. Or Les Ulanow, who has been waiting four years for a hearing to appeal a real estate assessment he considers outrageously high.

Listen to Diane Hendle, who became a foster mother to crack-addicted twins, only to have the city renege on a promise to pay for their day care. Or Mike Brown, who hasn't heard from the city after a snow plow ripped the side off his wife's car 14 months ago. Or Rufus S. Lusk III, whose real-estate information company has to wait 15 weeks to find out who bought a house in the District—by far, he says, the longest delay in the country.

Listen, in fact, to D.C. Council member Harold Brazil (D-Ward 6), who says he was stonewalled himself by District bureaucrats when he tried to get information from the Office of Campaign Finance—and he's chairman of the council's Committee on Government Oversight. Brazil said, "have a right—and an obligation—to demand more than they're getting from their government.

"There is a lack of mission," Brazil said. "I don't think we, the government, are that well focused."

Others are far less generous in their assessments. A recent study by the consulting firm KPMG Peat Marwick said the city government is "still perceived as bloated and inefficient;" Lawrence S. Herman, a Peat Marwick partner in charge of government reengineering services, went further.

"Frankly," he said, "the District has one of the highest ratios of civil servants to citizens in the world—and that probably includes even Moscow and the former communist countries."

"It's crazy," said Chalmers, who's been seeking the condominium-tax refund for six years. "We can't even get a response from them. We can't even get them to say they're looking for it. Total incompetence."

Twins' Unpaid Day Care

The D.C. Department of Human Services was paying $1,200 a day to keep twin crack babies in the hospital when Diane Hendle fell for them. It's an occupational hazard at the Hospital for Sick Children, where she works as a pediatric nurse.

Abandoned by their mother after six days of life, the twins were eight months old when Hendle first laid eyes on them. No D.C. social worker had ever visited, she said, even though the twins were eligible for placement at three months.

It took five months, four hearings and, ultimately, a court order to get the twins released to her care. Now, a year after she became the babies' guardian, the District has fallen $3,187 behind in their day-care bill, which it promised to pay.

That care is desperately needed. One twin, a girl, has chronic lung disease and has battled four separate cases of pneumonia in the last 11 weeks. The other, a boy, is blind in one eye and losing sight in another.

But Hendle says her experience with the D.C. Department of Human Services has been dispiriting from the start. "There are no foster parents or adoptive parents who, once they work with the department, will ever want to work with the department again," she said.

Indeed, Hendle's experience is so commonplace that a federal judge took control of a large segment of the foster care system in September, after finding conditions in the system "horrific."

Two other city agencies, the departments of Corrections and Housing, also have been slapped with court orders.

Information Bottleneck

For Rufus Lusk, the man who trades in real-estate information, there was good news and bad news last week down at the D.C. Recorder of Deeds office.

The good news was that, for the first time since early December, there were 11 rolls of microfilm available for his data clerk to review. The bad news, as the clerk sat before a microfilm viewer, was that the film was blurry and difficult to read.

The viewer next to her—like the firetruck that's supposed to rescue the president—wasn't good for much. A hand-scrawled sign covered the screen with a one word epithet: "Broke."

"D.C. is, sad to say, far and away the most difficult area in the country in terms of access to data," said Lusk, a regional vice president of Lusk/TRW REDI. "We have been unable to publish anything for the last five weeks—nothing at all. It really is totally inexcusable."

Such lack of control over information, and a lack of systems to gather information quickly, are widespread in city government. Russell Smith, the District's auditor, says the city's cash management system was "archaic" 20 years ago. D.C. Inspector General Samuel McClendon found last year that in fiscal 1994 alone, city administrators conducted 481 separate transactions totaling $31 million without written contracts.

Smith also said the city does not have the technology that would enable it to manage personnel efficiently. "We don't have a system that allows us to know how many people are on board and whether their salaries are within our budgeted salaries amounts," he said.

Unresolved Tax Dispute

Down at ABC Salvage Corp., on N Street SE near the Washington Navy Yard, Les Ulanow and his father, Sam, are still waiting for their day in court.

Five years ago, when the coming of a Metro stop raised land values in the neighborhood, the city reassessed their property, sending their real estate taxes surging from $8,350 to $18,400 a year, according to Sam Ulanow. The next year, the property was reassessed again, and again the taxes skyrocketed, this time to a whopping $55,000 a year.

They've pretty much remained at that level, Ulanow said, even though real estate values have since plummeted. "I know damn well we're going to win something back, and it won't be small," Ulanow said.

"If I could sell this property and get the hell out of D.C., I'd be gone," Les Ulanow said. "You get nothing for your taxes. I can't even get people in the D.C. government to return my calls. It's a totally unresponsive government—and it's always been that way."

Others, too, believe they have been wronged by the city government but have failed to get even a hearing. Mike Brown doesn't think he'll ever get paid for the $900 claim he filed 14 months ago after a D.C. snow plow ripped the side of his wife's car off "like a can of sardines."

"Obviously," he said, "there is no government—it's anarchy. Apparently, they have no intention of paying anybody."

John G. Doherty worked for more than 25 years as a District police officer, but he says that when he took early retirement in September, the city owed him $16,909 in compensatory time. Four months later, he has yet to receive the check.

"I think it's absolutely disgusting," he said. "You were dedicated to your work—and this is what you get for it?"

Money is also the reason the city is without Tower 10, the firetruck that is supposed to protect the White House. The D.C. government is not yet delinquent in paying the $2,300 repair bill for that vehicle, but it is behind on others being fixed at the Johnson Towers garage in Beltsville. So, according to service manager Randy Hart Tower 10 won't be released until the bill is paid.

The Clintons will be relieved to know they won't be stranded if something catches fire at the White House in the meantime. According to D.C. Fire Department Capt. Alvin T. Carter, the department has contingency plans to send another ladder truck.

Hart says that when city officials come to get Tower 10, they should bring cash.

For a Few Dollars More

Santiago Testa has learned to cope with the District's service cuts, but he had to take matters into his own hands.

After pruning 33 trees on his property in Chevy Chase-D.C., he wrapped the leaves and branches into neat little bundles and put them in his driveway. There they sat for the next six weeks, untouched by D.C. sanitation workers. He ultimately discovered that the days of monthly bulk pickups were over.

So what did he do?

He took a morning off from work, waited for a trash truck to come by and gave the sanitation workers a few bucks, and they took care of it, Testa said.

"Just like in Latin America."

Do you know of jobs that are not being done or services that are not being rendered because of problems in the D.C. government? Tell us. Call Post-Haste at 202-334-9000 and leave a message.

Analysis of Chapter 3 Case Studies

Based on the above discussions of major issues and problems in fiscal management institutions, what advice can we provide to those charged with fixing the District's problems (known in this case as the Federal Financial Control Board) to improve basic policy results? What are the costs and benefits of strengthening particular functions (e.g., internal controls) as opposed to seeking wholesale reform through integrated fiscal systems? What sequence of reform would one suggest given the severe institutional constraints to policy results in Washington, D.C.? How can the principles of financial management institutional development noted above guide solutions to these problems?

This case study points to major institutional systems' deterioration that affect the delivery of basic services and internal operations. A full analysis of organizational structures and functions ("root and branch" review) or management audit is needed. One should ask immediately whether this should be done in house or by an outside management consultant. The purpose of the review should be to clarify lines of authority to tighten links between policies, management, and results. Effective policy results require (1) sufficient discretion and authority to allocate resources, (2) sufficient funds, and (3) valid and timely information—on orders flowing down and feedback activities. One should remember that the major theme of this chapter is that policy analysis cannot limit itself to prospective costs and benefits without considering the institutional environment.

Since a client (hypothetically the District government or the control board) seeking analysis is unlikely to pay for a full-blown study at the outset, it is important to offer several phases of increasing activity. The phases should be sequenced so that each can be stand alone but implicitly require that one goes on to the next. For example, the first step here could be to review workloads of target agencies. Since all the workload of the city cannot feasibly be reviewed in a reasonable period of time, one might focus on transactions, such as purchasing equipment, hiring staff, or issuing licenses. The major work areas of the city can be broken down into a series of transactions requiring legal authorization, staff resources, and a series of procedural steps leading to expected results. Structural and management issues could be the initial focus of the study. Managerial discretion and legal authority to take appropriate actions would be the critical variables here. Next, one could examine how the financial management functions and information systems support management authority. Legal authority without funds or information on past results and expected activities would not be very useful. Attention may be focused on the major financial management functions first—budgeting and accounting, followed by personnel, procurement, and internal control. As noted, integration of financial management systems should proceed in stages. Given the uncertainties and the costs, the most reasonable course (with the highest likely impact) would be to focus on strengthening particular functions, followed by limited integration. The analyst needs to work out in advance how much funding is available and plan accordingly.

BLOATED STAFF

This case study raises at least five major issues to which five kinds of policy-program analysis methods and tools can be applied. First, the case indicates that the city's bureaucracy is oversized, having "one of the highest ratios of civil servants to citizens in the world" (Loeb 1995). A common technique used in civil service reforms around the world is work programming that includes development of staffing ratios. Civil service reforms involve review of structures and functions of government and the roles and responsibilities of departments and their managers to produce cost-effective and accountable program delivery. This is a big order and often is subsumed under "reinventing government" to "empower" employees through "reinvention laboratories" and other buzz words. Many times the starting place is the size of the government itself in relation to tasks to be performed. Merely downsizing aggregate numbers to reduce payroll will of course lower expenditures, reduce fiscal deficits, and appear to satisfy fiscal rectitude criteria. A recent Brazilian civil service reform allows workers to be sacked when payroll costs exceed 60 percent of total revenues. But often this merely hides needed expenditures for services, operations and maintenance, and construction needs that cost more later.

Work programming or analysis of staffing needs is a critical element in both building personal services budgets (up to 60 percent of total costs in some jurisdictions). To do this analysts could follow these steps.

1. Estimate workload (e.g., student enrollment, number of tax returns, number of bus passenger miles, number of unemployment claims). Demand analysis should also link incoming workload to resource allocation—for instance, deployment of police in response to call patterns or demand for business licenses and redeployment of department personnel to accommodate the demand (Ammons 1991, 22)

2. Estimate unit time and costs (e.g., number of tax examiners per 100,000 returns, student-faculty ratios by discipline, administrative overhead rule of thumb based on past experience [8–10 percent]).

Developing of time-output and staffing ratios runs into problems with professional groups that oppose measurement on the grounds that this development ignores quality, is based on statistical averages, ignores task complexity, becomes a straitjacket, and ends up displacing the goal itself. That is, the measurement of work becomes the goal rather than delivering quality services that require judgment and flexibility. Nevertheless, if used as a rough guide, work programming can limit budget damage and enable agencies to rid themselves of redundant personnel and/or redeploy labor for particular tasks (Axelrod 1995). In the case of Washington, D.C., it should be noted that even though the city has one of the highest personnel-to-citizen ratios in the world, the public works department is understaffed for construction management and maintenance tasks that it must accomplish: staffing ratios indicate that the bureau is only half as large as cities of similar size (Reid 1996).

GLACIAL BUREAUCRACY

It is clear that even though they were strapped for cash, many services cut personnel but left in place bureaucratic management and clearance systems. This destroyed any savings achieved in salaries by creating longer term cost liabilities for services and facilities. While the public works department has lost hundreds of staff members in the past five years, it still had to answer to a layered city bureaucracy that delayed projects by up to six months (Reid 1996). Staffing cuts that saved budget funds in the short run were then squandered by bureaucratic constraints, driving up transaction costs for remaining personnel. Analysis could proceed to first review existing functions to determine whether or not cost-effective service delivery is possible or necessary under existing institutional conditions. Measurement of costs and revenues per employee should be a first step in determination of rates of change in the average costs of service delivery. Although the case study does not provide data to perform this measurement, there is anecdotal evidence that costs per employee are high. Analysis could focus on the structures of roles and responsibilities for program delivery. Departments could be restructured. Should roles be consolidated? Should management be delayered? Should processes be streamlined? Again, ratios are helpful as a guide to focus systematic reform. The city of Milwaukee, for example, reduced its building inspection management:staff ratio from 0.15 to 0.13 in seven years (Milwaukee 1995, 59). This may be important in improving policy delivery, or it may not. Clearance and approval systems may have been held intact.

Deregulation of existing systems is often needed to take advantage of staff reductions, allowing them to exercise more judgment and responsibility for outcomes. For this purpose, analysis should focus on the flow of work. Often, it is assumed that those who have performed a particular function for years and are intimately associated with the legalities and procedures of the process are most qualified to design the best procedures to carry out that function. In fact, they are often immersed in the details and are unable to view the matter systematically from the perspective of clients and other users (Ammons 1991). Processes such as public procurement/purchasing should be diagrammed and examined for redundant and cost-ineffective steps. Most policy processes and systems become routinely clogged and could use such flowcharting on a regular rolling basis.

FRAGMENTED INFORMATION

Fragmented information systems means that budget planning and controls are weakened. In Washington, D.C., "islands of information" exist that permit transactions to fall through the cracks, such as paying employees without budgeted slots before it becomes clear that a department has exceeded its personnel costs (Flaherty 1995). Evidence of the failure to link payroll with personnel rosters and budget goes further. The city used an employee identification numbering system to safeguard against fraud, but audits found 1,734 people on the payrolls without numbers who were paid anyway. Nearly 200 people shared numbers, and personnel numbers existed for eight dead people. Individuals appeared on the payroll file but were not listed on personnel and budget files, meaning that although they were paid there was no audit trail in the files to document their existence (Horwitz and Strauss 1997). Integration of fiscal and personnel data could prevent this. It is clear from the case that the city has major problems in several components of financial management: budget planning is weakened by incomplete information flowing in from multiple sources; procurement systems purchase a financial management information system that was not geared to either the capacities or needs of local organizations; information aggregation does not serve the needs of operational units, preventing managers from using information to control resources and deliver services properly; budget administration is weakened by a system that allowed deficits to be financed by withholding entries without detection by internal controls.

Many of the District's policy problems result from a growing institutional problem: the tendency to go for the quick-fix computerized information system. The city procured a "gold-plated Cadillac" system that ignored the incapacities of departmental personnel to meet new system requirements. System design also ignored the need for clear authority structures and chains of command to act on information that revealed fiscal and policy problems. The assumption peddled by many salespeople in information technology is that the system will take care of all these problems. This leads in many cases, and not just in Washington, D.C., to computerization of bad systems that will take more funds to fix later. In particular, the computerized system did not require the very reporting essential to its design.

But as this case study indicates, managers lacked feedback information on their own service performance. Senior managers can avoid the hard choices of running deficits by failure of internal controls to act upon cash flow information. Balances are not reported or acted upon in many cases because there are no penalties for failure to do so. An integrated system could improve control and allow managers to reprogram resources to meet service targets. Note that a premise of an integrated financial management system (IFMS) is that standards should be defined centrally and operational responsibility decentralized. Implementation of standards should be delegated to operational units. Where operational responsibility is not decentralized, this acts as a disincentive to generate or share information across programs, cost categories, or institutions.

Installation of an IFMS is not a simple task that can be handled by a "cookbook" manual. In some ways, it offers a comprehensive conceptual solution to all problems that does not happen in reality. Failure to consider design and installation issues have produced substantial fiscal and management problems in many jurisdictions. For example, policymakers need to consider the level of integration and flexibility desired. A jurisdiction may purchase an inflexible system that generates far more information than it can use in the foreseeable future, and it may have been designed for one jurisdiction and require many changes before it can be adapted to a new one (e.g., Argentina's to Nicaragua's). A jurisdiction may only need basic budgeting and accounting integration with better internal controls and institutional incentives to utilize them. While installation problems are being worked out an IFMS can create new opportunities for fraud and waste.

In practice, integrated systems can generate dependence on a sophisticated system that can crash when any of the subsystems fail. Substantial management time and talent is needed to implement the system and to exploit its information fully to improve policy results. A new IFMS may create inflexibility. Governments frequently change appropriations codes, funding sources, projects and responsibility centers. Such changes require modification of posting logic: to the extent that classification definitions are hard-coded into computer posting routines, each change can require modification of whole data processing steps (impeding linkages and information sharing). This can be avoided by using tables to process each transaction rather than hard-coding definitions (Hayes et al. 1982, 136).

Also, decentralization of input and output data makes inconsistencies and errors more likely. Politically, integrated systems are based on clarity and accountability; this means that institutions should share information to accomplish common tasks. But in the context of line-item annual budgeting and segmented policymaking in the United States and elsewhere, this is somewhat naïve. Most governments are deliberately fragmented, stratified by departments and staff-line roles. Positively, this avoids accumulation of too much power and encourages checks and balances, as well as allowing multiple access points for public inputs. But this may also hide information from other institutions viewed as competitors: in high-trust cultures such as in this country this is less of a problem than in low-trust societies of the former Soviet Union. In the latter, however, integration of systems would be more difficult because this is perceived as a threat to existing power relations.

There are four basic components needed to installing an IFMS. Note that the major ones are not based on technical expertise in such areas as budgeting and accounting. Management expertise and leadership are needed to break down institutional barriers and forge consensus.

First, there should be a uniform chart of accounts in which budgeting and accounting classifications are the same. The most basic level of integration ties together these two functions. This prevents basic problems, such as classification of teachers as administrators and others as employees that had worked at closed schools (Horwitz and Strauss 1997). The major advantage of an IFMS is that once classifications and accounting principles are defined, financial transactions and performance events need to be entered only once rather than multiple times (which creates opportunities for multiple errors) (Hayes et al. 1982, 132). But financial data for budgeting and management often lack standardization. Definitions of types of maintenance such as "routine," "periodic," "major rehabilitation," or "minor" may vary widely by jurisdiction and agency. This allows slippage in the accounts, possibly resulting in artificial savings through financing current expenses (e.g., minor maintenance classified as major) by borrowing—also known as capitalization of operating expenses. If budgetary accounting is inconsistent, integrating other functions and spreading information around to different institutional levels will merely multiply uncertainty and confusion. More tightly integrated systems link in payroll, purchasing, internal control and cash management.

Second, there should be a single unified bank account. Treasury control of finances based on timely reporting of cash balances of payments and receipts and controls on appropriations is essential. This provides creditors with confidence in the ability of the government to pay bills on time.

A single account that contains all public expenditure transactions in subaccounts also allows credit rating institutions to assess creditworthiness accurately. There are no hidden debts and payables that could compromise both policy performance and debt service.

Third, there should be a single database. Consistent with decentralization of operational responsibility, data entry occurs at dispersed locations closer to where the transaction occurs (Bartel 1996, 15). There may be several databases that include fiscal and physical results measures. These databases are related by computers to permit data sharing and improved decisionmaking.

Fourth, there should be a coordinating group. As is evident in this case study, an IFMS must meet the needs of various agencies in their efforts to allocate resources to achieve policy results. A coordinating group composed of representatives from each user must exercise oversight and implementation. It is also critical that the group contain line-level officials that work in existing systems. They are the ones who must be convinced of the value of new data entry routines and classifications. Utilizing their insights into strengths and weaknesses of the existing process can avoid expensive design errors at the outset.

WEAK INTERNAL CONTROLS

To reform policy systems, adequate internal controls must be in place. Inadequate controls over budget transactions can be traced to the failure of many policies, including fiscal decentralization efforts in many parts of the world. Washington's failure to exercise its local authority accountably and the growing effort to remove local discretion and recentralize power in Congress or a control board can be traced to the fiscal control problem. As noted in this case study, weak budgetary controls over budget modification allow the major reprogramming of funds during the year, not so much for management flexibility as for meeting salaries. Changes in budget are necessary throughout the year. The basic rule is that increases in a particular line-item or appropriation accounts should be offset by decreases in other accounts or line items. Where the transfer will increase aggregate budget amounts legislative approval is often required. However, in some jurisdictions approvals are required for even minor changes or those of little budgetary significance. This raises the issue of cost-effectiveness of controls that restrict managerial flexibility. In many cases, ex-post auditing is a more cost-effective control than trying to prevent noncompliance with intrusive clearances and approvals (Hayes et al. 1982, 66).

Having said this, budget modification controls in Washington, D.C., appear to be below the minimum. The $7.3 million budgeted for job training ended up in salaries and failed to produce a single trained person (Harris 1997). Since the $7.3 million was still insufficient to cover deficits within the agency created by other expenditures, the Department of Employment Services asked for $3 million more. This request revealed an inability to track basic outlays, transfers, reprograms, and results of the training program. Part of the problem is that unplanned budget cuts during the year create fiscal instability and produce a rash of reprogramming to meet mainly salary costs. Given the uncertainty, the departments could withhold program expenditures and cover salaries directly or indirectly through transfers from other accounts. This "repetitive budgeting" is well known in resource-poor environments (Caiden and Wildavsky 1975). But without accounting controls, budget administration cannot function properly to track and compare variances with previous quarters and fiscal years. Lack of controls makes policy planning difficult and virtually ensures that previous mistakes will be recycled into the next year. Financial systems can provide internal edits (rejections) for such obvious errors as obligating funds without available balances and submitting vouchers for purchase orders that have not been entered into the system, but someone has to act on the information. Otherwise overruns, arrears, and total budget transformations can continue unnoticed.

Part of the problem is that incentives need to exist for controls to be exercised. Enforcement of regulations as part of the job, driven by commitment to improved policy results, has not proven effective where other countervailing incentives exist (like getting one's salary). Put another way, there are institutional limits to control "by direction," which implies considerable centralization (Premchand 1983, 152). By contrast, control "by incentives" relies on decentralized discretion. In such countries as Australia, public-sector managers have incentives to control expenditures in the form of receiving maximum trust and discretion to change their budgets. Managers are given lump-sum budgets for "running costs" to achieve policy performance targets ("forward estimates") set by the finance department. In exchange for this trust from the finance department, department managers can shift funds (with finance department approval) between line items and across fiscal years (carryover authority) (Keating and Rosalky 1990).

Consistent with the principle cited above of centralized policy standards and decentralized operational responsibility, the Australian system succeeds in creating budgetary institutions that reflect policy. More important, these incentives have increased the value of the budget to the point where it is the key instrument of public policymaking. That is, shifts in the composition of expenditures and reductions reflect genuine shifts in public policy. Controls are exercised on postaudit to permit managers maximum discretion to achieve policy targets. But solid reporting and accounting are performed to permit an audit trail. Better reporting is rewarded with more discretion, which leads to more innovative policy approaches. Policy successes (or failures) can be traced back to performance measures and expenditure composition in the budget.

The Australian example demonstrates the need to design controls to avoid mismatching subjects of controls and their timing. As noted by Fred Thompson (1993, 311), the costs of overcontrol or micromanagement affect policy results. He suggests that mismatched controls can add 5 to 20 percent to the real cost of supplying services; overcontrol can add even more. Substitution of after-the-fact (post facto) controls for before-the-fact (precontrols) can produce substantial productivity gains. Precontrols sever any link between potential performance gains and rewards to officials. Thompson recommends moving from traditional government budgets relying on line-item precontrols to "outlay" budgets where, as in Australia, departments supply services in exchange for a guaranteed allotment of funds (1993, 307). It should be noted that the system functions well in Australia in part because the central finance department rigorously monitors performance and demands regular reporting from departments. Part of the departmental obligation in exchange for guaranteed funds and release from precontrols over spending during the fiscal year is that it must provide regular detailed reports of balances. The central finance department responds to reporting irregularities in a timely and efficient fashion. Again, the Washington, D.C., system is one of no concentrated responsibility, with Congress, the mayor, and several subsystems diffusing accountability and responsibility for expenditures and program results.

QUESTIONABLE EXPENDITURE CONTROLS

Programs such as primary and secondary education suffer from weaknesses in expenditure control. The success of education policy turns on many factors, but supplies, computers, books, and support equipment are critical tools needed by teachers everywhere. In the District of Columbia, financial institutions allowed unfettered reprogramming of funds from supplies and equipment to salaries. Since salaries were not tied to budgeted positions, massive overspending occurred for fictitious employees (Horwitz and Strauss 1997). In the context of the highest per pupil expenditures in the United States, mostly for administrative personnel and related salaries, policy outputs, and outcomes, however defined, are dismal.

Analysis of this problem should focus on budget formulation and accounting and reporting systems. Budgets should be based on realistic numbers that allow the allocation of fair shares through reasonable cuts and adds. The District school system budget offered unreasonable numbers (e.g., $75,000 for garbage pickup when actual costs exceeded $1 million in previous years). Council cuts and adds were essentially arbitrary, providing incentives for administrators to perpetrate more budget games. There is also evidence that capital expenditures were not planned on a multiyear basis to allow financing that would not threaten the sustainability of current expenditures. Projects were approved and dropped without adequate analysis. The system persists because reporting is not required. Failure to report does not result in cuts or personal reprimands. So, the Washington, D.C., school system operates a fragmented fiscal management system that allows transactions to go unreported and payments to be made, the latter adding to arrears and future obligations. The school system operates two unlinked financial tracking systems. The budget tracking system linked to the treasurer and chief financial officer is not linked to the Resource Management Control and Information System, which is controlled by the school district administration. Essentially, this means that the school system is an independent special fund with unreported balances to the city administration. But the city administration (general fund) is ultimately responsible for payment of obligations incurred by the school district. This is a common pattern with city enterprises and special funds.

But, usually, interfund transfers and balances are regularly consolidated to give the treasurer a comprehensive picture of total finances. In the District this does not happen for several reasons. First, there are no penalties imposed for failure to report unapproved transfers and obligations against unencumbered balances. Failure to enforce data entry requirements can destroy the purposes of any system no matter how expensive. Second, the District government can track obligations and appropriations status against budgets for particular cost centers, but this tracking does not extend to such program areas as the schools. In effect, the city budget is fictional and not comprehensive. This is more than a technical issue of redefining budget codes and classification. It means more than "integrating" data systems. It means developing functional expenditure controls over obligations, payments, and transfers. Internal controls, as noted above, must be exercised within departments and results reported to chief financial officers. Officials should withhold approval for payments to cover unbudgeted personnel slots and should deny transfers from supplies to salaries when performance targets are obviously not going to be met with such a budget modification.

Failure of internal control systems (like other problems cited in this chapter) are not unique to the Washington, D.C., government. The nonintegrated computer system of the Department of Defense (DOD) requires personnel to make manual entries of data, leading to such major errors as massive overpayment to contractors. In one case, a contractor was overpaid $7.5 million and this remained outstanding for eight years with an estimated loss of $5 million in interest. There is no cost-effective control of the DOD payments process. According to Senator Tom Harkin (D-Iowa), "The Pentagon's accounting system is in the Stone Age. DOD uses a magnifying glass to check a Tootsie Roll purchase and misses million dollar problems" (*Washington Post,* 1997). This underscores the point that internal controls are the glue that holds the financial management system together (Bartel 1996, 53). The controls should be management tools, and not simply audit exercises, to ensure that financial information generated by the system is materially correct and that applicable rules and regulations have been complied with. In the instances cited above, evidence points to massive failure of internal controls and the need for redesign to improve management and policy performance. This is not a difficult task and merely requires political will to carry it out. The financial control board of the District of Columbia may overrule the tendency of the mayor's office to ignore fiscal problems. Continuing sweetheart relationships, however, between the DOD and its contractors makes this problem more intractable: the present system of overpayment may be too beneficial to too many interests to be countered by techniques such as IFMS or training courses in internal controls.

Notes

1. The efficiency-effectiveness distinction in public administration is often confusing to economists, who define both as subcategories of "efficiency." "Technical efficiency" refers to least cost and maximization of output per unit of input; "allocative efficiency" refers to client access and service quality that satisfies consumer preferences (World Bank 1995, 30).
2. A common problem in policy analysis today is the simplistic assumption that information can always improve decisionmaking quality. Going on this assumption, considerable sums are expended on information reporting systems, the implicit assumption being that some manager will use data for some purpose. But more timely and accurate fiscal and economic "data" flows may not produce valuable "information" for better decisionmaking. Many management and policy problems derive from issues of organizational structure. Having more data available does not necessarily help policymakers articulate the questions that need attention in the solution to problems. A fundamental presumption of information technology is that more and better information increases public-sector control over costs and service

performance. Public management theorists and practitioners presume that the more and better the information on project cost, schedule, and quality in computer systems, the greater the project control and the less the actual performance variances.

In an empirical study of management control systems for ninety-nine defense contracts, E. Sam Overman and Donna Loraine (1994, 195) found that the "quality, detail, timeliness and cost of information do not have a positive effect on project control." Despite these findings, "most managers still believed that collecting and reporting information led to project control." In short, data are collected and processed into information largely to "support the illusion of control" or for "symbolic value." Given this disturbing finding, there should likely be an upper limit or hard budget constraint on generation of information as a management tool for most organizations. Rather, organizations should likely emphasize incentives that help management engage in critical policy thinking and to turn the most important data into useful information for decisions. Information, it seems, can guide better policymaking. But it cannot prevent problems caused by the modern tendency to demand all data and the failure to demand more precise data around defined questions and problems.

References

Ammons, David N. (1991). *Administrative Analysis for Local Governments* (Athens: University of Georgia, Carl Vinson Institute of Government).

Axelrod, Donald. (1995). *Budgeting for Modern Government,* 2d ed. (New York: St. Martin's).

Banks, William C. and Jeffrey D. Straussman. (1999). "Defense Contingency Budgeting in the Post-Cold-War Period," *Public Administration Review* (March/April) pp. 135–45.

Barr, Stephen. (1997). "AID's $71 Million Global Computer Link Sidelined by Software, Design Problems," *Washington Post,* 5 May, A9.

Bartel, Margaret. (1996). "Integrated Financial Management Systems: A Guide Based on the Experience in Latin America" (draft) (Washington, D.C.: World Bank).

Blustein, Paul. (1997). "Thinking Globally, Punishing Locally: States, Cities Rush to Impose Their Own Sanctions, Angering Companies and Foreign Affairs Experts," *Washington Post,* 16 May, G1.

Boyne, George A. (1998). "Bureuacratic Theory Meets Reality: Public Choice and Service Contracting in U.S. Local Government" *Public Administration Review* 58, 6 (November/December).

Byrnes, Patricia, Mark Freeman, and Dean Kauffman. (1997). "Performance Measurement and Financial Incentives for Community Behavioral Health Service Provision," *International Journal of Public Administration* 20, 8–9, pp. 1555–78.

Caiden, Naomi and Aaron Wildavsky. (1975). *Planning and Budgeting in Poor Countries* (New York: John Wiley).

Chandler, Clay. (1997). "Medicare Accounting Dispute Could Threaten Early Budget Accord," *Washington Post,* 10 January, A12.

Coe, Charles K. (1989). *Public Financial Management* (Englewood Cliffs, N.J.: Prentice Hall).

Economist. (1999). "Government in Disgrace: Bilking the Tribes" (13 March), pp. 34–35.

———. (1997a). "Just What the Doctors Ordered?" (26 July), p. 63

———. (1997b). "Fraudulent Behavior" (26 July), p. 25.

———. (1997c). "Ukraine, A Glint of Hope?" (26 July), p. 45.

———. (1997d). "Bridge-Building in Washington" (25 January), p. 23.

———. (1993). "Government in California: Buckling Under the Strain," pp. 21–23.

Flaherty, Mary Pat. (1995). "Failure to Compute Adds to D.C.'s Bills," *Washington Post,* 5 May, A1 and A8.

Gianakis, Gerasimos A. and John G. Davis. (1998). "Reinventing or Replacing Public Services? The Case of Community-Oriented Policing," *Public Administration Review* 58, 6 (November/December).

Government Finance Officers Association. (1978). *An Operating Budget Handbook for Small Cities and Other Governmental Units* (Chicago: Government Finance Officers Association).

Haarmeyer, David and Ashoka Mody. (1997). "Private Capital in Water and Sanitation," *Finance and Development* 34, 1, pp. 34–37.

Harris, Hamil. (1997). "City Diverts Money from Job Training," *Washington Post,* 10 March, A1 and A21.

Hayes, Frederick O'R., David A. Grossman, Jerry E. Mechling, John S. Thomas, and Steven J. Rosenbloom. (1982). *Linkages: Improving Financial Management in Local Government* (Washington, D.C.: Urban Institute).

Heclo, Hugh. (1978). "Issue Networks and the Executive Establishment," in Anthony King (ed.) *The New Political System* (Washington, D.C.: American Enterprise Institute), pp. 87–124.

Horwitz, Sari and Valerie Strauss. (1997). "A Well-Financed Failure: System Protects Jobs While Shortchanging Classrooms," *Washington Post,* 16 February, A1 and A24–25.

Jeter, Jon and Susan Levine. (1997). "Montgomery Agency Handled Boy's Case Correctly, Officials Say (But Child Protection System Has Problems, Task Force Finds)," *Washington Post,* 2 May, B1

Keating, Michael and David Rosalky. (1983). "Rolling Expenditure Plans: Australian Experience and Prognosis," in A. Premchand. *Government Budgeting and Expenditure Controls, Theory and Practice* (Washington, D.C.: International Monetary Fund).

Kory, Ross C. and Philip Rosenberg. (1984). "Costing Municipal Services," in John Matzer. *Practical Financial Management* (Washington, D.C.: International City Management Association), pp. 50–60.

Lehan, Edward. (1984). *Budgetmaking: A Workbook of Public Budgeting Theory and Practice* (New York: St. Martin's).

Levine, Susan and Manuel Perez-Rivas. (1997). "Montgomery Targets Services Watchdog, Accountability Office is in Line for 50% Budget Cut," *Washington Post,* 14 May, B1.

Lipton, Eric. (1998). "A Cleanup Job Left Unfinished," *Washington Post,* 9 December, B1.

Loeb, Vernon. (1995). "In an Ailing City, Vital Services Cease to Function: Dozens of Departments Failing D.C. Residents," *Washington Post,* 29 January, A1 and A22.

Matzer, John. (1984). *Practical Financial Management* (Washington, D.C.: International City Management Association).

McAllister, Bill. (1996). "Bottom Line or By-the-Book: Postal Services Public-Private Identity Crisis," *Washington Post,* 25 December, A1.

Milwaukee, City of. (1995). *1995 Plan and Budget Summary* (Wisconsin: City of Milwaukee).

North, Douglass C. (1990). *Institutions, Institutional Change and Economic Performance* (Cambridge: Cambridge University Press).

Overman, E. Sam and Donna T. Loraine. (1994). "Information for Control: Another Management Proverb?" *Public Administration Review* 54, 2 (March/April), pp. 193–96.

Pearlstein, Steven. (1997). "The Thriving Economy That Keeps on Surprising," *Washington Post,* 3 May, H1.

Premchand, A. (1990). *Government Financial Management: Issues and Country Studies* (Washington, D.C.: International Monetary Fund).

———. (1983). *Government Budgeting and Expenditure Controls, Theory and Practice* (Washington, D.C.: International Monetary Fund).

Raimondo, Henry J. (1978). *The Economics of State and Local Government* (New York: Praeger).

Reid, Alice. (1996). "Public Works Positions Cut But Management Layers Remain," *Washington Post,* 27 March, B1 and B3.

Schiavo-Campo, Salvatore. (1994). "Institutional Change and the Public Sector in Transitional Economies," World Bank Discussion Paper 241 (Washington, D.C.: International Bank for Reconstruction and Development).

Schlosser, Eric. (1998). "The Prison-Industrial Complex," *Atlantic Monthly* (December), pp. 51–77.

Schmitt, Eric. (1997). "Panel Urges Abolishing Immigration Agency," *International Herald Tribune,* 6 August, p. 10

Thompson, Cheryl W. (1998). "Homicide Unit to Return Officers to Headquarters: Study of Other Cities' Departments Prompts Police Officials to Abandon Decentralization Effort," *Washington Post,* 21 January, B12.

Thompson, Fred. (1993). "Matching Responsibilities with Tactics: Administrative Controls and Modern Government," *Public Administration Review* 53, 4 (July/August).

Washington Post. (1997). "Report Faults Accounting at Defense Department, GAO Says Contractors Get Big Overpayments," 13 May, A4.

———. (1996). "D.C., U.S. Streamline Road-Project Approval Process" (7 June).

World Bank. (1997). *The Public Expenditure Management Handbook* (Washington, D.C.: World Bank).

———. (1995). "Better Urban Services: Finding the Right Incentives" (Washington, D.C.: International Bank for Reconstruction and Development).

Forecasting Policy Options

In the process of acquiring data, the analyst decides whether an actionable policy problem exists. Through assessment of data trends the analyst structures the policy problem, reviewing its degree complexity and stakeholder involvement as well as its potential solubility in the short or medium term. At this stage, evidence mounts to show whether a problem is well or ill structured, whether a problem exists at all, and, if it does, just how actionable it is. The conclusion that a problem does or does not exist is the product of the first part of the "diagnostic" phase of policy analysis.

The second part of the policy analysis process seeks to uncover the future behavior of variables used to define the problem. Clearly, the two phases are related because additional diagnosis might not be warranted if preliminary data indicate that the "problem" will solve itself in the near future. As a lurid example to emphasize this point, there is the 1997 film *The Beast,* in which marine experts recommended a do-nothing option to the police, arguing that the giant squid that was eating local fishermen was simply "passing through" and that any police actions could result in further actions by the monster against the town. Conceptually, we are still at the problem definition phase. Data forecasts and projections are necessary for proper determination of costs and benefits of a problem solution. Thus, forecasting options should be treated as a bridge between problem definition (chapter 2), forecasts of institutional capacities and constraints to policy performance (chapter 3), and applications of formal analytic techniques (chapters 5–7).

In this chapter we focus on the future behavior of policy problems. The development of reliable data forecasts can then give us a baseline from which to develop policy options. As we learned in chapter 2, an improperly defined problem (which should not be confused with an ill-structured one) can lead to such costly and inefficient omnibus approaches as throwing dollars at the problem. Similarly, the failure to establish how problem variables will behave in the future can result in public expenditures that could worsen the problem by failing to control for unanticipated consequences. If, for example, drug abuse is still a "problem" based on past trends, then setting out viable policy alternatives will depend on the accuracy of forecasts of the problem's various components' behavior in the future. Being able to project trends accurately depends on experience (judgment), the accuracy of past data (time-series), and a thorough understanding of such drug abuse determinants as hunger and homelessness (causal model).

Based on the needs of decisionmakers who are often faced with "messy" policy problems, this chapter will discuss (1) the purposes of forecasting, (2) the kinds of forecasts commonly developed, and (3) useful techniques for forecasting data. This information will then be applied to the case study of a public policy consultant forecasting sales tax receipts required for the development of the annual budget for the Metropolitan Atlanta Rapid Transit Authority (MARTA).

Predicting the Future, Cautiously

Before examining the range of techniques needed to predict the future, we need to know the objectives of forecasting. Public-sector stakeholders, such as a municipal credit-rating agency, want such specifics on financial condition as the precise level of operating expenses for maintenance of capital investment projects five years from now, or what clients will want to know about the level of sales tax revenues in a given city for the year 2005. To forecast gasoline tax revenues, the stakeholders might want to know what the level of gas consumption will be in 2005. Such clients as regulators and other stakeholder institutions regularly want to know current and future fiscal condition of public-sector agencies. Just as important, public agency managers themselves want to know revenues and expenditures so that they can manage their budgets for the year and deliver services effectively. They cannot do so without accurate forecasts based on sound methodology and supplemented by good monitoring of the budget to determine when they should alter expenditure plans in response to forecasts. Finally, at the operations policy level, federal land managers need to know the behavior of forest fires to prevent loss of firefighter life and property damage. For this purpose, researchers at the Los Alamos National Laboratory have been developing "crisis forecasting" techniques based on predictive computer simulations (Lane 1998).

Typically, the policy analyst will begin work developing "projections" (or a range of forecasts based on extrapolations of current and historical claims into the future) to avoid being pinned down on one figure (or forecast). "Forecasts" are single projections chosen from the process of developing a series of possible projections based on currently plausible assumptions. Policy analysts tend to avoid the term *prediction* (or forecasts based on explicit theoretical assumptions) because it implies "a statement of certainty about future events that obscures the conditional basis on which each of the projections, including the forecast, are based" (Klay 1983, 289). William Klay notes, for example, that the U.S. Bureau of the Census publishes several series of projections based on different assumptions about fertility, mortality, and migration, "but it resists identifying any one of these projections as an official forecast" (1983, 289).

One could reasonably ask how accurate statistical forecasting techniques are before learning about them. William Dunn (1994, 192) notes, for example, that the larger econometric firms had an average forecasting error as a proportion of actual changes in gross national product (GNP) (1971–1983) by 50 percent. He suggests that the accuracy of predictions based on complex theoretical models has been no greater than the accuracy of projections and conjectures made on the basis of simple extrapolative models and informed judgment.

On the other hand, shorter term forecasts of U.S. budget deficits have been more accurate even when obvious political incentives exist to vary the final figures. Between 1993 and 1996, the difference between the four sets of projections and ten fiscal deficit forecasts of the U.S. Office of Management and Budget (OMB) and the Congressional Budget Office (CBO) was only $13 billion. More surprisingly, both OMB and CBO projected higher deficits than actually came to pass (Congressional Budget Office 1997, 58). Several months later, CBO discovered with new revenue data that its forecasts were actually off by $45 billion per year, or $225 for its five-year forecast (Chandler 1997). Instead of continued fiscal deficits, the budget would actually be in surplus. CBO now projects budget surpluses to rise from 1.4 percent of gross domestic product (GDP) in 2000 to 2.8 percent of GDP in 2009 (*Economist* 1999a, 42).

The forecasting problem was likely a combination of overreliance on technical models, normal bureaucratic caution, and CBO interest in jacking up the size of the deficit to make the Clinton administration look bad. By requiring forecasts by both CBO and OMB, the Congressional Budget Impoundment and Control Act of 1974 institutionalized competitive forecasting and increased the overall accuracy of results. This suggests that greater forecasting accuracy lies in balancing the technical assumptions of any method against political and historical contextual factors. In this case, policy changes enacted after the forecasts were issued by both CBO and OMB had the net effect of reducing the deficit. Thus, good forecasting and wise use of techniques pays off. It should also be recognized that use of high-powered forecasting techniques requires valid data based on adequate sample sizes. As we will see below with the MARTA case, a problem with forecasting policy options is that revenue receipts are often based on small sample sizes that can compromise the power of statistical tests (Nelson and Cornia 1997, 42).

How important are revenue forecasts for budget policy and national politics? One might do worse than to ask French president Jacques Chirac. To qualify for the European single currency, the euro, the Maastricht Treaty required that the French 1998 budget (and those of other applicants) be no larger than the target of 3.0 percent of GDP. But Chirac's treasury forecast a budget deficit of 3.7 percent in 1997 and 4.5 percent in 1998. Based on this forecast, he questioned even trying for adoption of the single currency. He then called an election ten months early in which his Gaullist Party supporters suffered major losses. For the new government of Socialist prime minister Lionel Jospin, the latest treasury forecasts point to deficits of 3.1 percent in 1997 and 3.0 percent in 1998, based largely on higher economic growth (3.0 percent) and major cuts in defense spending (*Economist* 1997b). If these forecasts turned out more accurate than those in the last batch, Jospin would reap major political gains. In short, policy forecasters can actually make or break governments! Much can turn on the single number forecast by competent professionals.

The forecast can literally mean life or death for governments and individuals. This is especially true for providing the public with flood warnings based on forecasts. Unlike earthquake predictions, which remain in the realm of discontinuous phenomena, storms and flood patterns are regular—and they and their effects on surrounding populations can be discerned with appropriate forecasting methods. A good example of this is the Northern California floods of 1996. California's 1,400 dams and reservoirs are operated by a network of federal, state, and local agencies, plus power companies, irrigation districts, and water agencies. At its river forecast centers, the National Weather Service uses an orographic-hydrological model fed by information from the U.S. Geological Survey (USGS) and the California Department of Water Resources at more than 200 hydrometeorological measuring stations in rivers and streams.

The model forecasts precipitation produced by air lifted over mountains. Predictions of wind, temperature, and humidity up to 20,000 feet are combined with land elevation data at three-mile intervals to pinpoint precipitation amounts and locations in the mountains. Data from satellite pictures and Doppler radar are collected and used to track storms needed for flood management decisionmaking. (Flood management consists of juggling inflows and releases from reservoirs and dams to control the level of runoff.) While much of the guesswork in the models has been eliminated, "flood forecasting remains an inexact science" (Kiester 1997, 36). In December 1996, based on observations and predictions from an orographic model and a good bit of experience, a major storm was forecast. Even though the timing of rainfall occasionally eluded forecasters, the total amount forecast for the three storms was exceptionally close to what actually fell (Kiester 1997, 44). The hydrologists came up with mostly accurate predictions of not only amounts but locations as well. Although the floods swept out several critical USGS stations, the management of flood control space by the U.S. Army Corps of Engineers saved countless dollars of flood damage.

Purposes of Policy Forecasting

The purposes of policy forecasting vary according to the goals and objectives of policy and definitions of the problem. William Dunn (1994, 192) distinguishes between forecasts of existing and new policies. Clients may want to know the behavior of new macroeconomic policies, present policies without changes, and new policies on stakeholder groups.

MACROPOLICY IMPACTS

Policy forecasts may have macropolicy objectives, such as determination of energy policy. Forecasts of new policy trends, in which new government actions are taken in response to market forces, tend to allow a wide range of assumptions and conclusions. For example, oil pricing forecasts often seek the point at which drilling becomes profitable. Based on a price of $15 to $20 for a barrel of oil, U.S. oil production declined by 2 percent from 1985 while imports increased by 8 percent in the same period. If these trends had continued until a stable $22/barrel price was reached, that would have been the profitability point for drilling in the United States (Daniels 1986). Economists employ theory-based policy forecasts at the macro level: they try to forecast aggregate demand in the economy and how much the inflation or output gap will be. Using an income determination model of aggregate demand, or the likely amount of expenditures by government, investors, and consumers from their respective incomes, economic policy analysts try to predict how much inflation or unemployment will occur from this level of predicted demand. From this they recommend appropriate fiscal and monetary policies.

EXISTING POLICY IMPACTS

Forecasts may take existing policies as a given. The U.S. budget process begins with expenditure forecasts based on no changes in existing policy. "Current services estimates" of expenditures consider real, nonpolicy changes in expenditures with modifications only for changes in agency workloads. Forecasts of existing revenue trends, where no new government actions are taken to change tax or fee structures, typically will seek one figure (e.g., a 4 percent increase in revenues for the next three fiscal years). In the case study for this chapter, MARTA requires exact knowledge of sales tax revenues for at least the following four years to avoid budget deficits or surpluses that would rouse the enmity of differing stakeholders, which include public-sector unions, bondholders, the appointed MARTA board, riders who would face a fare increase, and such bond-rating agencies as Standard and Poor's. To recognize the seriousness of revenue forecasts in the determination of policy, in FY 1987 the sales tax forecast of $155.8 million was high by $8.8 million. The resultant budget deficit had to be financed by a fare increase in June 1987 (Roughton 1987). Fare increases are always dangerous, because if patronage falls, increased deficits may be created. In the late 1980s the entire fleet of new buses of Birmingham, Alabama, was warehoused because of exactly such a downward spiral in ridership caused by fare increases, followed by more fare increases to make up the shortfall, thus causing further ridership reductions, and so on. Knowledge of price elasticities of demand is required to make revenue forecasts of alternate fare structures. The concept of elasticity will be discussed in detail in chapter 5.

IMPACTS ON STAKEHOLDERS

Forecasts are also made about the contents of new policies and the behavior of policy stakeholders. Much of this is "judgmental" despite the forecasts' often heavy quantitative foundation. Two examples should suffice here, one from a political and the other from an economic policy. First, "high" policy analysis increasingly attempts to forecast the political stability of nations as a service to investors and other interested patrons. This involves forecasting the relationship between economic and political stability based on past patterns and the quality of the current government. "Political risk analysis" is an effort to forecast the behavior of policy stakeholders by using such techniques as "political feasibility assessment" of professors (*New York Times* 1986; Coplin and O'Leary 1986). By this technique, data are examined from multiple sources covering a variety of structural and policy questions and the country is given a rating from a panel of experts. The rating is converted into an index or multiplier for forecasting existing trends into the future. Foreign investors then have an indicator of the political, as well as economic and financial, risk of success or failure.

In some cases, economists try to forecast the effects of existing policies for both investors and policymakers. For example, an important current question for both groups is whether there will be a currency crisis in Eastern Europe. A currency crisis would involve speculative attacks on currencies that have increased greatly in real terms, leading to a policy of forced devaluation. Economists, using the cases of Mexico and Thailand, which have both suffered in recent currency crises, use a matrix of variables (including current account deficit as percent of GDP; percent of current account financing in short-term capital; import coverage months of foreign exchange reserves; budgetary balance as percent of GDP; and money supply increase past twelve months) to develop a weighted score of currency risk (*Economist* 1997c, 71–75). Using data on the past behavior of core variables in comparative cases, analysts can provide warning signals to policymakers and guidance on when to tighten fiscal and monetary policies. Hence, the purposes of forecasting can vary about whether a policy is a new initiative or an ongoing program.

We now turn to the basis (set of assumptions or data) for forecasting. A major purpose of this book is to provide a working knowledge of policy techniques and their bases. For this we will critically examine techniques commonly used. In addition, we will suggest that theoretical elegance and technical sophistication are less important than providing a reasonably accurate answer in the least possible time with a minimum of resources. There are three major approaches to policy projection:

- *Judgmental,* which means an intuitive or qualitative approach that lead to conjectures from analysis of hard data.
- *Time series,* which is trend extrapolation that leads to projections.
- *Causal* or *econometric modeling,* which is based on regression analyses that lead to predictions (Dunn 1994, 202).

These are important similarities and differences between these three approaches, but it should be stressed that in practice most policy analysts use some combination of all three. Choice of method or methods often turns on the quality of the available data. Interval data allow for more sophisticated techniques than nominal ordinal-level data. But analysts often have to decide whether interval data are actually "interval enough" to justify interval methods. Analysts like to use interval statistical methods often with ordinal data, which can bias results (Hedderson 1991, 92–93). Choice of method often boils down to a combination of data quality and the analyst's judgment. Nevertheless, it is prudent to compare forecast results obtained from the use of each method, if possible. We will illustrate this in this chapter's case study analysis.

Professional forecasters such as the Economic Forecasting Center of Georgia State University in Atlanta (see the MARTA official statement below) employ multivariate recursive and nonrecursive (causal) models, linear and nonlinear extrapolative techniques, and judgment to overcome weaknesses in the data and uncertainties about policymaker behavior. Policy analysts should recognize that forecasting policy options, such as revenue policy, involve more than mathematics and technique. Frequently, more depends on the administration of numbers and institutional issues of accounting by the client. In final analysis, forecasting policy options is really an exercise in explaining how people behave in institutions, a subject eminently suited for economic and public administration analysis.

Judgmental Forecasting

The wise practitioner uses judgment to some extent in all forecasting. All forecasts involve some judgment, but judgment should not produce all forecasts. *Judgmental, intuitive, qualitative,* and *subjective* are applied where "theory and/or empirical data are unavailable or inadequate" (Dunn 1994, 200) or where one finds "the failure to use the data in systematic, mathematical projections (Toulmin and Wright 1983, 221). The basis of judgmental forecasting can be causal and deductive, observational and inductive, or experiential and "retroductive" (Dunn 1994, 200).

CAUSAL AND DEDUCTIVE FORECASTS

The first type is based on deductive logic, which involves reasoning from general statements or laws to specific (sets of) information. This can be deceptive for policy analysis. In his *Devil's Dictionary*, Ambrose Bierce gives a nice absurdist example of deductive logic for working out labor productivity. "Major premise: 60 people can do a piece of work 60 times as fast as one person; Minor premise: one person can dig a post hole in 60 seconds; Conclusion: therefore 60 people can dig a post hole in 1 second." U.S. Defense Department policy forecasts, for example, based on kill ratios and nuclear deterrence often have this sense that absurd conclusions follow from sound major premises that have been lost somewhere in the chain of reasoning.

OBSERVATIONAL AND INDUCTIVE FORECASTS

Forecasts can be based on trend extrapolation from inductive logic. Inductive logic involves reasoning from particular observations (such as time-series data) to general conclusions that include trend extrapolations. For example, a major policy issue in the late 1990s in California has been how to accurately forecast public-service burdens, particularly in education, caused by recent immigration to that state. Answers require trend extrapolation from time-series data on immigration, school enrollments, and public expenditures.

EXPERIENTIAL FORECASTS

"Retroductive" logic is used where theory and data are unavailable and the need is to work backward to the information and assumptions necessary to support claims. When data patterns are irregular, discontinuous, noncyclical, and sudden, analysts are in the unenviable position of trying to forecast abrupt changes or "catastrophes," such as military surrenders, weather systems, stock market collapses, or sudden changes in the density of liquids as its boils (Dunn 1994, 213).

In William Boyd's novel *Brazzaville Beach*, mathematician John Clearwater believed that sudden "divergence syndromes" from linearity could not be explained by "writing endless and ever more complicated differential equations for the flow of fluids...because their connection to the basic phenomenon grew more tenuous." He believed that one needed to "look at the shapes of turbulence" to understand it, but unfortunately, this did not get him very far in forecasting abrupt changes. In the real world, to develop improved responses to earthquakes—provision of advance public notice and after-event response—better earthquake prediction methods are needed. Despite almost daily forecasts on the radio from "experts" in California (using, say, such techniques as surveys of animal behavior), the current state of earthquake forecasting is mostly conjectural and the field is populated with quacks who alarm both the public and government. Clearly, a breakthrough is needed or new techniques and scenarios that allow for more informed judgments on when and where they will occur.

CONSTRAINTS TO ACCURATE JUDGMENTAL FORECASTING

For policy forecasting, the problem is that in the real world life and history are not linear. Like water slowly and predictably coming to a boil, we expect events to do the same thing. In fact, many events are more analogous to critical masses triggering radical change. The temperature of pure water can be lowered to below the freezing point and the water will still remain a liquid. But touch the water and it suddenly will turn to ice. In public policy small changes feed on themselves, causing people and institutions to behave differently. At a "tipping point," there is a crystallization suddenly into huge shifts that are hard to predict (Samuelson 1998). Judgmental forecasting of budget behavior provides good examples of the "tipping point" problem.

UNANTICIPATED AGENCY ACTIONS

As one would expect, judgmental policy projections are used to a greater extent on the expenditure rather than the revenue side of the budget. The difficulty in projecting fiscal deficits has already been noted. Expenditures depend on some combination of unanticipated agency actions (to purchase goods or employ personnel) and individual decisions (e.g., to claim retirement, unemployment, welfare, or medical benefits) that are based on laws (e.g., creating trust funds for future expenditures and providing entitlements). Expenditures for the common messy-problem-derived policy are often affected by institutional interventions and changes in laws. By contrast, revenue decisions are fixed by laws or authority board decisions. Revenue decisions persist long enough to generate linear data patterns, while expenditure levels can change almost daily. In general, revenue estimation allows examination of individual sources from past-year actuals, current-year probables, and budget-year estimations. More important, analysts can review potential causes of variance that will affect revenue yields, such as changes in tax base (e.g., types of buildings subject to property tax assessment) or economic conditions that could affect sales tax receipts (McMaster 1991, 99).

ADMINISTRATIVE ACCOUNTING PROCEDURES

In a strict sense revenue receipts data can also be flawed, preventing calculation of formal statistics. As noted, part of the problem is small sample size. A more basic one is that it is difficult to sort out the measurement noise produced by administrative and accounting procedures on time-series and trend data. Tools to forecast the variable effects of institutional and financial management practices on public policy were reviewed in chapter 3. "Because of late filing and incorrect accounting procedures, monthly receipts may not occur independent of each other. For example, untimely closing of the books during one month may induce an arbitrary assignment of revenue in subsequent months. Such an instance may cause one month of unexpectedly large receipts followed by several months of lesser revenue" (Nelson and Cornia 1997, 47). In short, one must pay particular attention to the source of time-series data before applying forecasting techniques. This is a data quality issue.

Related to the data quality issue is one of technical capacity. The agency may not know how to predict from obvious data trends. The Australian national treasury made an "embarrassing blunder" in 1997 and underestimated company tax collections by $1.6 billion over two years. According to the secretary of the treasury, the "department clearly did not look carefully enough in analyzing trends in company tax collections." There had been a surge in 1995 tax collections ahead of an increase in company tax rates, followed by an erroneously predicted sharp collections decline for 1997 (Cleary 1997).

Further, receipts may be affected by collection efficiency for such basic services as water, sanitation, public transit, parking, electricity, urban markets, and telephone. For this reason, policy analysts should periodically examine the relationship between collection efficiency of and charges for such services. Billings may not match collections because of pipe leaks and underbilling. For other services, such as fire and recreation, demand (and thus revenues) may be constrained by inefficient agency workload patterns. Agency personnel may not be matched to demand patterns for service, thus constraining potential demand and potential revenues. In this case, analysts can forecast increased revenues from changes in staffing patterns and workload routines of agencies (Ammons 1991). As stated in chapter 2, institutional constraints can affect both policy forecasts and results. Policy forecasts need to take the operations of institutions into account in forecasting revenues as well as improving collection efficiency.

In practice, attempts to forecast results and to explain variation in program performance, whether physical or purely fiscal, involve a lot of judgment. To simplify these tasks in government budgeting offices, expenditure forecasters normally employ different rules of thumb for each line item. For example, salaries and benefits can be estimated by payroll but must include the flow of retirements, new hires, and official retrenchments to be accurate. Operations and maintenance expenditures (e.g., for roads) require estimation of vehicle demand, varying road conditions from inventory or maintenance information systems, and allocation of workloads to road crews and their vehicles. Each line item carries its own forecasting and evaluation methodology. Aggregating line items plus workload and inflation can provide a reasonable estimate of planned expenditures for the year. Unfortunately, forecasts are often limited to one year and ignore downstream recurrent costs or savings of future investment projects. Rarely are multiyear estimates made of how new investments will generate new operation expenditures or save maintenance costs (McMaster 1991, 108).

VARIATIONS WITHIN YEARS

Expenditure variation within a year for particular programs is even harder to predict. This might be difficult to believe in spite of the enormous amount of expenditure data available. But, because of the intervention of political and legal factors, public expenditure time-series data are often nonlinear (Dunn 1994, 212). There may be oscillations within persistent patterns, such as the regular variation of education budgets from seasonal factors. Or variation in expenditures may reflect departures from annual linearity but regularity when compared with quarter-on-quarter expenditures between years.

This pattern may reflect agency workloads, such as bus and rail ridership or snow removal service patterns within an urban area. Without careful understanding of these background factors, such expenditure patterns could create havoc for analysts relying solely upon their linear, nonlinear, and causal forecasting models.

Oscillations and cycles are hard to predict for such social phenomena as homelessness. For example, a city's policymakers may want to forecast the number of shelter users in order to calculate operating subsidies to the shelters. The number of "homeless" people that will take advantage of shelter programs might be a function of the following:

- Personal needs (it being more feasible to use a nearby shelter than live in an apartment)
- The economy, usually meaning the level of unemployment and consumer expenditures for housing and food (based on other "aboveground," or empirical, and "underground," or emotional, forecasts) (Silk 1986)
- Other factors, such as the local real estate market (affecting the construction and maintenance of single occupancy hotels)

This may be an excessively muddy or complex picture for forecasters. Actual homeless demand may be less difficult to forecast than the coverage of total homeless (potential demand) by existing programs. "The more uncertain the future chain of events, the more likely that judgmental forecasting will be the only basis for making expenditure projections" (Toulmin and Wright 1983, 221). Put another way, it would be difficult to forecast potential homeless demand or the number of eligible homeless people without a modicum of program experience (expert judgment). Still, even the inexperienced analyst with solid grounding in methodology should be able to arrive at reasonably sound judgments on shelter demand for the year based on past patterns of demand. The best policy analysts use their experience to judge the results of quantitative techniques. In the words of William Dunn (1994, 203), "They know their technical assumptions but do not strictly or rigidly rely upon them. Over-reliance on method alone could produce numbers that, as one consultant put it, 'get us all fired!'"

In most public-sector organizations, forecasts often boil down to expert judgments because of the simple reality that practitioners are often the only ones who know their business. They also know better than most the limits of their own professions in terms of measurement and prediction. For instance, who is in a better position to describe present and future maintenance needs for a rail transit system than the crews in the maintenance department? Would the average budget or program analyst be likely to know the point at which "tunnel fan" operating efficiency would decline from absence of regular maintenance? Maintenance people can provide the best judgmental forecasts of such phenomena, and with improved databases they could probably provide both extrapolative and causal forecasts as well. The question is, what incentives do they have to avoid inflating requests? If the budget process is punitive, maintenance personnel may know how to accurately forecast maintenance costs but inflate the costs to avoid being caught short later. A big scandal, where those in technical positions exploit their technical knowledge to inflate budget requests, naturally generates suspicion of experts. More seriously, this can result in elaborate attempts to control, or at least counter, experts' judgmental claims by the use of detailed regulations and/or panels of other experts. And, not infrequently, public-sector experts end up scaring or outraging the public with their overtechnical and seemingly arrogant explanations to the public of accidents, problems, and other events. However, the politically sensitive policy analyst with sound technical credentials should have a bright future in any public agency, for the process of managing expert judgments can either produce better forecasts or, paradoxically, hamstring the experts, making everything harder to manage effectively.

INTERVENING VARIABLES

In many cases good data may exist, but the uncertainty of intervening variables demands explicit use of judgment. For example, in developing budget requests for the county budget office, department heads must use their judgment to forecast even the next year's costs of salary and fringe benefits. This will be based on their more intimate knowledge, for instance, of who is leaving in midyear and whether a new employee has decided to join the pension plan. Department staff members often know the probable effects of inflationary changes on particular line items, such as purchases of supplies and equipment for health and education services, based on past actual changes in expenditures. But they may know less about how to predict future price changes in these items. Estimates from the budget personnel are often challenged by other officials, such as an assistant county manager or members of a county commission (who will usually compare the estimates with private-sector forecasts).

What about intervention by management in policy decisions? Suppose managers alter budgets because planned receipts do not materialize from accounting and processing errors, such as premature closing of the books noted above (Nelson and Cornia 1997, 38). Suppose, alternatively, that managers take corrective action based on midyear price increases that will inflate expenditures. Under the first set of internal conditions managers should probably not take corrective action: if they do, it will likely contaminate the very accuracy of their revenue and expenditure forecasts. In the latter case of external influences, such as reduced purchases leading to lower sales tax collections, corrective action would be justified. The problem, of course, is sorting out the effect of combined influences on budget execution for later forecasts.

In some cases public expenditure patterns are affected by more "iffy" intervening variables, such as powerful weather cycles. Peruvian budget policy forecasters, for example, have to include the likely effects of El Niño. This welling up of warm water will likely drive away the anchovies and much of the next few years' industrial and employment activity based on the fishes' appearance. El Niño is also likely to cause droughts and floods: Peruvians know that it cost them 10 percent of GDP and cut farm output by 8.5 percent and that of fisheries by 40 percent in its last arrival 1982/1983. So, forecasters include funds for infrastructure and higher current expenditures for FY 1998 to cover unemployment. But the expenditure effects of climatology still require lots of judgment (*Economist* 1997a). To cover these kinds of uncertainties in policy forecasting, technical methods should be supplemented by "expert group consensus" methods (Toulmin and Wright 1983, 223), such as the "Delphi technique" (Dunn 1994, 242) or a "bargaining approach" to generate a constructive clash of projections that can lead to agreement on a realistic forecast.

The policy consensus approach to forecasting is similar to "political risk analysis" in which data produce normally conflicting projections on the future behavior of such variables as groups in conflict (e.g., unions, political parties), different economic trade policies, and long-term debt repayment scenarios that are hashed out among experts into one forecast. This kind of forecasting produces a "workable" science rather than an exact one; but this may not be fatal. As noted, even the most sophisticated methods and tools do not ensure precision in the policy-forecasting business. William Dunn notes that "method" alone does not ensure that assumptions are made explicit, meaning that subjectivity levels are high and that "facts" are actually often "values" (1981, 210). Further, expert judgmental forecasts for new programs or countries in volatile states of political conflict presume that "the positions of stakeholders are independent and that they occur at the same point in time. These assumptions are unrealistic, since they ignore processes of coalition formation over time and the fact that one stakeholder's position is frequently determined by changes in the position of another" (Dunn

1981, 210). But with little else to rely on to forecast the future of policy expenditures, the analyst has little choice than to apply "expert group consensus" to existing data sources.

Ongoing public policies are driven by the budget cycle that makes forecasts at the margin potentially more rigorous and successful. Existing programs often seem immune to the major political and economic vicissitudes that affect new programs, and they permit more systematic and quantitative treatment of data (meaning proportionately less judgment mixed into the final forecast). The fact that most governments budget their future annual resources "incrementally," from the previous year's base, under pressure from staff budgetary "guardians" who want to cut their requests and to allow "spenders" to achieve no more than their "fair shares," means that to a large extent the following year's appropriations will be around 5–15 percent of the last year's for most line items (Wildavsky 1984). This conservative feature of the budget policymaking process helps expenditure forecasters.

Annual budgeting tends to stabilize policy planning and financing. This underscores the unity of public budgeting and policy decisions noted in chapter 3. Policy decisions are driven by the budget cycle, and budgets require accurate revenue and expenditure forecasts. Such knowledge may please some forecasters, such as those who need simple levels of budget authority for the year, but it will not help those who need to know actual outlays, since some outlays may occur months or even years after obligations. Nevertheless, forecasters know that in most cases, barring unforeseen political changes, expenditures will change only incrementally up or down for existing policies. Again, this is generally not true for new programs or policies.

Governments need revenues to finance budgets, and budgets are the political expression of what policies are going to be in the next year. Since revenues involve collection and receipt numbers, one would expect forecasters to have a field day, applying the latest high-technology methods available with the most exact results. Unfortunately, as noted above, even revenue projections contain many imprecise numbers. Although expenditure forecasts are the aggregate of incremental changes in programs, revenue forecasts are the aggregate expression of interlocking economic variables and administrative collection practices—and are riskier because once made, they cannot be changed until the next fiscal year. Program expenditures can always be added or cut during the year by supplemental appropriations or rescissions. That is, "Revenue policy, in the short run, is a given fact or a constant rather than a variable, and the ensuing collections result from forces that are largely beyond the forecaster's control" (Klay 1983, 289).

Revenue forecasting is made even more tenuous by its deceptive air of certainty. Economic forecasters, on which the accuracy of public revenue forecasting ultimately rests, often overwhelm clients with their macroeconomic prognostications of consumer prices, growth, debt, inflation, and recession on a daily basis. These forecasts often represent clusters of micro-consensus, which, when magnified across institutions such as CBO, OMB, Federal Reserve, and even Salomon Brothers, can reveal substantial disagreement. For example, as in current forecasts for the late 1990s, the "aboveground" forecast for 1987 of slow but steady growth for the United States next year was "rational and based on what (could) be observed in the economic data, on consumer's behavior to date, on the lack of panic in the markets, and on the assumption that the Administration and the Federal Reserve (would) hold things together" (Silk 1986).

Specifically, performance of the economy is said to be cyclical. Cycles are "caused by people and governments unknowingly acting in concert" (Kilborn 1987). While cycle theory would predict economic expansion based on declining interest rate and dollar data, it did not happen in the late 1980s. Why? One economist explains the death of the expansion cycle as "an accidental counterbalancing of developments in different sectors" (Kilborn 1987). What this means is that econometric forecasters can understand cyclical patterns but cannot predict their timing: major economic expansion in the United States began instead in the early 1990s. "The economy can go from one trough to another in less than a year, or it can take almost a decade or so" (Kilborn 1987). In more technical terms, "Cycles may be unpredictable or occur with persistence and regularity. While the overall pattern of a cycle is always nonlinear, segments of a given cycle may be linear or curvilinear" (Dunn 1994, 212). This puts the policymaker in a precarious position. Policy expenditures in this case can be pared back if available revenues do not materialize, but revenue projections are fixed and based on several levels of economic assumptions. If forecasters make a 1 percent error in a $5 billion projection, this amounts to almost $50 million that has to be found to finance programs, that could be added to the federal deficit, or that will simply result in fewer services produced by public agencies (e.g., more homeless people on the streets).

Hence, viewed as a strictly number-crunching activity, revenue projection is amenable to more sophisticated statistical techniques. But most fiscal forecasters would also admit that there are insufficient data points to precisely link receipts with revenue determinants like income and employment. The small sample size of revenue receipts as a constraint on use of statistical tests has already been noted by Nelson and Cornia (1997). Because of major variations between and within years of revenues and expenditures, analysts must also use some combination of data transformation techniques, hunches, and judgment (subject always to expert consensus) to make up for missing data and smooth out the curves. In the first edition of this book we used data interpolation to generate more observations. For monitoring expenditures and forecasting revenues, use of cumulative monthly data rather than individual monthly receipts smoothes out the data into a natural seasonal pattern and reduces noise from the accounting process that distorts true data patterns (Nelson and Cornia 1997, 47). Such data techniques are used by most professional forecasters to avoid overreliance on the blind results of their forecasting methods.

Perhaps the basic difference between expenditure (program and policy) and revenue (tax policy) projection is that judgment is applied both at the front and back end of the former and only at the back end of the latter. Revenue forecasts are mostly technique and some judgment. Despite incrementalist budgetmaking, expenditure forecasts are largely judgmental. Both types, when subject to the tests of professional group judgment, tend, as Ambrose Bierce noted, to project the future as "that period of time in which our affairs prosper, our friends are true and our happiness is assured." Regardless of the end to which the judgment is applied, agency managers need reliable forecasts that would allow them to alter budget plans at the beginning of the year rather than at the end, when most policy options are closed.

It should be noted before passing to the subject of trend forecasting that judgmental forecasts also require hard data. The "accounting identity-based" technique (Toulmin and Wright 1983, 224) or "deterministic" approach (Schroeder 1984, 272) forecasts revenues or expenditures by developing a multiplier (usually a ratio) to be attached to last year's base—for example, the price of a gallon of gasoline (rate) times the number of gallons of gasoline sold (base) should provide a multiplier from which to accurately forecast the next year's tax receipts (if the price of gasoline behaves as estimated). The sum of the base and this rate then equals the forecast for the required period. For revenues, development of the "rate" often presumes knowledge of the determinants of future revenue-producing behavior for each revenue source (e.g., sales, property and income taxes), such as consumer spending, population migration, and inflation. Unless one employs trend or causal forecasting techniques to find the unknown at this point, use of a mathematical percentage for the rate then cloaks the essentially "judgmental" process in scientific aura. For this reason, the deterministic approach is included under judgmental approaches to forecasting rather than as a separate topic. The question begged by the deterministic approach remains: How do you reliably estimate the rate that is to be added to the base?

The deterministic approach is more commonly used for expenditure forecasting. Schroeder suggests that "nearly all cities . . . use basically a deterministic method to forecast spending" (1984, 272). Again, the purpose is to develop a per capita cost multiplier for the base to relate inputs to planned outputs or expenditures (average cost of providing given levels of service). "In San Antonio, while the price assumptions are made centrally, departments are requested to produce documented projections of how many units of the several types of inputs will be required to produce services over the forecast period" (Schroeder 1984, 272).

In practice, this means beginning at a microlevel of analysis or task within a cost center. For example, with a bus maintenance cost center in a transit agency it can be calculated that below a certain level of inputs (pay hours), the ratio of bus miles to mechanical breakdowns decreases—which jeopardizes ridership. By decreasing farebox coverage ratios, this will decrease agency fiscal integrity and perhaps future bond ratings. Thus, using the deterministic method, the percentage increase in pay hours required to maintain service levels (the per capita cost multiplier) could be added to the last year's base as the forecast for the future. This method combines empirical data from past expenditures with judgments on the relationship between service outputs and required new expenditures. Again, these are expert opinions, derived from experience and group bargaining on their validity. These data, which are primarily useful for expenditure reporting and control of budget implementation purposes, may also be very useful for analysis of policy cost-effectiveness and cost-benefits (this will be discussed further in chapters 5 and 6). But the problem is that such quality data are not often available for these kinds of analyses.

Trend Extrapolation

There's a strange rhythm to the Ripper murders. There are cyclical rhythms which control other things. There are rhythms which control the sun spots. Every 17 years a particular kind of locust swarms and flies. Every 14 years the price of nutmeg peaks then drops again. But in the Ripper murders, it is always 126 days between the first and second murder, but only 63 days between the second and last.

"Isn't it weird? I've heard of these rhythms. What causes them?"

"Ah, that is one of the mysteries of the universe!"

– Yours Truly, Jack the Ripper episode
of Boris Karloff's *Thriller* series.

In contrast to judgmental forecasting, which is based largely on post hoc rationalizations of claims about the future that are often founded on limited data, trend forecasting is based on inductive logic—reasoning from particular observations such as time-series data. Trend forecasting is usually based on some form of time-series analysis or numbers collected at multiple and chronological points in time. According to Dunn (1994, 203), the aim of time-series analysis is "to provide summary measures (averages) of the amount and rate of change in past and future years."

Trend or "extrapolative" forecasting can be accurate only where three assumptions hold: (1) past observed patterns will persist into the future, (2) past variations will recur regularly in the future, and (3) trends are measured validly and reliably. According to Larry Schroeder (1984, 272), "Trend techniques extrapolate revenues or expenditures based purely on recent history. Most commonly, linear trends or linear growth rates are used as the underlying 'model.' Again, while relatively low-cost in terms of its data and computational costs, the approach is incapable of forecasting downturns if the past is characterized by continuous growth." As noted, "tipping points" at which, for example, multiple factors combine to produce a plunge in crime rates from what had been a small but steady drop, are hard to predict (Samuelson 1998). But, as we shall see, this weakness also applies to nonlinear trend forecasting and causal models. The only difference is that in the latter case, we have more confidence in the techniques because they can ostensibly take account of a more dynamic reality.

COMPUTER SOFTWARE APPLICATIONS FOR FORECASTING

Public policy tool kits have been compared with equipment needed for plumbing jobs. One selects tools until the leaking pipes are isolated and fixed. Much has been made of this analogy: Analysts bring the wrong tools, or use them improperly, or do not know when to try less mechanical approaches—such as actually finding out what needs are beforehand. Approaches to the description of analytic tools might also be compared with the housing construction industry. It may be faster to ignore such topics as wall construction and methods of customizing external appearance. After all, modular construction techniques have advanced to the point where builders can construct homes from prefabricated parts. But, when things go wrong, such as parts or materials not being available, it is useful to know the topic from the ground up.

In trend forecasting, much of the statistical "grunt" work has been eliminated by the widespread availability of user-friendly software packages.

For example, the 1997 version of "Excel" provides full-service options for analysis of statistical data: F-tests, *t* tests, correlation analysis, and an exponential smoothing tool to predict values based on forecasts of the prior period, adjusted for error in that prior period. Other software packages combine statistical, fiscal, and demographic analyses for use by governments. For example, "FISCALS" (Tischer and Associates, Bethesda, MD) calculates the fiscal impact of changing public service demands on municipal budgets, revenue rates, and bonding capacities from land use and demographic changes in the community. FISCALS generates budget summaries to show tax rates required to balance total revenues. Like Lotus 1-2-3, Excel, and SPSS packages (see Hedderson 1991), it allows exploration of "what-if" scenarios by varying underlying revenue and expenditure assumptions. Despite the ready availability of these computer tools for statistical analysis, we still provide the raw data and calculations here to cover the topic of trend analysis from the ground up. More advanced readers can simply skip to the conclusions.

TIME-SERIES DATA ANALYSIS

Beginning with a discussion of classical time-series analysis as the foundation for examination of more complex techniques of policy forecasting, it should be noted that time-series data are affected by four components: secular trends, seasonal variations, cyclical fluctuations, and irregular movements.[1] Secular trends are long-term growth or decline in a time series, such as reductions in arrests per 1,000 people. Seasonal variations consist of periodic variations in a time series recurring within a one-year period or less, such as patterns of sales and holidays. Cyclical fluctuations could periodically extend unpredictably over a number of years, such as the Ripper murders did. Irregular movements are irregular fluctuations in a time series, such as strikes and natural disasters (Dunn 1994, 205).

The effects of these components on forecasting accuracy may be demonstrated by a simple example. Past data trends are important in establishing whether, for example, a drug abuse policy problem exists. Weighing the costs and benefits of alternative policy responses to time-series data requires an estimate of future data behavior, in this case cocaine use. Looking at Figure 4.1, we see that the time-series variable cocaine use on the Y axis or vertical ordinate, had been leveling off for blacks, whites, and Hispanics from 1988 to 1995. These trends follow periods of increased rates of cocaine episodes in 1990–1991 and 1993–1994. Do data suggest a growing cycle of use that will recur? The question is whether we can validly forecast

Figure 4.1: Trends in Cocaine-Related Emergency Department Episodes, 1988–1995

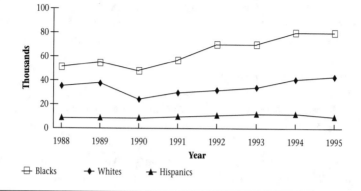

Source: National Institutes on Drug Abuse.

future trends in use and hospital visits on the X axis or horizontal abscissas from these data.

Similar time-series data could be plotted to determine whether public health policies should focus on control and elimination of cockroaches in inner cities. The results of a 1992–1993 study published in the *New England Journal of Medicine* showed that youths allergic to cockroaches and exposed to the insects at home were three times more likely to be hospitalized than other asthmatic youths. The pattern is unique in the United States because inner-city young people were most afflicted by cockroach allergens. For those under eighteen years of age, asthma cases per 1,000 persons increased from 41 to 69 percent in the ten-year period of 1984–1994: 62 percent of the cases were in inner cities, where 78 percent of the 1,500 cases analyzed happened to be black (Suplee 1997). Although the study did not examine cost-effectiveness in detail, one implication of the time-series data is that a relatively small expenditure in cockroach control could result in substantial public health benefits. Reducing the population of cockroaches through control of food and water sources and regular cleaning and routine use of insecticides (similar to dealing with the rat problem in New York City cited in chapter 3) would lead to fewer school days missed by and less hospitalization of inner-city children.

Simpler time-series techniques, such as the classical time series, visual estimation (also called the "black thread" technique), moving averages, exponential smoothing, and regression analysis, rely on the assumption that the ordinate and abscissa will move together. This is assumed whether or not substantive or specious causality exists, such as in the notion that sun spots produce changes in stock market prices. How the two axes move together depends on the degree of impact by the above four trend components. Where the other three components reveal irregular variation over time, other variables need to be included in a causal model to develop forecasts in which we can have greater confidence.

For example, the cocaine episodes for the three groups in Figure 4.1 seem to exhibit a secular trend, or "smooth long-term growth or decline in time-series" (Dunn 1994, 203). If so, one might have confidence in the results of averaging techniques to produce a forecast of future trends. There does not seem to be any "seasonal variation" (within a one-year period) or "cyclical fluctuation" (regular long-term changes that can change trends) that would upset assumptions of regularity and persistence of trends. To forecast cycles, one must know how the many determinants of drug abuse, such as price, enforcement, or user susceptibility, will affect the pattern of ultimate use. This means utilization of a causal model.

But closer inspection of Figure 4.1 indicates that for blacks and whites cocaine use exhibits "irregular movements." In 1996, 54 percent of cocaine-related episodes occurred among blacks, 29 percent among whites, and 8 percent among Hispanics. Between 1994 and 1995, there was no change in cocaine-related episodes by gender or race/ethnicity except for Hispanics, among whom there was a decrease of 13 percent (from 13,400 to 11,600) (National Institutes of Drug Abuse 1997, 1). The curious shifts in use (1989 drop, 1990 increase, 1993 increase) may have been due in part to measurement problems, enforcement practices, social mores, or family structures. Whatever their causes, forecasting cyclical fluctuations or describing trends is thus made much more difficult. This underscores our earlier assertion that good data are essential both for defining a policy problem and for analyzing policy options. Later shifts in trends that reveal irregular events to actually be part of regular cycles are important in redefining the problem, perhaps midway in the enforcement period. Such new data trends, turned up as part of a midterm policy forecast, are important in redefining policy and ultimately in improving policy results.

Despite the benefits of regular forecasts with new data during the problem definition or policy implementation phases, forecasters often assume that trends will continue for the short term. They also assume that changes in underlying variables, such as migration and birth rates affecting population trends, will "not change dramatically or unexpectedly over short periods of time" (Liner 1983, 84). Given the relative freedom to engage in short-term trend forecasting, let us apply several simple techniques to the drug use data. Where application is made difficult by data limitations, we will employ alternative data for "whiskey excise taxes" in a small city in the United States.

PROPORTIONATE CHANGE OR AVERAGING TECHNIQUES

At the lowest level on any policy forecaster's scale of technical sophistication are averaging techniques. These are also called "moving average" (Toulmin and Wright 1983, 226) or "proportionate-change" methods (Rabin, Hildreth, and Miller 1983, 35). As we will see, simplicity and accuracy are not necessarily opposites. Averaging techniques are rudimentary time-series analysis methods widely used because of their simplicity and ease of calculation. Moving averages can be applied whenever it is necessary to make an estimate of a variable value for a short-term forecast of one to three time periods (e.g., months, years). "The concept of the moving average is based on the assumption that the past data observations reflect an underlying trend that can be determined, and that the averaging of these data will eliminate the randomness and seasonality in the data. The averaging of the data to develop a forecast value provides a 'smoothing' effect on the data" (Toulmin and Wright 1983, 226). Averaging depends on the assumption that past patterns will continue and that "turning points" (irregular components) will not take place in the period to be forecast.

Suppose that we were asked to forecast cocaine use (Table 4.1) for users age twenty-six and older for 1996. We know from the difficulty of defining the problem in chapter 2 that past trends are affected by both cyclical and irregular components so that linear or nonlinear forecasting techniques may boil down to nothing more than sophisticated guesswork. Nevertheless, we need some kind of reading based on the usual caveats of uncertainty that apply to all forecasting efforts. Applying the averaging technique to Table 4.1 data, we must find the percentage changes in use for preceding years, average them, and multiply the average percentage change by the last year to obtain the forecast for the next year.

How did we calculate the percentage changes? First, we found the differences in reported use between each year. The difference between 1991 and 1992 was a drop of –1.7 percent. To find the percentage change from 1991 to 1992, we divided 1.7 by the base year (7.8) and found it to be .217 or –22 percent. We then averaged the percentage changes by totaling the column (= –5.2) and dividing it by the number of changes (5). The average percentage change was found to be –1.04 percent. Since this will be our

Table 4.1: Reported Trends in Cocaine Use by High School Seniors, 1991–1996

YEAR	REPORTED USE	% CHANGE
1991	7.8	0
1992	6.1	–22
1993	6.1	0
1994	5.9	–3.2
1995	6.0	1.7
1996	7.1	18.3
1997	—	—

multiplier, we took the product of the last data year (7.1) and –1.04 and found the expected level of use in 1997 to be 7.4 percent or a 0.3 increase over 1996. The total reported percentage use for 1997 should then be 7.4 percent = 7.1 × 1.04. Thus, by this method change in projected cocaine use for 1997 will be 4.2 percent more than in 1996.

The same moving average technique is often used by municipal revenue forecasters for annual budgeting. The accuracy of the revenue forecast will affect budget management during the year as managers attempt to manage cash flow. It will also determine the size of any budget deficit that needs to be financed (through arrears, carry-overs, or short-term financing). The success of entire policies can depend upon this technique. For example, such cities as San Diego and Pittsburgh are basing their economic development strategies on new sports stadiums. Local bond repayments from the budget will depend largely upon earmarked revenue sources such as the hotel tax (*Economist* 1999b, 39). Whether revenues from this tax will grow or decline needs to be included in the analysis of proposed economic development policies. Hotel tax receipts are often successfully forecast by using the moving average method. In the annual budget document, assumptions underlying the revenue forecast will determine whether the city attains its financial goals.

Proportionate change trend analysis is an easy and reasonably accurate statistical technique for predicting future revenues from revenue base or collection data over the past five to six years. This method allows determination of the average rate of change from collections over a trend period of years and application to the last year. Suppose we want to estimate anticipated revenue from building permit receipts for FY 1997. The following five steps will provide an answer (Guess 1996):

1. Needed are monthly receipts data for the building permits revenue source. Add this up for a yearly total, e.g., $1,000 for 1991.

2. To come up with the rate of change, calculate the difference in amount collected between each fiscal year. This can be done with a simple hand calculator. For six years, there will be five rates of change:

$$\frac{\text{Current Year (CY)} - \text{Past Year (PY)}}{\text{Past Year}} = \text{rate of change}$$

1. $\dfrac{\text{FY 1992} - \text{FY 1991}}{\text{FY 1991}} = \dfrac{1{,}200 - 1{,}000}{1{,}000} = .2$ or 20 percent

2. $\dfrac{\text{FY 1993} - \text{FY 1992}}{\text{FY 1992}} = \dfrac{1{,}300 - 1{,}200}{1{,}200} = .08$ or 8 percent

3. $\dfrac{\text{FY 1994} - \text{FY 1993}}{\text{FY 1993}} = \dfrac{1{,}500 - 1{,}300}{1{,}300} = .15$ or 15 percent

4. $\dfrac{\text{FY 1995} - \text{FY 1994}}{\text{FY 1994}} = \dfrac{1{,}900 - 1{,}500}{1{,}500} = .26$ or 26 percent

5. $\dfrac{\text{FY 1996} - \text{FY 1995}}{\text{FY 1995}} = \dfrac{2{,}100 - 1{,}900}{1{,}900} = .10$ or 10 percent

3. Add all rates of change and compute average rate of change for the period FY 1991–FY 1996.

   20 percent
     8
   15
   26
   <u>10</u>
   79 = 79/5 = 16 percent average rate of change

4. Multiply average rate of change by the past year collections: 2,100 × .16 = 336

5. Add 336 to past year collections of 2,100 to obtain the estimated revenue from building permits for FY 1997. 2,100 + 336 = $2,436: estimated FY 1997 building permit revenue.

Using the $2,436 figure in this case requires two assumptions. The accuracy of every revenue source estimate will require assumptions, and local policymakers should make them explicit in the budget document. First, there is no change in permit fees over the last year (or change in rates), and second, there is no local ordinance in the near future that would encourage or discourage people from building new structures or adding to existing ones. In addition, local tax offices should consider other factors affecting the accuracy of revenue estimates, such as inflation rates (price changes) and other regulatory ordinances.

It should be evident from the two examples that the strength of the averaging technique is also its telling weakness. It is based on a straight-line projection of average past changes that assumes that average differences between years will be a guide to next year. Specifically, as in regression analysis to be discussed next, the averaging technique gives each data point the same weight in the analysis "whereas, in actuality, the latest data may be of more importance because they may indicate the beginning of a new trend" (Toulmin and Wright 1983, 234). Note that after increasing from 60 to 100 percent between 1974 and 1977, the percentage change in cocaine use dropped from 90 to 11 percent in the two most recent data years. Nevertheless, this method gives the 11 percent the same weight as 100 percent for forecasting purposes. What this means is that a "turning point" may have occurred in 1985 and that the 65 percent figure may be too high for next year. In fact, as was indicated in chapter 2, there is evidence that use may have stabilized or even declined despite increases in incarceration rates for drug offenders (with attendant jail overcrowding) caused mainly by rigid state three-strike laws.

Causal or Regression Analysis

Moving up the scale of time-series forecasting sophistication, better results should be obtainable through regression analysis. Even though many refer to linear regression as "causal analysis" (Toulmin and Wright 1983; Klay 1983), we use the latter term in reference to deductive theory-based, often econometric analyses that employ linear multiple regressions and correlational analyses (Dunn 1981, 150). All regression is "linear" in the sense that it is "curve fitting" and a straight line is one form of a curve.

The results of multiple and correlational analysis do not prove causation. For example, suppose one finds that a linear regression line closely links changes in food consumption (Y) with changes in family income (X). The data on the scattergram fall into a linear pattern with a beta, 'b,' slope or "regression coefficient" that tells us how much the dependent variable will change in 'a,' or alpha, for changes along that line. It could be concluded that higher food consumption depends on higher income, that higher income depends on higher food consumption, or that they are both influenced by some other factor(s). Since both X and Y increase together at a specific magnitude, any of these relationships could be supported (Schroeder, Sjoquist, and Stephan 1986, 22). Causal models will be discussed in the next section.

Here, we illustrate how regression analysis can aid forecasting. According to Dunn (1981, 154): "The most accurate technique for extrapolating linear trend is least-squares trend estimation, a procedure that permits mathematically precise estimates of future social states on the basis of observed values in a time series. While least-squares regression is technically superior to the black-thread technique, it is based on the same assumptions of persistence, regularity and data reliability."

The regression model also assumes that there are no measurement errors. Unless this assumption is challenged, forecasting results can be distorted. The ordinary least-squares (OLS) regression model assumes that (1) the error term associated with one observation is uncorrelated with the error term associated with all other observations, (2) error terms can be small or large but are not related to the independent variables used, and (3) error terms are not correlated with the independent variables. The most common problem associated with these errors for time-series data (successive time periods) is termed "autocorrelation" or "serial correlation." In such a case the residual error terms from different observations are correlated. Autocorrelation can be caused by such factors as omission of important explanatory variables or from the tendency of effects to persist over time. Clues to the existence of autocorrelation can be provided by use of a test statistic called the Durbin-Watson coefficient. This coefficient can be used to test the null hypothesis that successive error terms are not autocorrelated. When serially correlated error terms are detected, such techniques as the generalized least-squares regression technique can be used (Schroeder, Sjoquist and Stephan 1986, 74–75).

Policy analysts first need to focus on the exploratory task of finding which variables are related to a given variable, such as population growth, per capita income, and consumer expenditure patterns in relation to sales tax collections. This gives us the "correlation coefficient"—a "descriptive statistic that measures the degree of linear association between two variables" denoted "r" for each pair of variables (Schroeder, Sjoquist, and Stephan 1986, 25). The correlation coefficient only measures the degree of association. It says nothing about the reasons for the correlation, which may be cause and effect, mutual causation, both related to a third variable, and coincidence. However, the correlation coefficient (r, which ranges from –1.0 to +1.0 and indicates the direction of the relationship) and the coefficient of determination (R^2, which is an index of the amount of variation in the dependent variable explained by the independent variable) can supplement regression analysis and enable it to provide "much more information of direct relevance to policymakers than other forms of estimation" (Dunn 1981, 195).

The analyst uses correlation coefficients to search for the "significant variables" (Blalock 1972, 361). After finding, for example, that per capita income growth (X or the independent variable) and sales tax collections (Y or the time-series variable) are positively correlated (e.g., r = 0.584), one can then turn their attention to "regression analysis in which we attempt to predict the exact value of one variable from the other" (Blalock 1972, 361). Let us examine the regression technique more closely and indicate its strengths and weaknesses for forecasting. According to David Nachmias (1979, 113), "The objective of regression analysis is to formulate a function by which the researcher can predict or estimate the scores on a target variable from scores on independent variables."

From Figure 4.2, we note that each pair of X and Y values is a "coordinate" and where all coordinates fall on a straight line, the function relating X to Y is a linear function. The regression equation is $Y = \alpha + \beta(X)$. This suggests that Y is a linear function of X. The slope of the regression function (β) indicates how many units in Y are obtained for each unit change in X. The more rigorously we can estimate a regression line, the better chance of predictive accuracy for the future. The symbol (α) represents the point where the regression line crosses the Y axis (where X = 0).

The regression equation hypothesizes that observed coordinates will fall along a straight line. But a regression line cannot minimize the distance between all observed points simultaneously. Thus, we need a means of averaging the distances to obtain the best fitting line. "Goodness of fit" tests such as the coefficient of determination (R2), discussed above, indicate the strength and direction of the relationship between the variables. The most common form of regression analysis is "least-squares" regression, which focuses on the need to minimize errors (differences between observed and actual points due to randomness in behavior of other factors). By squaring

Figure 4.2: The Regression Equation

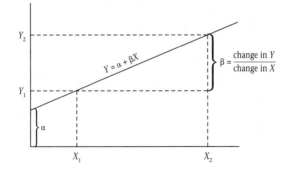

errors, the possibility that distances above and below the line would cancel is eliminated. By not squaring errors, that is, by not using least-squares, we could use several lines to minimize the sum of nonsquared errors (Schroeder, Sjoquist, and Stephan 1986, 20). "Thus, if we draw vertical lines from each of the points to the least-squares line, and if we square these distances and add, the resulting sum will be less than a comparable sum of squares from any other possible straight line" (Blalock 1972, 371). According to Nachmias, "The least-squares method is a way for finding the one straight line that provides the best fit for an observed bivariate distribution." Put more simply, the line will minimize the "residual" distance between the function line and any observed point on the scattergram (see Figure 4.3). Simply averaging, as we did before, ignores the possibility that several lines could "fit" if we ignore the need to minimize residual distances.

Let us now turn to an application of least squares regression to extrapolate a trend from the data. Since the technique requires valid data, employing cocaine use data, for example, might be problematic. Cocaine use data are often based on a small sample to generalize to large populations. In one case, cocaine use data based on a sample of only 4,000 to 8,000 users were used to project the behavior of about 12 million admitted users (Kerr 1986). Let us therefore use whiskey excise tax collected receipts from a small city for five years to project collections for the following fiscal year. This is more realistic and useful for our case exercise below in that many commodity and excise tax projections must often be aggregated into one comprehensive sales tax revenue projection.

Based on the assumptions and formulas for least squares regression, where a and b are calculated it is possible to estimate the Y variable (revenues here) in the observed time-series or in any projected time period. While we are demonstrating how this and other forecasting techniques can

Figure 4.3: A Geometrical Interpretation of Residuals

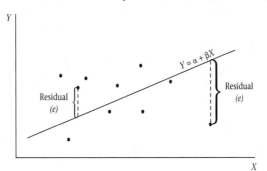

be performed with little more than hand calculators, in most cases policy analysts will use software that requires data entry according to the programs. The calculations to project whiskey tax collected receipts for FY 1997 are illustrated in Table 4.2.

Calculating the trend values according to $Y = a + b(x)$, we now have enough data to calculate both a and b. The formula for a (termed "level in the central year" in Table 4.3) =

$$\frac{\Sigma Y}{N} \text{ or } \frac{489.1}{5} = 97.8 \quad \text{and for } b = \frac{\Sigma(xY)}{\Sigma(x^2)} \text{ or } \frac{11.9}{10} = 1.19$$

With a and b, we can now compute the values for the trend line for each fiscal year in the past series and project the trend line for FY 1996 and 1997 (Table 4.3).

We are now ready to graph the least-squares line (Figure 4.4). Two questions arise on the utility of the least-squares method now that we have our forecasts. First, how confident can we be in the forecast values? Second, how useful are linear methods such as least-squares, when most ill-structured policy problems have data that are "often nonlinear, irregular, and discontinuous" (Dunn 1981, 160)? The first we will attempt to answer by using a method known as "percentage calculation of trend." The second we will answer by changing the linear least-squares equation for secular trends to one suitable for nonlinear growth trends.

To measure our confidence in the forecasts just obtained, we need to see how far past receipts data varied from the trend line (Table 4.4). According to Charles Liner (1983, 41),

> Cyclical components will show up as high or low percentage of trend values during years of expansion and contraction. Major irregular components will show up as one-time deviations.... Confidence in the accuracy of the trend is gained if the percentage of trend values are close to 100%, and the assumption can be made that the variation in actual collections is due to the underlying trend. In contrast, if the percentage of trend values varies significantly above or below 100%, many other factors might account for the collections.

The calculated percentages of trend values suggest that we should have a relatively high level of confidence in our forecasts since the past has been largely unsullied by cycles or irregular (nonlinear) events. However, where past observations reveal a nonlinear pattern—"the amounts of change increase or decrease from one time period to the next" (Dunn 1981, 158)—other techniques must be used to forecast future time-series values.

Table 4.2: Least-Squares Regression of Whiskey Tax Collected Receipts, 1992–1996

(X) FISCAL YEAR	(Y) COLLECTIONS	CODED TIME VALUE (x)	CROSS-PRODUCTS (xY)	YEARS SQUARED (x^2)
1992	$98,751	–2	–197.5	4
1993	95,075	–1	–95.0	1
1994	94,131	0	0	0
1995	97,794	+1	+97.7	1
1996	103,354	+2	+206.7	4
N = 5	ΣY = $489,105	Σx = 0	$\Sigma(xY)$ = +11.9	$\Sigma(x^2)$ = 10

It was noted that generally public expenditure trends are less irregular than revenues, but problems exist that make it difficult to fit a curve or line to revenue data. The small sample and internal accounting procedure problems were noted above. Revenue cycles may be nonlinear fluctuations—or, since segments of a cycle may be linear or curvilinear, revenue cycles may occur with persistence and regularity. Trends or cycles within time-series data can confuse cumulative receipts from year to year, and this can weaken forecasts. Growth or decline curves (S-shaped patterns) can occur between years, decades, or longer periods. If we use a linear regression equation for data (according to the scattergram) that appears to be increasing, our forecast will be off. For example, if the data suggest a growth curve, such

Table 4.3: Whiskey Tax Receipts Forecast for FY 1996 and FY 1997

FISCAL YEAR	(a) LEVEL IN CENTRAL YEAR	+	(x) NUMBERS FROM CENTRAL YEAR		(b) SLOPE	=	Y TREND LINE
1991	97.8	+	(–2	×	1.19)	=	95.4
1992	97.8		–1		1.19	=	96.6
1993	97.8		0		1.19	=	97.8
1994	97.8		+1		1.19	=	98.9
1995	97.8		+2		1.19	=	100.2
1996	97.8		+3		1.19	=	101.4
1997	97.8		+4		1.19	=	102.6

Figure 4.4: Plot of Least-Squares Line for Whiskey Tax Receipts

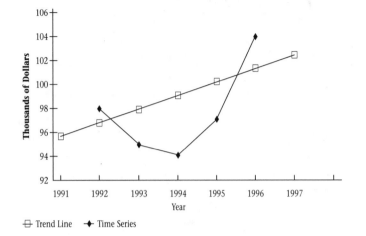

⊟ Trend Line   ◆ Time Series

as the growing increases of $1,000 gaining compound annual interest, a linear equation would produce a forecast appropriate only for constant increases, such as putting in $100 each year on a $1,000 account.

Causal Forecasting

Policy analysts will typically have large portfolios of techniques that can be used for extrapolating linear and nonlinear trends from past data. Unfortunately, the techniques themselves can produce different results. For this reason, forecasting is part technical method and part judgment—an art and a science. Causal forecasting is one of the more complex and sophisticated. A cautionary note on the word *cause*. Statistical techniques such as regressions do not prove causation; they merely associate variables from which

Table 4.4: Calculation of Percentage of Trend

FISCAL YEAR	ACTUAL COLLECTIONS	CALCULATED TREND VALUE		PERCENT OF TREND
1991	($98,751	95.4) × 100	=	103.5
1992	95,075	96.6 × 100	=	98.5
1993	94,131	97.8 × 100	=	96.2
1994	97,794	98.9 × 100	=	98.9
1995	103,354	100.2 × 100	=	103.1

inferences about causation can be made. A droll illustration of this is the link between "mad cow disease" and beef consumption. The former, through the latter, has lead to human illness and death. Turning this around, Bolling (1997) notes that a single factor, human consumption of beef due to increased barbecuing, may be increasing the rate of cattle mortality.

Similarly, economic policymakers grapple with the causes of current account deficits in order to predict dangerous capital flight from a country. To predict changes in the current account (e.g., trade balance, flow of transfers, foreign income flows), the policymakers often refer to sophisticated economic models that tend to be both static and excessively hard to use. Many have found that such sophisticated models as the Mundell-Fleming framework, which includes multiple variables, are rarely used. In fact, economists find that good rules of thumb (e.g., don't worry about current account deficits under 5 percent of GDP) work just as well to predict when capital flight might occur (*Economist* 1998).

Trend extrapolation has little to do with policy theory, other than in the exploratory phase of suggesting variables for possible correlation coefficients. Causal forecasting, by contrast, makes use of empirically testable laws or propositions that make predictions (Dunn 1981, 148). Causal modeling is useful for identifying determinants of public policies (Dunn 1994, 229). As opposed to subjective, inductive, or retroductive logic, this approach is deductive, reasoning from general statements and propositions to particular sets of information and claims. Deduction and induction are related logics in that deductive arguments are strengthened by empirical research, often turning the deductive statement into an inductive generalization. Deduction implies a "model" or systematic set of propositions that can be empirically affirmed or rejected.

Above we used the example of income and food purchases to illustrate regressions. On a more complex plane, the regression could serve as a test of economic pricing theory. Such a theory would postulate that the quantity of a good purchased by an individual depends on both their disposable income and the price of the product (Manning and Phelps 1979, cited in Schroeder, Sjoquist, and Stephan 1986, 29). An empirical test would verify or reject both the theoretical proposition and the statistical relationship. The purpose of using a model or theory is not simply elegance. According to William Klay (1983, 299), for example, "The advantage of building formal revenue-forecasting models is that it forces the participants to think clearly about the relationships and assumptions which underlie their forecasts." The inductive methods applied so far do not require thinking about underlying causal relationships—only whether the curve or line fits the data.

Two kinds of causal models exist for revenue forecasting that will be discussed here:

- Single-equation regression models that may have one or more explanatory variables.
- Multiple-equation models that incorporate several regression equations (Klay 1983, 299). Multiple-equation models are useful for causal forecasting because "they more nearly approximate the real world situation in which several factors may influence and act on a dependent variable" (Toulmin and Wright 1983, 233).

SINGLE-EQUATION REGRESSION MODELS

An example of a single-equation multiple-regression model is that developed for forecasting sales tax receipts of the city of Mobile, Alabama (Figure 4.5).

The regression equation on which this model is based ($Y = a + b1X1 + b2X2 + b3X3$) states that based on past relationships, the city's sales tax can be forecast by the sum of a constant ('a', or the Y intercept) and three products. Put another way, there are three multiple, independent causes of Y. The regression coefficients in multiple regression are interpreted as "partial slopes" (Nachmias 1979, 129). Partial slopes indicate how much change in Y is expected for each independent variable when all others are held statistically constant. Assuming no intercorrelation among independent variables, the regression coefficients will be the same as if the independent variables were regressed one at a time with Y. As in bivariate regression, the intercept and regression coefficients are estimated by the least-squares method (Nachmias 1979, 130). Since we are solving for three unknowns (a, b_1, and b_2),

Figure 4.5: Single-Equation Multivariate Projection Model for Sales Tax Receipts

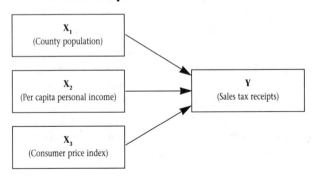

three equations must be solved by using the following least squares formulas (which will again be used in our MARTA sales tax case below):

$$b_1 = \frac{(\Sigma\, x_1 y)\,(\Sigma\, x_2^2) - (\Sigma\, x_1 x_2)}{(\Sigma\, x_1^2)\,(\Sigma\, x_2^2) - (\Sigma\, x_1)}$$

$$b_2 = \frac{(\Sigma\, x_1^2)\,(\Sigma\, x_2 y) - (\Sigma\, x_1 x_2)}{(\Sigma\, x_1^2)\,(\Sigma\, x_2^2) - (\Sigma\, x_1 x)}$$

$$a = \frac{\Sigma\, Y - b_1 \Sigma\, X_1 - b_2 \Sigma\, X_2}{N}$$

Once the regression values are obtained, various measures of "goodness of fit" should be calculated as in the two-variable case. As noted, these measures enhance the utility of regression analysis by telling us the direction and strength of the relationships. More technically, goodness of fit tests indicate how close the regression line minimizes the sum of the squared error term (Schroeder, Sjoquist, and Stephan 1986, 26). For example, the difference between the actual and estimated value is "the error, also called the residual" and "these are analyzed through computation of a statistic such as the "standard error of the estimate" (or SEE) to develop judgment as to how well the model fits the past relationships" (Klay 1983, 300).

The SEE would be 0, for example, where the regression line fits actual observations and the residual sum of squares is minimized (Nachmias 1979, 116). The SEE must be first calculated to develop another measure of fit commonly used by policy analysts that is called the "coefficient of determination" or R2. This is a measure of "relative closeness" of the fit between the regression line and the data points which, as indicated by the "R2," is also the square of the correlation coefficient. In this case, "R" would be the multiple correlation coefficient (Blalock 1972, 454). The R2 measures variation in the dependent variable Y explicable by X1, X2, and X3 as a percentage of total variation in Y (Nachmias 1979, 133).

MULTIPLE-EQUATION REGRESSION MODELS

Policy analysts can also forecast policy options by using causal models with several regression equations. Single-equation models assume that the value of each independent variable is determined independently of the dependent variable. So, for example, Mobile's sales tax receipts do not affect consumer personal income to the extent that they could contribute indirectly to the levels of receipts themselves. This is similar to the Laffer assumption that beyond a certain point tax incidence reduces the propensity to save and invest, which also affects tax receipts (Browning and Browning 1983, 440). But in reality, "some of the independent variables might be causes of others" (Nachmias 1979, 145), meaning that we need to construct more complex multivariate models. Such models require development of equations for each dependent variable that include "disturbance terms" (E) allowing for the possibility that they are also independent variables (affected by exogenous forces, or variables not explicitly defined in the model). The equations are then solved simultaneously as simultaneous structural equations.

Structural equation models can be "recursive" and "nonrecursive." Recursive models assume that the direction of influence from any variable does not feed back to it, meaning that each variable is an independent cause but can be influenced by prior variables. "Path coefficients" are often used in recursive models to measure the magnitude of linkage between two or more variables (Nachmias 1979, 149). Path analysis is used in casual modeling "to identify those independent variables (e.g., income) that singly and in combination with other variables (e.g., political participation) determine changes in the dependent variable (e.g., welfare expenditures)" (Dunn 1994, 230). For example, Gary L. Tompkins (1975, cited in Nachmias 1979, 154–56) found that ethnicity exerts a strong direct effect on welfare expenditures, but that income level also has a strong indirect effect via ethnicity and party competition. To derive forecasts of the next year's welfare expenditures, it would be extremely useful to employ such a recursive model, assuming that it could be used post hoc to forecast past spending levels. However, in reality, variables often feed back into other variables. Welfare expenditures, for example, would also affect income, party competition, and even ethnicity (migration patterns). Nonrecursive models permit the use of both exogenous and endogenous variables via simultaneous equations (Nachmias 1979, 156).

The use of causal modeling may be more appropriate for advanced policy analysis, such as that conducted by CBO or the Brookings Institution. Since few expenditure and revenue forecasting assignments at the state or local levels of government would ever require techniques of such immense time, cost, and sophistication, we will end the discussion of these methods here and move on to a less complicated and more likely forecasting assignment.

CHAPTER 4 CASE STUDY

MARTA Forecast

18 January 1996 Report of Economic Forecasting Center, Georgia State University, Economic Consultants

January 18, 1996

Mr. Terry L. Griffis
Director of Treasury Services
MARTA
2424 Piedmont Rd, N.E.
Atlanta, GA 30324

Dear Mr. Griffis:

Enclosed is our analysis of MARTA sales and use tax revenues including projections through 2015. In making these projections, we have re-estimated the coefficients of our model to generate budget estimates for MARTA operating purposes. Projections of relevant variables used to generate those estimates are explained in this report.

When data derived from state or federal data sources were used in this analysis, no attempt was made to verify the accuracy of that data. Traditionally, changes in definitions and new benchmarks will alter some of the historical data. This, in turn, could alter the projections. However, such adjustments in the past have not be sufficient to substantially change such projections, and are assumed to be of minor significance in the future.

Although MARTA receives revenue from both sales and use taxes, separating these two sources of revenue is useful for analytical purposes. The use tax fluctuates considerably from more than 20% of gross MARTA collections to less than 6% in recent years. Moreover, use taxes have fallen from more than $21 million in Fulton and DeKalb as recently as 1985 to less than $10 million today even as use taxes have increased by nearly 5% in the state over the same period. Tax avoidance, especially in the airline and utility use taxes, accounts for most of this change. No reversal of such avoidance is anticipated. Indeed, further tax avoidance is possible, but the magnitude of the use tax for airlines and utilities probably has reached a minimum. Until further avoidance by commodity grouping can be identified, stabilization of the use tax collections near current nominal levels was assumed. In inflation adjusted terms, this leads to further declines in the use tax over time. This is a conservative approach to projecting future trends in the use tax.

Unlike use taxes, sales tax receipts relate closely to economic conditions in Fulton and DeKalb counties. Some sales are made to visitors, such as tourists and conventioneers. Other sales are made by residents to vendors that are not taxed locally. Also, the percentage of purchasing power that is saved fluctuates during the business cycle and has trended downward for U.S. households in recent years. More significantly, an increasing percentage of all purchases by households has been in services or exempted items that are not subject to sales taxes.

No sales tax projections can adequately capture all these influences. However, surprisingly strong relationships have been developed between economic conditions in

Fulton and DeKalb counties and the sales tax receipts MARTA receives from activity in those counties.

To capture cyclical changes in sales tax receipts, our model assumes that savings rate shifts are reflected in the purchases of durable goods. As a result, our model includes purchases of durable goods locally as a contributor to sales relative to income. Using durable purchases as derived from the Department of Commerce's report on Retail Trade substantially improves the model's accuracy. In generating our projections, we have included durable goods projections on the basis of a five year acquisition cycle. Reality may differ from projections for any given year, but the projections should be valid over time.

Sluggishness in durable sales in the past has been responsible for a substantial reduction in sales tax receipts. A cyclical rebound in durable sales has continued well above long run sustainable rates in recent months (gains are more than 20% above previous year levels in recent months), and that explains much of the improvement in sales tax collections.

Definitions

Every month, MARTA receives a share of the sales and use taxes collected from vendors in Fulton and DeKalb counties. This contribution reflects collections based upon economic activity two months before. However, some accounts may be set aside because of reporting or auditing problems. Income from these accounts will not be forwarded until any issues are satisfied. No systematic delay in such accounts is apparent. Therefore, except for some random factor, payments to MARTA can be assumed to reflect economic conditions two months previously.

Some collections are based upon estimates of prevailing conditions. For example, public utilities may pay estimated tax liabilities. Large chain retailers tend to estimate their monthly tax liabilities, which are then adjusted at the end of the fiscal year. Obviously, these estimates will not conform to changing monthly economic conditions, but they should have little impact upon the correlation between collections and annual economic conditions, as used in this report.

Collections are augmented by penalties but reduced by 3% vendor compensation and a 1% state preparation fee.

Unfortunately, income and employment data at the county level are not available on a timely basis. (Employment and Income data for Fulton and DeKalb are only available through 1993). Fulton and DeKalb's share of the MSA's personal income and taxable sales have declined by 20% from 1969 through 1993. However, taxable sales have improved relative to the MSA in two of the past three years, while population growth also appears to have improved.

Durable goods sales for Atlanta are derived from the Department of Commerce report on Retail Activity by subtracting nondurable sales from total sales. The data then is converted to real expenditures historically by the United States personal consumption deflator. All sales tax projections are in real dollars, which are then converted to projected collections by imposing an estimated inflation rate.

Employment data use the historical relationship between the reported county employment developed by the Bureau of Economic Analysis and the more timely MSA data generated by the Bureau of Labor Statistics. As mentioned above, both employment and income for Fulton and DeKalb have declined by the same share of the total MSA during the past twenty years. Not only does this suggest that congestion in the major counties will limit their growth relative to counties farther out, but also suggests that employment is interchangeable with income for statistical purposes. For this reason, the more timely MSA employment was used in the analysis.

Trends

In addition to the cyclical variations in sales tax revenues, longer-term trends in collections are apparent. Part of the slowing in the growth of sales tax revenues in the 1980s reflects the slowing of inflation. During the 1970s, the personal consumption deflator rose an average of 7.3% per year. In the 1980s, the deflator increased 4.7% annually. In recent years, inflation as measured by the consumption deflator has increased only 2.7%. Thus, sales tax revenues would grow more than 4 percentage points slower than in the 1970s merely by the reduction in inflation.

Clearly, inflation is not the only factor leading to a slowing in revenue growth. Between FY1986 and FY1993, only FY1988 experienced an increase in inflation adjusted sales tax revenues. Obviously, the recession of 1990 accounts for some of this sluggishness, which was reversed when the recovery began in earnest. An extended slump in purchases of consumer durables also accounted for some of the sluggishness. The strong rebound in durables sales in recent months reflects the strong replacement needs of Atlanta households. When those needs are fulfilled, a more normal growth of less than 5% gains in durable goods sales should be expected.

A national slowing in the growth of new households is less significant in Atlanta, where migration accounts for more than 70% of population growth. However, a reduction in that population which forms new households could reduce the migration to Atlanta. Recent population trends have strengthened to more than 3% growth per year, but some slowing to 2% gains is again expected in the next decade.

Several tax changes also altered the collection pattern. When Fulton county added the local option sales tax in 1983, incentives to avoid tax payments were enhanced. Many auto dealers shifted sales from Fulton soon after. In 1984, the airlines decided to establish fueling subsidiaries in Clayton county to avoid the use tax in Fulton county. In July, 1985, prescription drugs were exempted from sales taxes, causing a $1 million reduction in collections. Another $1 million reduction occurred when food stamps were exempted October 1986. NOTE: In making our projections, we have assumed that the local option portion of the state sales tax will not be exempted for food, as contained in the current legislation. However, exemption of food on the state's portion certainly increases the possibility that a convenience argument will be used to extend that exemption to special use sales taxes in the future.

A change in the timing of collections added a thirteenth collection period in 1980. Data have been adjusted to make FY1980 comparable to other years. In 1985, administration changes, including passage of a reciprocity amendment, led to a sharp drop in net sales receipts. Because of the different magnitudes and frequency of these tax adjustments, our models were not altered to reflect these changes. In 1985, however, the model overestimated collections by 5.1% because of the administrative changes. Eliminating that error would reduce model errors to less than 1% for the fiscal years of the 1980s despite the myriad tax base changes that have been made.

Also, revenue growth has slowed because of the maturation of the retail economy, especially in Fulton County. Fulton accounts for 16% of taxable sales in Georgia.

Combined with DeKalb, nearly a fourth of Georgia's retail activity is reflected in the two counties. (Earlier data on taxable sales showed even stronger concentrations in Fulton, but a revision of the methodology used to estimate taxable sales substantially reduced estimates of such sales).

Congestion has restrained population growth in the two counties. Retail activity continues to expand around North Pointe Mall, the latest regional mall to open in Fulton county. Also, Phipps and Lenox Malls in Buckhead have recently added nearly a million square feet (combined) to their available space. An explosion of retail space around Perimeter mall in DeKalb county also is adding to vendors. Whether these centers will attract purchases from residents outside the two counties or substitute for alternative retail activity within the two counties remains to be seen. The slowing of population growth within the two counties suggests that relatively slower growth in taxable sales and in sales tax receipts is likely in the years ahead.

Modeling Tax Collections

Ideally, sales taxes would be related to changes in retail sales and to any tax base or tax rate changes that develop. Although further erosion of the base is possible if food exemptions are again legislated in the future, no such base erosion has been assumed. Moreover, no rate changes are expected until 2032.

Sales tax collections have been growing nearly 1.3 times as fast as retail sales. Either the estimates of retail sales are too low, or taxes are being collected on services within a retail transaction. This ratio has been relatively constant over time but dipped during the recession.

One accepted approach would be to use standard economic relationships to estimate per capita sales after adjustment for inflation, use estimates of population to convert those projections into retail sales, and then derive sales tax receipts by using some ratio to sales. Unfortunately, some of the variables that would be used to derive real per capita sales, such as wealth, are not easily available at the county level. Inflation adjusted incomes depend upon earnings, transfer payments, and property incomes in the county. As table 2 shows, income estimates are available historically by county . However, a model would be needed to project personal incomes before sales could be derived. Furthermore, population changes would be related to employment opportunities as well as residential selection within the metropolitan area.

In short, any model would need employment estimates to derive income and population estimates. These estimates then would be used to derive retail sales. Sales tax receipts then would be developed from retail sales projections. When all the steps are consolidated, employment becomes the basic determinant of net sales tax receipts. Therefore, a consolidated model that directly derives net sales tax receipts from employment was preferred to the development of a set of relationships, all of which depended upon employment projections.

Historically, employment for individual counties is available with a lag along with employment for the Atlanta MSA. However, a relatively consistent reduction in employment shares by counties has developed in recent years. Therefore, a variable that incorporates this shifting share of Atlanta employment would be used in any projection model. Moreover, the Economic Forecasting Center at Georgia State University has been forecasting Atlanta employment since 1975 with some considerable degree of success. In order to exploit this metropolitan forecasting competence and also capture the shifting shares of employment in Fulton and DeKalb, our forecasting model used Atlanta employment projections and a share shifting time variable.

Over time, cyclical factors are overwhelmed by underlying trends. However, the Atlanta economy rebounded from a moderate recession that reduced metropolitan employment by 21,800 in 1991. Starting the forecast after 1995 and then superimposing long-range forecasting techniques would emphasize only the upside recovery from this recession. Of course, our employment projections capture some of this cyclical adjustment, but sales also change relative to income and employment during a recovery. We have discovered that using estimates of changes in real durable sales has substantially reduced the natural tendency to overestimate receipts during a recession and understate them during a boom. Indeed, recent receipts above our forecasted values reflects the explosion of sales in durable goods. Thus, our final forecasting model includes Atlanta employment, a variable to capture shifting shares, and an estimate of real durable goods sales.

Once forecasts are derived for Atlanta employment and real durable sales, the model estimates real net sales tax receipts. An inflation factor must be included to gross up these sales to actual values. Our estimates of use taxes are then added to the sales tax receipts to determine total MARTA receipts

Use taxes have continued to fall to only slightly more than $9 million in 1993. Instead of relating the use tax for Fulton and DeKalb to the use tax statewide, we chose to assume that avoidance would continue to drift upward, preserving the nominal value of use taxes at $9 million. In the past three years, this assumption slightly understated use tax collections.

Because the sales tax estimates are so sensitive to inflation projections, forecasted values for inflation from the Georgia State University Forecast of the Nation were used to determine inflation through 1997. In 1996, the personal consumption deflator is expected to increase only 2.0% but should accelerate to a 2.5% gain in 1997. This compares with gains of 2.2% in 1994 and 1995. From 1996 through 2015, the inflation adjustment was assumed to average 3.0%. These are slightly lower than in our previous projection, causing sales tax projections to grow slightly less per year than previously projected.

Employment estimates were adjusted to reflect the strong boom in Atlanta employment which is expected to persist through the Olympics in 1996 as contained in the Economic Forecasting Center estimates in its November forecast. Adjustments also were made to include Olympics operations in 1996. In the post-Olympics period after 1996 to 2000, employment gains were projected at 2.6% annually. Subsequent estimates averaged 2.3% annually. These higher estimates than in previous reports were generated by detailed projections of cyclical fluctuations in population and economic activity over the forecast period.

Aided by the Olympics and an explosion of computer sales, durable sales averaged 16.6% gains per year during the early 1990s. In a projected post Olympics slump, real durable sales were assumed to show moderate growth of 3.9% through 2000. Between 2000 and 2015, real durable sales are expected to grow an average of 4.2% per year. This slightly increases the share of durable goods in economic activity as a projected 1.5% per employee gain in productivity per year leads to implied real economic gains of 4.1% annually during the forecast period.

The Olympics arrives when a downturn normally would be projected with this methodology. Therefore, the durable goods expansion is extended by a year because of the Olympics. The five year cycles resume after the projected post-Olympics slump in durable goods sales is completed.

Finally, our forecasts of sales and use tax receipts correspond with the June 30 fiscal years used by MARTA. Of course, economic conditions reflect calendar years. The estimated coefficients of the model were used but the economic conditions were adjusted relative to sales and use tax receipts to assure comparability.

****Gains projected for the current fiscal year reflect conditions to date and above normal growth next year as well. Inflation rates are slightly higher than originally expected. Combined, the sales tax performance is above our previous anticipations. Stronger job and population growth this decade than previously projected is expected to be followed by slower growth rates early in the new century.

Assumptions

The relationships discussed above constitute the major assumptions used in these projections. Assumptions about employment and real durable goods sales were discussed above and are contained in tables 5 and 6.

- Employment growth is expected to slow but remain more than 1.8 times the national average during the forecast period. However, higher service employment was expected in 1996 to reflect the Olympics. A post Olympics slump was assumed, implying no lasting structural changes in Atlanta because of the Olympics. This certainly is a conservative assumption.
- No significant changes in boundaries, government structure, or state involvement in local governance was assumed.
- Although regional shopping malls were assumed for DeKalb in the next five years, no significant changes in the relative importance of sales tax receipts was expected from these developments. In other words, the malls exhaust alternative retail activity within the counties. Again, this is a conservative assumption.
- No further changes in tax rates or base changes were assumed. However, further erosion in taxable sales relative to income was assumed because of the relative growth of services in consumer spending patterns. The food tax exemption was assumed to not impact special use tax collections.
- Alternative tax changes in non-MARTA counties was not assumed to alter the shopping patterns in the metropolitan area.
- No government or resource induced limits to growth were assumed in the projections.
- No additional counties were assumed to provide revenue to MARTA during the forecast period.

Important Economic Characteristics

Fulton and DeKalb experienced less employment decline than the Atlanta MSA during the recession, and then rebounded more slowly according to our estimates. However, employment, income, and taxable sales have been growing less than in the Atlanta MSA over time. Part of this is caused by reduced available land, especially in DeKalb, while part reflects population and employment shifts away from the Atlanta center. However, substantial potential for development remains in Fulton county and some of the more vigorous development areas, such as Midtown, Buckhead, and part of the 400 corridor are in Fulton. Therefore, complete limits to income, employment, and population growth are not likely to be reached through 2015.

Atlanta's employment growth in the early 1990s was especially vigorous. Economic conditions responsible for this growth include consolidation of Atlanta activity as the economic center of the southeast region. As lawyers, accountants, consultants, and convention business met needs of a growing service base, and as that base also was growing faster than the United States, Atlanta grew exceptionally fast. The southeast continues to grow more rapidly than the nation but in some instances, such as conventions and finance, new competition has arisen within Atlanta's service area. However, Atlanta remains competitive in attracting new business.

TABLE 1:   Trends in Non-Farm Wage and Salary Employment, Atanta MSA, Fulton, and DeKalb, 1980–1992

	Average Annual Employment (000's)			Annual Percent Change		
	Atlanta	Fulton	DeKalb	Atlanta	Fulton	DeKalb
1981	1145.4	549.3	220.8	1.9%	–1.0%	2.7%
1982	1155.8	546.9	225.2	0.9%	–0.4%	2.0%
1983	1210.8	561.7	235.5	4.8%	2.7%	4.6%
1984	1322.5	596.1	258.1	9.2%	6.1%	9.6%
1985	1409.1	608.3	281.1	6.6%	2.1%	8.9%
1986	1486.5	623.1	294.1	5.5%	2.4%	4.6%
1987	1551.4	639.7	297.4	4.4%	2.7%	1.1%
1988	1611.4	658.2	305.1	3.9%	2.9%	2.6%
1989	1637.4	659.3	306.6	1.6%	0.2%	0.5%
1990	1659.4	662.1	303.1	1.3%	0.4%	–1.1%
1991	1626.8	627.9	297.8	–2.0%	–5.2%	–1.7%
1992	1666.9	630.5	294.3	2.5%	0.4%	–1.2%
1993	1751.5	650.5	303.0	5.1%	3.2%	3.0%

Source: U.S. Department of Commerce, Bureau of Economic Analysis, and Georgia State University, Economic Forecasting Center.

This data differs from the payroll estimates provided on a more timely basis by including the self employed who have no other employees and household help. The data are from the Bureau of Economic Analysis rather than from the Bureau of Labor Statistics. The reason for this unusual data source is the comparison with county performance. Although this source shows considerably smaller employment for Fulton and DeKalb than previous estimates (partially because migration patterns showed a smaller residence portion of the jobs in the two counties than originally expected), the percentage changes have been similar to previous reports, except in the past year. Also, the Atlanta data have been revised to show the historical impact of the new 20 county MSA designation. Unfortunately, the 20 county designation could not be pushed back before 1980 because of data limitations.

Fulton suffered all the employment loss during the previous recession as a result of the restructuring of large corporations, that are heavily concentrated in Fulton county. Also, government budget constraints reduced government workers in the government intense locations of Fulton county. Only modest recovery has occurred since then. DeKalb grew dramatically early in the 1980s but has begun to experience some land saturation problems that have slowed development in recent years. Light manufacturing also is leaving the county, causing the unusually slow rebound from recession. Together, the concentration of employment has dropped from 68.5% in 1980 to an estimated 54.4% in 1992. By 2015, this ratio will fall to less than 40% according to current projections. However, this still will permit employment gains of almost 2% per year in Fulton and slightly more than 1% annually in DeKalb over that period.

TABLE 2: Trends in Personal Income for Atlanta, Fulton and DeKalb, 1980–1992

| | Average Annual Income (Billions) | | | Annual Percent Changes | | | |
	Atlanta	Fulton	DeKalb	Atlanta	Fulton	DeKalb	Ratio
1981	25.703	7.259	5.823	12.9%	10.9%	12.0%	50.9%
1982	27.822	7.752	6.242	8.2%	6.8%	7.2%	50.3%
1983	31.073	8.597	6.850	11.7%	10.9%	9.7%	49.7%
1984	35.986	9.862	7.768	15.8%	14.7%	13.4%	49.0%
1985	40.424	10.950	8.598	12.3%	11.0%	10.7%	48.4%
1986	44.842	12.045	9.263	10.9%	10.0%	7.7%	47.5%
1987	48.826	13.104	9.817	8.9%	8.8%	6.0%	46.9%
1988	53.330	14.535	10.416	9.2%	10.9%	6.1%	46.8%
1989	56.620	15.629	10.877	6.2%	7.5%	4.4%	46.8%
1990	60.882	16.835	11.406	7.5%	7.7%	4.9%	46.4%
1991	63.543	17.579	11.762	4.4%	4.4%	3.1%	46.2%
1992	68.383	18.968	12.388	7.6%	7.9%	5.3%	45.9%
1993	73.206	20.181	13.070	7.1%	6.4%	5.5%	45.4%

Source. U.S. Department of Commerce, Bureau of Economic Analysis and Economic Forecasting Center, Georgia State University. Revised to include new definitions of income and the twenty counties for the MSA in April 1993.

Because of the large commuter activity for workers into the central city, income of county residents has not been comparable to employment. However, the rate of decline in income concentration has been comparable to the decline in employment's importance. By 2015, slightly more than a third of the income generated in the MSA will be held by residents in Fulton and DeKalb counties. Incomes are growing more slowly in DeKalb than in Fulton in recent years, and this trend is not expected to change. Income gains improved in the MARTA area following the recession. Even so, the concentration of income in the two counties continues to fall relative to the region. Most of this decline is in DeKalb. To a large extent, the relative reduction in employment importance of Fulton has been offset by increased income of Fulton residents relative to the MSA.

Obviously, this decline in concentration leads to slower growth in retail activity in the MARTA area than in the MSA. On the other hand, a high proportion of sales to non-residents occurs in Fulton and DeKalb. Taxable sales as a percentage of the metropolitan area has stabilized even as income proportions continue to decline. Any change in the relative importance of convention, tourist or day commuter purchases at work would alter this relationship.

TABLE 3: Trends in Population for Atlanta MSA, Fulton and DeKalb, 1980–1992

	Average Annual Population (000's)			Annual Percent Change			
	Atlanta	Fulton	DeKalb	Atlanta	Fulton	DeKalb	Ratio
1981	25.703	7.259	5.823	12.9%	10.9%	12.0%	50.9%
1981	2299.1	597.0	487.2	2.3%	0.9%	0.6%	47.2%
1982	2344.1	598.4	490.5	2.0%	0.2%	0.7%	46.5%
1983	2402.9	606.3	492.4	2.5%	1.3%	0.4%	45.7%
1984	2475.5	610.4	500.7	3.0%	0.7%	1.7%	44.9%
1985	2565.6	615.6	514.8	3.6%	0.9%	2.8%	44.1%
1986	2662.9	631.2	526.2	3.8%	2.5%	2.2%	43.5%
1987	2754.4	636.1	532.3	3.4%	0.8%	1.2%	42.4%
1988	2834.0	639.0	537.2	2.9%	0.5%	0.9%	41.5%
1989	2906.9	644.9	542.3	2.6%	0.9%	0.9%	40.8%
1990	2977.7	649.2	548.2	2.4%	0.7%	1.1%	40.2%
1991	3054.0	655.7	555.6	2.6%	1.0%	1.3%	39.7%
1992	3135.1	664.6	562.0	2.7%	1.4%	1.2%	39.1%
1993	3228.6	676.7	568.9	3.0%	1.8%	1.2%	38.6%
1994e	3331.0	690.2e	575.7e	3.2%	2.0%e	1.2%e	38.0%e

Source. U.S. Department of Commerce, Bureau of the Census, County data by the Atlanta Regional Commission.

A sharp slowing in population growth in 1990 reflects an undercounted Census. Worksheets from the Department of Commerce clearly show that substantial undercounting occurred in Fulton county. Moderate undercounting also occurred in DeKalb. The Atlanta Regional Commission had to put the population estimates back on track.

Increased density, especially in south DeKalb is responsible for the relative slowing of population in that county. Also, the migration must be of lower income groups, as per capita incomes are growing more slowly in DeKalb than in Fulton. Fulton is benefitting from strong community developments near the newly constructed North Pointe Mall. Following gains of 3.3% at annual rates in the 1980s, population gains will slow to 2.6% in the 1990s for the metro area and slow further to 1.8% from 2000 to 2015. Employment growth will remain stronger than that, however, because of continued growth in labor force participation.

Population gains in Fulton county were slightly less than 1% annually during the 1980s. Growth above that level is expected for the 1990s as activity migrates around the new regional mall in Alpharetta. Modest slowing to only 1.0% gains per year are expected between 2000 and 2015. In DeKalb, population has grown 1.4% per year at annual rates in the 1980s. Gains of 1% per year are expected in the 1990s and beyond. As a result, the concentration of Atlanta population in the two MARTA counties should fall from 38.0% in 1994 to slightly more than a third by 2015.

TABLE 4: Non-Farm Employment by Major Industry Group Atlanta, MSA 1983–1993

| | No. of Employees | | Periodic Change | | 1984 | 1994 |
	1984	1994	Number	Percent	% Dist	% Dist
Mining	1.7	1.6	–0.2	–10.8%	0.1%	0.1%
Construction	65.9	75.9	9.9	15.1	5.3	4.4
Manufacturing	194.0	205.5	11.5	5.9	15.7	11.9
T.C.U.	102.1	144.4	42.2	41.4	8.3	8.3
Trade	345.6	462.7	117.1	33.9	27.9	26.7
Wholesale	125.3	145.2	19.9	15.9	10.1	8.4
Retail	220.3	317.5	97.2	44.2	17.8	18.3
F.I.R.E	83.5	116.2	32.7	39.2	6.8	6.7
Services	267.8	483.3	215.5	80.5	21.7	27.9
Government	175.8	242.8	67.0	38.1	14.2	14.0
Total Non-Ag Empl:	1236.4	1732.2	495.8	49.2	100.0%	100.0%

Source: Bureau of Labor Statistics, Department of Labor, and Georgia Department of Labor.

In the past ten years, employment grew an average of 4.1% per year. The largest increase of 107,400 jobs occurred in 1984, but all years were positive until jobs were lost in 1991. The composition of employment changed dramatically away from manufacturing and construction to services. Retail activity maintained its share of employment, which probably reflects normal expansion of retail servicing of the economic area. This shift in employment composition reflects the surge in Atlanta's service area as accountants, lawyers, and consultants in Atlanta increased their service to clients outside the metropolitan area. The fastest growing service sector in importance is business services, which increased its share of total employment from 7.6% to 8.0% in the latest full year. Many of these jobs are from the employment agencies and are difficult to classify. Health services also have expanded in the area from 6.0% to 6.1% in the past year. Consolidations in that sector probably will prevent further rapid relative gains in the next few years.

Unless activity rebounds in manufacturing or another growth sector emerges, such as finance or health following the near term consolidations, employment growth should slow in the next two decades. Table 5 shows our current projections of employment by five year increments through 2015.

These data are different from the employment estimates of Table 1 because they reflect payrolls rather than employment by residents (the measure used for county comparisons). They also incorporate the new twenty county MSA and are therefore higher than previous employment estimates.

Estimates have been revised upward again for the most recent interval to capture the stronger employment gains that already are developing. As much of this gain does not appear to be Olympics related, the post Olympics slump has been modified. Eventually, employment growth rates are projected to slow, as the factors leading to stronger than national growth slowly dissipate with the maturing of the Atlanta economy. The 100,000 gains of the past three years clearly reflected catch-up following the recession. Our estimates show that the underlying employment growth for

TABLE 5: Employment Projections for the Atlanta MSA, 1990–2015

	Number of Employees Latter Year (000's)	Annualized Change	Annualized Percentage Change
1980–1985	1262.2	43,900	3.9%
1985–1990	1528.8	53,320	3.9%
1990–1995	1826.1	59,460	3.6%
1995–2000	2129.4	60,660	3.1%
2000–2005	2414.8	57,080	2.5%
2005–2010	2704.9	58,020	2.3%
2010–2015	3004.4	59,900	2.1%

"Latter" in this and subsequent tables refers to estimates in the last year of any noted interval. Thus, the 1262.6 for 1980–1985 is the 1985 estimate, not the interval average.
Source: Department of Labor, Bureau of Labor Statistics, and Economic Forecasting Center, Georgia State University.

Atlanta is about 60,000 jobs per year. Of course, in the year following the Olympics, growth will slow to 29,000 before regaining that more sustainable rate.

Any reduced competitiveness of Atlanta industry that slows relocations and hinders competition in the convention and services industries could lead to considerably slower employment gains than currently projected. On the other hand, no long term international relocations or convention activity was assumed because of the Olympics. Employment growth presented here is substantially less than in the past two decades, and could be as easily understated as excessive.

TABLE 6: Retail Trade Atlanta MSA 1978–1990 and Projections to 2015

	Retail Sales (Millions) (Latter)	%ch a.r.	Nondurable Sales (Millions) (Latter)	%ch a.r.	Durable Sales (Millions) (Latter)	%ch a.r.
1978–1980	9604	8.4	7147	14.0	2457	–4.1
1980–1985	21886	17.9	13122	12.9	8764	29.0
1985–1990	22917	0.9	14382	1.8	8535	–0.5
1990–1995	30741	6.1	18221	4.8	12520	8.0
1995–2000	40630	5.7	23477	5.2	17153	6.5
2000–2005	53609	5.7	30107	5.1	23502	6.5
2005–2010	70928	5.8	38425	5.0	32503	6.7
2010–2015	94415	5.9	49041	5.0	45374	6.9

Source: U.S. Department of Commerce, Bureau of the Census, and Economic Forecasting Center, Georgia State University.

Government estimates of retail trade in Atlanta were subject to reporting and definitional errors in the early 1980s. Changes in what constituted durable goods vendors are as responsible for the fluctuations during the decade as actual spending on durable goods. Even nondurables appear to be distorted in the five year segments of the eighties. However, some reduction in sales growth clearly developed as the decade progressed. In durable goods, large changes occurred in 1985, and must be related to definitional changes in the surveys. Although we use durable goods sales after adjusting for inflation in our model to capture shifting savings patterns over the cycle, our five year projections show little fluctuation after the post-Olympics slump. In other words, we use the durable goods sales to reflect cyclical factors but do not expect durable goods to be a significant factor in explaining sales tax receipts over time.

More significantly, data distortions that clearly existed early in the decade preclude the use of retail sales to determine sales tax receipts. Reduced growth in the sales of durable goods reflects reduced inflation for commodity goods in the next ten years as well as the slowing of population growth and some reduction in the growth of real spending per capita.

Because durable goods currently are rebounding from a major slump, current growth cannot be sustained. In general, durable goods are expected to follow a five year cycle. However, as explained above, the Olympics in 1996 will generate some moderate prosperity that should prevent the durable cycle from slumping until 1997. Then a moderate slump is expected to partially offset this unusually long expansion. The strong gains in durable sales occurring and projected to continue through 1995 are partially responsible for the higher actual and projected sales tax receipts in our forecast. We also slightly raised the growth of durable goods for the remainder of the forecast period to reflect stronger anticipated growth in durable goods than previously expected.

However, actual retail trade for 1995 is falling below our expectations. Therefore, our projections of retail sales through 2015 is lowered by the reduction in initial levels and the reduced growth in prices currently expected.

Until 1991, taxable sales never declined in the Atlanta MSA and only declined in 1975 in Fulton county. Over the 20 year period, taxable sales increased at an annual rate of 10.1% for Atlanta, 11.5% for DeKalb, and 7.6% for Fulton. In recent years, however, Fulton sales have remained comparable with Atlanta and have exceeded taxable sales in Georgia. As a result, the rapid decline in the share of Atlanta's taxable sales in Fulton and DeKalb has vanished. Part of the difference is the introduction of Underground Atlanta in 1989, the expansion of Phipps Plaza in 1992 and the opening of North Pointe Mall in 1993. The expansion at Lenox in 1995 also should contribute to strong taxable sales growth. Unfortunately, the series currently is not being published because of concerns about changes relative to previous history.

Taxable sales are expected to stabilize in Fulton and DeKalb relative to the metropolitan area. Concentrations will again fall when malls are opened outside the MARTA counties in the new century.

Slowing in net sales tax receipts during the recession has been replaced by strong growth in durable sales and tax collections in the subsequent expansion. Although not sustainable, these strong gains appear to be structural as well as cyclical. The growth of computer sales has partially added to the explosion of durable sales. Additions to retail activity in Alpharetta in North Fulton and further retail expansion near Perimeter and Lenox malls also appear to have temporarily arrested the downward drift in Atlanta sales concentration in the MARTA counties. In short, our forecast is stronger partially because recent growth has been stronger than anticipated.

TABLE 7: Taxable Sales in the Atlanta MSA and Fulton and DeKalb, 1970–1993

| | Atlanta Taxable Sales | | Fulton Taxable Sales | | DeKalb Taxable Sales | | |
	(Millions)	%ch	(Millions)	%ch	(Millions)	%ch	Ratio
1970	4819	6.3	2953	4.4	864	9.1	79.2
1971	5521	14.6	3281	11.1	1038	20.1	78.2
1972	6368	15.3	3592	9.5	1323	27.5	77.2
1973	7321	15.0	3981	10.8	1594	20.5	76.2
1974	7813	6.7	4216	5.9	1698	6.5	75.7
1975	8062	3.2	3851	-8.7	2042	20.3	73.1
1976	8936	10.8	4206	9.2	2229	9.1	72.0
1977	10176	13.9	4723	12.3	2552	14.5	71.5
1978	11638	14.4	5333	12.9	2914	14.2	70.9
1979	13025	11.9	5849	9.7	3262	11.9	70.0
1980	14884	14.3	6598	12.8	3782	15.9	69.7
1981	16477	10.7	7183	8.9	4217	11.5	69.2
1982	17539	6.4	7501	4.4	4542	7.7	68.7
1983	19868	13.3	8179	9.0	5140	13.2	67.0
1984	23985	20.7	9432	15.3	5849	13.8	63.7
1985	26411	10.1	10149	7.6	6319	8.0	62.4
1986	28206	6.8	10494	3.4	6874	8.8	61.6
1987	29990	6.3	11434	9.0	6976	1.5	61.4
1988	31925	6.5	12156	6.3	7350	5.4	61.1
1989	32406	1.5	12483	2.7	7574	3.0	61.9
1990	33134	2.2	12673	1.5	7614	0.5	61.2
1991	32921	-0.6	13102	3.4	7582	-0.4	62.8
1992	34538	4.9	13722	4.7	8124	7.1	63.3
1993	38648	11.9	14925	8.8	8937	10.0	61.7

Source: Georgia Department of Revenue. (A new methodology for taxable sales was begun in 1993 which showed that too much had been allocated to Fulton and DeKalb. We chose to maintain the older methodology as it was continued through 1993. Subsequent reports probably will require an adjustment downward in sales in 1993 and beyond to reflect this methodology).

However, our estimates of longer term sales activity also has been strengthened. Although Fulton and DeKalb will continue to lose retail share to other counties, absolute sales should continue to grow as incomes expand. Our national forecasts have assumed higher productivity gains than in previous projections, which should also be true in Atlanta. As those productivity gains gradually are reflected in higher compensation per capita, stronger sales gains are likely.

The only forecast segment that shows greater growth than any of the segments prior to the forecast period is the five year segment after the turn of the century. This growth reflects a rebound following a post Olympics correction. Slower but orderly growth in Atlanta employment and the continued employment and retailing importance of Fulton and DeKalb counties then is expected in the following decade.

Following the post Olympics stall, these projections grow stronger than previously expected at the turn of the century. Growth then slows. However, that period of

TABLE 8: Inflation Adjusted Net Sales Receipts in Fulton and DeKalb, 1980–2015

	Real Receipts (000's) (Latter)	Annualized Change (000's)	Percent Change a.r.
1975–1980	111250	4224	4.3%
1980–1985	128969	3544	3.0%
1985–1990	144498	3106	2.3%
1990–1995	177602	6621	4.2%
1995–2000	197271	3934	2.1%
2000–2005	220034	4553	2.8%
2005–2010	242869	4567	2.0%
2010–2015	261283	3683	1.5%

Source: Real net receipts are derived from the sales and use tax collections provided by MARTA minus the use taxes estimated by the Georgia Department of Revenue. The results were then divided by the implicit price deflator for consumer
expenditures provided by the Department of Commerce, Bureau of Economic Analysis. These data have been adjusted
from a 1982 base to a 1987 base. As a result, all real receipts appear larger than in previous reports. A look at the percentage changes will show that the history has not been altered, at least not before the first half of the 1990s. Projections came from our forecasting equation which relates real net sales receipts to Atlanta employment, real durable sales,
and a time variable to reflect changes in concentration from Fulton and DeKalb.

TABLE 9: Historical and Forecasted Values for MARTA Sales and Use Tax Receipts

	Net Sales Tax (000's)	Net Sales Tax %ch	Use Tax (000's)	Use Tax %ch	Total Receipts (000's)	Total Receipts %ch	Additions (000's)
FY							
1973	40644	3176	43820				
1974	44804	10.2	5697	79.3	50501	15.2	6681
1975	41979	−6.3	8967	57.4	50946	0.9	445
1976	47354	12.8	5465	−39.5	52819	3.7	1873
1977	47125	−0.5	10808	97.8	57933	9.7	5114
1978	53148	12.8	12972	20.0	66120	14.1	8187
1979	62475	17.5	12997	0.2	75472	14.1	9352
1980	71303	14.1	17039	31.1	88342	17.1	12870
1981	81695	14.6	18141	6.5	99836	13.0	11494
1982	83916	2.7	20769	14.5	104685	4.9	4849
1983	92858	10.7	19150	−7.8	112008	7.0	7323
1984	103676	11.7	19730	3.0	123406	10.2	11398
1985	112254	8.3	22647	14.8	134901	9.3	11495
1986	131914	17.5	15235	−32.7	147149	9.1	12248
1987	135834	3.0	12748	−16.3	148582	1.0	1436
1988	147962	8.9	10587	−17.0	158549	6.7	9967
1989	153014	3.4	9529	−10.0	162543	2.5	4114
1990	156521	2.3	9201	−3.4	165722	2.0	3179
1991	159085	1.6	9000	−2.2	168085	1.4	2363
1992	158016	−0.7	9000	0.0	167016	−0.6	−1069
1993	172345	9.1	9000	0.0	181345	8.6	14329

Continued on facing page

TABLE 9: Historical and Forecasted Values for MARTA Sales and Use Tax Receipts *(continued)*

FY	Net Sales Tax		Use Tax		Total Receipts		Additions
	(000's)	*%ch*	*(000's)*	*%ch*	*(000's)*	*%ch*	*(000's)*
1994	189490	10.0	9000	0.0	198490	9.5	17145
1995	213475	12.7	9000	0.0	222475	12.1	23985
Forecast							
1996	234175	9.7	9000	0.0	243175	9.6	20700
1997	244397	4.4	9000	0.0	253397	4.3	10222
1998	246021	0.7	9000	0.0	255021	0.6	1624
1999	254198	3.3	9000	0.0	263198	3.2	8177
2000	269357	6.0	9000	0.0	278357	5.9	15159
2001	286435	6.3	9000	0.0	295435	6.2	17078
2002	295159	3.0	9000	0.0	304159	2.9	8724
2003	299764	1.6	9000	0.0	308764	1.5	4605
2004	317558	5.9	9000	0.0	326558	5.8	17794
2005	335529	5.7	9000	0.0	344529	5.6	17971
2006	353505	5.4	9000	0.0	362505	5.3	17976
2007	370468	4.8	9000	0.0	379468	4.7	16963
2008	392682	6.0	9000	0.0	401731	5.9	22263
2009	407731	3.8	9000	0.0	416731	3.7	15000
2010	420044	3.0	9000	0.0	429044	2.9	12313
2011	439147	4.5	9000	0.0	448147	4.4	19103
2012	452616	3.1	9000	0.0	461616	3.0	13469
2013	465087	4.9	9000	0.0	474087	4.8	12471
2014	487793	4.9	9000	0.0	496793	4.8	22706
2015	502712	3.1	9000	0.0	511712	3.0	14919

Source: As in Table 8, the data were supplied historically by MARTA, and the Georgia Department of Revenue. Projections were based upon the model explained earlier with an inflation rate superimposed upon projections of real activity.

stronger gains along with the higher initial values lead to considerably higher estimates of revenues by 2015. Inflation rates remain contained, although they are higher than previously projected at the turn of the century. We have eliminated some of our pessimism of the post Olympics performance of the area. Our projections also differ from ones presented previously because of more cyclical adjustments to the model. These projections almost certainly are conservative. Some nominal growth in use taxes should be expected during the forecast period. The inflation rates assumed in the next twenty years are reasonable, but are significantly lower than inflation in the 1970s and 1980s. Substantial inflation changes would dramatically alter the revenue projections, but they also would change operating costs in the same direction.

Conclusion

Using a forecasting model of sales tax receipts and making assumptions about the future performance of the volatile and shrinking use tax, we have derived estimates of MARTA sales and use tax receipts between now and 2015 The current recovery has been sharper than the recession. All our analysis suggests that this current expansion reflects both structural as well as strong cyclical changes following the recession. Productivity gains nationwide are expected to be higher than previously expected, and that should also be true in Atlanta. As a result, real per capita spending should grow more than previously expected.

Of course, any projections depend upon the assumptions used to drive the analysis. We believe the assumptions are reasonable based upon previous historical relationships and normal behavior related to the development of cities. Of course, reality can deviate substantially from those assumptions, and the resulting tax receipt estimates could change materially.

Sincerely,

Donald Ratajczak, Director
Economic Forecasting Center
Georgia State University

Appendix A

October 7, 1996, Report of Economic Forecasting Center, Georgia State University, Economic Consultants

October 7, 1996

Mr. Terry L. Griffis
Director of Treasury Services
MARTA
2424 Piedmont Rd, N.E.
Atlanta, GA 30324-3330

Dear Mr. Griffis:

This is our latest analysis on projected sales tax revenues for MARTA in the next two fiscal years through June of 1999, quarterly projections through 2002 and annual estimates to the year 2020. I hope this fits your planning needs.

Two factors are worthy of note. Because of the two month lag from activity to collections, we do not yet have a clear picture of the impact of the Olympics upon revenues. We do not think that the strong June estimates reflected Olympics activity. Of course, our estimates for the next few months are based upon speculations of the Olympics impact. After that, we feel more comfortable about the post-Olympics picture. We already have some post-Olympics employment estimates, which suggest that employment will slow to less than 50,000 gains in the fourth quarter. In the months overlapping Olympics activity in 1997, little employment growth from previous year levels is likely, although seasonally adjusted growth still is expected. For 1997, employment gains of less than 40,000 are likely.

Second, our equations consistently over-estimate sales tax revenues in 1994 and 1995 and then under-estimate them in 1996. This could be caused by the reporting problems at the state level. Apparently, our allocation was less than expected according to our economic performance for nearly two years and now has been above economic conditions in the past year. If this is caused by allocation problems, then above normal allocations might be expected for another year before allocations return to those predicted by economic conditions.

Our model remains robust. After adjustment for inflation forecasted collections are as follows:

$$\text{Price adjusted collections (000)} = 1549 + 39475 * \text{Atlanta Employment (000)}$$
$$(715) \quad (9062)$$
$$+ 3368 * \text{Price adjusted durable goods sales (\$000)} - 421293 * \text{time.}$$
$$(943) \qquad\qquad\qquad\qquad (102575)$$

All the relationships except the constant are robust. Durable goods sales have become more important in recent quarters while time also has become more significant. This reflects both the unusually strong durable goods sales in the area and the continued growth in relative importance of areas outside the MARTA region. (The numbers in parentheses reflect the standard error of the estimate of coefficients).

Our latest projections by quarter through 2002 are as follows:

1996–3	$70,129	1998–1	$73,451	1999–3	$75,742	2001–1	$83,250
1996–4	65,204	1998–2	73,139	1999–4	72,514	2001–2	82,783
1997–1	70,746	1998–3	73,585	2000–1	79,185	2001–3	83,581
1997–2	66,328	1998–4	69,978	2000–2	79,327	2001–4	80,081
1997–3	67,360	1999–1	71,827	2000–3	79,980	2002–1	86,917
1997–4	67,526	1999–2	75,158	2000–4	76,560	2002–2	86,707
						2002–3	87,458
						2002–4	84,006

This leads to the following projections for the fiscal years:

Fiscal Year	Receipts (000's)	% Change	Previous Estimates (000's)	% Change	Additions (000's)	Previous Additions (000's)
1996	251668	13.2%	243175	9.6%	29193	20700
1997	272407	8.2%	253397	4.3%	20739	10222
1998	281476	3.3%	255021	0.6%	9069	1624
1999	290548	3.2%	263198	3.2%	9072	8177
2000	306768	5.6%	278357	5.9%	16220	15159
2001	322573	5.2%	295435	6.2%	15805	17078
2002	337286	4.6%	304159	2.9%	14713	8724

Our higher projections are partially because of a stronger economy than used in our January forecasts. Also, we added slightly more inflation. In addition, we adjusted the forecasts upward in the next fiscal year to capture the higher payouts from the state that were discussed above.

Our monthly projections for the remainder of this year and through 1999 are as follows:

	1996	1997	1998	1999
January		$23,396,417	$24,314,870	$23,778,796
February		24,996,198	25,977,709	25,405,190
March		22,353,385	23,158,298	22,643,460
April		21,375,131	23,572,284	24,225,127
May		22,310,264	24,603,400	25,284,694
June		22,642,751	24,963,564	25,648,426
July	$23,572,788	22,644,499	24,736,909	25,464,663
August	23,861,506	22,921,155	25,041,723	25,777,606
September	22,695,811	21,794,774	23,806,065	24,499,624
October	21,768,161	22,545,442	23,365,989	24,215,205
November	21,968,244	22,752,585	23,581,564	24,439,055
December	21,467,718	22,228,887	23,030,700	23,859,868

We continue to caution that the monthly projections around the Olympics are difficult to determine because of the one time nature of that event. We certainly could be too low in our estimates for the Olympics months. However, the subsequent estimates appear to be realistic. We assume no changes in spending patterns, and therefore in collections, because of the state's removal of sales taxes on food over the next three years. As this is not altering the tax base for MARTA, the additional spending generated by that tax reduction might lead to higher collections than estimated. We did not consider that impact, however, in order to preserve conservative estimates for the forecast.

We have also made projections to the year 2020. We have not included the detail to support those estimates that we would in a bond report, but we have increased both real growth and inflation in our estimates. These changes are not large, but they accumulate over twenty years. We also are including the previous estimates and additions as contained in our January study to show how our outlook has changed with these minor adjustments.

Fiscal Year	Receipts (000's)	% Change	Previous Estimates (000's)	% Change	Additions (000's)	Previous Additions (000's)
1996	251668	13.2%	243175	9.6%	29193	20700
2003	348471	3.3%	308764	1.5%	11185	4605
2004	365853	5.0%	326558	5.8%	17382	17794
2005	375605	2.7%	344529	5.6%	9752	17971
2006	391128	4.1%	362505	5.3%	15523	17976
2007	420062	7.4%	379468	4.7%	28934	16963
2008	447929	6.6%	401731	5.9%	27867	22263
2009	474461	5.9%	416731	3.7%	26532	15000
2010	492160	3.7%	429044	2.9%	17699	12313
2011	510474	3.7%	448147	4.4%	18314	19103
2012	537253	5.3%	461616	3.0%	26779	13469
2013	560149	4.3%	474087	4.8%	22896	12471

Continued on facing page

Fiscal Year	Receipts (000's)	% Change	Previous Estimates (000's)	% Change	Additions (000's)	Previous Additions (000's)
2014	566200	1.1%	496793	4.8%	6051	22706
2015	585928	3.5%	511712	3.0%	19728	14919
2016	615480	5.0%			29552	
2017	650522	5.7%			35042	
2018	685704	5.4%			35182	
2019	720852	5.1%			35148	
2020	756276	4.9%			35424	

Apparently, my assumptions have not generated a business cycle toward the end of the period. We probably will be able to more readily see where our estimates are off after a complete analysis such as those done for the bond reports. In the meantime, we believe the estimates to 2020 provide a reasonable projection of probable revenue growth in the absence of any tax base changes.

I hope these results will aid you in your planning process.

Sincerely,

Donald Ratajczak, Director
Economic Forecasting Center
Georgia State University

Analysis of Chapter 4 Case Study

For our third case, assume that we are consultants hired to forecast sales tax receipts for a transit authority for the next two years. This forecast is essential to enable the public transit authority to set its farebox policies and plan for transit services and improvements for the coming years. How typical is this kind of activity for policy analysts? Given the relative stability of tax rates and the fact that interval-level data exist for both tax receipts and its causes, such as income and taxable sales, one might expect this to be a narrow, technocratic, and perhaps trivial kind of policy exercise—in contrast to a meaty policy option issue like defense, poverty, or the environment. Sales tax forecasting may not seem messy enough, but, in fact, revenue forecasting is plagued with many of the same kinds of uncertainties as expenditure forecasting, proving that the availability of numbers does not cure every disease.

More important, revenue forecasting permits less room for error. While expenditures (outlays) can be varied throughout the year by supplemental appropriations, rescissions, deferrals, earmarks, and decisions not to obligate, revenue decisions are usually made only once each year. It is true that revenue estimates have to be updated monthly and both the true data trends and procedures for doing this will affect expenditure forecasts. The trends and procedures will also affect planned corrective actions for expenditure management during budget execution. But the structure (relative contribution of each tax) and incidence (or the politics of who pays) of major state and local revenue sources are normally locked in at the beginning of the fiscal year.

It might be argued that an agency such as MARTA that relies on a portion of sales tax receipts for 50 to 60 percent of its annual revenues effectively relies on a single revenue source and would be difficult to predict revenues for. The problem is that specialized, single-source revenues, such as mineral lease receipts, are subject to catastrophic revenue losses caused by economic cycles and political action (Nelson and Cornia 1997, 38). This structural feature profoundly affects both revenue estimates and budget management. While MARTA relies on sales tax receipts for much of its revenues, evidence from time-series data going back almost twenty-five years shows that average year-on-year variation in total receipts is only 7.8 percent (Metropolitan Atlanta Rapid Transit Authority 1996, A-14). Since substantial and successful experience exists with sales tax revenue forecasting, MARTA's revenue data and budget management actions are more amenable to statistical tests than those of agencies dependent on minor, single sources of revenues. Further, in contrast to those of federal programs, MARTA's expenses are mostly fixed and thus actually easier to project than revenues.

At the state and local levels, most budgets are developed on the basis of revenue availability. Rather than calculate needs and work out the most cost-effective means of attaining them for different levels of expenditure (the "rational" approach), budget preparation in most governments works from available revenues back to allowable expenditures. Under such real-world conditions, budget forecasters may be more critical to policymaking than policy analysts. As indicated, MARTA is especially dependent on sales tax receipts for its operations. The Metropolitan Atlanta Rapid Transit Authority Act of 1965 (amended 1983) provides for a 1 percent sales tax to be levied by the two member counties. The proceeds of the tax are used for bond debt service and operating costs. However, the act provides that no more than 50 percent of the sales tax proceeds can be applied to subsidy of operating costs (60 percent after year 2032).The act also provides that after 2032 sales tax receipts may not subsidize more than 50 percent of MARTA system operating costs.

Where sales tax receipts are too low (either because expenses increase or forecasts were too low), MARTA must carry over prior reserves to make up the difference. In FY 1987, because expenses were higher than expected,

MARTA had to carry over $4.0 million to cover the sales tax subsidy rate of 52.6 percent for that year. Should that level of carry-over reserves have been insufficient, MARTA would have been required by the 1965 act to adjust fares so that operating revenues would cover at least 35 percent of projected operating costs for the year. MARTA can raise fares or cut its bus/rail services to attain this level of coverage—but either action would be highly unpopular political decisions! So, MARTA policymakers rely upon timely and accurate sales tax revenue forecasts. Such stakeholders as riders, bond-holders, board members, labor unions, senior managers, and bond-rating agencies like Standard and Poor's, all rely on this information for planning the next year's activities.

Special fund, autonomous transit authorities, which are also called public or state enterprises, such as MARTA, depend on accurate sales tax forecasts. But the quality range of available forecasts from consultants and in-house experts varies widely. Some forecasters (often in house) hide a growth premise in their calculations in hopes that they (or their clients) will receive more money to pay for capital projects. Inflated operating expenditure forecasts are often made in the public sector to satisfy constituents on the theory that revenues can always be found later, through such vehicles as supplemental appropriations.

Sales tax revenue forecasting is an appropriately messy but actionable policy problem because one must make decisions on which variables to include and how to measure them. Suppose now that a consultant is asked to develop a "multiyear" forecast of FY 1996–1998 sales tax receipts for MARTA. [Larry Schroeder and Roy Bahl classify three-to-five-year forecasts as multiyear (1984, 7).] At the consultant's disposal are the data and current forecasts of the Economic Forecasting Center (EFC) of Georgia State University. Because time is money in the context of this task, the consultant considers simpler and less time-consuming methods than used by EFC.

Policy forecasters typically include elastic disclaimers to cover such unpredictable events as changes in tax laws or political interventions. The EFC forecast for MARTA notes accordingly that "... any projections depend upon the assumptions used to drive the analysis. We believe the assumptions are reasonable based upon previous historical relationships and normal behavior related to the development of cities. Of course, reality can deviate substantially from those assumptions, and the resulting tax receipt estimates could change materially" (Ratajczak 1996, 15). This is indicated in Table 4.5 in which a comparison was requested by the MARTA board of directors of estimated receipts with actual receipts as reported by the Georgia Department of Revenue.

Table 4.5: Comparison of Sales Tax Receipts Projections ($ millions)

ACTUALS	%	YEAR	SERIES D $	SERIES D %	SERIES E $	SERIES E %
112.0	6.99	1983	111.3	6.3	—	—
123.4	10.18	1984	121.6	10.5	119.1	6.36
134.9	9.31	1985	130.6	7.4	128.1	7.53
147.1	9.08	1986	140.4	7.4	138.1	7.78

Source: Memorandum from R. J. McCrillis to S. L. Barth, "Sales Tax Receipts 'Official' Estimates," 4 November 1986, MARTA.

EFC forecasts are found in the 1996 "Official Statement," which was issued by MARTA at the time of bond sale to provide information on financial condition and security pledged for securities offered, to enable investors to judge the quality of securities being offered, reproduced here as the chapter 4 case study. The case challenges us to supply the missing data and to apply the appropriate techniques in an attempt to replicate EFC answers. We are just as interested in "right answers" as we are in an analyst's ability to substantiate the use of methods and to explain any answers.

To demonstrate knowledge of the use of policy forecasting techniques, one should be able to answer two questions related to the case. First, one needs to know which variables determine sales tax receipts. As noted, correlation analysis serves the purpose of finding the "significant" variables. Most sales tax forecasters use roughly the same variables to link "retail trade sales in constant dollars to sales tax receipts with varying degrees of success." For example, MARTA's previous forecaster, the firm of Hammer, Siler, George Associates (HSGA), used this approach (Guess and Farnham 1989, 73). For this reason, we will eliminate this step and assume we have the variables. According to HSGA, six factors affect sales tax receipts: employment, population, income, inflation, retail sales, and taxable sales.

The analyst should apply a range of techniques relating these variables to sales tax yields (receipts) before judging the accuracy of the forecast. Here we need an appropriate "function," such as linear least squares regression or even simple averaging, to predict future receipts from the independent variables. Note that the function may also be obtained from "guesstimates" and hunches as well as multivariate regressions, and the first two may be just as accurate! The best analyst will combine critical use of the most sophisticated techniques with hunches based on experience.

Unfortunately, sufficient data on key variables for regression purposes here are difficult to obtain. For example, employment and income data are available only through 1993 (MARTA 1996, A-1). Such a data lag can affect forecasting where "turning points" start to develop and current data are unavailable to note them. The experience of the previous MARTA forecaster (HSGA) suggests that the key to HSGA's forecasting accuracy was the behavior of variables over any preceding six months, which means that forecasting from the previous several years with interpolated data into the future would to some extent be blind. Further, some of the data include benchmarks for the national and state levels but not for counties or localities. This means that sales and income had to be estimated by extrapolation from national data and available local data. Dallas, Texas, for example, forecasts its sales tax receipts from trends in the Dallas consumer price index and population (Klay 1983, 305). Despite some data problems, EFC notes that "surprisingly strong relationships have been developed between economic conditions in Fulton and DeKalb counties and the sales tax receipts MARTA received from activity in those counties" (Ratajczak 1996, A-1). For this reason, we will not have to resort to extrapolation or interpolation.

Additionally, forecasting accuracy can be weakened by the existence of county revenue competition. As in many metropolitan areas in the United States composed of multiple counties, the Atlanta metropolitan region contains several counties in competition with each other for sales tax revenues (e.g., Fulton and DeKalb counties). This complicates the projection process in that fiscal decisions of each county may be based on what it perceives the other is doing, such as provision of incentives for regional malls. Unfortunately, no consistently accurate methodology exists to project the results of "zero-sum games" into the future. Nevertheless, EFC assumes no alternative tax changes in non-MARTA counties that would alter shopping patterns in the Atlanta metropolitan area (MARTA 1996, A-5).

More important, in order for regression analysis to be of any value, according to Llewellyn Toulmin and Glendal Wright (1983, 234), "The data must contain sufficient observations so that a statistical relationship can be clearly established. This means that for most practical purposes at least 20 or more data points (that is, observations) should be available." Other than for taxable sales, the other variables contain less than fifteen observations. Under these conditions, some suggest the need to use a technique to "estimate missing data," such as interpolation or extrapolation (Simon 1978, 251). But where basic relationships are established, as here for economic activity and sales tax receipts, and where the aim is to specify the relationships more precisely into a forecast, use of interpolated data may not add anything. Use of such effectively "manufactured" data can only add to the aura of certainty. Interpolated data are not an independent draw from any distribution that would contribute to actual hard data. In fact, it could invalidate other statistical tests such as regressions.[2] Thus, one method to ostensibly improve data could actually invalidate other statistical methods. In short, it is better to use hard data even if there are fewer data points than strictly required for correlation tests. Also, since regression techniques treat all data equally we may want to "shed" earlier data and emphasize more recent trends. This will be illustrated below.

Additionally, many of the independent variables relate to each other (which is the intercorrelation or "multicollinearity" problem) and to other exogenous variables. Population and sales do not correlate highly, but the income, employment, and retail sales variables do. And taxable sales and retail sales exhibit a close relationship. Where correlation coefficients of all independent variables explain only slightly more than partial correlations of each independent variable, the multicollinearity problem exists (Toulmin and Wright 1983, 234). According to David Nachmias (1979, 134), "The problem can be remedied to some extent by combining highly correlated independent variables into a single variable (for example, an index) or by eliminating all but one of the highly correlated independent variables." The related problem of serial correlation or "autocorrelation" is discussed above.

Beyond multicollinearity is the problem of exogenous variables' determining the values of the endogenous variables. For instance, the value of the dollar and level of inflation both affect the propensity to consume certain durable and nondurable items, which would then affect sales tax receipts. This means that often inflation alone is a major determinant of the actual dollar amount of retail sales and sales tax receipts. As noted, the technical solution to such a problem is development of a nonrecursive model. But the costs of such an effort may not be worth the increases (if any) in forecast accuracy. Faced with this dilemma, the analyst may simply average each time-series variable until a reasonable line or curve develops.

The second issue we need to resolve is what technique(s) should be employed to obtain an accurate forecast. Different techniques will produce different forecasts. To some extent selection is determined by the quality of the data. Where good "interval"-level data exist and one can presume that past trends should continue for the short term, one should develop as elegant a model as time and resources permit. As is known, nominal data are dichotomous (e.g., male, female) and cannot be ranked. Interval data consist of units of equal size that can be ranked (e.g., tax receipts in dollars). But data may be available only at the "ordinal" level, meaning that categories can be ranked but the distance between units is not precise (e.g., "very happy," "somewhat happy"). Some statistical techniques are designed only for use with interval variables because they are better at handling multivariable analyses and detecting weak associations between variables (Hedderson 1991, 92). Much depends also on the good judgment of the policy analyst in selecting a method and interpreting the meaning of the results. Fortunately, tax receipt data are at the interval level and are typically available for many years. Let us then compare the results one may obtain on revenue forecasting by using simple averaging and exponential smoothing and a "soft" causal approach that combines interpolated data and linear least-squares with those obtained by EFC.

The least cost method, as noted, is to simply average past data for fiscal years using such techniques as the "proportionate change" method. We know from the chapter 4 case study that we have more data points (twenty-three) for receipts (collections paid to MARTA by the state from the two counties) than any of the other variables. We therefore begin our quest for the latest forecast by averaging this data and forecasting receipts for 1996 through 1999. As indicated, we first need to calculate the percentage change in receipts between fiscal years (Table 4.6).

Using the same procedure for FY 1997 through 1999 we forecast:

- FY 1997 $257,098 million
- FY 1998 $276,380 million
- FY 1999 $297,108 million

Note that the proportionate change or averaging method requires the assumption that FY 1997–1999 increases will grow at a constant 7.5 percent rate because this is the average of the previous fiscal years. As indicated in Figure 4.6 below, this forecast is (except for FY 1996) higher than that developed by EFC. Should we want to stick with this method, it may be improved by exponential smoothing, using "alpha weights" to rectify the difference. As noted by Toulmin and Wright (1983, 227–28), where considerable randomness in actual observations is expected, one should use a higher alpha factor. Comparing EFC forecasts with those just obtained, the percentage difference is not constant but increasing: FY 1996 (–1.7 percent lower than EFC), FY 1997 (1.5 percent higher than EFC), FY 1998 (8.4 percent higher) and FY 1999 (9.1 percent higher). In the first edition of this book, we found that use of the proportionate change method produced differences that were also increasing and higher than that found by the official forecaster (then HSGA) by FY 1987 (9.8 percent), FY 1988 (8.1 percent), FY 1989 (11.7 percent), and FY 1990 (14.4 percent). To increase accuracy,

Table 4.6: Time-Series Trend Analysis: Proportionate Change Method

FISCAL YEAR	PAYMENTS TO MARTA ($000)	PERCENT CHANGE
1973	$43,820	
1974	50,501	15.2
1975	50,946	0.9
1976	52,819	3.7
1977	57,933	9.7
1978	66,120	14.1
1979	75,472	14.1
1980	88,342	17.1
1981	99,836	13.0
1982	104,685	4.9
1983	112,008	7.0
1984	123,407	10.2
1985	134,902	9.3
1986	147,149	9.1
1987	148,582	1.0
1988	158,549	6.7
1989	162,543	2.5
1990	165,722	2.0
1991	168,085	1.4
1992	167,016	–0.6
1993	181,345	8.6
1994	198,490	9.5
1995	222,475	12.1

$$\frac{171.5}{23} = 7.5 \quad \text{FY } 1996 = .075 \times 222,475 = \$16686 + 222,475 = \$239,161$$

alpha weights would have to be varied each year to match this curvilinear pattern.

Let us now move to an application of a "soft causal" approach to see whether our accuracy (always assuming greater accuracy on the part of EFC professionals) can be improved. Although this is hardly state of the art, in principle it should enable us to get closer to EFC results. More sophisticated

Figure 4.6: Comparison of Averaging and Least Squares Forecasts with EFC Results

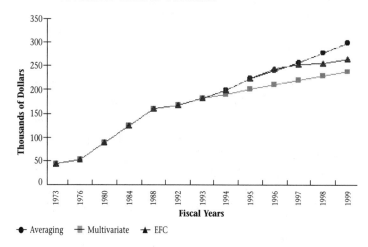

forecasters, such as the Georgia State Department of Revenue and Taxation, use recursive multivariate models with complex vectors on a year-round basis to project and track sales tax receipts. Such econometric forecasters rely more on method than judgment and claim to produce sophisticated, highly accurate results (Figure 4.6).

These models are so sensitive that where monthly forecasts diverge slightly from actuals, potential residual error correlation analysis (autocorrelation) begins immediately. According to Schroeder, Sjoquist, and Stephan (1986, 75), "Autocorrelation can be caused by several factors, including omission of an important explanatory variable or the use of an incorrect functional form. It may also simply be due to the tendency of effects to persist over time or for dependent variables to behave cyclically." The most common technique for determining whether autocorrelation exists is the Durbin-Watson coefficient, which is "used to test the null hypothesis that successive error terms are not correlated" (Schroeder, Sjoquist, and Stephan 1986, 75). If autocorrelation exists, forecasters can then transform the variables through use of generalized least squares regression.

At the introductory level, the policy analyst needs an approach that is more accurate than simple averaging but not as costly and time consuming as recursive model building. If that is the objective, given the sales tax problem we need to perform three prior tasks. First, where fewer than twenty data points exist, data need to be improved for key variables by interpolation (Simon 1978, 251). In the first edition (1989), only three to four data points existed, and there we extrapolated sales tax receipts as growth rates or ratios from a combination of population and income data. We reasoned that since taxable sales are often a function of income, we could do the forecast off income growth or a ratio of taxable sales to income. The same reasoning applies here. But when we wrote the book in 1987, population, taxable sales, and personal income variables contained only three or four data points. We needed more data points, especially for the more recent years. Additionally, the client (MARTA) needed sales tax data for fiscal years because it budgets on this basis. However, 90 percent of the base data, such as income, sales, population, and employment, are calculated on a calendar year basis. To be precise, we would have had to convert calendar year to fiscal year data. But proving that time heals most technical problems, by the time of the revised edition (1998) each key variable contained what we consider sufficient data points for regressions: employment (13), population (14), per capita income (13) and taxable sales (24). For our multiple-regression test, we should use 13 data points (1980–1993).

Second, we need to take a more deductive or econometric approach to the determination of sales tax receipts. So far, our calculations have assumed that time alone causes changes in sales tax receipts, but this is a questionable methodological approach. As noted, EFC suggests that six variables determine receipts—but it also suggests that taxable sales and per capita income are the key variables. This conclusion is suggested by the following statements in the "Official Statement" or "OS": sluggishness in durable sales in the past has been responsible for a substantial reduction in sales tax receipts (A-1), and decline in income concentration leads to slower growth in retail activity in the MARTA area than in the Atlanta Metropolitan Statistical Area (MSA) (A-7). EFC also relies on employment data to drive its model. "Any model would need employment estimates to derive income and population estimates. These estimates then would be used to derive retail sales. Sales tax receipts then would be developed from retail sales projections. When all the steps are consolidated, employment becomes the basic determinant of net sales tax receipts" (A-3). With existing data for these two key variables, then, we should be able to forecast sales tax receipts.

Third, we should use a method such as exponential smoothing or ordinary least squares regression for each variable. Use of such simpler techniques before applying multivariate regressions recognizes that the future may not be like the past and that old data should not be accorded the same weight as more recent data. This means that we probably should apply some exponential smoothing to the least squares results as well. A ratio of taxable sales to income should give us the basis for extrapolating sales tax receipts.

A forecast of greater comprehensiveness (and probably accuracy) would include the effects of such factors as legislative changes, county competitive positions in relation to other metro counties, sales to nonresidents, service-sector growth (one-third of taxable sales), use tax (utilities and manufacturing activities), and changing retail structure (mail order and other resident expenditure patterns). An $8.8 million forecasting difference for FY 1987 was largely due to the assumption (apparently erroneous) that the utility and manufacturing component (whose sales taxes fluctuate widely from month to month) would cancel out and grow at the same rate as the rest of retail sales. Another surprise for forecasters was the pattern of use tax avoidance. In 1984 airlines established fueling subsidiaries in Clayton County (a non-MARTA county) to avoid the use tax in Fulton County (MARTA 1996, A-2). This resulted in overestimation of tax receipts. For our less ambitious purposes in this book, it is important to recognize that the policy analyst must trade the cost of developing totally comprehensive multivariate models with the time necessary to do so and the potential gains in forecasting accuracy. To date, models of lesser sophistication had served client purposes admirably (Table 4.7).

Using the above data, let us try forecasting receipts first with the ratio of per capita income to taxable sales (Figure 4.7), second with population growth, and third with (a) regression coefficient(s) of forecast income and sales using a multiple-regression model. The ratios are indicated in Table 4.8. If any of these three methods approximates what EFC obtained we have accomplished our purposes. Whether or not we obtain close results, for consistency they should be compared with those obtained by more complex techniques, such as multivariate regression, which we shall perform below.

Figure 4.7: Forecasts Using Population and Ratio of Income to Taxable Sales

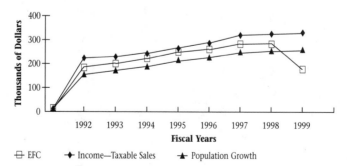

Table 4.7: Annual Percentage Changes in Basic Data for Atlanta Metropolitan Statistical Area, 1977–1994

YEAR	1977	78	79	80	81	82	83	84	85	86	87	88	89	90	91	92	93	94
Employment	—	—	5.7	3.1	1.9	0.9	4.8	9.2	6.6	5.5	4.4	3.9	1.6	1.3	-2.0	2.5	5.1	—
Population	—	—	—	—	2.3	2.0	2.5	3.0	3.6	3.8	3.4	2.9	2.6	2.4	2.6	2.7	3.0	3.2
Per Capita Income	—	—	—	—	12.9	8.2	11.7	15.8	12.3	10.9	8.9	9.2	6.2	7.5	4.4	7.6	7.1	—

YEAR	1970	71	72	73	74	75	76	77	78	79	80	81	82	83	84	85	86	87
Taxable Sales	6.3	14.6	15.3	15.0	6.7	3.2	10.8	13.9	14.4	11.9	14.3	10.7	6.4	13.3	20.7	10.1	6.8	6.3

YEAR	1988	89	90	91	92	93
Taxable Sales	6.5	1.5	2.2	-0.6	4.9	11.9

Table 4.8: Ratio and Growth Rate Projections Versus EFC Results

YEAR	RATIO OF SALES:INCOME	1992–1993 POPULATION	EFC
1992	$(1.1 \times 168.1 = 186.6)$	$(2.9 \times 168.1 = 216.8)$	167.0
1993	185.4	215.4	181.3
1994	201.2	233.9	198.5
1995	220.3	256.1	222.4
1996	246.8	286.9	243.2
1997	270.0	313.7	253.4
1998	281.3	326.6	255.0
1999	283.1	329.0	263.2

Observing the time-series data as trend lines, the first question the analyst should ask is whether the data indicate any major turning points that could throw off a linear projection. Since visually and from the discussion in the OS, a "turning point" seems to have begun in the 1992–1993 period, we could use the ratio of these two years. The average ratio of taxable sales to income for 1992 and 1993 is 8.4/7.4 or 8/7 = 1.1. Using this ratio, and the 2.9 percent growth rate from the 1992–1993 population growth figures, we see from Table 4.8 and Figure 4.7 that all figures are too high but lower than those obtained by using the population growth rate. As indicated in the Official Statement (1996, A-8), population figures may in fact reflect undercounted census by the U.S. Commerce Department in 1990. Compared with the EFC forecast, then, the ratio of sales to income for the 1992–1993 period serves as our best predictor function to this point. Naturally, this may or may not approximate the real-world behavior of sales tax receipts.

Let us now try a multiple-regression model using taxable sales and income as independent variables to see if their regression coefficients with the dependent variable, sales tax receipts, can improve on what we have obtained so far. We are justified in using a linear multiple-regression model because taxable sales, per capita income, and sales tax receipts seem to exhibit linear growth patterns (even though their rates vary). Multiple regression allows us to develop partial slopes of taxable sales to receipts and per capita income to receipts. This method allows us to estimate the effect of changes in per capita income on changes in sales tax receipts, taking into account (or holding constant) the effects of taxable sales. Conversely, income could be held constant and the effects of taxable sales on receipts examined. Using the multiple-regression equation, we can then select the highest regression coefficient as multiplier for forecasting purposes. The model can be described as:

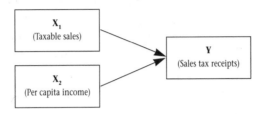

The predicted equation would be:

$$y = a + b_1 X_1 + b_2 X_2$$

Using real data for taxable sales (1970–1993) and for per capita income (1981–1993), we can now estimate the intercept (a) and regression coefficients for both independent variables. The data are presented in Table 4.9. Using these data and the multiple-regression formula provided, the analyst should perform the simple mathematics necessary to obtain the multiplier. Assuming that multicollinearity (intercorrelated independent variables) has been remedied, the variable explaining the greatest variation in sales tax receipts should be used as the multiplier. In this case, since per capita income explains 0.32 and taxable sales only .012, let us try 0.32 as the multiplier to see whether EFC estimates can be replicated (Table 4.9).

Using the regression equation (Nachmias 1979, 130–31), we obtain the following:

$$\Sigma X_1{}^* = \Sigma X_1{}^* - \frac{(\Sigma X_1)^2}{N} = 1,364.7 - \frac{1,862,406}{13} = 264,693.3$$

$$\Sigma X_2{}^* = \Sigma X_2{}^* - \frac{(\Sigma X_2)^2}{N} = 2,003.2 - \frac{4,012,810.2}{13} = 306,674.5$$

$$\Sigma X_1 X_2 = \Sigma X_1 X_2 - \frac{(\Sigma X_1)\,(\Sigma X_2)}{N} = 1,342.9 - \frac{(115.0)\,(137.9)}{13} = 123.0$$

$$\Sigma X_1 Y = \Sigma X_1 Y - \frac{(\Sigma X_1)\,(\Sigma Y)}{N} = 14,954.7 - \frac{(115.0)\,(1,968.8)}{13} = 2,461.6$$

$$\Sigma X_2 Y = \Sigma X_2 Y - \frac{\Sigma (X_2)\,(\Sigma Y)}{N} = 17,769.8 - \frac{(137.9)\,(1,968.8)}{13} = 3,114.6$$

$$b_1 = \frac{(\Sigma X_1 Y)(\Sigma X_2{}^*) - (\Sigma X_1 X_2)(\Sigma X_2 Y)}{(\Sigma X_1{}^*)(\Sigma X_2{}^*) - (\Sigma X_1 X_2)^2}$$

$$= \frac{(14,954.7)(2,003.2) - (1,342.9)(17,769.8)}{(1,364.7)(2,003.2) - (1,342.9)(1,342.9)} = \frac{609,414}{930,386} = 0.65$$

$$b_2 = \frac{(\Sigma X_1{}^*)(\Sigma X_2 Y) - (\Sigma X_1 X_2)(\Sigma X_1 Y)}{(\Sigma X_1{}^*)(\Sigma X_2{}^*) - (\Sigma X_1 X_2)^2}$$

$$= \frac{(1,364.7)(17,769.8) - (1,342.9)(14,954.7)}{(1,364.7)(2,003.2) - (1,342.9)(1,342.9)}$$

$$= \frac{(24,250,446) - (20,068,268)}{(2,733,494) - (1,800,964)} = \frac{4,182,178}{932,530} = 4.5$$

$$a = \frac{\Sigma Y - b_1 \Sigma X_1 - b_2 \Sigma X_2}{13} = \frac{1,968.8 - 74.8 - 620.6}{13} = 98.0$$

$$y = 98.0 + 0.65 \text{ (taxable sales)} + 4.5 \text{ (per capita income)}$$

$$y = 103.2$$

Table 4.9: Calculations For Multivariate Least-Squares Forecast

	Y	X^1	X^2	Y^2	$X_1{}^*$	$X_2{}^*$	$X_1 Y$	$X_2 Y$	$X_1 X_2$
1980	95.1	14.3	15.2	9,044.0	204.5	231.0	1,359.9	1,445.5	217.4
1981	99.8	10.7	12.9	9,960.0	114.5	166.4	1,067.9	1,287.4	138.0
1982	104.8	6.4	8.2	10,983.0	41.0	67.2	670.7	859.4	52.5
1983	112.0	13.3	11.7	12,544.0	176.9	136.7	1,489.6	1,310.4	155.6
1984	123.4	20.7	15.8	15,227.6	428.5	249.6	2,554.4	1,949.7	327.1
1985	134.9	10.1	12.3	18,198.0	102.0	151.3	1,362.5	1,659.3	124.2
1986	147.1	6.8	10.9	21,638.4	46.2	46.2	1,000.3	1,603.4	74.1
1987	148.6	6.3	8.9	22,081.2	39.7	79.2	936.2	1,322.5	56.1
1988	158.5	6.5	9.2	25,122.3	42.3	84.6	1,030.3	1,458.2	59.8
1989	162.5	1.5	6.2	26,406.3	2.3	38.4	243.8	1,007.5	9.3
1990	165.7	2.2	7.5	27,456.5	4.8	56.3	364.5	1,242.8	16.5
1991	168.1	-0.6	4.4	28,257.6	0.4	19.4	-100.9	67.2	-0.2
1992	167.0	4.9	7.6	27,889.0	24.0	57.8	818.3	1,269.2	37.2
1993	181.3	11.9	7.1	32,869.7	141.6	50.4	2,157.5	1,287.2	84.5
	1,968.8	115.0	137.9	287,677.6	1,364.7	2,003.2	14,954.7	17,769.8	1,342.9

Table 4.10: Multivariate and Proportionate Change Forecast Versus EFC Results ($000)

YEAR	MULTI-VARIATE	EFC	DIFFERENCE ($ MILLIONS)	PROPORTIONATE CHANGE	DIFFERENCE FROM EFC ($ MILLIONS)
1994	189.4	198.5	9.1	198.5	0
1995	199.9	222.4	22.5	222.4	0
1996	208.8	243.2	34.4	239.1	(4.1)
1997	218.1	253.4	35.3	257.0	21.7
1998	227.8	255.0	27.2	276.3	49.1
1999	238.1	263.2	25.1	297.1	33.9

Thus, we obtain: $y = 103.2 + 0.65X1 + 4.5X2$. Based on a comparable model used by Schroeder, Sjoquist, and Stephan (1986, 31), this means that for a $1.00 increase in per capita income, we can expect a 4.5 cent increase in sales tax receipts. Using 4.5 as our multiplier (.045 x added to the 1993 projection of $181.3 million by EFC), we forecast the following receipts. Using data obtained from the earlier proportionate change method, we can also compare them with those obtained generated by EFC (Table 4.10).

From the growing difference between multivariate and EFC numbers, it is evident that the equation is taking us in a linear path away from what EFC predicts as the future. Based on a comparison of the growth rate and both multiple-regression and proportionate change techniques, one could conclude that methodological elegance does not always purchase forecasting relevance. As indicated in Table 4.8, use of the proportionate change method gets us closer to the EFC estimates than use of the more sophisticated multiple-regression approach. More likely, one could conclude that we made mistaken assumptions about the behavior of key determinants (e.g., wrong "turning points" or further problems with utility and manufacturing sales contributions to the use tax) that led to major differences with EFC forecasts. Assuming that EFC is more accurate, we would need to try other turning points and different assumptions. This would likely improve the forecast accuracy of the multiple-regression technique. Note also in Appendix A of the chapter 4 case study that EFC revises its forecast upward to add in more inflation and added payouts from the state related to the 1996 Olympics in Atlanta. This points to professional flexibility and the need to constantly revise forecasts with better data. Unfortunately, it also increases the yearly difference between our multivariate forecasts and those of EFC.

Conclusion

Policymakers would like to control the consequences of public expenditures consistent with programmatic objectives. Techniques for forecasting alternative policy consequences can serve policy objectives by providing advance notice for redesign and reprogramming during policy implementation. But even with the best of past data, most techniques presume the future will look something like the past. So, even with the best sales tax receipts forecasts, MARTA policymakers cannot be certain that they can avoid the politically costly policy changes of raising fares or cutting back services to cover revenue shortfalls. Even more sophisticated econometric models can only describe such phenomena as the cyclical patterns of the economy. Since they cannot usually predict cyclical timing (Kilborn 1987), policymakers cannot know with precision how to pull the levers of government power to produce stabilization and growth by changes in public spending, taxation, transfer payments, and interest rates to develop the best stabilization and growth policies.

Hence, the quest continues for the genie of forecasting certainty. In this chapter, we have noted several basic techniques that can be applied to hard data to provide forecasts. At the most basic level, we can average time-series data to develop trends by such techniques as proportionate change. More sophisticated extrapolative and causal techniques employ bivariate or multivariate least-squares regression equations to try to fit the data. The equations are used to try to explain both variation and residual variation in target variables. Where the techniques do not seem to fit, as in our sales tax problem, we can employ a more basic averaging-ratio method with exponential smoothing or move to nonlinear regression.

Notes

1. For an excellent discussion of analysis of longitudinal data ("time-series"), see Susan Welsh and John Comer. *Quantitative Methods for Public Administration: Techniques and Applications,* 2d ed. (Chicago: Dorsey 1988), pp. 289–304.
2. Interview with Dr. John Blomquist in Jalal-Abad, Kyrgyz Republic, 1 November 1997, during work on TA No. 2688-KGZ Social Services Delivery and Finance Project, financed by the Asian Development Bank. Dr. Blomquist is now senior economist at Development Alternatives, Inc. (DAI), in Bethesda, Maryland.

References

Ammons, David N. (1991). *Administrative Analysis for Local Governments* (Athens: University of Georgia, Carl Vinson Institute of Government).

Blalock, Hubert M. (1972). *Social Statistics* (New York: McGraw-Hill).

Bolling, Ruben. (1997). "Tom and the Dancing Bug Presents: America's Consumption of Beef May Be Killing Cows," *Washington Post* (12 September).

Brinkley, Joel. (1986). "Drug Use Held Mostly Stable Or Lower," *New York Times* (10 October) 10.

Browning, Edgar K. and Jacqueline M. Browning. (1983). *Public Finance and the Price System,* 2d ed. (New York: Macmillan).

Chandler, Clay. (1997). "Hitting the Jackpot on Capitol Hill," *Washington Post* (3 May)

Cleary, Paul. (1997). "Red Face Over $5 Billion Slip-Up in Deficit Figures," *Sydney Morning Herald* (27 February).

Congressional Budget Office. (1997). *An Analysis of the President's Budgetary Proposals for the Fiscal Year 1998* (Washington, D.C.: Congressional Budget Office).

Coplin, William D. and Michael K. O'Leary. (1976). "Teaching Political Strategy Skills with 'The Prince,'" *Policy Analysis* 2, 1 (Winter), pp. 144–60.

Daniels, Lee A. (1986). "U.S. Oil Output Is Declining," *New York Times* (11 December).

Dunn, William N. (1994). *Public Policy Analysis: An Introduction,* 2d ed. (Englewood Cliffs, N.J.: Prentice Hall).

———. (1981). *Public Policy Analysis: An Introduction* (Englewood Cliffs, N.J.: Prentice Hall).

Economist. (1999a). "Social Security Reform" (13 March), pp. 41–43.

———. (1999b). "Are Stadiums Good For You?" (13 March), p. 39.

———. (1998). "Figures to Fret About" (11 July), p. 84.

———. (1997a). "Fujimori Against El Niño" (27 September), pp. 35–36.

———. (1997b). "France's Budget: Circle Squared" (27 September), p. 53.

———. (1997c). "Something Horrible Out There" (18 October), pp. 71–75.

Guess, George M. (1996). "Revenue Surveying and Forecasting," technical note no. 6 (Skopje: USAID Public Administration Program for Macedonia).

Guess, George M. and Paul G. Farnham. (1989). *Cases in Public Policy Analysis* (New York: Longman).

Hedderson, John. (1991). *SPSS/PC+ Made Simple* (Belmont, Calif.: Wadsworth Publishing Company).

Kerr, Peter. (1986). "Anatomy of an Issue: Drugs, The Evidence, The Reaction," *New York Times* (17 November) 1.

Kiester, Edwin, Jr. (1997). "Water Water Everywhere," *Smithsonian* 28, 5 (August), pp. 34–46.

Kilborn, Peter T. (1987). "The Business Cycle Rolls Over and Plays Dead," *New York Times* (11 January) 6F.

Klay, William Earle. (1983). "Revenue Forecasting: An Administrative Perspective," in Jack Rabin and Thomas D. Lynch (eds.) *Handbook on Public Budgeting and Financial Management* (New York: Marcel Dekker), pp. 287–317.

Lane, Earl. (1998). "Crisis Forecasting Offers New Ways to Predict Natural or Human Events," *Washington Post* (2 January).

Liner, Charles D. (1983). "Projecting Local Government Revenue," in Jack Rabin, W. Bartley Hildreth and Gerald J. Miller. *Budget Management, A Reader in Local Government Financial Management* (Athens: University of Georgia Press), pp. 83–92.

McMaster, James. (1991). *Urban Financial Management: A Training Manual* (Washington, D.C.: World Bank).

Metropolitan Atlanta Rapid Transit Authority. (1996). *Sales Tax Revenue Bonds, Second Indenture Series, Refunding Series, 1996A* (Atlanta: Metropolitan Atlanta Rapid Transit Authority).

Nachmias, David. (1979). *Public Policy Evaluation, Approaches and Methods* (New York: St. Martin's).

National Institutes of Drug Abuse. (1997). *Annual Trends in Cocaine-Related Episodes* (Washington, D.C.: National Institutes of Drug Abuse).

Nelson, Ray D. and Gary C. Cornia. (1997). "Monitoring Single-Source Revenue Funds Throughout the Budgeting Process," *Public Budgeting and Finance* 17, 2 (Summer), pp. 37–57.

New York Times. (1986). "Two Syracuse Teachers Rank Political Climate in 85 Nations" (7 December).

Rabin, Jack, W. Bartley Hildreth, and Gerald J. Miller. (1983). *Workbook* and *Data Sourcebook* (Athens: University of Georgia).

Rabin, Jack and Thomas D. Lynch (eds.) (1983). *Handbook on Public Budgeting and Financial Management* (New York: Marcel Dekker).

Ratajczak, Donald. (1996). *January 18, 1996 Report of Economic Forecasting Center* (Atlanta: Georgia State University).

Roughton, Bert. (1987). "MARTA Fare to Be $0.75 This Sunday," *Atlanta Constitution* (23 June).

Samuelson, Robert J. (1998). "The Way the World Works," *Washington Post* (7 January).

Schroeder, Larry D. (1984). "Multi-Year Forecasting in San Antonio," in Carol W. Lewis and A. Grayson Walker, *Casebook in Public Budgeting and Financial Management* (Englewood Cliffs, N.J.: Prentice Hall), pp. 268–300.

Schroeder, Larry D. and Roy Bahl. (1984). "The Role of Multi-Year Forecasting in the Annual Budgeting Process For Local Governments," *Public Budgeting and Finance* 4, 1 (Spring), pp. 3–14.

Schroeder, Larry D., David L. Sjoquist, and Paula E. Stephan. (1986). "Understanding Regression Analysis: An Introductory Guide," Sage Paper no. 57 (Beverly Hills: Sage).

Silk, Leonard. (1986). "A Season of Cassandras," *New York Times* (10 December) 32.

Simon, Julian L. (1978). *Basic Research Methods in Social Sciences, The Art of Empirical Investigation,* 2d ed. (New York: Random House).

Suplee, Curt. (1997). "Most Serious Youth Asthma Cases Linked to Roaches, Study Finds," *Washington Post* (8 May) A12.

Toulmin, Llewellyn M. and Glendal E. Wright. (1983). "Expenditure Forecasting," in Jack Rabin and Thomas Lynch (eds.), *Handbook on Public Budgeting and Financial Management* (New York: Marcel Dekker), pp. 208–87.

Welsh, Susan and John Comer. (1988). *Quantitative Methods for Public Administration: Techniques and Applications,* 2d ed. (Chicago: Dorsey).

Wildavsky, Aaron. (1984). *The Politics of the Budgetary Process,* 4th ed. (Boston: Little, Brown).

CHAPTER 5

Pricing and
Public Policy
The Case of Cigarette Taxes

In this chapter we combine the issues of problem definition and structuring discussed in chapter 2 with the empirical techniques covered in chapter 4 to analyze the role of pricing as a public policy tool. We are thus moving from the diagnostic phase of public policy analysis to the analytic phase. How prices are set in the private sector is often of concern to public decisionmakers and regulatory agencies. In addition, changing these prices through public-sector subsidies and taxation programs is a key element of many public policies. The goal of many public-sector programs is to modify the prices established in the private sector to influence individual behavior. Since economics is the primary discipline that focuses on analyzing the role of prices in the economy, this chapter will draw much more substantially on economic analysis than the previous chapters. The issues raised in this chapter will also serve as a background for the following two chapters, which discuss the economic program evaluation tools of cost-effectiveness analysis and cost-benefit analysis. These are two major analytic tools that are used to help make resource allocation decisions about funding different public-sector programs. The quantitative techniques used in all three of these chapters will draw upon the basic microeconomic analysis of market operation and its impact on the consumers and producers in the economy. However, the economic analysis will also be related to the political environment, for both of these are crucial elements of overall public policy analysis.

Smoking is generally considered to be a major public policy problem in the United States. Since 1964, reports of the surgeon general of the U.S. Public Health Service have repeatedly listed cigarette smoking as one of the country's most significant sources of death and disease. An estimated 47 million adults smoke cigarettes. Particular concern is focused on teenagers, since this group comprises the bulk of new smokers. Tobacco use is responsible for more than 430,000 deaths each year (U.S. Department of Health and Human Services 1999). Smoking is considered responsible for am estimated 30 percent of all cancer deaths, including 87 percent of lung cancer; 21 percent of deaths from coronary heart disease; 18 percent of stroke deaths; and 82 percent of deaths from chronic obstructive pulmonary disease (U.S. Department of Health and Human Services 1989). The economic burden of tobacco use is estimated at more than $50 billion in medical expenditures and another $50 billion in indirect costs (U.S. Department of Health and Human Services 1999). There has been ongoing litigation by both individuals and state governments to force the tobacco industry to pay compensation for smoking-related medical costs. During this litigation, thousands of formerly secret documents have revealed how tobacco companies suppressed research on the health hazards of smoking and sought to attract teenagers as "replacement" smokers (Meier 1998b).

There are a variety of public policies that can and have been used to limit smoking in the population, including moral suasion from the publicity surrounding the various surgeon generals' reports on smoking produced over the past twenty-five years; restrictions on cigarette advertising; policies limiting how cigarettes can be sold, such as restrictions on the use and location of vending machines; and cigarette taxation that changes the price, and therefore affects the consumption, of cigarettes. Public policy analysis focuses on which of these policies are most effective in reducing cigarette consumption, particularly in light of the costs of implementing the policies. All these policies can be described in economic terms as being designed to affect either the demand for or the supply of cigarettes and, thus, the amount consumed. However, only taxation operates by changing the price of cigarettes. The other policies operate by changing individuals' attitudes toward smoking, their knowledge about cigarettes, or the availability of the product. Thus, a comparison of the policies involves evaluating the role of prices versus other influences on human behavior. Economic analysis provides particular insights into the role of pricing and human behavior.

This chapter explores how the prices of goods and services affect individual behavior and how they can be useful tools for public policy. The case study focuses on cigarette taxes as a public policy to reduce the rate of smoking, particularly among teenagers and young adults. Antismoking advocates argue that preventing teenagers from starting to smoke may be the most effective means of controlling smoking overall, given that most smokers begin during their teenage years and given the addictive nature of the process. Thus, any public policy that prevents teenagers from starting to smoke may limit both current consumption of cigarettes and potential future consumption.

In this chapter we will analyze why cigarette taxes may be such a potent weapon in the fight against teenage smoking. We first explore the basic role of prices in a market economy and how they influence behavior through the forces of supply and demand. The means by which economists quantify the effect of prices—the price elasticity of demand—will then be described. Drawing on the statistical issues presented in chapter 4, there will be a discussion of the methods for empirically estimating price elasticities and for separating the influence of price from that of all other factors on cigarette consumption. We then present the case and summarize the issues that relate to these theoretical concepts. We also discuss the results of the major empirical studies that have estimated the response of teenagers and adults to changes in cigarette prices and taxes. The chapter ends with a discussion of how the technical information from economic analyses does or does not influence the policy process and how information from other methodological approaches may also be necessary for a complete evaluation of the policy questions.

Prices and Markets: The Role of Demand and Supply

Pricing is the key element in an economic system based on the market place. Prices are the factors that help determine the answers to the fundamental resource allocation questions that all economies face: What goods and services should be produced from the vast range of available inputs? How should these goods and services be produced if more than one method of production is feasible? How should the output of the economy be distributed among the individuals in the society? In a market economy those goods and services that are the most profitable, or where there is the largest difference between their price and the costs of production, tend to be produced. Yet when profits are earned in particular industries, other firms are attracted to produce the same or similar goods, thus causing prices to decrease. If more than one method of production is feasible for a particular good or service, firms in a market economy have an incentive to find the least-cost means of production. This strategy involves using larger quantities of inputs whose prices are lower. The prices received by the owners of the factors of production (e.g., labor, land, capital equipment) help determine the distribution of income among the individuals in a society and thus influence the ability of these persons to purchase market-produced goods and services. This is the essence of the pricing system in a market economy.

Public policies are often created to influence either the process by which market prices are established or the final prices themselves. For example, some prices, such as those for agricultural products or the wages paid for low-skill jobs, may be considered "too low." Thus, legislators have enacted both farm price support and minimum wage programs. When prices are thought to be "too high," various forms of price controls have been implemented, which would include rent controls passed by various city councils and the general controls temporarily enacted under the Nixon administration's Economic Stabilization Program in the early 1970s. Sometimes the market prices of particular goods and services are subsidized through the use of food stamps, housing vouchers, or the federal Medicare program. This government intervention into the pricing system is undertaken for reasons related to income distribution or equity issues. The policy concern is whether certain groups of people have the necessary resources to purchase particular goods and services.

Public policy influences prices through the regulation of business activity. Some of this regulation occurs because of concern over the acquisition of market or monopoly power by firms, thus allowing companies to charge prices that are substantially higher than the costs of production. The Antitrust Division of the U.S. Department of Justice analyzes the behavior of different firms and industries to determine whether the general public is being harmed by the pricing policies and other strategies of these firms. In the case of regulated electric or gas utilities, a government commission or agency explicitly determines how prices are set in relation to costs. Some of this regulation relates to problems of income distribution. Other utility-price-setting policies focus on the efficient use of gas or electricity where there is a peak-load problem. In these cases, the demand for and the cost of producing gas or electricity varies substantially by time of day or season of the year. Efficient use of these resources requires the use of higher prices during the peak-load periods. Problems with the utility regulatory process, however, have led to a much greater use of competitive markets in the past decade (Viscusi, Vernon, and Harrington 1995).

Other regulation arises because businesses may not always consider the full costs of production when determining prices. Pollution occurs when companies use the air or water for waste disposal without recognizing that they may be imposing costs on other groups of individuals. The prices of these companies' products may not reflect these environmental costs. Environmental policy is concerned with correcting this problem either through taxation, regulation, or, more recently, the use of markets for trading allowances or the rights to pollute (Barthold 1994; Hyman 1996).

Finally, certain services (i.e., public goods) such as national defense are provided by government through a political process because they will not be provided in the marketplace. Markets will fail to provide these goods because people cannot be excluded from consuming them once they are provided: therefore, a market price cannot be charged for these goods. In these cases, the government must explicitly decide what the services are worth to the citizens of the country and what tax price to cover the costs of production should be imposed. Any form of taxation will cause a further burden on consumers and influence the prices of goods and services established in the private marketplace (Hyman 1996).

In a competitive marketplace with many buyers and sellers, prices are established through the forces of demand and supply. We will briefly review these basic economic concepts, and then focus in more detail on demand since that is the concept most relevant for analyzing the public policy issues in this case. Demand incorporates variables affecting the behavior of the consumers of a good or service, while supply reflects producer behavior. This analysis uses the fundamental economic approach of examining the relationship between two variables while holding everything else constant.

Although demand and supply are used in everyday language, these concepts have very precise meanings in economics. Demand is a functional relationship between the price of a good and the quantity demanded of the good, *all else held constant*. The Latin phrase *ceteris paribus* is often used in place of the "all else held constant." A demand function shows, either symbolically or mathematically, all the variables that influence the demand for a particular product. It can be represented as follows:

(1) Q_{XD} = f (P_X, T, I, P_Y, P_Z, ...) where
Q_{XD} = quantity demanded of good X.
P_X = price of good X.
T   = variables representing an individual's tastes and preferences.
I   = income.
P_Y, P_Z = prices of goods Y and Z, which are related in consumption to good X.

Equation 1 is read: the quantity demanded of good X is a function of the variables inside the parentheses. Dots are placed after the last variable to signify that many other variables may also influence the demand for a specific product. These may include variables under the control of a producer, such as the size of the advertising budget, or variables not under anyone's control, such as the weather. Every consumer has a demand function for a particular product. We can also define a market demand function that shows the quantity demanded by all consumers in the market at any given price.

Equation 1 shows the typical variables included in a demand function. Socioeconomic variables such as age, sex, race, and level of education are often used to represent an individual's tastes and preferences for a particular good. An individual's income also affects demand because the concept of demand incorporates both an individual's willingness and ability to pay for the good. If the demand for a good varies directly with income, that good is called a *normal* good. If the demand varies inversely with income, the good is termed an *inferior* good. There are two major categories of other goods whose prices influence the demand for the given good: *substitute* and *complementary* goods. If the price of a substitute good increases, the demand for the given good will increase. If the price of a complementary good increases, the demand for the given good will decrease.

Demand is a functional relationship between alternative prices and the quantities demanded at those prices. This is most easily seen when graphically drawing a demand curve for a particular product, as in Figure 5.1.

Demand curves are generally downward sloping, showing an *inverse* relationship between the price of a good and the quantity demanded at that price, *ceteris paribus*. Thus, when the price falls from P_1 to P_2 the quantity demanded is expected to increase from Q_1 to Q_2, if nothing else changes. Likewise, an increase in the price of the good results in a decrease in quantity demanded. This movement between points A and B along the given demand curve in Figure 5.1 is called a *change in quantity demanded*. It results from a change in the price of the good, all else held constant. It is also possible for the entire demand curve to shift, which results when the values of one or more of the other variables in equation 1 change. For example, if consumers' incomes increase, the demand curve for the good generally shifts outward or to the right, assuming that individuals purchase more of the good if their incomes increase. This shifting of the entire demand curve is a *change in demand*. It occurs when one or more of the variables held constant in defining a given demand curve changes.

The demand curve in Figure 5.1 has been drawn as a straight line, representing a linear demand function. This is used both as a simplification and because it is often believed that this form of a demand function best represents individuals' behavior. Not all demand functions are linear. The implications of the particular form of demand function will be discussed in greater detail below when the *price elasticity of demand,* an important concept for analyzing the issues in this chapter's case study, is presented.

Figure 5.1: The Demand Curve for a Product

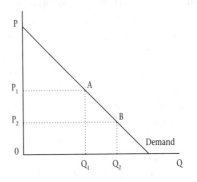

A supply function for a product is defined in a similar manner. Supply is the relationship between the price of a good and the quantity supplied, all else held constant. A supply function is shown as follows:

(2) Q_{XS} = f (P_X, TX, P_I, P_A, P_B, . . .) where
    Q_{XS} = quantity supplied of good X.
    P_X = price of good X.
    TX = technology.
    P_I = prices of the inputs of production.
    P_A, P_B = prices of goods, A and B, which are related in production to good X.

As with the demand function, we can distinguish between the supply function for an individual producer or a supply function for all producers in a given market.

Equation 2 shows the variables typically included in a supply function. The state of technology is included because it determines how the good is actually produced and affects the costs of production. Input prices are the prices of all of the factors of production—labor, capital, land, and raw materials—used to produce the given product. These input prices will affect the costs of production and, therefore, the prices at which producers are willing to supply different amounts of output. The prices of other goods related in production are also included in a supply function. Supply curves generally slope upward, showing a positive relationship between the price of the product and the quantity producers are willing to supply. A higher price typically gives producers an incentive to increase the quantity supplied.

In a competitive market, it is the interaction of demand and supply that determines the *equilibrium price,* the price that will actually exist in the market or toward which the market is moving. Figure 5.2 shows the equilibrium price for good X.

The equilibrium price is the price at which the quantity demanded of good X by consumers just equals the quantity producers are willing to supply. At any other price, there will be an imbalance between quantity

Figure 5.2: Demand, Supply, and Equilibrium

demanded and supplied. Forces will be set in motion to push the price back toward equilibrium.

Reactions of both consumers and producers to changes in prices and the other variables in the demand and supply functions cause changes in the equilibrium quantities of different goods. Thus, the quantity and price of cigarettes can be influenced by changes on either the demand or the supply side of the market. If the public policy goal is to reduce cigarette smoking among teenagers, the relevant policy questions are these: Will supply- or demand-side variables have the greatest impact on cigarette consumption? What is the role of cigarette price versus the other variables in the demand and supply functions in influencing cigarette consumption? To answer these questions, we need to develop a quantitative measure, *elasticity*, to measure the responsiveness of cigarette consumption to changes in prices and the other variables, and we need to determine how to disentangle the effects of all the variables influencing the consumption of cigarettes.

Demand Elasticities

An elasticity quantitatively measures the responsiveness of the change in quantity demanded of a particular product to a change in one of the variables included in the demand function for that product. Thus, an elasticity can be calculated with regard to product price, consumer income, the prices of other goods and services, advertising budgets, education levels, or changes in the weather, depending on which of these variables are in the demand function. The important point is that an elasticity measures this responsiveness in terms of percentage changes in both variables. Thus, an elasticity is the ratio of two percentage changes: the percentage change in quantity demanded relative to the percentage change in the other variable. Percentage changes are used so that comparisons can be made among elasticities for different variables and products. The elasticity that is most analyzed in economics and which is most important for this case is the *price elasticity* of demand. The price elasticity is defined as the percentage change in the quantity demanded of a given good, X, relative to a percentage change in its price and is shown as follows:

(3) $e_p = (\% \Delta Q_X) / (\% \Delta P_X)$
$e_p = (\Delta Q_X / Q_X) / (\Delta P_X / P_X) = (\Delta Q_X / \Delta P_X)(P_X / Q_X)$ where
e_p = price elasticity of demand.
Δ = the absolute change in the variable: $(Q_2 - Q_1)$ or $(P_2 - P_1)$.
Q_X = the quantity demanded of good X.
P_X = the price of good X.

A percentage change in a variable is the ratio of the absolute change to a base value of the variable. The price elasticity of demand is illustrated as the movement from point A to point B in Figure 5.1.

Economists and policy analysts are interested in the size of various price elasticities to determine how responsive the quantity demanded is to a change in the price of a product, such as cigarettes. Since the calculated value of *all* price elasticities for downward-sloping demand curves will be negative (given the inverse relationship between price and quantity demanded), it is customary to drop the negative sign and examine the absolute value ($|e_p|$) of the number. This leads to the definitions shown in Table 5.1.

As shown in Table 5.1, demand is elastic if the number is greater than 1 in absolute value and inelastic if the number is less than 1. Elastic demand implies a larger consumer responsiveness to changes in prices than does inelastic demand. The fourth column of Table 5.1 shows the relationship between price elasticity, changes in prices, and total revenue (which is defined as price times quantity). Total revenue to a producer also equals the total expenditure on the good by consumers. If demand is elastic, higher prices result in lower total revenue, while lower prices result in higher total revenue. This results from the fact that the percentage change in quantity is greater than the percentage change in price. If the price increases, enough fewer units are sold at the higher price so that total revenue actually decreases. The opposite holds for inelastic demand: in this case, if the price increases, the total revenue increases also because the percentage change in quantity is less than the percentage change in price. If the price increases, enough units are still sold at the higher price to cause total revenue to

Table 5.1: Values of Price Elasticity of Demand

VALUE OF ELASTICITY	ELASTICITY DEFINITION	RELATIONSHIP AMONG VARIABLES	IMPACT ON TOTAL REVENUE
$|e_p| > 1$	Elastic demand	$\% \Delta Q_X > \% \Delta P_X$	Price increase results in lower total revenue. Price decrease results in higher total revenue.
$|e_p| < 1$	Inelastic demand	$\% \Delta Q_X < \% \Delta P_X$	Price increase results in higher total revenue. Price decrease results in lower total revenue.
$|e_p| = 1$	Unit elastic or unitary elasticity	$\% \Delta Q_X = \% \Delta P_X$	Price increase or decrease has no impact on total revenue.

increase. If demand is unit elastic, changes in price have no impact on total revenue because the percentage change in price is exactly equal to the percentage change in quantity.

The price elasticity of demand is an extremely important concept for producers, since it tells producers what will happen to revenues if the price of the product is changed. It can also help firms develop a pricing strategy that will maximize their profits. For example, the price elasticity of demand for airline travel for pleasure travelers is around –1.9, while that for business travelers is around –0.8 (Morrison 1998). The airlines typically charge business travelers much higher fares because they know that these travelers are not very price sensitive. The number of trips the business travelers take will not decrease substantially if fares increase. The price elasticity of demand has been estimated to be less than 1 in absolute value (inelastic) for many local public services such as education, police and fire, and parks and recreation (Fisher 1988). User charges for these services could be a valuable source of revenue to a local government because citizens are not very sensitive to changes in prices. Price elasticity is also a key concept for this chapter's case because estimates of the price elasticity of demand for cigarettes will tell a policy analyst how sensitive individuals are to changes in cigarette prices and whether elasticities differ between teenagers and adults. Price elasticity estimates can also be used to calculate the tax revenue flowing to the government from increased cigarette taxes.

Although price elasticities are of great importance, economists also want to know the size of the other elasticities in the demand function for a given product. Two other commonly used elasticities are the *income elasticity* and the *cross elasticity* of demand. These are shown in Table 5.2.

The income elasticity of demand shows how consumers change the quantity demanded of a particular product in response to changes in income, all else held constant. If an increase in income results in an increase in the quantity demanded or vice versa (a positive income elasticity of demand), the good is called a *normal good*. If an increase in income results in a decrease in quantity demanded or vice versa (a negative income elasticity), the good is termed an *inferior good*. Thus, the *sign* of the income elasticity of demand is important as well as the *size* of the elasticity, which measures the responsiveness of the demand to income changes. The cross elasticity of demand measures how the demand for one good, X, varies with changes in the price of another good, Y. Two goods with a positive cross elasticity of demand are said to be *substitute goods*. An increase in the price of good Y will cause consumers to demand more of good X because they are substituting good X for good Y. If two goods have a negative cross elasticity

Table 5.2: Other Demand Elasticities

ELASTICITY NAME	ELASTICITY DEFINITION	ELASTICITY VALUE	IMPACT ON DEMAND
Income elasticity: e_I	$(\% \Delta Q_X) / (\% \Delta I)$	$e_I > 0$: Normal good	Increase in income results in increase in quantity demanded and vice versa.
		$e_I < 0$: Inferior good	Increase in income results in decrease in quantity demanded and vice versa.
Cross elasticity: e_C	$(\% \Delta Q_X) / (\% \Delta P_Y)$	$e_C > 0$	Increase in the price of good Y results in increase in the quantity demanded of good X: substitute goods.
		$e_C < 0$	Increase in the price of good Y results in decrease in the quantity demanded of good X: complementary goods.

of demand, they are called *complementary goods.* An increase in the price of good Y will result in a decrease in the quantity demanded of good X if the two goods are used together or are complements.

All the discussion in this section of the chapter is conceptual. The important point for policy analysis is determining the actual signs and sizes of the relevant elasticities for different variables in a demand function. This is necessary for analyzing the validity of taxes on cigarettes compared with other policies for reducing cigarette consumption. Before discussing the case, we will briefly explain how economists and policy analysts empirically estimate demand functions and the various elasticities of demand for different products. This will help us evaluate the empirical studies of the factors influencing cigarette consumption by teenagers and adults.

Estimating Demand Functions

In chapter 4 we examined the use of various statistical and econometric techniques to focus on the issue of forecasting the future values of policy variables such as sales tax receipts for Atlanta's MARTA transportation system. Many of these same techniques are appropriate for examining the factors that affect cigarette consumption by teenagers and whether these factors differ between teenagers and adults. The analysis here falls under the heading of causal forecasting in chapter 4 because the empirical analysis is based on a deductive model of behavior (i.e., the economic theory of demand). This analysis differs from the use of correlation and regression analysis simply to explore relationships among variables, which was also discussed in chapter 4. The goal of this analysis is to estimate the magnitude of the effect (the elasticity) of each policy-relevant variable on cigarette consumption while holding constant the effects of all other relevant variables. In the physical sciences, many of these types of relationships can be tested experimentally in the laboratory. However, an experimental approach is not possible for most of the policy questions addressed in this book. Experiments in the social and policy sciences are very expensive, time consuming, and complex to perform. Although a few experimental approaches have been undertaken to examine such questions as the impact of welfare payments on individuals' willingness to work and the impact of different types of health insurance plans on individuals' consumption of medical and health care services, these approaches are the exception in the social sciences. Most research relies on econometric techniques, such as multiple-regression analysis, to examine the relationship between two variables while statistically holding constant the effect of all other variables.

Equation 1 above gave a generalized form of a demand function for a particular good. To obtain information useful for the policy question of cigarette taxes, we must estimate a specific demand function for cigarettes. This requires specifying the form of the demand function to be estimated, the variables to be included in the estimation process, and the data to be used in the analysis.

Economists typically estimate two major forms of demand functions: the linear function and the log-linear function. These functions are used because they are believed to appropriately model individuals' behavior and they permit a relatively easy calculation of the relevant elasticities.

A simple linear demand function is shown in equation 4:

(4) Q_X $= a + bP_X + cI + dP_R + \varepsilon$ where
Q_X = quantity demanded of good X.
P_X = price of good X.
I = consumer income.
P_R = price of a related good (substitute or complement).
a = constant term.
b, c, d = estimated coefficients.
ε = an error term.

The economist or policy analyst collects data on the variables to be included in the demand function. In this simple case, the economist or analyst would need data on the price of good X, the quantity of good X demanded, consumer income, and the price of a good related in consumption to good X. These data could represent either the behavior of individuals across time (time-series) or the differences among individuals at a point in time (cross-section). There needs to be a large enough sample of observations and sufficient variation among the observations to permit estimation of the desired relationships. The economist then uses a multiple-regression analysis program in one of the standard statistical software packages to estimate the coefficients, b, c, and d, which best fit the sample data. Details of this estimation process were given in chapter 4.

In the linear model, these coefficients represent the change in the quantity demanded of good X resulting from a one-unit change in the independent variable (price of good X, consumer income, or price of the related good), *ceteris paribus*. Multiple-regression analysis coefficients show the effect of each independent variable while statistically holding constant the effects of the other variables hypothesized to affect the quantity demanded of good X. Thus, in equation 4, the estimated coefficient, $b = (\Delta Q_X / \Delta P_X)$, holding constant the effects of consumer income and the price of good R. Referring back to equation 3, this term is part of what is needed to calculate the price elasticity of demand. The coefficient, b, can then be multiplied by a specific value of (P_X / Q_X) to determine the price elasticity at a specific point on the demand curve. The other estimated coefficients, c and d, can be used to calculate the income and cross-elasticity of demand in a similar manner.

The linear demand function (4) implies both that there is some maximum price that drives consumers' quantity demanded of the product back to zero and that there is some maximum quantity that people demand at a zero price. The price elasticity of demand also changes at different prices along a linear demand curve, since $(\Delta Q_X / \Delta P_X)$ is constant, but (P_X / Q_X) varies along the curve. These outcomes may not always adequately represent the behavior of different groups of individuals.

It is often hypothesized that a nonlinear demand function of the following form better represents individuals' behavior:

(5) $Q_X = (a) (P_X^b) (I^c) (P_R^d)\varepsilon$

where the variables are defined as above. This function is often called a log-linear demand function because it can be transformed into a linear function by taking the logarithms of all the variables in the equation. This function is also called a constant-elasticity demand function. It can be shown that the elasticities are constant for all values of the input variables and are represented by the exponents b, c, and d, in equation 5. Thus, the price, income, and cross-elasticities can be directly read from the statistical results if this type of function is used in the estimation process. No further calculation is needed to determine the elasticities.

Demand functions estimated for actual products are obviously much more complex than the simple examples presented in equations 4 and 5. However, the estimation process and the choice of functional form is similar to what has been presented here. The policy analyst must decide which variables to include in the analysis. Various types of statistical problems can arise if relevant variables are excluded from the analysis or if irrelevant variables are included. The choice of variables is derived from economic theory, real-world experience, the policy problem under consideration, and common sense. Variable choice can also be influenced by data availability; in many cases, analysts would like to include certain variables, but a consistent set of observations for all individuals included in the analysis may not be available. Analysts may also have to use other variables as proxies for the variables of greatest interest.

Every multiple-regression analysis study is also influenced by the sample of data, either time-series or cross-sectional, which is used. The policy analyst wants to estimate behavioral relationships that can be generalized beyond the sample of observations included in the analysis. Yet large-scale data collection can be very expensive and time consuming. Thus, the analyst has to be concerned that the estimated relationships may only hold for the sample of data analyzed, and not the larger population. The analyst engages in hypothesis testing to determine how much confidence can be placed in the results of a particular analysis and whether these results can be generalized to a larger population. An analyst usually focuses on whether an estimated coefficient from the regression analysis is statistically significant, that is, whether it is statistically different from zero. If it is, then the independent variable actually has an influence on the dependent variable in the larger population. The statistical results are then believed to be not simply a function of the data used in the given analysis. Standard tests for statistical significance can be found in any econometrics textbook (Pindyck and Rubinfeld 1998). These issues were also discussed previously in chapter 4.

Data for demand estimation are often drawn from large-scale surveys undertaken by the U.S. federal government, universities, or nonprofit groups. Not every relevant variable for a given analysis may be included in a single data source, so the results of various surveys may need to be combined. Some data sources may have better information on economic variables, while others may have more data on personal characteristics of the individuals included in the analysis.

Although the details of demand estimation are very technical and can be found in standard sources, the policy analyst is often more concerned with interpreting the results of these analyses than with performing them. Variations in the functional form of the estimating equations, the variables included, and the data sets employed can all influence and cause differences in the results of various statistical analyses of the same problem. Thus, researchers, policymakers, and advocates can criticize and attack the results of any empirical study. These issues are discussed in the chapter 5 case study of cigarette demand and the estimates of the impact of taxes on that demand. The study is taken from a *New York Times* article by David Cay Johnston (1997).

CHAPTER 5 CASE STUDY

Anti-Tobacco Groups Push For Higher Cigarette Taxes

David Cay Johnston

In a drive to reverse a recent surge in teen-age smoking, anti-tobacco forces are pushing for a combination of state and Federal tax increases that could raise the cost of a pack of cigarettes by more than $1.

Buoyed by public revulsion at disclosures that tobacco companies have been aiming at teen-agers for years with sophisticated advertising and marketing techniques, advocates are lobbying for tax increases in 19 states and hope to have campaigns going in all 50 states by next year.

Also, Congress is considering a bill introduced last month by Senators Orrin G. Hatch, Republican of Utah, and Edward M. Kennedy, Democrat of Massachusetts, to nearly triple the Federal excise tax on cigarettes, to 67 cents a pack from 24 cents.

With polls showing that a vast majority of Americans—and even most smokers—support raising taxes to discourage adolescents from lighting up, politicians from both parties are rushing to attach their names to that rarity, a tax rise that seems not only safe, but positively virtuous.

"Raising tobacco taxes is our No. 1 strategy to damage the tobacco industry," said John D. Giglio, manager of tobacco-control advocacy for the American Cancer Society. "The tobacco industry has found ways around everything else we have done to reduce smoking by teen-agers, but they can't repeal the laws of economics."

The anti-tobacco lobby's goal is to raise state cigarette taxes to a uniform $2 a pack nationwide in the next several years, from the current range of 2.5 cents in Virginia to 81.5 cents in Washington State.

If the Federal Government increases its tax to 67 cents as well, the average cost of a pack of cigarettes would rise to $4.23, from $1.80, as the result of the tax increases alone. That, opponents of smoking believe, would be enough to drive millions of smokers, adults and teen-agers alike, to kick the habit and dissuade hundreds of thousands of young people from taking it up.

Cigarette Taxes Across the Nation

Anti-smoking activists are lobbying for higher state cigarette excise taxes to discourage teen-age smoking, hoping to raise the average state tax to $2 a pack from 34 cents in the next few years. Economists say that for every 10 percent rise in the overall price of cigarettes, 12 percent fewer teen-agers will start smoking.

Current Excise Tax on Cigarettes (Per Pack)

Proposed Increases State by State Present Ranking	State	Average Price Per Pack*	1996 Excise Tax	Increase Being Considered
42	Alabama	$1.64	16.5 cents	18.0 cents
28	Alaska	2.14	29.0	100.0
18	California	2.00	37.0	20.0
9	Connecticut	2.08	50.0	25.0
25	Florida	1.83	33.9	10.0
5	Hawaii	2.43	60.0	50.0
43	Indiana	1.56	15.5	49.5
18	Maine	1.90	37.0	100.0
20	Maryland	1.91	36.0	100.0
3	Michigan	2.34	75.0	Unspecified
38	Mississippi	1.69	18.0	75.0
38	Montana	1.65	18.0	18.0
23	Nebraska	1.85	34.0	10.0
30	New Hampshire	1.77	25.0	25.0
35	New Mexico	1.76	21.0	10.0
7	New York	2.23	56.0	50.0
46	Wyoming	1.64	12.0	25.0
Already Passed This Year				
8	Utah	1.86	26.5	25.0
23	Arkansas	1.81	31.5	2.5

*As of the end of 1996. Generics included in price calculation. In addition to excise tax, figure includes state sales tax and federal cigarette tax of 24 cents per pack.
Sources: Tobacco Institute; American Cancer Society.

Utah and Arkansas have already approved small cigarette-tax increases this year, and increases of as much as $1 a pack are being debated in Maryland, Alaska and Maine. Anti-smoking forces say chances are good for passage in those states and in Alabama, Hawaii, New Hampshire and perhaps New Jersey, Wisconsin and Wyoming as well. South Dakota, Virginia and Wyoming have rejected cigarette tax increases this year, but the Wyoming measure is expected to be revived.

While the number of states considering higher taxes is lower than in some previous years, both advocates and opponents of the measures say the energy and money behind the current effort make it more formidable than ever.

"Any legislator can introduce a bill," said Walker Merryman, a vice president of the Tobacco Institute, the industry trade association. "What is different is the seriousness of these efforts. Our industry is the subject of a coordinated, energetic campaign to raise cigarette taxes. All we can do is redouble our efforts."

The anti-tobacco forces say the campaign has strong grass-roots support. State Representative Con Bunde, a Republican who is sponsoring Alaska's bill, agrees. Three years ago, he would have got nowhere if he had pushed such a measure, he said.

"But now the debate is not about if we will raise the tax, but whether it will be a dollar a pack or $1.29," Mr. Bunde said.

Mr. Bunde, a bush pilot, said he thought the same forces that shaped the debate in his state were at work across the country. "What changed is that Republicans went home for the election last fall and found that while generally speaking no one likes more taxes, tobacco taxes are an exception," he said.

Opponents of smoking say they turned to the cause of higher cigarette taxes after the industry blunted efforts to limit cigarette vending machines, restrict where people can smoke and, in California and Massachusetts, broadcast government-financed anti-smoking messages intended for teen-agers. By next year, they say, they hope to have campaigns under way in every state. They expect support for their cause to grow as the result of the Liggett Group's break with the industry last month. Liggett, the maker of Chesterfields and L & M's, acknowledged that nicotine was addictive and that the industry had long picked young people as targets.

The movement to make cigarettes more expensive comes as many states, flush with budget surpluses, are considering cuts in income or sales taxes or one-time refunds. But even champions of lower taxes like the looks of this increase. In Maryland, Gov. Parris N. Glendening, a Democrat, is backing a bill to double cigarette taxes in tandem with a bill to cut state income taxes by 10 percent. Last week, Maryland legislators rejected the cigarette tax increase, but the bill could be revived this week.

"The issue the Governor is raising is, What can we do to prevent kids from starting to smoke and to get those who have started to stop?" said Ray Feldmann, a spokesman for Governor Glendening.

The two main groups behind the current drive are the Robert Wood Johnson Foundation in Princeton, N.J., which has committed $100 million to anti-smoking efforts, and the American Cancer Society, which has committed $10 million. The money is being used to hire organizers, distribute voter education materials, hold conferences and take surveys. The two organizations are also the main financial backers of the Campaign for Tobacco-Free Kids, a national tobacco-control advocate.

"Legislators read polls," said Dr. Steven Schroeder, the foundation's president, "and the polls tell them that this is probably the only tax that has widespread appeal. People know it is a deterrent and that the longer you can delay kids from starting smoking, the less likely they are to become smokers."

That is a truism that the tobacco industry has long understood—and worried about. A memo inside the Philip Morris Companies from 1981 said the company should "take seriously" a statement by the National Bureau of Economic Research in Cambridge, Mass., that higher Federal excise taxes could be used to reduce smoking by young people.

"It is clear that price has a pronounced effect on the smoking prevalence of teenagers," the memorandum said, adding that the bureau's estimate that a 10 percent increase in cigarette prices would lead to a 12 percent decline in the number of teen-agers taking up smoking was "of greatest significance to the company."

Asked about the memorandum, a Philip Morris spokeswoman, Mary Carnovale, said, "We don't want kids to smoke and we want stricter enforcement of state laws, restrictions on vending machines, stopping cigarettes through the mail, stopping sampling, things of that nature."

An informal survey of teen-age smokers in New Jersey, however, suggests it will not be easy to get them to stop. At the Monmouth Mall in Eatontown, Wanda Morales, 18, of Long Branch, said a 50-cent or $1 increase would be enough to make her discard her pack-a-week habit because "I want to quit anyway." But hardened puffers said they would be more resistant. Thirteen-year-old Karl Becker of Atlantic Highlands, who started smoking at the age of 11 when a friend offered him a ciga-rette, conceded that $5 a pack "would make me rather upset." But, he added, an extra dollar or two would not bother him.

And in Union City, teen-agers taking lunchtime drags at a bodega two blocks from their high school said nothing could induce them to quit.

"It kills all the stress, you know?" said Robert Diaz, a 17-year-old sophomore. "It makes me feel good."

One of his friends, Mike Perez, 14, pulled a package of Djarum cigarettes out of his pocket.

"These cost $4 a pack already, but that's what I like," he said. "Those companies, you know, they make it all look so nice—bright colors, lots of kids smiling. I just can't let my grandma find out I smoke."

In Albany, bills that would raise cigarette taxes from a nickel to a quarter per pack, with the money going to finance health care for children of the working poor, have been introduced by Democrats but are not moving toward passage.

Smoking by teen-agers had been declining for years, but that trend has reversed in the 1990's. According to annual surveys by the University of Michigan, the portion of high school seniors who indulge went up to 34 percent last year, from less than 28 percent in 1992.

Part of that increase, Mr. Giglio of the American Cancer Society said, reflects an upward swing in drug and alcohol use, but part of it results from steep price reduc-tions on Marlboros and other heavily advertised cigarettes in 1994. The median price of a pack of cigarettes, including taxes, has fallen since 1993, a Tobacco Institute report shows, to $1.80 last year from $1.84 in 1993. Adjusted for inflation, the decline would be even greater.

Even William F. Shughart, who has served as an expert witness for the cigarette industry, said that raising cigarette taxes would reduce teen-age smoking. "They are more price-sensitive than adults," said Mr. Shughart, a senior fellow with the Inde-pendent Institute, a libertarian research center in Oakland, Calif., and the Self Profes-sor of Economics at the University of Mississippi. He added, though, that higher tax-es could not be justified because the costs to society of smoking were more than covered by existing cigarette taxes.

Mr. Merryman of the Tobacco Institute complained about the anti-tobacco lob-by's embrace of popular programs to spend the extra tax money on, like mandatory kindergarten in New Hampshire.

"Who is going to say they are against kindergarten for kids?" he asked.

But Eric Gally, an organizer with the Campaign for Tobacco-Free Kids, said public awareness that cigarette companies had sought to attract children was "beginning to erode the enormous clout that the tobacco industry has in state legislatures, and it is no secret how they have gained that clout—through decades of contributions, by hiring the best lobbyists, by wining and dining legislators, sponsoring golf outings, giving tickets to sporting events."

Most teen-agers do not smoke, and some are vocal in their distaste for tobacco. Joe Lewis, 17, a senior at Wootton High School in Rockville, Md., and a member of a local group, Students Opposed to Smoking, says bumping up taxes by a nickel or a dime would have little effect. He advocates the full shock treatment.

"If cigarette prices went up by a dollar, a lot of kids would still try cigarettes once, like I did," he said. "But the younger ones, the seventh and eighth graders, couldn't afford it and wouldn't become addicted."

Raising cigarette taxes to increase the price of cigarettes and thus affect consumption appears to be the method of choice for those individuals and groups, such as the American Cancer Society, who are trying to reduce cigarette smoking, particularly among teenagers. Even the tobacco industry has acknowledged the importance of price on cigarette consumption. The case study states that antitobacco groups are pushing for a combination of federal and state tax increases, which could increase the price of a pack of cigarettes by more than $1. In March 1997, Senators Orrin G. Hatch (R-Utah) and Edward M. Kennedy (D-Mass) introduced a bill to nearly triple the federal excise tax on cigarettes from $.24 a pack to $.67. These combined efforts could raise the price of a pack of cigarettes from $1.80 (at the time of writing) to $4.23. It is believed by supporters of such efforts that such tax increases will persuade millions of individuals to stop smoking and deter hundreds of thousands of teenagers from beginning to smoke.

Both the pro- and antitobacco forces believe that these tax increases have strong grass-roots support, and that the question is not if there will be a tax increase, but when it will happen. The Robert Wood Johnson Foundation and the American Cancer Society are both making substantial monetary contributions to fund current antismoking efforts. The case study notes that the tobacco industry has hindered or blocked such antismoking strategies as limiting cigarette vending machines, restricting where people can smoke, and broadcasting antismoking messages specifically aimed at young people. Thus attention has turned to the use of taxes and prices to influence human behavior. Many antismoking advocates also suggest that any increased tax revenues be spent on popular programs (e.g., in New Hampshire, for mandatory kindergarten). Thus the appeal of using the taxing mechanism to influence behavior is increased.

The case study also presents several anecdotes about the expected effect of cigarette price increases on teenage behavior and how the tobacco industry influences demand for its products. Some teenagers surveyed said that nothing would make them quit smoking, arguing that smoking "kills the stress" and "makes [them] feel good." A thirteen-year-old who started smoking at the age of eleven, conceded that a tax increase "would make [him] rather upset," but would not "bother" him. Others noted the role of the tobacco industry in influencing demand through advertising and the positive images created by strategic marketing. One teenager stated that the tobacco companies "make it all look so nice—bright colors, lots of kids smiling." Teenagers in the case who support the antismoking campaign argued that large price increases of $1 or more would be needed to change the behavior of their contemporaries. They note that younger children in the seventh and eighth grades would not be able to afford these price increases and would not become addicted. These are anecdotal descriptions of the technical concept of price elasticity of demand.

All these stories illustrate the fundamental economic issues involved with this case:

- How prices influence individual behavior
- What the quantitative effect of a given price increase is on the consumption of cigarettes (i.e., price elasticity of demand)
- How important price is versus other factors in influencing cigarette consumption
- What the implications are of the importance of price for the design and implementation of different public policies to reduce cigarette smoking
- Why a policy based on taxation and pricing may be favored by antismoking advocates for political reasons (i.e., the policy's being less susceptible to manipulation by the tobacco industry than other types of policies)

We will now discuss the empirical studies that can help provide answers to these public policy questions.

Estimating Cigarette Demand Functions

Table 5.3 summarizes the results of the major empirical studies of the demand for cigarettes.

Table 5.3: Empirical Estimation of Cigarette Demand Functions: Selected Recent and Often-Cited Studies

| | | | RESULTS | |
STUDY	DATA SET	PRICE ELASTICITY ESTIMATES	EFFECT OF OTHER ANTISMOKING VARIABLES	EFFECT OF OTHER VARIABLES
Chaloupka and Wechsler (1997)	1993 Harvard College Alcohol Study. N = 16,570 students at 140 U.S. four-year colleges and universities.	−0.906 to −1.309. Half of decreased consumption from reduced smoking participation; the other half from a reduction in the number of cigarettes consumed by smokers.	Relatively strong restrictions on smoking in public places, particularly restaurants and schools, discourage college students from smoking.	Age, gender, race, marital status, religion, parental education, on-campus living, fraternity/sorority membership, employment, college characteristics, regional indicators included. Results not reported. Sample also adjusted for students crossing borders to low tax/price localities.
Chaloupka and Grossman (1996)	1992, 1993, 1994 surveys of eighth, tenth, and twelfth grade students from Monitoring the Future Project, Institute for Social Research, University of Michigan. N = 110,717 youths.	−0.846 to −1.450 for full sample. −1.254 to −1.702 for sample adjusted for border-crossing problem. −1.313 is average estimate. Half of smoking reductions from decrease in probability of a youth smoking; half from reduction in average daily cigarette consumption.	Relatively strong restrictions on smoking in public places, such as workplaces, restaurants, or retail stores, reduce the probability of smoking but have little impact on average daily cigarette consumption. Restrictions on smoking in schools are significant for this sample.	Variables decreasing likelihood of smoking: race; religious attachment; rural location; families with both parents present; greater parental education. Variables increasing likelihood of smoking: age; higher incomes (e_i = +0.294); employed; working mothers.

Continued

Table 5.3: Empirical Estimation of Cigarette Demand Functions: Selected Recent and Often-Cited Studies (*continued*)

STUDY	DATA SET	PRICE ELASTICITY ESTIMATES	RESULTS EFFECT OF OTHER ANTISMOKING VARIABLES	EFFECT OF OTHER VARIABLES
			Limits on availability of tobacco products, such as minimum legal purchase age and restrictions on vending machine sales, have little effect. These laws may not be well enforced. Educational antismoking activities appear to reduce youths' smoking.	
Becker, Grossman, and Murphy (1994)	Time-series of state cross-sections of per capita cigarette consumption from 1955 to 1985. Assume the data reflect the behavior of a representative consumer. N = 1,517.	−0.75 for long-run response to permanent change in price. −0.40 for short-run response to permanent change in price. −0.30 for temporary change in price.		Control for income and differences in state taxes, which influence smuggling incentives among states.
Keeler et al. (1993)	Monthly time-series data in California from 1980 to 1990. Per capita adult consumption	−0.30 to −0.50 in the short run. −0.50 to −0.60 in the long run.	Antismoking ordinances have a significant negative effect on cigarette consumption, but	Effects of income are weak, insignificant, and negative. Negative income elasticity may be due to su-

	Data/Methods	Results	Conclusions
	(ages 15 years and older). Cigarette tax increase from 10 cents to 35 cents per pack occurred on 1 January 1989.	they do not overshadow the effects of price.	perior education of higher-income groups. (Earlier data—positive elasticity). Cigarette consumption increases around holiday periods and before a tax increase. Bootlegging due to state tax differentials can be an important determinant of demand.
Wasserman et al. (1991)	Study uses *National Health Interview Survey* data from 1970 and 1985. N = 207,647. Assume all consumption is underreported by one-third. Also used *National Health and Nutrition Examination Survey II* for teenage smoking between 1976 and 1980. N = 1,960. Discuss use of individual versus state data in other studies.	−0.017 in 1974 to −0.226 in 1985 for adult sample. +0.859 for teenagers. Yet cannot reject hypothesis that teenage elasticity is significantly different from adult estimate of −0.23 in 1985. Teenage estimate much lower than other studies. For adults, price changes have greatest effect on decision to become a smoker rather than on number of cigarettes smoked.	Adult sample: Antismoking regulations would decrease consumption but did not affect decision to smoke. Teenage sample: Antismoking regulations have strong negative and statistically significant effect on consumption. Major effect was on the probability of being a smoker. Price elasticity results affected by inclusion of regulatory variables. Public sentiment against smoking may be related to the regulation variables.	Adult sample: Price and income elasticities are changing over time. Income elasticities change from positive to negative. Cigarette consumption declines as education increases. Cohort effects (especially for males) are important. Whites smoke more than nonwhites. Married people smoke less than nonmarried. Teenage sample: Cigarette consumption negatively related to family income and parental education. Study shows distributional consequences of taxing cigarettes.

Continued

233

Table 5.3: Empirical Estimation of Cigarette Demand Functions: Selected Recent and Often-Cited Studies (continued)

| | | RESULTS | | |
STUDY	DATA SET	PRICE ELASTICITY ESTIMATES	EFFECT OF OTHER ANTISMOKING VARIABLES	EFFECT OF OTHER VARIABLES
Lewit and Coate (1982)	1976 *Health Interview Survey*. N = 19,266 individuals age 20 to 74 years.	−0.42 overall, −0.26 for participation rate, and −0.10 for quantity demanded. −0.89 for 20–25-years age group, twice as large as estimate for other age groups. −0.74 for participation rate in this age group.		Control for family income, education, age, sex, marital status, race, and health status. Results not reported.
Lewit, Coate, and Grossman (1981)	Cycle III of the *U.S. Health Examination Survey*. National sample of 6,768 noninstitutionalized youths age 12 to 17 conducted from 1966 to 1970.	−1.2 for the decision to smoke; −1.4 for the quantity smoked equations.	Substantial negative effect of antismoking messages on participation rates.	Border-crossing problem likely to be smaller for teenagers than adults because quantity of cigarettes smoked is smaller and teenagers are less likely to be able to drive. Control for real family income, number of children in family, parents' schooling, whether mother works, age, race, sex, student status, working status, region. Results not reported.

Other studies of cigarette demand functions have been summarized in the reports *Reducing Health Consequences of Smoking: 25 Years of Smoking* (U.S. Department of Health and Human Services 1989), *Preventing Tobacco Use Among Young People. A Report of the Surgeon General* (U.S. Department of Health and Human Services 1994), and by Viscusi (1992) and Grossman and Chaloupka (1997).

All these studies show that cigarette smoking by both teenagers and adults is sensitive to the price: that is, the price elasticity of demand is greater than zero in absolute value. Most of the studies conclude that young people are more sensitive to changes in price than are adults. The estimates by Frank Chaloupka and Michael Grossman (1996) suggest that the impact of a price increase on teenagers is about three times that on adults. Approximately half of the smoking reduction results from a decrease in the probability of a youth smoking, while half results from a reduction in average daily cigarette consumption.

This larger price sensitivity among young people would be expected for several reasons (Grossman and Chaloupka 1997). Teenagers are likely to spend a greater proportion of their disposable income on cigarettes than are adults. There are also substantial peer pressure effects operating on young people. Any change in cigarette taxes, and therefore prices, has both a direct negative effect on consumption as measured by the empirical studies and a peer pressure effect (i.e., fewer peers are smoking for a teenager to emulate). It is often argued that teenagers tend to discount the future by underestimating future health hazards and the likelihood of addiction. Given the nature of addiction, small reductions in cigarette consumption by young people due to price increases could have much greater future effects. Reducing teenage smoking appears to be an effective policy overall because few individuals begin smoking after the age of twenty.

It can be seen from the results in Table 5.3 that there is variation in the estimates of the price elasticity of demand for cigarettes. This variation relates to the issues discussed earlier in this chapter: the nature of the estimating equations, the data sets employed, and the other variables included in the estimations. In the smoking research literature, there are also disagreements about the behavioral theory underlying the empirical estimation.

Cigarette demand studies have been based on both aggregate data, typically at the state level or across a sample of states, and on microlevel individual data drawn from surveys of different groups in the population. The price elasticity estimates from the aggregate data studies typically fall in the range from –0.14 to –1.23, with the majority varying from –0.20 to –0.50 (U.S. Department of Health and Human Services 1994). Studies using cross-sections of state-level data must control for smuggling or border-crossing problems. If cigarette taxes or prices differ significantly among adjoining states, state cigarette consumption data may be inaccurate if there are substantial sales from the low price (tax) state to residents of the higher price (tax) states. At the aggregate level, researchers must also consider the interaction between supply and demand in determining cigarette prices. Ignoring this simultaneity could lead to biased estimates of cigarette price elasticities (U.S. Department of Health and Human Services 1994). This is an example of the distinction between single- and multiequation models that was discussed in chapter 4.

Using microlevel individual data avoids some of the above empirical problems. Since no individual smoker consumes enough cigarettes to affect the overall price, the simultaneity problem in the aggregate data studies is not an issue here. Individual data also allow researchers to model cigarette demand as the outcome of two separate, but interrelated, decisions: (1) the decision to begin smoking (estimating the probability of smoking or the participation rate); and (2) the number of cigarettes consumed, once a decision to begin smoking has been made. It is possible and quite likely that cigarette prices and other variables, including other antismoking policies, have different effects on these two decisions. Aggregate data studies can focus only on average cigarette consumption for some large geographic unit. Individual data allow researchers to examine the factors influencing smoking in various age or socioeconomic groups in the population and the decisions to both begin and quit smoking.

Examples of both aggregate and individual data studies are given in Table 5.3. Gary Becker, Michael Grossman, and Kevin Murphy (1994) have used a time series of state cross-sections of per capita cigarette consumption from 1955 to 1985. They assumed that the data reflected the behavior of a representative consumer. Theodore Keeler et al. (1993) used monthly time-series data on per capita adult cigarette consumption in California from 1980 to 1990. The event influencing smoking behavior in this study was the cigarette tax increase from $.10 to $.35 per pack in 1989. Individual-data studies by Jeffrey Wasserman et al. (1991), Eugene Lewit and Douglas Coate (1982), and Lewit, Coate, and Grossman (1981) use data drawn from the major ongoing health interview surveys sponsored by the federal government, the *National Health Interview Survey* and the *Health Examination Survey*, while other researchers have located university-based surveys. Frank Chaloupka and Henry Wechsler (1997) use the 1993 Harvard College Alcohol Study of nearly 17,000 students at 140 U.S. colleges and universities, while Chaloupka and Grossman (1996) use surveys of eighth, tenth, and twelfth grade students drawn from the Monitoring the Future Project at the University of Michigan's Institute of Social Research. As shown in Table 5.3, the sample sizes of the data sets in these studies vary substantially, also contributing to differences in the statistical reliability of the results.

The individual-data studies do show different impacts of cigarette price and other antismoking variables on the decision to smoke versus the quantity of cigarettes consumed. Chaloupka and Wechsler (1997) and Chaloupka and Grossman (1996) estimate that half of the reduced cigarette consumption from increased prices in their samples of college and high school students results from a reduced probability of smoking and half results from a decrease in the quantity of cigarettes consumed. This contrasts with the results of Wasserman et al. (1991) who found a very small price effect in their teenage sample: their actual estimated price coefficient was positive, the opposite of what is predicted by economic theory. However, they could not reject the hypothesis that the teenage price elasticity was significantly different from the adult sample estimate of –0.23. Wasserman et al. (1991) also found that for adults, price changes have the greatest effect on the decision to become a smoker rather than on the number of cigarettes smoked.

The effect of prices on cigarette demand may be intertwined with the effect of other antismoking policies. Disentangling these effects may be a substantial empirical challenge. Wasserman et al. (1991) argue that their low estimates of cigarette price elasticity resulted from the inclusion of an index of antismoking regulations in their estimating equations. They conclude that price elasticity estimates in other studies may have been biased upward because they were capturing some of the effect of antismoking regulations and public sentiment against smoking. Although this conclusion has been debated by other researchers, who also included both price and antismoking variables in their equations and found little effect on estimated price elasticities, the debate shows the influence of empirical estimation issues on policy conclusions. Recent studies are more likely to include variables measuring the effect of other antismoking policies, given the current interest in the full range of policies to reduce smoking. Chaloupka and Wechsler (1997) and Chaloupka and Grossman (1996) found that relatively strong restrictions on smoking in public areas such as work places, restaurants, and schools were effective in discouraging young people from smoking. There was a greater estimated effect on the probability of smoking than on the quantity of cigarettes consumed. Limits on the availability of tobacco products, such as a minimum legal purchase age and restrictions on vending machine sales, appeared to have little estimated effect, perhaps because these laws are not well enforced. Wasserman et al. (1991) found a difference in the effects of antismoking regulations on teenagers and on adults. For teenagers, the major impact was on the probability of being a smoker, whereas for adults, the regulations appeared to decrease consumption but did not affect the decision to smoke.

Developments in the economic theory of smoking have also affected the empirical studies of cigarette demand and price elasticity. The Becker and Murphy (1988) model of rational addiction has been applied to smoking behavior by Chaloupka (1991) and Becker, Grossman, and Murphy (1994). This model implies that current smoking decisions depend upon past smoking and that the future consequences of an individual's past and current smoking behavior are considered when making current choices. The rational addiction literature tends to find somewhat smaller differences between short-run and long-run elasticities than does the traditional literature (Gravelle and Zimmerman 1994). This theory has been subject to a variety of criticisms (Rice 1998) and also presents substantial econometric estimation problems (Gravelle and Zimmerman 1994). However, policymakers need to be aware that differences in underlying theory can cause variations in empirical estimates of parameters used for setting policy.

There may also be other changes in the behavior of smokers arising from increased cigarette taxation that partially offset the goal of the taxation policy. Grossman and Chaloupka (1997) note that in response to higher cigarette prices, smokers may switch to higher tar and nicotine brands, inhale more deeply, reduce idle burn time, or switch to the use of smokeless tobacco. It has also been argued that extremely high cigarette taxes will lead to a vast increase in black market activity and smuggling. None of these effects are addressed in the above empirical studies, and most have not been well researched. In many cases, the relevant data may not be available for examining these issues in a quantitative framework. However, policymakers must always consider compensating behavior and unintended consequences in the analysis of any policy problem, even if only on a qualitative basis. This consideration, which relates to the discussion of structuring policy problems in chapter 2, shows the limits of quantitative techniques in solving policy problems. Empirical results assist but never substitute for informed judgment.

As in many public policy areas, and as noted earlier in this book, there may be multiple goals of any particular policy, some of which are conflicting. Over the years cigarette taxes have been used as a means of raising tax revenue, reducing the federal budget deficit, and financing programs such as the health care reform proposed by the Clinton administration in the early 1990s, as well as for reducing smoking by teenagers and adults. The price elasticity issue discussed in this chapter has a major impact on the health benefit versus revenue-raising goals of taxing cigarettes. If cigarette price elasticities of demand are very small, using cigarette taxes to raise revenues is an efficient mechanism because there will be very little response from smokers in terms of quantities demanded or the decision to smoke. However, there would also be very little health benefit from the policy. Higher price elasticities imply a smaller revenue-raising potential for the tax, but a larger effect on public health (Warner et al. 1995). Differences between short- and long-run price elasticities also have an influence on these goals: a significant long-run elasticity could have a substantial negative impact on any tax revenues initially collected. This implication for tax policy led Grossman and Chaloupka (1997, 296) to note that one "would hardly like to see the development of a situation in which fiscal needs create pressure on the government to encourage smoking or at least not discourage it."

The potential conflict between these goals is illustrated by the case of New Jersey, which doubled its cigarette tax from $.40 to $.80 per pack in 1997 to pay hospitals for providing care to uninsured patients. Under a 1992 state law New Jersey hospitals are required to accept all patients, regardless of their ability to pay. The New Jersey Hospital Association reports that the number of uninsured increased from 700,000 to 1.3 million after the law was passed (Pallarito 1998). In 1996 New Jersey governor Christine Todd Whitman signed a bill that funded charity care payments primarily by using the state's unemployment insurance fund. New Jersey used $310 million from the fund for FY 1996 and $300 million for FY 1997 (Demenchuk 1997). The cigarette tax bill will phase out the state's reliance on unemployment contributions to fund charity care programs from 1998 to 2002. "The charity care provided by New Jersey hospitals and our subsidized health insurance programs are critical to the health and well-being of our families and children in need," Governor Whitman has said. "With the signing of these laws today, we now have a permanent revenue source to fund the charity care program, and we are putting an end to reliance on unemployment insurance" (Demenchuk 1997). Others have noted that the issue of price elasticity will influence how much revenue the new tax will generate. One health care analyst was quoted as saying, "Forty cents a pack is steep. You're going to have a change in the demand curve on packs of cigarettes with a 40-cent increase. It certainly puts a crimp in smoking habits" (Demenchuk 1997). State officials have claimed that both funding charity care and decreasing teenage smoking were goals of the legislation. They anticipate a 14 percent drop in the teen smoking rate. "We may not get all of the 18-year-old smokers in

New Jersey to stop, but a lot of 12-year-olds may indefinitely delay the decision to start" (Downs 1998).

If cigarette taxes are to be used as a policy tool to reduce smoking, and not simply for raising revenue or reducing the federal budget deficit, the taxes would probably have to be indexed for inflation to have the intended effect. The existing federal cigarette tax was fixed at $.08 per pack between 1 November 1951 and the end of 1982 when it rose to $.16 per pack. The tax was increased to $.20 per pack in January 1991, and $.24 per pack in January 1992. However, if the tax had simply been adjusted for inflation since 1951, it would be $.47 per pack today (Grossman and Chaloupka 1997). Since cigarette taxes account for only a small proportion of the total price of cigarettes, the price elasticity of demand for cigarettes would have to be multiplied by the percentage change in the price resulting from the tax change to determine the elasticity of demand with respect to the tax. This tax elasticity will be smaller than the price elasticity of demand (U.S. Department of Health and Human Services 1989)

Implications for Public Policy

The preceding discussion may leave students and policy analysts wondering what they can conclude from these differences in theoretical issues and empirical results for this one policy area. Although there are differences about the precise magnitude of the response to cigarette price increases, there is substantial consensus in the research literature that prices do reduce cigarette consumption, both in terms of the decision to smoke and the quantity of cigarettes consumed. These results have led two prominent cigarette demand researchers, Michael Grossman and Frank Chaloupka, to argue that a "substantial real tax hike to curb youth smoking should move to the forefront of the antismoking campaign" (Grossman and Chaloupka 1997, 297).

However, even in this policy area where there is a vast literature on policies to stop or prevent smoking, there will not be total agreement, particularly as new study results are announced. Moreover, various interest groups are likely to use weaknesses in the literature to advance their own position. For example, a *New York Times* article in May 1998 cited testimony from Lawrence H. Summers, U.S. deputy treasury secretary, that "every 10 percent increase in the price of a pack of cigarettes would produce up to a 7 percent reduction in the number of children who smoke" and that "children are far more sensitive to price increases than adults" (Meier 1998a). This was immediately contradicted by the citation of a recent Cornell University study, which found that price had little effect on smoking rates among youths when these issues were examined in a time-series rather than a cross-section framework. The Cornell researchers also argued that the size of the cigarette tax increases currently being debated lie outside the range of the estimated behavioral impacts in the empirical literature. This is an issue that was discussed as a forecasting problem in chapter 4 of this text. In the *New York Times* article, a U.S. Treasury Department official then responded that "the Cornell study had its own methodological flaws and that the earlier findings about prices supported the department's position" (Meier 1998a).

The headline article in the *Atlanta Constitution* of 31 July 1998 reports the results of a new study by the Centers for Disease Control and Prevention (CDC) that states that a 60.0 percent increase in cigarette prices would cut consumption among smokers by 12.5 percent (Aldag 1998). This implies a price elasticity of −0.21. The CDC study also found that lower income and minority smokers were more likely to reduce smoking in response to price increases than other groups. This announcement immediately brought a response from the tobacco industry. A spokesman is quoted in the article saying, "I just don't know if the mechanics of the marketplace are within the expertise of the CDC. On the surface it sounds simplistic."

A recent study of a \$.25 excise tax on cigarettes in Massachusetts has also attempted to examine smokers' perceptions of the impact of new tobacco taxes (Biener et al. 1998). The study analyzed adults' and teenagers' reports about whether the price increase affected them and, if so, whether it led them to quit, to consider quitting, or only to reduce the cost of continuing to smoke. The most commonly reported action by adults was to consider quitting (35 percent), followed by changing to a cheaper brand (28 percent), and then by reducing the number of cigarettes smoked per day (17 percent). For teenagers, the most commonly reported reaction was to buy fewer cigarettes (29 percent), followed by thinking about quitting (21 percent), and then by changing to a cheaper brand (19 percent). The authors of the study concluded that "a tax provides economic incentives to quit and may also send a potent message of societal disapproval that may affect smokers' behavior" (Biener et al. 1998, 1391).

Research, particularly the econometric literature discussed in this chapter, can never definitively "prove" a hypothesis about the relationship between two variables. It can, however, suggest that the weight of the evidence supports a given relationship. The policy analyst needs to review or find other surveys of the literature, sometimes called meta-analyses, which distill and analyze the results of numerous studies to determine whether there is a consensus about the impact of different policy variables. This is a relatively easy task in the area of smoking behavior, given the policy interest in the question since the first surgeon general's report on smoking in the 1960s. Major reports by the federal government (U.S. Department of Health and Human Services 1989; 1994) as well as key summary articles (Warner et al. 1995; Grossman and Chaloupka 1997) can help the policy analyst organize and summarize the existing literature and determine what empirical and policy questions still need to be addressed. For other policy areas, the literature may be very sparse or of poor quality. However, analysts can access a wide range of literature in a relatively short time using the variety of electronic data bases in most libraries and sources currently available on the Internet.

The great body of the smoking literature supports the hypothesis that raising cigarette prices through taxation will reduce smoking, particularly among teenagers—thus, pricing has a significant impact on human behavior in this case and can be used as a policy tool. The justification and desirability of doing so will depend upon the values of different policy advocates as well as the perspectives of different academic disciplines. For example, different policy recommendations can follow from the economic and the public health perspectives. Participants in a 1995 meeting of economics-based smoking researchers concluded that "economic analysis can inform but never resolve the debate on how much society should tax cigarettes" and that "neither the discipline of economics nor any other could determine what is socially 'right' or 'wrong'"(Warner et al. 1995).

It is likely that policies based on pricing will need to be combined with other approaches to behavior change to influence smoking behavior, particularly among teenagers. There is a large psychological, public health, and evaluation literature that attempts to directly measure the impact of anti-smoking interventions, such as education programs, bans on advertising, and restrictions on smoking in public places. Much of this literature is summarized in the major federal government reports on smoking by the Department of Health and Human Services (U.S. Department of Health and Human Services 1989; 1994). There is also a growing literature analyzing the cost-effectiveness of antismoking programs (Elixhauser 1990). Studies in this literature directly analyze specific interventions and alternative theories of behavior change to determine their effectiveness under idealized experimental conditions and in actual operation among different populations. This is a quite different approach than simply measuring the effects of these programs by determining the statistical significance of a dummy variable in an econometric estimation equation as in the literature discussed in this chapter. The use of program evaluation techniques, such as cost-effectiveness and cost-benefit analysis, will be discussed in the following chapters with applications to other policy areas.

Policy analysts may have to synthesize literature across a variety of academic disciplines to try to form a complete picture of the impact of pricing versus other variables in influencing human behavior. Analysts must be aware that the difficult task is to untangle the effects of multiple influences on human behavior. This can be accomplished through a variety of research approaches, each of which has its own strengths and weaknesses. It is clear from the issues discussed in this chapter that pricing policies do have an impact on smoking behavior and cigarette demand. Thus, pricing and taxation should be considered as one of the tools in this policy arena.

References

Aldag, J. Matthew. (1998) "Tobacco Pricing Linked to Habit," *Atlanta Constitution* (31 July), 1A.

Barthold, Thomas A. (1994) "Issues in the Design of Environmental Excise Taxes," *Journal of Economic Perspectives* 8, 1 (Winter), pp. 133–51.

Becker, Gary S. and Kevin M. Murphy. (1988) "A Theory of Rational Addiction," *Journal of Political Economy* 96, 4 (August), pp. 675–700.

Becker, Gary S., Michael Grossman, and Kevin M. Murphy. (1994) "An Empirical Analysis of Cigarette Addiction," *American Economic Review* 84, 3 (June), pp. 396–418.

Biener, Lois, Robert H. Aseltine, Bruce Cohen, and Marlene Anderka. (1998) "Reactions of Adult and Teenaged Smokers to the Massachusetts Tobacco Tax," *American Journal of Public Health* 88, 9 (September), pp. 1389–91.

Chaloupka, Frank. (1991) "Rational Addictive Behavior and Cigarette Smoking," *Journal of Political Economy* 99, 4 (August), pp. 722–42.

Chaloupka, Frank J. and Michael Grossman. (1996) "Price, Tobacco Control, and Youth Smoking," *NBER Working Paper Series, Working Paper 5740* (Cambridge, Mass.: National Bureau of Economic Research).

Chaloupka, Frank J. and Henry Wechsler. (1997) "Price, Tobacco Control Policies and Smoking Among Young Adults," *Journal of Health Economics* 16, 3 (June), pp. 359–73.

Demenchuk, Michael. (1997) "N.J. Looking to Smokers to Foot Bill for Hospital Care for Uninsured," *Bond Buyer* 322, 30298 (23 December), p. 3.

Downs, Larry. (1998) "Follow the Lead Set by N.J. and Hike the Cigarette Tax," *Philadelphia Business Journal* 17, 22 (10 July), p. 39.

Elixhauser, Anne. (1990) "The Costs of Smoking and the Cost-Effectiveness of Smoking Cessation Programs," *Journal of Public Health Policy* 11 (Summer), pp. 218–37.

Fisher, Ronald C. (1988) *State and Local Public Finance* (Glenview, Ill.: Scott, Foresman and Company).

Gravelle, Jane G. and Dennis Zimmerman. (1994) *Cigarette Taxes to Fund Health Care Reform: An Economic Analysis* (Washington, D.C.: Congressional Research Service, The Library of Congress).

Grossman, Michael and Frank J. Chaloupka. (1997) "Cigarette Taxes: The Straw to Break the Camel's Back," *Public Health Reports* 112 (July/August), pp. 291–97.

Hyman, David N. (1996) *Public Finance: A Contemporary Application of Theory to Policy,* 5th ed. (Fort Worth: Dryden Press).

Johnston, David Cay. (1997) "Anti-Tobacco Groups Push for Higher Cigarette Taxes," *New York Times* (3 April), A1.

Keeler, Theodore E., The-Wei Hu, Paul G. Barnett, and Willard G. Manning. (1993) "Taxation, Regulation, and Addiction: A Demand Function for Cigarettes Based on Time-Series Evidence," *Journal of Health Economics* 12, 1 (April), pp. 1–18.

Lewit Eugene M. and Douglas Coate. (1982) "The Potential for Using Excise Taxes to Reduce Smoking," *Journal of Health Economics* 1, pp. 121–45.

Lewit, Eugene M., Douglas Coate, and Michael Grossman. (1981) "The Effects of Government Regulation on Teenage Smoking," *Journal of Law and Economics* 24, 3 (December), pp. 545–69.

Meier, Barry. (1998a) "Politics of Youth Smoking Fueled by Unproven Data," *New York Times* (20 May), A1.

———. (1998b) "Remaining States Approve the Pact on Tobacco Suits," *New York Times* (21 November), A1.

Morrison, Steven A. (1998) "Airline Service: The Evolution of Competition Since Deregulation" in Larry L. Duetsch (ed.) *Industry Studies,* 2d ed. (Armonk, N.Y.: M. E. Sharpe), pp. 147–75.

Pallarito, Karen. (1998) "N.J. Smokers to Finance Charity Care," *Modern Healthcare* 28, 2 (12 January), p. 50.

Pindyck, Robert S. and Daniel L. Rubinfeld. (1998) *Econometric Models and Economic Forecasts,* 4th ed. (New York: McGraw-Hill).

Rice, Thomas. (1998) *The Economics of Health Reconsidered* (Chicago: Health Administration Press).

U.S. Department of Health and Human Services. (1999) *Targeting Tobacco Use: The Nation's Leading Cause of Death, At-a-Glance, 1999.* (Atlanta, Ga.: U.S. Department of Health and Human Services, Centers for Disease Control and Prevention.

U.S. Department of Health and Human Services. (1994) *Preventing Tobacco Use Among Young People: A Report of the Surgeon General.* (Atlanta, Ga.: U.S. Department of Health and Human Services, Public Health Service, Centers for Disease Control and Prevention, National Center for Chronic Disease Prevention and Health Promotion, Office on Smoking and Health). Reprinted with corrections, July 1994.

U.S. Department of Health and Human Services. (1989) *Reducing the Health Consequences of Smoking. 25 Years of Progress. A Report of the Surgeon General.* (Atlanta, Ga.: U.S. Department of Health and Human Services, Public Health Service, Centers for Disease Control, Center for Chronic Disease Prevention and Health Promotion, Office on Smoking and Health).

Viscusi, W. Kip. (1992) *Smoking: Making the Risky Decision* (New York: Oxford University Press).

Viscusi, W. Kip, John M. Vernon, and Joseph E. Harrington, Jr. (1995) *Economics of Regulation and Antitrust,* 2d ed. (Cambridge, Mass.: Massachusetts Institute of Techology Press).

Warner, Kenneth E., Frank J. Chaloupka, Philip J. Cook, Willard G. Manning, Joseph P. Newhouse, Thomas E. Novotny, Thomas C. Schelling, and Joy

Townsend. (1995) "Criteria for Determining an Optimal Cigarette Tax: The Economist's Perspective," *Tobacco Control* 4, pp. 380–86.

Wasserman, Jeffrey, Willard G. Manning, Joseph P. Newhouse, and John D. Winkler. (1991) "The Effects of Excise Taxes and Regulations on Cigarette Smoking," *Journal of Health Economics* 10, 1 (May), pp. 43–64.

CHAPTER 6

Cost-Effectiveness Analysis

The Case of Mother-to-Infant HIV Transmission

This chapter discusses the use of cost-effectiveness analysis to evaluate alternative public policies. The specific case chosen for the chapter is a cost-effectiveness analysis of the current guidelines from the Centers for Disease Control and Prevention (CDC) for preventing transmission of the human immunodeficiency virus (HIV) from mothers to infants. A health care example was chosen, given the vast increase in the number of cost-effectiveness studies in the health care area and the development and standardization of economic evaluation techniques that have occurred over the past decade. Preventing transmission of HIV is a major health policy concern both in the United States and around the world. Although the focus of the chapter will be the prevention of HIV transmission from mothers to children, the cost-effectiveness techniques discussed here are used in a wide variety of health and other policy areas. These techniques have been used to analyze alternative antismoking strategies which were discussed in the previous chapter.

We will begin by defining cost-effectiveness analysis and discussing how it compares with other program evaluation tools, such as cost-benefit analysis. The latter is the subject of chapter 7 in this book. Even though chapters 6 and 7 focus on different policy areas and evaluation techniques, there are many similar elements and linkages in the chapters. We will then discuss the features and problems that are common to all cost-effectiveness analyses. This discussion will draw on two major publications that summarize the issues regarding the application of cost-effectiveness analysis in health policy decisions: *Prevention Effectiveness: A Guide to Decision Analysis and Economic Evaluation,* which was developed to facilitate the analysis of disease prevention programs at the CDC (Haddix et al. 1996), and *Cost-Effectiveness in Health and Medicine,* a report by an expert panel appointed by the U.S. Public Health Service (Gold et al. 1996). These methodological issues will be examined in the context of this chapter's case study, "Preventing Perinatal Transmission of HIV—Costs and Effectiveness of a Recommended Intervention" (Gorsky et al. 1996).

What Is Cost-Effectiveness Analysis?

Cost-effectiveness analysis is one of a series of techniques that can be used to provide a systematic economic evaluation of alternative public policies. These economic evaluation techniques all focus on relating some measure of the output, outcomes, or consequences of a program with the costs of the inputs used to provide those outcomes. The techniques provide a decision-maker with a useful way to clearly identify alternatives to a given policy and to focus on the consequences of using scarce resources for one program instead of another. Like all economic analysis, these techniques derive from the fact that limited resources are available to fund any program and that choices must be made among alternatives.

Economic evaluation differs from other forms of program evaluation that concentrate on describing the process by which the program is implemented (Rossi and Freeman 1993). These evaluations may define their "outputs" simply as the number of clients served or the number of counseling sessions offered. Although these measures may be useful for describing and monitoring the operation of a particular program, they do not show the impact of the program on the population. Economic evaluation focuses on measuring the production process or "production function" inherent in the program—the relationship between the flow of program inputs and the resulting outcome that has an impact on the final consumers or clients.

Focusing on the final impact of the program on the population means that modeling is often used in economic evaluation. Modeling is particularly useful when some of the alternatives being considered have not actually been implemented or when there is great uncertainty about the actual effectiveness of the intervention. For example, in HIV prevention, decisionmakers might be interested in the costs and consequences of needle exchange programs in the United States or in a policy of mandatory HIV testing of pregnant women to prevent transmission of HIV to their infants. However, there has been only limited use of needle exchange programs in the United States, and there is no mandatory HIV counseling and testing of pregnant women, given the political, ethical, and legal issues surrounding these strategies. Therefore, little or no direct evidence exists about the costs and consequences of the programs. Researchers need to develop models of how these programs would work, using the best data available from comparable programs or making educated guesses about certain parameters.

Although modeling may seem like an academic exercise, models "can be very helpful in making assumptions explicit and in forcing examination of the logic and evidence for each step in the process" (Haddix et al. 1996, 6). Sometimes, simply the process of logically going through the steps inherent in a public policy will highlight issues that might otherwise have been overlooked, even if the model is never fully estimated. Modeling forces a decisionmaker to explicitly confront alternatives and to develop the logic of what might happen under each alternative. "Modeling may also help in identifying the important issues for which data are needed and thereby help to formulate a research agenda. . . . The use of models makes the decision process explicit and can help to clarify the criteria upon which the decisions are to be made" (Haddix et al. 1996, 6–7). This role for modeling relates to the problem definition issues discussed in chapter 2 of this book. We noted there that many public policy problems are only moderately or ill structured, and that one of the main tasks of policy analysis is the resolution of ill-structured problems. The use of decision analysis models to frame problems in this chapter relates directly to the discussion of classification and causal analysis in chapter 2.

ALTERNATIVE ECONOMIC EVALUATION TECHNIQUES

The various economic evaluation techniques differ in how the measurement, valuation, and comparison of costs and consequences are performed. In cost-effectiveness analysis, the program outcomes or consequences are measured in the most appropriate natural effects or physical units. In the health care area, the number of infections prevented or the number of life-years saved by a medical or prevention intervention are typical outcome measures. These are basic measures that can be simply counted to determine the effectiveness of the intervention. No valuation is placed on the outcome measures. Thus, cost-effectiveness analysis is most appropriately used where there is already general agreement on the nature of the program outcomes and where the outcomes of the alternatives being compared are the same or very similar. The decisionmaker wants to choose the alternative that has the lowest additional cost for achieving the additional outcomes. For example, one might compare the cost-effectiveness of two alternative strategies for preventing HIV infection. In this case, estimating the number of infections prevented under each strategy might be a sufficiently precise measure of program output, given the common goal of the alternatives.

Cost-effectiveness analysis becomes a less useful tool even in the health care arena when comparisons are made across broader program areas. Suppose that the question facing the decisionmaker is how to allocate resources between HIV and heart disease prevention programs. The question then is how to rank a case of HIV infection prevented in relation to a case of heart disease prevented. One could answer this question by analyzing the cost per life-year saved in each case. However, this measure focuses solely on the mortality outcome of the intervention, the extension in the number of years of life, and ignores major issues about the quality of those life-years saved and the values individuals attach to them. An individual with HIV infection could live with the disease for ten to twelve years or even longer, given the development of new antiretroviral therapies. The stigma that has been attached to HIV, as well as the inconvenience and side effects associated with following the current drug regimes, means that the quality of life for a person living with HIV is quite different from that of a noninfected individual. These differences are not incorporated if only the number of life-years saved by an HIV prevention program is measured. In evaluating cholesterol screening to prevent heart disease, the reduction in mortality is an important outcome. "But simply counting deaths, or even life-years gained, may leave out other important health outcomes, such as the morbidity repercussions of angina and heart attacks, as well as the psychological concerns that accompany a diagnosis of hypercholesterolemia" (Gold et al. 1996, 84). Thus, the use of cost-effectiveness analysis is limited when the decisionmaker is trying to compare programs across broad policy areas, when there are multiple outcomes of interest in each program, and when some outcomes are valued more highly than others.

In health care policy, cost-utility analysis has been developed as a modification of cost-effectiveness analysis to focus on these quality of life issues. In cost-utility analysis, the outcome measure is typically a quality-adjusted life-year (QALY), in which the number of life-years gained by an intervention has been adjusted for factors relating to the quality of those life-years. "In the QALY approach, the quality adjustment is based on a set of values or weights called utilities, one for each possible health state, that reflect the desirability of the health state" (Drummond et al. 1997, 140). Cost-utility analysis would be the economic evaluation technique to use when (1) health-related quality of life is *the* important outcome, such as in the treatment of arthritis, which has no expected impact on mortality; (2) health-related quality of life is *an* important outcome (evaluating neonatal intensive care for low-birth-weight infants); (3) interventions, such as many cancer treatments, affect both morbidity and mortality and the decisionmaker wants a single measure incorporating both effects; (4) the programs being compared have a wide range of outputs and a common unit for comparison is needed; and (5) a decisionmaker wants to compare a new program with one that has already been evaluated in terms of cost-utility analysis (Drummond et al. 1997, 141–42).

Although cost-utility analysis helps in making comparisons across alternative health prevention and treatment programs, decisionmakers may be asked to make even broader comparisons across more disparate activities. Legislators and other policymakers must make decisions regarding resource allocation to health care, national defense, education, job training, and a variety of other programs, all of which provide benefits to society and yet have outcome measures that are not directly comparable. In these cases, cost-benefit analysis may be the most appropriate economic evaluation technique. Cost-benefit analysis attempts to put a monetary valuation on the consequences of the intervention. This monetary measure is to reflect the amount of money society is willing to pay for the output of the program. Dollars then become the common metric for making comparisons about the outcomes of policies in a variety of programmatic areas and for comparing these outcomes with the costs of the programs. Policymakers can assess the benefit-cost ratios or the net benefits (benefits minus costs) of alternative programs to devise a rank ordering of priorities. However, as will be discussed in much greater detail in chapter 7, there are numerous conceptual and empirical problems in developing these willingness to pay estimates, including the task of placing a value on the lives saved by a particular program. Health researchers have often been averse to making these valuations, so that cost-effectiveness analysis and cost-utility analysis are used much more widely in the health care arena. For example, in a review of forty-three economic evaluations of HIV counseling and testing interventions, thirty-three studies were cost-effectiveness analyses, four were cost-utility analyses, and ten were cost-benefit analyses. Two studies contained a cost-effectiveness and a cost-utility analysis, whereas two other studies contained a cost-effectiveness and a cost-benefit analysis (Farnham 1998).

USE OF COST-EFFECTIVENESS ANALYSIS

The cost-effectiveness approach was used in the early years (1965–1968) of the planning, programming, and budgeting (PPB) era in the U.S. Department of Health, Education, and Welfare (now the Department of Health and Human Services). This federal agency undertook a number of studies of various disease control programs to determine which programs had the highest payoff in terms of number of lives saved and disabilities prevented per dollar of cost (Grosse 1970). For the cancer control program from 1968 to 1972, it was found that the cost per death averted ranged from a low of $2,217 for uterine-cervix cancer to $6,046 for breast cancer, $43,729 for cancer of the head and neck, and $46,181 for cancer of the colon and rectum. These figures were used to compare the return from investments in these programs with other programs designed to save lives, such as seat belt education and the prevention of drunk driving (Grosse 1970, 532–36).

Applications of cost-effectiveness analysis in health care began to expand during the 1970s (Weinstein and Stason 1977; Shepard and Thompson 1979). Much of this literature was clinical in nature, and some of it was controversial. For example, Duncan Neuhauser and Ann Lewicki (1975) studied a recommended protocol for screening cancer of the colon. The procedure consisted of six sequential stool tests for occult blood: if any of the tests were positive, a barium enema would be administered. Sherman Folland, Allen Goodman, and Miron Stano (1997, 579) summarize the marginal and average cost per case of colon cancer detected drawn from the study. The marginal cost per case detected is calculated by dividing the incremental or additional screening cost of the next test by the additional number of cancer cases detected, while the average cost per case is calculated by dividing the total screening costs by the total number of cases detected. Neuhauser and Lewicki (1975) showed that the average cost per case was small and increased relatively slowly to $2,451 after six tests. However, the marginal cost rose much more rapidly and exceeded $47 million for the sixth test. Although criticisms have been raised about the Neuhauser and Lewicki study (Brown and Burrows 1990; Gastonis 1990), the example shows how cost-effectiveness analysis can help alert health policymakers to issues regarding program costs and outcomes that might otherwise have remained obscure.

The federal government began to use cost-effectiveness analysis to examine public health policies much more extensively in the late 1970s and 1980s. This trend led to the publication in the 1990s of two federally supported guides to the use of cost-effectiveness analysis. *Prevention Effectiveness: A Guide to Decision Analysis and Economic Evaluation* was originally written "to introduce Centers for Disease Control and Prevention staff to the concepts of decision and economic analysis, to provide guidance on methods to maximize comparability of studies, and to provide access to frequently used reference information. It has been adapted to meet the need of scientists and managers in state and local health departments and managed care organizations as well as students in public health" and other disciplines (Haddix et al. 1996, ix). Similarly, the Panel on Cost Effectiveness in Health and Medicine, a group of experts appointed by the U.S. Public Health Service, was charged with "assessing the state of the science in cost-effectiveness analysis; with identifying methodologic inconsistencies and fragilities in the technique; with fostering consensus, where possible, with respect to standardizing the conduct of studies; and with proposing steps that can be taken to address remaining issues and uncertainties in the methodology" (Gold et al. 1996, vii). The outcome of this panel was the book *Cost-Effectiveness in Health and Medicine*. Much of the material in this chapter is drawn from these two works and from the work of Michael Drummond et al. (1997), the second edition of a book that has greatly influenced the use of economic evaluation techniques in health care.

The economic analysis of disease prevention programs, as compared with programs focusing on the treatment and cure of disease, was stimulated in part by Louise Russell's work (1986). Prevention is often argued to be the better policy, given the advantages of avoiding disease rather than repairing the damage it causes. Pain and suffering can be avoided and possible death may be averted. Furthermore, it is typically argued that prevention costs less than treatment, given the savings in medical treatment costs from the cases of disease prevented. In a 1979 surgeon general's report, President Jimmy Carter wrote that prevention "can substantially reduce the suffering of our people and the burden on our expensive system of medical care" (U.S. Department of Health, Education, and Welfare 1979).

Louise Russell notes that it is unclear whether the cost savings argument is valid in all cases or whether it is even the appropriate criterion for evaluating disease prevention programs. The costs of a disease prevention program relate to the size of the population at risk, while the benefits are received by a much smaller group that would have contracted the disease in the absence of prevention. The costs and benefits of a treatment program are focused only on those who have actually become ill. Thus, the costs per person of acute care may be much higher than those for prevention, while still producing the same or lower cost per life saved or case avoided. There are also risks with the preventive treatment, such as side effects of vaccines or possible misdiagnoses. Whether these side effects are worth the possible gain in length of life is a question of individual values. Furthermore, the time span between preventive measures and their associated health benefits may be considerable, whereas there is a much more direct association between incurring costs and receiving the benefits in the treatment of disease (Russell 1986, 7–9; Russell 1993; 1994). Investment in prevention can be worthwhile, even if costs are not saved by the particular intervention. What matters is the comparison between the additional health impact and the added costs of the intervention. If these comparisons are similar to investments in other policy areas, then investment in prevention activities is a sound economic decision. These issues will be discussed in more detail in the following sections of this chapter and in the case study to be analyzed.

The Components of a Cost-Effectiveness Analysis

The following are the major steps to be undertaken in any cost-effectiveness analysis (Haddix et al. 1996):

1. Frame the problem and identify the options to be considered.
2. Identify the appropriate outcome measures for the problem.
3. Identify intervention and outcome costs.
4. Construct a decision tree, the tool most commonly used to analyze the alternatives under consideration.
5. Identify the probabilities and other data needed to construct the decision tree.

6. Analyze the results of the decision tree.
7. Perform sensitivity analysis on key parameters in the model.
8. Prepare results for presentation.

FRAMING THE PROBLEM

The first step, framing the problem, might seem to be basic and obvious. However, the policy analyst often has to give considerable thought to this stage of the analysis. As we noted with the examples given in chapter 2, most policy problems are not well structured. In the news media a particular public program or strategy is often said to be "cost-effective." The real question, however, is whether the program or strategy is cost-effective compared with an alternative. Cost-effectiveness analysis always involves a comparison of outcomes and costs of one or more alternatives. In some cases, the alternative may be the status quo or no policy. For example, in the case study for this chapter to be discussed below (Gorsky et al. 1996), the cost-effectiveness of the CDC guidelines for voluntary HIV counseling and testing of pregnant women and offering zidovudine (ZDV) to prevent HIV transmission from mother to child is compared with a policy of no program, the situation that existed before the effectiveness of the ZDV intervention was known and the guidelines were established. In a follow-up study, researchers compared alternative policies for administering this intervention, such as the mandatory testing of pregnant women or the mandatory testing of all newborns (Farnham et al. 1999). In this latter case, the current CDC guidelines for voluntary counseling of pregnant women become the alternative against which the other policies are compared.

In other health policy areas, researchers have compared the costs and effects of screening women for cervical cancer versus a policy of no screening, but also screening every five years versus every three or two years or even annually. This is known as extending screening on the intensive margin (Phelps 1997). Other alternatives could be compared, such as extending cervical cancer screening to groups of women, particularly the elderly and women of Hispanic origin, who are currently not being screened (Russell 1994). For mammography screening for breast cancer, protocols typically focus on women over fifty years old, where the incidence of the disease is the greatest. The cost-effectiveness of extending this screening to women between the ages of forty and fifty or between thirty and forty years old could then be considered. Applying the procedure to different groups would be extending the screening on the extensive margin (Phelps 1997). In extending a screening policy on either the intensive or extensive margin, it would be expected that the additional benefits of the extension, such as the number of additional cases of breast or cervical cancer detected, would decline as the intervention was being extended to populations where the prevalence of the disease was lower. Since the additional costs of these extensions would probably increase, a policy that might be cost-effective in one population could easily become less desirable from the cost-effectiveness perspective when extended elsewhere.

In all of these studies, analysts need to consider what may happen under the different policy alternatives regarding such issues as the behavior of the participants, the quality of the screening procedures used, and the prevalence of the health condition in various populations. Each of these factors will influence the costs and outcomes of the alternatives. The question is always what would happen with the given policy compared to what would happen without the policy or with a specific alternative. Thus, cost-effectiveness analysis involves a "with and without" comparison, not a "before and after" comparison. Since there are often no empirical data on what might have happened if the policy had not been in place or what could happen under some hypothetical alternative, the policy analyst must often use a modeling technique, such as decision analysis, to compare alternative policy options. The logic of a decision analysis model forces the analyst to clearly think through the steps by which a policy option could be implemented and how these steps differ among policies under consideration. In health care policy, the counterfactual, or what would have happened under another scenario, may be difficult to determine, given the uncertainties and lack of knowledge associated with many health care events (Rice 1998). However, this uncertainty for many individual decisions about health care may be reduced in the study of populations, since describing the prevalence of disease in probability terms for different populations is the task of epidemiologists.

PERSPECTIVE OF THE ANALYSIS

Choosing a perspective for the analysis is an integral part of framing the problem and selecting the alternatives. The perspective recommended by both Haddix et al. (1996) and the Panel on Cost-Effectiveness in Health and Medicine (Gold et al. 1996) is the societal perspective. Using the societal perspective means that all costs and effects of the programs must be included regardless of who pays the costs and who receives the benefits. This approach is the most comprehensive and the most relevant for making policy decisions influencing the allocation of society's resources among competing activities. Using the societal perspective may have a particular impact on the definition and measurement of program costs. Program costs are often listed in an agency's budget or in the financial statements of a private-sector firm: these costs could simply be added together and compared with the program's output. However, from the societal perspective in economic program evaluation, monetary costs in these types of documents may not adequately reflect the true economic costs of the program or measure all the costs to society related to the provision of the program's output.

In examining both the private and public sectors of the economy, economists usually employ the societal perspective that measures the opportunity costs of producing various types of output. These costs must be included when using the societal perspective for either cost-effectiveness or cost-benefit analysis, and so this discussion is relevant for both this chapter and the one that follows. Opportunity costs measure the cost of using society's resources in one activity in terms of the opportunities foregone or the activities not undertaken. In some cases these costs are equal to the monetary costs found in an agency's budget. However, in other cases budgetary costs reflect an accounting definition rather than an economic definition of costs. Furthermore, some opportunity costs are not found in a given agency's budget and may not easily be evaluated in monetary terms. By definition, certain external costs, such as those resulting from pollution, are imposed on other individuals from the production of a given output and are not recognized by the producer. Opportunity costs include resources not available to society due to an illness or injury. The loss of a person's contribution to the work force is often considered in a cost-effectiveness analysis since it is an opportunity cost, as would be the value assigned to a person's healthy time that has been lost (Haddix et al. 1996). Issues in measuring opportunity costs from the societal perspective will be discussed in more detail below.

Although the societal perspective is recommended as the standard for cost-effectiveness analysis, decisionmakers may also want to adopt other perspectives for various studies. These perspectives include those of

> (1) *federal, state, and local governments* (the impact on the budgets of specific agencies undertaking a prevention program or on programs such as Medicaid and Medicare, which fund the purchase of health services); (2) *health-care providers* (the costs imposed on various types of hospitals, health maintenance organizations [HMOs], or other providers because of the adoption of particular prevention programs; (3) *business* (the impact of illnesses or prevention activities on health-related employee benefits); and (4) *individuals* (the costs of undertaking a current prevention activity with uncertain future benefits or the costs of illness paid out-of-pocket) (Haddix et al. 1996, 16).

For example, to answer questions from the business community about the impact of HIV in the workplace and to engage the business community in HIV prevention, the CDC requested a study of the costs to business of an HIV-infected worker (Farnham and Gorsky 1994). This study focused on the impact of HIV on employee health and life insurance, company retraining costs, and employee pension plans, factors typically not considered when estimating the costs of illness from the societal perspective.

IDENTIFYING OUTCOME MEASURES

The second step in a cost-effectiveness analysis is to identify the outcome measures appropriate for the analysis. Outcome measures must be relevant to the interventions analyzed and must be the same for all interventions. Ideally, a cost-effectiveness analysis should focus on the final outcomes resulting from an intervention, such as life-years gained, rather than any intermediate outcomes, such as the number of cases identified or the number of persons treated under a given intervention. Intermediate outcomes may be used if data on final outcomes are not available or if it is difficult to make a link between the intermediate and final outcomes. For example, the outcome of a clinical intervention to treat hypertension could be measured by the amount of blood pressure reduction achieved, while the treatment of high cholesterol could be measured by the percentage of serum cholesterol reduction. Outcomes of HIV-screening programs could be measured by the number of infections identified. Although these intermediate outcomes may have value in their own right, such as confirming the correct diagnosis of cases of HIV infection, the object of interest is typically the final outcome and the links between intermediate and final outcomes. The relevant questions are (1) how reduced blood pressure or serum cholesterol affects the length and quality of an individual's life, and (2) how many cases of HIV infection are prevented and/or how many life-years are saved by a prevention strategy. Links between intermediate and final outcomes may be derived directly from the results of clinical trials or by extrapolation of clinical trial data. "For example, Oster and Epstein (1987) used an epidemiological model, based on the risk equations in the Framingham Heart Study, to link reduction in total serum cholesterol with coronary heart disease risk and survival" (Drummond et al. 1997, 103). This is a good example of how analysts confront the issue of problem complexity discussed in chapter 2.

In some cases, there may not be a well-established link between the intermediate and final outcome. For example, in evaluating an intervention designed to reduce the blood-lead level in children, the number of children with blood-lead levels less than a certain amount may be selected as the outcome measure. The final outcome measure of interest would more likely relate to the gains in IQ points from lowering blood-lead levels. Because the relationship between blood-lead levels and IQ has not been definitively established, the intermediate outcome may be more appropriate in this case (Haddix et al. 1996). Thus, in using intermediate outcome measures, the policy analyst should either "(1) make a case for the intermediate endpoint having value or clinical relevance in its own right, or (2) be confident that the link between intermediate and final outcomes has been adequately established by previous research" (Drummond et al. 1997, 103).

The choice of outcome measures can also influence the results of the analysis. For example, the use of survival statistics can bias evaluation results in favor of a screening intervention. The results of a prostate cancer screening intervention may be reported in terms of the length of time the patient survived after diagnosis resulting from a screening exam or blood test. Yet this screening exam may simply serve to identify the cancer early, while having little or no impact on life expectancy. This is called "lead-time bias," and it can be an important factor in prostate cancer screening, where many cancers may be slow in growing and never result in the patient's death and where treatment for the disease is uncertain in effectiveness and has many unpleasant side effects (Russell 1994).

Serious side effects should be included in the cost-effectiveness analysis if they exist. For example, it has been proposed to fortify cereal grains with folic acid to increase the intake of women of childbearing age to try to prevent neural tube defects. Since the increased intake of folic acid by older persons may complicate the diagnosis of vitamin B-12 deficiency and ultimately result in permanent neurological complications and death, these side effects should be included in an economic evaluation of alternative strategies for preventing neural tube defects (Haddix et al. 1996).

The choice of outcome measures can also be difficult if program goals have changed over time. This is a particular problem in the evaluation of HIV counseling and testing programs. When it was first licensed in 1985, the primary function of the enzyme-linked immunosorbent assay (ELISA) to detect HIV antibodies was to screen the blood supply so that HIV-infected units of blood could be discarded or set aside for research purposes. However, the ELISA test became part of a nationwide HIV counseling and testing program whose objectives were to help uninfected persons initiate and sustain behavior change to prevent them from becoming infected and to assist infected persons from transmitting the infection to others. A further shift in the goal of HIV counseling and testing programs occurred in 1989 with the introduction of drugs such as ZDV when greater emphasis was placed on the early detection of infected persons so that they could be referred for medical monitoring. These twin goals of behavior change and early detection have been intertwined in both the operation and evaluation of HIV counseling and testing strategies (Farnham 1998).

This conflict is illustrated by Healton et al. (1996) in their analysis of New York state's voluntary HIV counseling and testing program in women's health care settings in 1991. The dual goals of case finding (identifying HIV-infected women) and HIV prevention may work at cross-purposes. "An agency which focuses on case-finding by emphasizing the testing component of the process may achieve its results by sacrificing progress on education and prevention goals, particularly if the testing emphasis reduces the number of women who agree to pretest counseling. Programs that focus on prevention counseling may understate the benefits of early access to medical care services achieved through testing and knowledge of serostatus" (Farnham 1998, 73).

This conflict among goals in program operation has led to a similar confusion and divergence in the definition of program outcomes by analysts performing economic evaluations of these counseling and testing programs. Some studies simply measure the number of persons screened or the number of infections identified by a screening process. Others make assumptions about the number of HIV infections that will be prevented by a particular screening process. Substantial variation exists in these economic evaluations of HIV counseling and testing in different settings (Farnham 1998).

DEFINING AND MEASURING COSTS

Defining and measuring the relevant costs for a cost-effectiveness analysis is also not an unambiguous exercise. The net cost of a disease prevention intervention is typically defined as the cost of the intervention minus the cost of illnesses averted minus the productivity losses averted. Thus the net cost measures the cost of the intervention, including the cost of side effects and the costs to the participants, while netting out the costs of diagnosis and treatment associated with cases of the health problem averted and the productivity losses averted as a result of the intervention (Haddix et al. 1996).

> An ideal cost-effectiveness analysis begins by identifying all of the consequences of adopting one intervention or another, including use of resources (medical services use, public health program costs, informal caregiving, and patient time costs...) and the effects of the intervention on health status... The amount or magnitude of each change is measured. Finally, these changes are

> valued: Changes in resource use are converted into a summary
> cost using dollar values for each input (Gold et al. 1996, 178).

We discussed the importance of cost accounting systems for public policy implementation in chapter 3 of this book. Many of the issues discussed
there, such as the focus on costs per unit of production, on marginal
changes in cost per result, and on accounting for the full pattern of costs
over time, are relevant for cost-effectiveness analysis. However, some costs
necessary for the economic evaluation of public programs are different from
those used for management and control. Ideally, economic evaluation of a
program is incorporated as the program is developed and implemented, so
that relevant cost information can be obtained from the program's accounting system. In reality, economic evaluation is often added on later and analysts must contend with little or no data collected on the relevant costs.

Some of the costs for economic evaluation (explicit) are easily measured since they result from market transactions, while other types of costs
(implicit) may have to be imputed for the analysis. This is particularly
important if the analysis is performed from the societal perspective as discussed above. Intervention costs typically include the costs of tests, drugs,
supplies, health care personnel, and medical facilities. Other nonmedical
costs that may be relevant include child care costs for a parent attending a
smoking cessation program, the increased costs of a special diet, the costs of
transportation to and from a clinic, and the implicit costs of the time spent
by family members or volunteers in providing home health care (Gold et al.
1996). Peter Arno (1986) has argued that the implicit costs of volunteer time
were very important in the early years of the AIDS epidemic. Since the use
of volunteers was much more widespread in the San Francisco area than in
other parts of the country, these implicit costs could have accounted for
geographic differences in the estimated money costs of treating HIV/AIDS.

The value of the patient or client's time is another important implicit
cost that is often not measured but that may be important. Failure to
include these implicit costs could bias the results of economic evaluations
against those that required greater use of market-purchased inputs and less
use of patient time, since the measured money cost of these interventions
would be higher than for those that required a greater mix of patient time.
This could be important in evaluating the cost-effectiveness of street outreach HIV prevention programs versus those located at a particular site
(Wright-DeAguero, Gorsky, and Seeman 1996). A crucial difference between
these programs would be the use of professionals' time versus that of the
patients. More than one-half of the studies surveyed in an analysis of HIV
counseling and testing programs in various settings used only aggregate cost

figures with *no* breakdown among the categories of counseling and testing costs. Outreach costs that may be incurred to find HIV-infected and high-risk persons who do not appear for counseling and testing in established settings have typically not been analyzed. Only two of the forty-three studies surveyed included any valuation of patient or client time (Farnham 1998).

When measuring costs from the societal perspective, opportunity costs must truly reflect the value of using the resource in a particular activity. This value must be included in a cost-effectiveness analysis even if the agency conducting the analysis does not have to pay this cost. For example, a city might be considering two alternative sites for a proposed park. In one case the city already owns the vacant plot of land, while it has to purchase the land in the other case. It might be tempting to argue that the cost of providing the first alternative is lower than for the second option. Although it is true that the monetary cost to the city is lower in the first case, the opportunity cost of using the first plot of land is not necessarily lower. The city needs to determine the value of the first plot of land in its next best alternative use or what price it would command in the market place. This opportunity cost must be included in a cost-effectiveness analysis because the city could lease or sell that plot of land. The cost of using that land to provide park and recreation services is not zero unless there is no alternative use for the land. Of course, the city might not want to include this implicit opportunity cost if, for political or other reasons, decisionmakers were already in favor of the one park option. The decisionmakers might also argue that the implicit cost is not understandable by, nor relevant to, their constituents, since this is not an out-of-pocket cost.

A similar example from the private sector would be the treatment of time incurred by the owner of a company in the production of a good or service. In a family-operated business the owner may not explicitly be paid a salary, so that the costs of his or her time may not be included as a cost of production. This practice will result in an overstatement of the firm's profits. If the owner could earn $40,000 per year by working in some other activity, that figure represents the opportunity cost of the individual's time in the family business, but this cost may not be reflected in any existing financial statement.

In a competitive market economy where resources are fully employed, the market price that an agency must pay for its inputs typically reflects their opportunity costs. For example, if the wages of construction workers are determined by the forces of supply and demand (as discussed in the previous chapter) and if all workers who want to work are able to do so, the monetary cost of hiring those workers for a public-sector program, which is reflected in the agency's budget, should equal the opportunity cost of employing the workers. The only way to draw workers into the public sector is to pay them what they could earn in the private sector. However, if certain types of workers face the prospect of continuing unemployment, the opportunity cost of employing them for a public-sector project may be less than the monetary cost in the agency's budget.

In a detailed study of construction projects, Robert Haveman (1983) estimated the proportion of labor and capital that was drawn from an idle pool of these resources by comparing the pattern of resource demands with the occupational and regional pattern of labor unemployment and the industrial pattern of excess plant capacity. He argued that the opportunity cost of the expenditures for these projects in 1960 varied between 70 and 90 percent of the monetary costs. The validity of adjusting monetary costs to reflect problems of unemployment depends upon whether the opportunity cost of using unemployed labor is zero or extremely low. The value of that nonworking time may not be zero if it is used, for instance, for family activities or going to school. Furthermore, macroeconomic conditions also influence the rates of unemployment. Edward Gramlich (1981, 67) argues that the opportunity cost of unemployed labor is less than its monetary cost only if

> (1) the reduction in unemployment can be sustained. Inflationary pressures will not be set up which require other cutbacks in spending demand, generating corresponding increases in unemployment somewhere else in the economy. (2) The project is responsible for reducing unemployment. Tax reductions, monetary policy, or price flexibility would not have done so anyway. (3) It can be persuasively argued that the supply curve or some other notion of social externality makes the opportunity cost below the market wage.

Since valuing labor costs below their monetary costs makes a public-sector project look more favorable, advocates of a project will often be tempted to follow this procedure. Gramlich argues that this approach must be resisted if the above three conditions are not met. Otherwise, public-sector projects either do not really create jobs, or they are not the only way to do so, or they create jobs that do not have much social value (Gramlich 1981, 1990).

A good health care example of the problems of adjusting budgetary costs and of measuring all costs associated with a program is given by Burton Weisbrod (1983) in his comparison of hospital- with community-based treatment of the mentally ill. He argues that the costs of inpatient care at the Mendota Mental Health Institute (MMHI) provided by Wisconsin differ from the true social or opportunity costs in three respects: "(1) *the opportunity cost of the land* on which the hospital is located had been disregarded; (2) *the depreciation of the hospital buildings* was based on historical cost rather than replacement cost; and (3) *research* carried out at MMHI was included in the per diem cost figure for the hospital" (Weisbrod 1983, 237). The land valuation problem was discussed above. Depreciation presents a problem because accounting procedures typically involve the use of historical costs. Yet it is the current cost of replacing the asset that best reflects the opportunity cost of using the asset to provide output. Research costs were included in the per diem figure for accounting purposes, but these costs were not directly related to the treatment of patients. Thus, the per diem cost estimated by the state "was adjusted upward to allow for an opportunity cost of 8 percent on the estimated value of the land and the depreciated replacement cost of the physical plant, and it was adjusted slightly downward to account for research services." (Weisbrod 1983, 237).

Other costs that Weisbrod attempted to measure included secondary treatment costs by other agencies, institutions, and professions; law enforcement costs associated with the different modes of treatment; external costs caused by the patients' illnesses, and patient maintenance costs. Secondary costs included those of other hospitals and psychiatric institutions, halfway houses, visiting nurses, and counseling services. Law enforcement costs were obtained from patient interviews about the number of police and court contacts, the number of nights spent in jail, and the number of contacts with probation and parole officers. External costs related to members of the patients' immediate families or other individuals who suffered from the illegal or disruptive behavior of the patients. It was impossible to place monetary values on these costs. However, family members were asked whether they had experienced work or school absences, disruption of domestic or social routines, trouble with neighbors, or stress-related physical ailments as a result of the patient's illness. They were also questioned about expenses incurred that were related to the patient. These responses were used to categorize each family as suffering a "severe," "moderate," "mild," or "no" burden from the patient's illness. Although the attempt was made to count only the incremental patient maintenance costs associated with the outpatient program, data limitations meant that all maintenance costs were actually included in the analysis (Weisbrod 1983, 239–41). Thus, implementation problems may prevent analysts from calculating all costs as theoretically desired or from valuing all costs in monetary terms. These problems should be noted and their implications discussed, so that decisionmakers have full information about the limits of the analysis.

Another cost measurement issue that may be of importance in evaluating health care policies is the difference between costs and charges of medical and health care services. There may be substantial differences between the fees that hospitals and other institutions charge for their services and the actual economic costs of providing the services (Finkler 1982; Drummond et al. 1997). Hospitals engage in cost shifting both to maximize their revenues from various public and private third-party payers and to provide services for those patients without insurance who are unable to pay. Different individuals or groups may, therefore, be charged fees that are more or less than the actual cost of providing the service to them. Many studies do not provide a clear distinction between these two terms. For example, in estimating the lifetime cost of HIV and AIDS, Fred Hellinger (1993, 474) uses the term *cost* but defines this to mean "total charges for services." Data on provider charges are generally much more readily available than data on the actual opportunity cost of providing the services. However, *cost-to-charge ratios* are often used to make the adjustment between these two sets of concepts. One hospital-level ratio may be used, or a more detailed approach may be taken: "(1) The patient's detailed bill is reconfigured into a set of exhaustive charges, or billing, categories; (2) each charge category is assigned to a specific hospital cost center; (3) the cost-to-charge ratio for each center is used to convert these assigned charges to their corresponding cost estimates; and (4) the latter are summed to yield the cost of admission" (Gold et al. 1996, 205). Gold et al. (1996) provide further details on how this approach has been implemented for different health care services.

TIMING OF COSTS

A final issue in the measurement of the costs of an intervention involves the timing of the costs if they extend a number of years into the future. Since this issue also relates to a stream of future health outcomes or benefits of a program measured in monetary terms, this discussion is relevant for the issues of cost-benefit analysis presented in the following chapter. As noted above, these issues may be particularly relevant for evaluating health prevention interventions with either cost-effectiveness or cost-benefit analyses, since the outcomes or benefits of these interventions may occur many years in the future, while many of the costs may arise in the present. The issue is how to compare costs and benefits that arise during different periods.

We discussed the issue of multiyear costs from the budgeting perspective in chapter 3. There we argued that decisionmakers must consider the difference between capital costs and current operating costs to fully account for all the costs of a program and to correctly plan the methods of financing multiyear projects. The issues here are similar but are now being discussed from a program evaluation perspective.

The timing problem arises because individuals weigh benefits and costs that occur now or in the near future more heavily than those that occur in the distant future. A dollar that I receive next year is worth more than a dollar that I receive ten years in the future because I can invest next year's dollar so that it will be worth more than $1 in ten years. This argument relates to the productivity of capital and investments and has nothing to do with the inflation rate. It would be relevant in a world of zero inflation. Thus, it is necessary to calculate the present value of both costs and benefits in real terms to make them comparable in terms of the time dimension. This present value calculation involves the choice of a discount rate. What discount rate to choose is an extremely controversial question that can have a major impact on the results of a cost-effectiveness or a cost-benefit analysis.

The calculation of the present value of a flow of costs or benefits is the reverse of the compound-interest problem. Compound interest attempts to determine what a given amount of money will be worth n years in the future at a given interest rate for compounding. Thus, $100 will be worth $110 one year from now if the interest rate is 10 percent. If this amount is left to compound for another year, it will grow to $121. Alternatively, the present value of $110 received one year from now is $100 using a discount rate of 10 percent. This result can be calculated from the following formula: Present value = $110 / (1 + 0.10) = $100. The present value of $121 received two years from now is also $100 and can be calculated as $121 / (1 + 0.10)^2. Thus, the present value of an annual stream of costs or benefits flowing n years in the future can be derived as follows: Present value = $R_1 / (1 + i) + R_2 / (1 + i)^2 + \ldots + R_n / (1 + i)^n$ where R_n is the dollar amount of the cost or benefit in the nth year and i is the discount rate.

The choice of a discount rate can have a significant impact on the resulting present-value calculations. Suppose that benefits from Project A equal $100 in year 1 and zero thereafter, whereas benefits of Project B are zero in the first 19 years and $100 in year 20. This is an extreme example of a short-term versus a long-term project with equal monetary benefits. Using the above formulas and a discount rate of 5 percent, the present value of benefits for Project A is $95.23, while for Project B it is $37.89. Thus, benefits one year from now are weighted much more heavily than benefits received 20 years from now. If a discount rate of 20 percent is used, the present value of the benefits of Project A is $83.33, while the present value for Project B is only $2.61. The present value of benefits for both projects decreases, but there is a much larger drop for Project B. Thus, raising the discount rate favors the short-term investment project. Low rates favor long-term investments.

The following more realistic example shows how changing the discount rate can significantly affect the relationship between a project's benefits and costs. Suppose that the project life is 25 years and that the initial capital cost is $5 million. The annual operating cost is $100,000 per year for 25 years and the annual benefits are $600,000 per year. Table 6.1 shows the benefits, costs, benefit-cost ratio, and net benefits (benefits minus costs) calculated for four different discount rates ranging from 0 percent (no discounting) to 10 percent.

It can be seen in Table 6.1 that the undiscounted benefits of $7.5 million drop to $3.7 million when a discount rate of only 3 percent is used in the example. The net benefits keep decreasing with a higher discount rate and become *negative* when a 10 percent rate is used. Thus, raising the discount rate alone can change the net benefits of a project from positive to negative. These issues are of particular importance to many health care interventions whose benefits and costs may extend over a significant period of time.

Given this importance of the discount rate, the question becomes this: What rate should be used in cost-effectiveness and cost-benefits studies? In cost-effectiveness analysis, there is also the question of whether health outcomes, which are not measured in dollar terms, should be discounted. These questions are controversial both in theory and in actual practice.

It is often argued that the opportunity cost or the rate of return that resources could earn in the private sector is the appropriate choice for a discount rate (Baumol 1970; Gramlich 1981; 1990). If resources are drawn from the private sector of the economy into the public sector, they should provide a rate of return in the public sector at least as great as what could have been earned in the private sector. However, the question still remains of

Table 6.1: The Effects of Discount Rates on Project Evaluation

	DISCOUNT RATES			
	0.00%	3.00%	5.00%	10.00%
Benefits (B)	$15,000,000	$10,448,000	$8,456,000	$5,442,000
Costs (C)	$7,500,000	$6,741,000	$6,409,000	$5,906,000
B / C	2.00	1.55	1.32	0.92
B–C	$7,500,000	$3,707,000	$2,047,000	–$464,000

B, benefits; C, costs; B / C, benefit-cost ratio; B–C, net benefits.

what rate measures this opportunity cost, since interest rates vary with the source from which the project's resources are drawn. A variety of interest rates in the private sector reflect differences in risk, the impact of distortionary taxes, and imperfections in the market place. Government monetary and fiscal policies in pursuit of various macroeconomic goals also influence interest rates. A weighted average of different rates may be most appropriate, although the choice of rates is unclear.

There is another viewpoint, which argues that a social discount rate derived through the political process should be used instead of any market-related rates (Baumol 1970; Gramlich 1981; 1990; Gold et al. 1996; Krahn and Gafni 1993). Arguments for the use of a social discount rate lower than market rates reflect concern about whether society overvalues present consumption relative to future consumption and whether individuals have preferences for social outcomes that differ from their preferences for private market outcomes. Even if these arguments are accepted, there is still the question of determining the optimal social discount rate.

There has also been considerable debate about whether nonmonetary health outcomes should be discounted: that is, should a year of life gained ten years from now be valued differently than a year of life gained one year from now? Marthe Gold et al. (1996) and Anne Haddix et al. (1996) present comprehensive summaries of the literature on this debate. A consensus seems to have developed that future health outcomes should be discounted at the same rate as monetary costs and benefits.

> Future health outcomes are also discounted, not because health outcomes realized today are more valuable than health outcomes realized tomorrow, but because in prevention-effectiveness studies, if health outcomes are not discounted but costs are discounted, the cost per health outcome prevented will decrease over time. Thus discounting health outcomes at the same rate as monetary outcomes creates an "exchange rate" for dollars and health outcomes that is time invariant (Haddix et al. 1996, 79).

The actual range of discount rates used in cost-effectiveness and cost-benefit analyses reflects the uncertainties in the theoretical discussions. Robert Lind (1982) recommended a rate of 1 percent for "safe investments" and 2 percent for "safe long-term assets." J. A. Lesser and R. O. Zerbe (1994) argued for a real discount rate of 2.5 to 5.0 percent for public projects. The British National Health Service uses a real discount rate of 6 percent (Parsonage and Newburger 1992), while the World Bank (1993) has settled on a 3 percent rate. The U.S. Office of Management and Budget has recommended rates between 2 and 3 percent for cost-effectiveness studies that focus on the least-cost means for the government to achieve some predetermined objective, and a 7 percent real rate for cost-benefit analyses where all outcomes and costs are measured in monetary terms (Gold et al. 1996). The two major guidelines for health care economic evaluations have reached a reasonable consensus on this issue. Haddix et al. (1996) recommend either a 3 or 5 percent real rate with sensitivity analysis undertaken with rates ranging from 0 (no discounting) to 8 percent. Gold et al. (1996) recommend 3 percent with sensitivity analysis ranging from 0 to 7 percent. However, these authors also recommend using a 5 percent rate, at least in the near future, given the large number of recent studies that have employed this rate.

USE OF DECISION ANALYSIS

Decision analysis is the key quantitative tool used to derive the relationships between costs and outcome measures in a cost-effectiveness analysis. "Decision analysis is an explicit, quantitative, and systematic approach to decisionmaking under conditions of uncertainty" (Haddix et al. 1996, 27). It is a tool that can be used to calculate the expected utility, cost, or benefit of different policies or alternative courses of action. For use in cost-effectiveness analysis, most decision analysis programs can be run so as to simultaneously calculate both the expected cost and the expected outcome of each policy being analyzed. Expectation means that the various costs and consequences of different policy options are influenced by the probability of certain events occurring that are not under the control of the decisionmaker. An expected outcome is calculated by multiplying the value associated with that outcome times the probability of that outcome occurring. This may be done repeatedly, depending upon the chain of events associated with each policy option.

As outlined by Haddix et al. (1996), the basic steps in a decision analysis are the following:

1. Structure the problem.
2. Develop a decision tree.
3. Estimate the relevant probabilities.
4. Value the outcomes or consequences.
5. Average out and fold back the decision tree.
6. Interpret the results in light of the inherent uncertainty.

A decision node is the first point of choice in a decision tree that shows the alternative decision options or policies being evaluated. Chance nodes are then built into the tree reflecting events whose outcomes are not under the control of the decisionmaker. Probabilities, based on literature searches, the results of scientific studies, estimates made by a panel of experts, or educated guesses, are assigned to each chance node. Outcome measures are assigned to each terminal node or endpoint of the sequence of events. To obtain measures of expected costs and consequences, decision trees are averaged out or folded back. This means that the value of the outcome for each branch is multiplied by its respective probability. At each chance node, the products for the entire set of branches emanating from that node are summed. This process, which is repeated until the analyst has arrived at the decision node, then gives a measure of the expected costs and outcomes associated with each decision option or policy.

Because the decision tree underlying any cost-effectiveness analysis usually contains numerous input variables (probabilities, cost, and outcome measures) and because the values of many of these variables may not be known with great certainty, sensitivity analysis is used to determine how much the expected costs and outcomes of the model are affected by changes in the input variables. Sensitivity analysis can be used to show how much an expected cost or outcome changes if the numerical value of a probability or outcome measure is changed or how much an estimated input value would have to change to produce a different result for the entire analysis. It can also show what value a variable would have to take for two policy options to have equal expected value (threshold analysis) or what happens to the results of the model if "best case" or "worst case" scenario estimates are used (Haddix et al. 1996). These issues are very similar to the effects of uncertainty on revenue forecasting discussed in chapter 4.

Constructing a decision tree is such a useful tool for cost-effectiveness analysis because it forces the policy analyst to explicitly outline the various policy options and identify the costs and consequences associated with each option. The decision tree can provide a much more comprehensive analysis than simply using intuition because it uses more information and can consider many more options. Decision analysis can help an analyst understand and convey information about policy options more clearly: it lends structure, organization, and reason to what are often very difficult decisionmaking processes (Haddix et al. 1996). We noted these advantages of modeling in the problem definition discussion in chapter 2 and in the analysis of causal revenue forecasting techniques in chapter 4.

In the health care arena the policy analyst is very fortunate to have the three major references cited in this chapter, Haddix et al. (1996), Gold et al. (1996), and Drummond et al. (1997), to provide more details on all aspects of decision and cost-effectiveness analysis. These guides have been produced both to reflect the major developments in the methodology of estimating costs and consequences of health care programs over the past decade and to try to standardize the procedures used in these analyses. Readers interested in other policy areas should consult the relevant literature to determine how these techniques have been applied in those areas.

CHAPTER 6 CASE STUDY

Preventing Perinatal Transmission of HIV—Costs and Effectiveness of a Recommended Intervention

Robin D. Gorsky, PhD; Paul G. Farnham, PhD; Walter L. Straus, MD MPH; Blake Caldwell, MD MPH; David R. Holtgrave, PhD; R. J. Simonds, MD; Martha F. Rogers, MD; Mary E. Guinan, MD PhD

SYNOPSIS

Objective. To calculate the national costs of reducing perinatal transmission of human immunodeficiency virus through counseling and voluntary testing of pregnant women and zidovudine treatment of infected women and their infants, as recommended by the Public Health Service, and to compare these costs with the savings from reducing the number of pediatric infections.

Method. The authors analyzed the estimated costs of the intervention and the estimated cost savings from reducing the number of pediatric infections. The outcome measures are the number of infections prevented by the intervention and the net cost (cost of intervention minus the savings from a reduced number of pediatric HIV infections). The base model assumed that intervention participation and outcomes would resemble those found in the AIDS Clinical Trials Group Protocol 076. Assumptions were varied regarding maternal seroprevalence, participation by HIV-infected women, the proportion of infected women who accepted and completed the treatment, and the efficacy of zidovudine to illustrate the effect of these assumptions on infections prevented and net cost.

Results. Without the intervention, a perinatal HIV transmission rate of 25% would result in 1750 HIV-infected infants born annually in the United States, with lifetime medical-care costs estimated at $282 million. The cost of the intervention (counseling, testing, and zidovudine treatment) was estimated to be $67.6 million. In the

Dr. Gorsky, who had been with the Department of Health Management and Policy at the University of New Hampshire and the Division of HIV/AIDS Prevention at the Centers for Diseases Control and Prevention in Atlanta, is deceased. Dr. Farnham, Dr. Straus, Dr. Caldwell, Dr. Simonds, Dr. Rogers, and Dr. Guinan are all with the Division of HIV/AIDS Prevention at the Centers for Disease Control and Prevention. Dr. Farnham is also with the Department of Economics, Georgia State University, Atlanta. Dr. Holtgrave is with the Center for AIDS Intervention Research, Medical College of Wisconsin, Milwaukee. Address correspondence to Dr. Guinan, Mail Stop D-01, Centers for Disease Control and Prevention, 1600 Clifton Road N.E., Atlanta, GA 30333; tel. 404-639-4475; fax 404-639-4463; e-mail <meg3@epo.em.cdc.gov>.

base model, the intervention would prevent 656 pediatric HIV infections with a medical care cost saving of $105.6 million. The net cost saving of the intervention was $38.1 million.

Conclusion. Voluntary HIV screening of pregnant women and ziovudine treatment for infected women and their infants resulted in cost savings under most of the assumptions used in this analysis. These results strongly support implementation of the Public Health Service recommendations for this intervention.

In the United States, nearly all new human immunodeficiency virus (HIV) infections in children are acquired through perinatal (mother-to-infant) transmission. Each year, approximately 7000 infants are born to HIV-infected women in the United States.[1] Without intervention, an estimated 15–30% of these infants would become infected.[2]

In 1994, results of the AIDS Clinical Trial Group (ACTG) Protocol 076 showed that treatment of infected pregnant women and their infants with zidovudine (ZDV) reduced the rate of perinatal HIV transmission from 25% to 8%.[3,4] Following these findings, the Public Health Service (PHS) issued recommendations for ZDV therapy to prevent perinatal HIV transmission[5] and for HIV counseling and voluntary testing of pregnant women.[6]

The potential cost of HIV counseling and voluntary testing of pregnant women in the United States has not been determined, nor has the cost-effectiveness of such screening combined with recommended ZDV treatment for preventing perinatal HIV transmission.[4] Because medical care for HIV infection is costly, savings resulting from HIV infections prevented can be substantial. The estimated annual costs for an HIV-infected adult are $5,000 for persons who have not developed AIDS and $35,000 for those with AIDS.[7] For an HIV-infected child, direct costs per year are $9,400 before development of AIDS and $38,000 after AIDS.[8]

Data from various sources were used to calculate both the intervention costs and the resulting pediatric medical care cost savings. The intervention costs included HIV counseling and voluntary testing services for pregnant women, ZDV treatment prenatally and during labor and delivery for those who are infected, ZDV treatment for their infants, and recommended laboratory testing during ZDV treatment.[5,6] To determine the savings from preventing pediatric infections, the costs associated with treatment for infants perinatally infected without the intervention were compared with treatment costs for infants who became infected despite the intervention.

Methods

Actual costs for HIV counseling, testing, ZDV treatment, and medical treatment of infected infants were included without regard to who would pay for them (societal perspective). The time horizon for the intervention costs was one year. To determine the lifetime savings from prevented pediatric infections, we included the present value of medical care that would have been incurred in the future. We did not consider the additional costs of treating HIV-infected women who would not have learned of their infection until later in the course of their illness, nor any additional benefits resulting from the intervention (for example, reduced HIV transmission to sexual or needle-sharing partners of infected women).[9,10]

Intervention costs. The intervention was divided into two cost components: (a) the direct costs associated with HIV counseling and voluntary testing services for pregnant women receiving first and second trimester prenatal care; and (b) the costs associated with ZDV treatment (that is, oral ZDV prenatally and intravenous ZDV during labor and delivery for infected women, oral ZDV for HIV-exposed newborns, and recommended laboratory testing during ZDV therapy) (see Box).

HIV counseling and voluntary testing costs. The number of eligible women was defined as the number of pregnant women of more than 13 weeks gestation[11] who receive prenatal care.[12] We estimated this number by adding the fetal losses and induced abortions occurring after 13 weeks gestation[13] to the number of annual live births in the United States.[12] This sum was then multiplied by the proportion of women (.939) who receive first or second trimester prenatal care.[12]

We made the following assumptions for the analysis: (a) all pregnant women entering prenatal care during the first or second trimester would be offered HIV counseling and testing; (b) women who had previously tested HIV seronegative would require retesting during each pregnancy; and (c) the number of HIV-infected pregnant women who knew their serostatus at entry into prenatal care would be small compared with total births. Since empirical data were lacking, we also assumed that HIV screening would not affect reproductive decision-making and that HIV seroprevalence was the same for women accepting and those refusing HIV tests.

HIV counseling and testing costs for seropositive women differ from those for seronegative women. In addition, client-based[14,15] counseling costs are greater for uninfected women at high risk (more extensive counseling) than for those at low risk. To determine the cost of HIV counseling and testing of uninfected women, a weighted average was calculated as follows—since 55% of U.S. women who give birth reside in states with relatively high HIV seroprevalence rates (more than one HIV-infected pregnant woman per 1000 live births),[16] we assumed that all seronegative pregnant women in these states would receive full counseling with costs comparable to those found in publicly funded clinics, or $33 per person.[17] This included the cost of pretest counseling, one enzyme-linked immunosorbent assay (ELISA), and post-test counseling on a return visit. For the 45% of women who give birth in states with low seroprevalence rates (less than one HIV-infected pregnant woman per 1000 live births), we assumed the costs of counseling seronegative women to be subsumed into routine prenatal care. Therefore, we assigned a cost of $6 per person (the cost of the ELISA) for seronegative women in these states.[17] Thus, the overall national cost estimate for HIV counseling and testing of seronegative women was $19.50 per person. For seropositive women, the cost of HIV counseling and testing was $103, which included additional costs for post-test counseling and confirmatory tests (ELISA and Western blot).[17]

We also assumed that all HIV-infected pregnant women receiving prenatal care in the first or second trimester would be offered ZDV treatment, regardless of their CD4+ T-lymphocyte counts or prior use of ZDV. Women who experienced fetal loss, who chose to terminate their pregnancies, or who entered prenatal care during the third trimester or later were excluded.

ZDV treatment costs. Average duration of ZDV therapy used in the ACTG Protocol 076[4] and average weights for a woman (50 kilograms) and newborn infant (4 kilograms) were used in calculating the cost of the ZDV regimen. The defined regimen involved oral ZDV for infected women during pregnancy (100 milligrams per dose multiplied by 5 doses per day multiplied by 12 weeks [420 100-milligram capsules]); intravenous ZDV for women during labor and delivery (2 milligrams per kilogram

Annual Cost Estimates of HIV Counseling and Testing of All Pregnant Women in the United States and of Zidovudine (ZDV) Treatment of Infected Women and Their Infants

Counseling and testing	
Number of pregnancies[a]	4,522,823
Number in prenatal care[b]	4,246,930
Number counseled and tested[c]	3,312,606
Number positive[d]	5,666
Number negative[d]	3,306,940
(a)Total cost[e]	$65,068,921
ZDV treatment	
Number of women eligible[f]	4,958
Number accepting ZDV during pregnancy[g]	3,371
(b)Cost of ZDV during pregnancy[h]	$1,858,466
(c)Cost of laboratory monitoring[i]	$448,392
Number receiving ZDV during labor and delivery	2,849
(d)Cost of ZDV during labor and deliver[j]	$131,366
Number receiving neonatal ZDV	2,407
(e)Cost of neonatal ZDV[k]	$40,486
Total cost of ZDV regimen	$2,478,709
Total annual cost (a+b+c+d+e)	$67,547,629

[a]Including pregnancies terminated or ending in fetal loss after the first trimester; these women would be eligible for HIV counseling and testing (HIV CT).[11,13]
[b]Assumes all pregnant women entering prenatal care during the first two trimesters are offered HIV CT.[12]
[c]Assumes that pregnant women accept HIV CT in the same proportion as that reported for other populations, 78%.[20,21]
[d]Adjusted for the sensitivity and specificity of the HIV tests and recommended test sequence;[17] assumes HIV seroprevalence of 1.7 per 1000 births.
[e]Cost for HIV CT: positive, $103; negative, $19.50.[17] (Adjusted as described in paper.)
[f]Number positive adjusted for fetal losses and induced abortions occurring after 13 weeks gestation.[13]
[g]Assume 68% of infected pregnant women accept prenatal ZDV if offered.[22]
[h]ZDV treatment cost—$551.25 per woman during pregnancy.
[i]Complete blood count at $21 per test (2 per woman and 1 per child) and chemistry profile at $35 per test (2 per woman).
[j]ZDV treatment cost—$46.11 per woman during labor and delivery; assumes 84.5% of women receiving ZDV during pregnancy also receive ZDV during labor and delivery.[4]
[k]ZDV treatment cost—$16.82 per newborn; assumes 71.4% of children born to infected mothers receiving ZDV during pregnancy receive ZDV neonatally.[4]

plus 1 milligram per kilogram per hour for 12 hours [700 milligrams ZDV]); and oral ZDV for HIV-exposed newborns (2 milligrams per kilogram per dose multiplied by 4 doses per day multiplied by 6 weeks [134 cubic centimeters of syrup]).

We contacted five principal investigators of the original ACTG Protocol 076 (from geographically representative areas) to obtain the current wholesale costs of the recommended preparations of ZDV from their hospital pharmacies. The following average ZDV treatment costs per person were used: (a) $551 for maternal treatment during pregnancy; (b) $46 for maternal treatment during labor and delivery; and (c) $17 for newborn treatment. Costs involved in administering intravenous ZDV were not included.

Using standard hospital laboratory cost data, we estimated the costs for laboratory testing during ZDV therapy (two 20-test chemistry profiles for the mother, two complete blood counts (CBC) for the mother, and one CBC for the infant[5] as follows: (a) $35 for each chemistry profile; and (b) $21 for each CBC.

Costs of medical care treatment for HIV-infected infants. We adapted reported annual costs for HIV-infected children[8] to estimate lifetime costs for a perinatally infected child (Table 1). Based on information from the revised classification system for HIV infection in children[18] as well as reported symptomatic disease progression,[19] the following average profile was developed for a child infected at birth: no symptoms in the first 9 months of life followed by mild HIV symptoms in months 10 to 13, moderate symptoms in months 14 to 57, and AIDS development at months 58 to 113 (average life span, 113 months).

Because no data exist to differentiate between costs for children with mild versus moderate symptomatic HIV disease, the following percentages were used: 75% of reported monthly medical costs for mild-symptom months and 125% for moderate-symptom months. Using a discount rate of 5%, we estimated the present value of lifetime medical care treatment costs for one perinatally infected infant and determined that the medical care costs-saved from preventing one pediatric HIV infection were $161,137.

Assumptions affecting outcomes. The following assumptions were made for the base model: (a) 78% of pregnant women offered HIV counseling and testing will accept;[20,21] (b) 68% of HIV-infected women identified through such screening who are offered ZDV treatment will accept and complete the first treatment component (oral ZDV during pregnancy);[22] (c) perinatal HIV transmission rates were 8% with the complete (maternal and infant) ZDV regimen[4], 25% with no ZDV[4], and 16.5% with maternal oral ZDV during pregnancy and either maternal intravenous ZDV during

TABLE 1. Annual and Lifetime Medical Costs for Perinatally Infected Children

Year of Life	Symptoms by Age in Months[a]	Undiscounted Costs[b]	5% Discounted Costs
1	1–9, none; 10–12, mild HIV	$1,759	$1,675
2	13, mild; 14–24, moderate HIV	11,337	10,283
3	25–36, moderate HIV	11,728	10,131
4	37–48, moderate HIV	11,728	9,648
5	49–57, moderate HIV; 58–60, AIDS	18,278	14,321
6	61–72, AIDS	37,928	28,302
7	73–84, AIDS	37,928	26,955
8	85–96, AIDS	37,928	25,671
9	97–108, AIDS	37,928	24,449
10	109–113, AIDS	15,803	9,702
Total		222,344	161,137

[a]See references 18, 19.
[b]Medical costs for treatment of HIV infection before development of AIDS: $9382 per year = $782 per month × 0.75 = $586.38 per month (mild); $782 × 1.25 = $977.29 per month (moderate). Medical costs for treatment of AIDS: $37,928 per year = $3.161 per month. See reference 8.

labor and delivery or oral ZDV for the infant (based on evidence that some reduction in transmission can occur without completion of all three components of the protocol;[23,24] (d) ZDV efficacy in women with CD4+ T-lymphocyte counts more than 200 cells per milliliter or with prior ZDV therapy was the same as that for women with higher CD4+ counts and no previous ZDV therapy; and (e) the proportion of patients completing all components of the ZDV regimen (pregnancy, labor and delivery, neonatal) was the same as that observed in ACTG Protocol 076: 84.5% of women who completed oral ZDV during pregnancy received intravenous ZDV during labor and delivery, and 71.4% of infants born to women who completed oral ZDV during pregnancy received the oral ZDV newborn regimen.[4]

The assumptions from the base model were varied as follows: (a) in the no partial effect model, the perinatal transmission rate was 25% unless all three components of the ZDV regimen were completed, and (b) in the complete treatment model, all eligible women and infants completed all three ZDV treatment components and the transmission rate was 8%.

Four sensitivity analyses were developed on the base model only. First, because maternal HIV seroprevalence rates among states vary from more than 5 per 1000 (New York) to less than 0.1 per 1000 (Utah), this rate was varied from the national average of 1.7 per 1000. Next, the proportion of women who accept HIV counseling and testing was varied upward from the base case of 78%. Third, the proportion of women who receive ZDV treatment was varied upward from the base case of 68%. Finally, the lifetime cost of medical treatment for a perinatally infected infant was varied up and down from the base-case value, since the only published estimate of pediatric lifetime medical costs[8] is not based upon age-specific cost data.

Results

Without the intervention, 1750 HIV-infected infants would require treatment (7000 births annually to HIV-infected women, with a 25% perinatal transmission rate). Using the present value of lifetime medical treatment costs of $161,137 per infant, the total cost of treating these children was $282 million.

In the base model, the intervention would prevent 656 perinatally transmitted HIV infections (Table 2), resulting in medical care cost savings of $105.6 million (calculated from Table 3 as $282 million without the intervention less $176.4 million with the intervention). When these medical care cost savings are subtracted from the cost of the intervention ($65.1 million for HIV counseling and testing plus $2.5 million for the complete ZDV treatment regimen), the net cost of the intervention is -$38.1 million. Thus, the intervention is cost-saving.

In the no partial effect model, the costs to provide HIV counseling and testing and ZDV treatment were the same as in the base model, but only 574 infections were prevented (Tables 2 and 3). This resulted in a cost saving of $24.9 million.

In the complete treatment model, the counseling and testing costs were also the same as in the base model, but the ZDV treatment costs were higher ($3.7 million compared with $2.5 million), since all eligible HIV-infected women and -exposed infants received the complete ZDV treatment regimen (Table 3). In this model, a larger number of infections were prevented (1007), resulting in a greater medical care cost-saving ($162.3 million) and a net cost-saving of $93.5 million.

(Text continues on p. 280)

TABLE 2. Number of HIV-Infected Infants Resulting from Intervention Effects

Model	Mother Not Tested[a]	False-Negative Test Results[a]	No ZDV (Mother or Infants)[a]	Partial ZDV Treatment[b]	Full ZDV Treatment[c]	Infected Infants	Infections Prevented[d]
Base case[e]	343.3	2.8	396.6	159.1	192.6	1094.4	655.6
No partial effect[f]	343.3	2.8	396.6	241.0	192.6	1176.3	573.7
Complete treatment[g]	343.3	2.8	—	—	396.6	742.7	1007.3

[a]25% transmission rate.
[b]16.5% transmission rate [50% reduction—includes maternal ZDV during pregnancy plus either maternal ZDV during labor and delivery or neonatal ZDV].
[c]8% transmission rate.
[d]Infected infants without intervention (1750) minus total infected infants.
[e]Assumes parameters of ACTG protocol 076 and 50% efficacy from partial ZDV treatment.
[f]Assumes parameters of ACTG protocol 076 and no effect from partial ZDV treatment.
[g]Assumes parameters of ACTG protocol 076 and that women eligible for ZDV complete all components.

TABLE 3. Cost and Effectiveness of Intervention for Pregnant Women in the United States[a]

Model	Counseling and Testing	ZDV Treatment	Medical Costs With Intervention	Medical Costs Without Intervention	Medical Cost Saved[e]	Net Costs[f]	Infections Prevented
Base case[b]	$65,068,921	$2,478,709	$176,346,305	$281,989,750	$105,643,445	–$38,095,816	655.6
No partial effect[c]	65,068,921	2,478,709	189,552,758	281,989,759	92,436,992	–24,889,363	573.7
Complete treatment[d]	65,068,921	3,704,444	119,679,701	281,989,759	162,310,049	–93,536,684	1007.3

[a]Negative net costs represent cost savings.
[b]Assumes parameters of ACTG protocol 076 and 50% efficacy from partial ZDV treatment.
[c]Assumes parameters of ACTG protocol 076 and no effect from partial ZDV treatment.
[d]Assumes parameters of ACTG protocol 076 and that women eligible for ZDV complete all components.
[e]Medical costs without intervention minus costs with intervention.
[f]Cost of counseling, testing, and ZDV treatment minus medical costs saved.

TABLE 4. Effect of Modifying Model Assumptions on the Net Cost of the Intervention

Modifications	Net Cost
Maternal seroprevalence	
0.00010	$58,590,167
0.00100	4,564,485
0.00170	–38,095,816
0.00200	–55,486,746
0.00300	–115,523,387
0.00500	–235,611,260
Proportion of pregnant women accepting HIV counseling and testing	
0.78	–38,095,816
0.82	–39,242,885
0.86	–40,389,955
0.90	–41,537,024
0.94	–42,684,093
Proportion of HIV-infected women accepting ZDV treatment during pregnancy	
0.68	–38,095,816
0.70	–40,350,747
0.75	–45,988,075
0.80	–51,625,403
0.85	–57,262,731
0.90	–62,900,058
0.95	–68,537,386
Lifetime medical care treatment costs for a perinatally infected child	
$125,000	–14,403,944
140,000	–24,238,133
165,000	–40,628,448
180,000	–50,462,636
195,000	–60,296,825
210,000	–70,131,014
225,000	–79,965,203

Table 4 shows the effect of varying rates of maternal HIV seroprevalence on the number of pediatric infections prevented and the net cost of the intervention. The net cost ranged from $58.6 million at a seroprevalence rate of 0.1 per 1000 to a cost-saving of $235.6 million at a seroprevalence rate of 5 per 1000. The intervention became cost-saving at an HIV seroprevalence rate of 1.1 per 1000.

The effects of changing other assumptions in the sensitivity analysis of the base model are also shown in Table 4. Increasing the proportion of women who receive counseling and testing during pregnancy had only a modest effect on the net cost of the intervention. The cost savings increased from $38.1 million with a 78% acceptance rate (the base model) to $42.7 million with a 94% acceptance rate. However, as the proportion of HIV-infected women receiving ZDV treatment increased from 68% (the base model) to 95%, the cost savings of the intervention increased substantially from $38.1 million to $68.5 million. Changes in the estimate of the lifetime medical costs of treating a perinatally HIV-infected child had a large impact on the net cost of the intervention. The cost savings varied from $14.4 million with a treatment cost of $125,000 per infected child to $80 million with a cost of $225,000 per child.

Discussion

We calculated the annual cost of HIV counseling and voluntary testing for pregnant women and the cost of ZDV treatment for HIV-infected women and their infants. These intervention costs were compared with the medical care costs saved from the resulting reduction in the number of pediatric HIV infections. For the United States, with a maternal HIV seroprevalence of 1.71 per 1000 births, the cost-savings of the intervention ranged from $24.9 million to $93.5 million, depending on the assumptions made regarding the effectiveness of ZDV and the participation of HIV-infected pregnant women (Table 3). Thus, the intervention was cost-saving for both the base and the alternative models. Sensitivity analyses of four major input parameters showed that the intervention remained cost-saving under most of our alternative assumptions (Table 4).

HIV counseling and testing of seronegative women constituted a primary cost component of the intervention, accounting for 95% of the total in the base case. The model was very sensitive to assumptions made about counseling costs. The time allotted for a client-based[14,15] HIV counseling session will depend on the client's risk, and the cost will vary according to session length. There are no data available on the cost of HIV counseling in the private sector and very little on cost in the public sector.[15,17] The purpose of counseling associated with HIV testing has gradually changed as the epidemic evolved[25] and may differ considerably among testing sites. In addition, the cost effectiveness of a HIV counseling and testing strategy has been shown to be dependent on the inherent goal of testing.[17] Therefore, to determine the cost and cost-effectiveness of implementing HIV screening of pregnant women and ZDV treatment for infected women and infants more precisely, it is imperative to clarify the purpose, time allotted, and cost for counseling associated with HIV testing in this setting and to define precisely the goal of HIV counseling and voluntary testing of pregnant women.

The number of children who will be perinatally infected and, thus, the total costs of pediatric HIV treatment as estimated by our model are affected both by the number of women who are not tested and the proportion who receive no or partial ZDV treatment. Data are needed on the independent effect of each component (pregnancy, labor and delivery, neonatal) of the ZDV regimen.

The overall cost-effectiveness of the intervention varies according to maternal HIV seroprevalence. In most geographic regions, the intervention was cost-saving except for areas with very low HIV seroprevalence rates. The intervention was also found to be cost-saving when a slightly different model and locally determined costs were analyzed in an urban setting.[26]

A similar cost-effectiveness analysis for the prevention of perinatally transmitted hepatitis B virus (HBV) infection[27] estimated that maternal screening and infant treatment would save more than $100 million annually if indirect costs from lost productivity and premature death were included. Our analysis was far more conservative, using only the direct costs of medical treatment for pediatric HIV infections and no indirect costs. The national maternal HBV seroprevalence is 2 per 1000, which is very similar to maternal HIV seroprevalence, and prenatal HBV screening is an accepted public health practice. In comparison, prenatal HIV screening is substantially more cost-effective and compares favorably with other life-saying interventions.[28]

This model may underestimate costs since it excluded those associated with a visit by a health-care professional to HIV-infected pregnant women identified through screening to explain the ZDV treatment regimen, obtain informed consent, explain the protocol, and prescribe the ZDV. Also, our ZDV treatment costs did not include administration costs or costs associated with additional visits by health-care professionals or complications resulting from therapy.

Benefits from HIV counseling of pregnant women that were not included in this analysis, such as behavior changes that can reduce HIV transmission to the sexual or needle-sharing partners of infected women, have been estimated to exceed the benefits for infants.[9,10] We limited our analysis to prevention of perinatal HIV transmission and, therefore, have underestimated the total benefits of the intervention.

We did not attempt to address the human costs of HIV infection such as the emotional and cost burden of infection for the patient as well as the patient's family, friends, and care givers. Nor did we address the indirect costs such as those associated with orphaned children and years of productive labor lost due to illness and premature death. The model focuses on the first year of the intervention only. Any changes in behavior or maternal seroprevalence resulting from the intervention are not included in the analysis. Finally, our model does not address any, as yet unknown, long-term detrimental health effects associated with ZDV given to uninfected children.

A reduction in the rate of perinatal HIV transmission through ZDV treatment represents a major breakthrough for HIV prevention. Translating the findings of the ACTG Protocol 076 into public health interventions that can maximize the opportunity for treatment of the 7000 HIV-infected U.S. women who give birth each year requires a number of systematic steps. The first steps of developing public health policies in response to the research findings have been taken. The ability to implement these policies into national and local prevention interventions depends in part on their cost. This analysis demonstrates a cost-savings to society when the costs of the intervention are compared with the medical care costs saved by reducing the number of pediatric HIV infections. These findings strongly support implementation of the PHS recommendations for the prevention of perinatal HIV infection.

References

1. Davis SF, Byers RH, Lindegren ML, Caldwell MB, Karon JM, Gwinn M. Prevalence and incidence of vertically acquired HIV infection in the United States. JAMA 1995;274:952–5.
2. Update: AIDS among women—United States, 1994. MMWR 1995;44:81–4. [Erratum MMWR 1995;44:135].
3. Zidovudine for the prevention of HIV transmission from mother to infant. MMWR 1994;43:285–7.
4. Connor EM, Sperling RS, Gelber R, Kiseley P, et al. Reduction of maternal-infant transmission of human immunodeficiency virus type 1 with zidovudine treatment. N Engl J Med 1994;331:1173–80.
5. Recommendations of the Public Health Service Task Force on the Use of Zidovudine to Reduce Perinatal Transmission of Human Immunodeficiency Virus. MMWR 1994;43(No. RR-11).

6. Public Health Service recommendations for human immunodeficiency virus counseling and voluntary testing for pregnant women. MMWR 1995:44(No. RR-7).

7. Hellinger FJ. The lifetime cost of treating a person with HIV. JAMA 1993;270: 474–8.

8. Hsia CD, Fleishman JA, East JA, Hellinger FJ. Pediatric HIV infection: Recent evidence on the use and costs of health services. Arch Ped Adol Med 1995;149:489–96.

9. Brandeau ML, Owens DK, Sox CH, Wachter RM. Screening women of childbearing age for human immunodeficiency virus: a cost-benefit analysis. Arch Intern Med 1992;152:2229–37.

10. Brandeau ML, Owens DK, Sox CH, Wachter RM. Screening women of childbearing age for human immunodeficiency virus: a model-based policy analysis. Mgt Sci 1993;39:72–92.

11. National Center for Health Statistics. Trends in pregnancies and pregnancy rates, United States, 1980–88. Monthly Vital Statistics Report 1992;41:1–11.

12. National Center for Health Statistics. Health, United States, 1992. Hyattsville, MD: U.S. Public Health Service, 1993.

13. CDC. Abortion surveillance—United States, 1990. MMWR 1993;42(SS-6):29–57.

14. Technical guidance on HIV counseling. MMWR 1993;42:11–17.

15. Doll LS, Kennedy MB, HIV counseling and testing: what is it and how well does it work? In Schochetman G, George JR, eds. AIDS Testing: a comprehensive guide to technical, medical, social, legal, and management issues. 2nd ed. New York: Springer-Verlag, 1994:302–9.

16. National HIV Serosurveillance Summary: update—1993. Vol 3. Atlanta, GA: Centers for Diseases Control and Prevention, 1995.

17. Farnham PG, Gorsky RD, Holtgrave DR, Jones WK, Guinan ME. Counseling and testing for HIV prevention: costs, effects, and cost-effectiveness of more rapid screening tests. Public Health Rep 1996; 111:44–53.

18. 1994 Revised classification system for human immunodeficiency virus infection in children less than 13 years of age. MMWR 1994;43 (No. RR-12):I–10.

19. Barnhart HX, Caldwell MB, Thomas PT, et al. Natural history of HIV disease in perinatally infected children: an analysis from the Pediatric Spectrum of Disease Project. Pediatrics, In press.

20. Barbacci M, Repke Jr, Chaisson RE. Routine prenatal screening for HIV infection. Lancet 1991;337:(8743)709–11.

21. Cozen W, Mascola L, Enguidanos R, et al. Screening for HIV and hepatitis B virus in Los Angeles County prenatal clinics: a demonstration project. J Acquir Immune Defic Syndr 1993;6:95–8.

22. Febo I, Scott G, Mitchell C, Diaz C. Assessment of the implementation of the recommendations for the use of zidovudine (ZDV) to reduce perinatal transmission of HIV-1. [Abstract #572] Abstracts of the 2nd Annual Conference on Human Retroviruses and Related Infections. Washington, DC, 1995.

23. Matheson PB, Abrams EJ, Thomas PA, Hernan MA, et al. Efficacy of antenatal zidovudine in reducing perinatal transmission of human immunodeficiency virus type 1. J Infect Dis 1995;172:353–8.

24. Boyer PJ, Dillon M, Navale M, Deveikis A, et al. Factors predictive of maternal-fetal transmission of HIV-1: preliminary analysis of zidovudine given during pregnancy and/or delivery. JAMA 1994;271:1925–30.

25. Rugg DL, MacGowan RJ, Stark KA, Swanson NM. Evaluating the CDC program for HIV counseling and testing. Public Health Rep 1991;106:708–13.
26. Lewis R, Obrien JM, Ray DT, Sibai BM. The impact of initiating a human immunodeficiency virus screening program in an urban obstetric population. Am J Obstet Gynec 1995;173:1329–33.
27. Arevalo JA, Washington AE. Cost-effectiveness of prenatal screening and immunization for hepatitis B virus. JAMA 1988;259:365–9.
28. Tengs T, Adams ME, Pliskin JS, et al. Five hundred life saving interventions and their cost-effectiveness. Risk Analysis 1995;15:369–90.

Preventing Perinatal Transmission of HIV—A Cost-Effectiveness Analysis

The case study for this chapter focuses on an evaluation of the costs and effects of an intervention to prevent the transmission of HIV from mothers to their infants (perinatal transmission). Nearly all cases of HIV infection in children in the United States are acquired through perinatal transmission. Over the past two decades perinatal transmission of HIV has become a major cause of illness and death in children, resulting in more than 15,000 infected children and more than 3,000 deaths (Simonds and Rogers 1996; Davis et al. 1995). In the early 1990s it was estimated that approximately 7,000 infants were born to infected mothers each year and that 15 to 30 percent of these infants would become infected with HIV without intervention (Gorsky et al. 1996).

The basis for the intervention was the National Institutes of Health announcement in February 1994 of the interim results of AIDS Clinical Trials Group (ACTG) Protocol 076, which had demonstrated that the drug zidovudine (ZDV) administered to a group of HIV-infected women during pregnancy and labor and to their newborns reduced the risk of perinatal transmission of HIV by two-thirds (Connor et al. 1994). Protocol 076 was a randomized, multicenter, double-blind, placebo-controlled clinical trial of the effectiveness of ZDV in preventing perinatal transmission of HIV. Since randomized controlled trials are the "gold standard" for measuring the effectiveness of new drugs, the results of these trials were heralded as a major breakthrough in preventing perinatal transmission of HIV. Indeed, the results were considered so significant that the trials were stopped after only the interim results were known. In June 1994, the U.S. Public Health Service convened a workshop of representatives from the medical, scientific, public health, and legal communities and interested professional, community, and advocacy groups to develop a set of recommendations for implementing ZDV therapy for HIV-infected pregnant women in the United States and for HIV counseling and testing to identify women infected with HIV. These workshops resulted in two sets of guidelines issued by the CDC in 1994 and 1995 (*Morbidity and Mortality Weekly Reports* 1994; 1995). The guidelines recommended voluntary HIV counseling and testing of all pregnant women in prenatal care in the United States and offering ZDV treatment to those who were found to be infected.

This intervention involved both the offering of a drug, ZDV, and numerous behavioral components, since pregnant women would already have to be in prenatal care to receive the HIV counseling and testing and to make the decision about the use of ZDV. Furthermore, the ZDV intervention itself is quite complicated. The complete intervention involves oral administration of 100 mg five times daily, initiated at 14 to 34 weeks of gestation and continued throughout the pregnancy; intravenous administration of ZDV during labor; and oral administration of ZDV to the newborn every six hours for the first six weeks of life, beginning eight to twelve hours after birth (*Morbidity and Mortality Weekly Reports* 1994).

Both practitioners and policymakers raised questions about the costs and cost-effectiveness of these guidelines as they were being implemented. Because the medical costs of treating HIV infection are high, there could be substantial cost savings from preventing infections transmitted from mother to child. During this period, the estimated annual medical costs for treating HIV-infected adults were $5,000 for persons who had not yet developed AIDS and $35,000 for persons with AIDS (Hellinger 1993). These annual costs were estimated to be $9,400 before development of AIDS and $38,000 after AIDS for an HIV-infected child (Hsia et al. 1995). There were also questions about whether women would participate in this intervention (i.e., accept HIV counseling and testing and agree to participate in all phases of the ZDV intervention for both themselves and their newborns). The study by Robin Gorsky et al. (1996), included as the case study in this chapter, was undertaken to try to answer these questions about costs and cost-effectiveness of this prevention intervention.

The first task, as noted earlier in this chapter, was to structure the problem and adopt a perspective for the analysis, which would influence how the costs and effects would be measured. The researchers decided to frame the analysis in terms of the costs and effects of applying the intervention to all pregnant women in the United States, since that was the intended goal of the CDC recommendations. The results would also be presented using national data estimates that policymakers might be able to understand more easily than the results of a hypothetical cohort of individuals, an approach often used in cost-effectiveness analysis. The societal approach was adopted to have a comprehensive measure of all costs and impacts of the intervention. The researchers chose this approach to conform with the recommendations being developed by the Panel on Cost-Effectiveness in Health and Medicine. The researchers recognized that this approach might not answer all relevant policy questions. For example, whether women were actually offered HIV counseling and testing and the ZDV treatment in various settings might depend upon whether such services were covered by private insurance or public-sector programs such as Medicaid, which finances health care for low-income individuals. These questions might be of more importance to hospital administrators, private physicians, and the pregnant women themselves than the more abstract measure of the opportunity cost of the intervention. However, the societal approach is necessary to draw implications about resource allocation among competing activities.

The researchers framed the analysis to measure the costs and effects of the intervention compared with no intervention. The intervention was divided into two cost components: "(a) the direct costs associated with HIV counseling and voluntary testing services for pregnant women receiving first and second trimester prenatal care; and (b) the costs associated with ZDV treatment (that is, oral ZDV prenatally and intravenous ZDV during labor and delivery for infected women, oral ZDV for HIV-exposed newborns, and recommended laboratory testing during ZDV therapy)" (Gorsky et al. 1996, 336). The outcome measure was the number of cases of HIV-infected infants with and without the intervention, or the number of cases prevented by the intervention. Thus, the researchers decided to adopt a strict cost-effectiveness approach by measuring intervention outcomes as the number of infections prevented, rather than use the quality-adjusted life-years (QALY) associated with cost-utility analysis. The use of QALYs to analyze HIV prevention interventions will be discussed in more detail below. One reason for choosing the more basic measure for this analysis was the lack of sound measures of QALYs for cases of HIV infection in children.

The time horizon for analysis of the intervention was set at one year. This meant that the analysis would focus only on the initial impacts on the population of the intervention and the intervention costs for the first year. The additional impacts of the program in subsequent years are likely to decline relative to the additional costs, since fewer additional pregnant women are likely to be identified as the program progresses. This relatively short time frame also means that any changes in the behavior of pregnant women or in the incidence of HIV infection among pregnant women that might result from the implementation of the program are not included in the analysis. Any detrimental long-term side effects from administering ZDV to infants, particularly those who prove not to be infected with HIV, are also not included in this time framework. However, research has not yet shown that any of these side effects actually exist, so there would be no real scientific basis for including them in a longer time frame.

Although the intervention costs were defined on the basis of one year, the medical costs of treating infants infected with HIV would extend for a number of years into the future, depending on the average survival rate of these children. These medical costs would be associated with cases of HIV infection the intervention failed to prevent, but would also represent a cost saving for those cases that were prevented. To incorporate these costs into the analysis, the researchers had to calculate the present value of these costs, using the methods described earlier in this chapter. Since the study on which these costs were based (Hsia et al. 1995) did not report the present value or discounted costs, the researchers had to combine the cost data from that study with other data on disease progression in HIV-infected children and choose an appropriate discount rate to derive the correct measure of these costs. This process is described in more detail below.

The researchers also made other limiting assumptions in framing the analysis. They did not consider the additional costs of treating HIV-infected women who would not have learned of their infection until later in the course of their illness if they had not received HIV counseling and testing during pregnancy. Administrative costs and costs associated with additional visits by health care professionals or from complications arising during therapy were also not included as part of the ZDV treatment costs. Since the analysis focused on the prevention of HIV transmission from mothers to infants, the researchers decided not to include any other benefits of HIV counseling and testing of pregnant women, such as the benefits from behavior change that could reduce transmission to the sexual or needle-sharing partners of HIV-infected women. Other researchers have shown that these benefits might actually exceed the benefits to the infants from the intervention (Brandeau et al. 1992; 1993). Thus, the total benefits of the intervention are probably underestimated.

The researchers noted that they "did not attempt to address the human costs of HIV infection such as the emotional and cost burden of infection for the patient as well as the patient's family, friends, and care givers. Nor did [they] address the indirect costs such as those associated with orphaned children and years of productive labor lost due to illness and premature death" (Gorsky et al., 1996, 340). These assumptions are necessary to make any analysis tractable or feasible to undertake. They are all part of framing the problem and may take substantial time before the analysis is even begun. If researchers from different disciplines and backgrounds are involved in the analysis, they may debate the importance of various assumptions. Since different researchers may make different limiting assumptions, this is one of the causes of variations in the results of alternative analyses of the same policy problem. Decisionmakers trying to use the results of these analyses to inform policy must be aware that there may be substantial variation in the scope of the research on the policy question.

Figure 6.1 shows the decision tree used to model this intervention. Since the intervention is simply being compared with no intervention, the "no intervention" branch of the tree shows the number of HIV-infected infants that would result in the absence of the intervention. This is calculated on the basis of an underlying HIV seroprevalence rate among pregnant women of 0.0017 and an HIV transmission rate from mother to child of 25 percent. In both branches, the true rate of HIV infection among pregnant women is the first chance node. This immediately divides the population into the categories which are relevant for influencing the final outcome (i.e., whether HIV infection is transmitted from an infected mother to her infant).

The "intervention" branch of the tree shows the various outcomes that can occur when the intervention is applied to all pregnant women in the United States. A woman must be in prenatal care in her first or second trimester of pregnancy to be offered HIV counseling and testing and to have adequate time for the ZDV treatment if accepted. On a national basis 94 percent of pregnant women are in prenatal care, so this percent was applied at the first chance node in the decision tree. It was then assumed that 78 percent of these pregnant women accept HIV counseling and testing, the same proportion as reported for other populations.

The next chance node of the intervention branch shows the proportion of women accepting HIV counseling and testing who test positive for HIV antibodies. The number of women in this category depends on both the rate of HIV in the population, assumed to be 0.0017 (the national seroprevalence rate), and the accuracy of the HIV testing process. There are two types of errors that can be made by any screening test: false negatives (incorrectly identifying a person with the condition as not having it) and false positives (incorrectly identifying a person without the condition as having it). The quality of a given test is measured by its sensitivity (e.g., the number of individuals who test positive as a fraction of the number who truly have the medical condition) and its specificity (i.e., the number of individuals who test negative as a fraction of those who truly do not have

Figure 6.1: Decision Tree for the Intervention

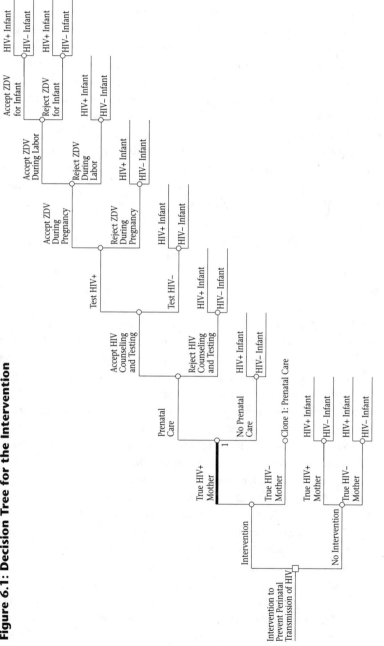

the medical condition). A perfect screening test would have both a sensitivity and specificity equal to one. The sensitivity and specificity of a single enzyme-linked immunosorbent assay (ELISA) used to screen for HIV antibodies was assumed to be 0.998 (George and Schochetman 1994). The researchers then assumed that a standard HIV testing protocol would be followed. This four-test algorithm can be assumed to be a perfect test for all practical purposes, thus simplifying the analysis (Farnham et al. 1996).

The subsequent chance nodes for those pregnant women testing HIV-positive show the probabilities of these women accepting the ZDV treatment during pregnancy, labor, and delivery, and for their newborns. As discussed in the case, these probabilities are 68.0, 84.5, and 71.4 percent, respectively. The number of HIV-infected infants at the end of each branch of the decision tree depends upon the HIV transmission rates associated with the ZDV intervention. The randomized controlled trials had shown that the ZDV intervention could reduce perinatal transmission rates from 25 percent without intervention to 8 percent with the complete maternal and infant ZDV regimen. After much discussion, the researchers decided to use a 16.5 percent transmission rate if two of the three components of the ZDV intervention had been completed. This was a controversial assumption because there was only limited evidence that some reduction in HIV transmission could occur if a woman did not complete all three components of the ZDV protocol. Given the uncertainty surrounding this assumption in the baseline model, two other models were also analyzed. In the "no partial effect" model, it was assumed that the HIV transmission rate was 25 percent unless all three components of the ZDV regimen were completed. In the "complete treatment" model, the researchers assumed that all eligible women and infants completed all three ZDV treatment components and that the transmission rate was 8 percent (Gorsky et al. 1996). These alternative models were analyzed in addition to performing the usual sensitivity analyses on individual parameters in the baseline model.

The costs of the intervention were divided into two components: the costs of HIV counseling and testing and the costs of the ZDV treatment. The costs of HIV counseling and testing depended upon whether a woman tested positive or negative on the initial ELISA screening test. Although the basic costs of HIV counseling and testing were derived from previous research (Farnham et al. 1996), an issue arose regarding how much of the HIV counseling and testing costs would be part of normal prenatal and obstetric care and how much would be additional costs. Only the additional costs should be included in the cost-effectiveness analysis. The researchers decided to use a weighted average of the full additional costs of HIV counseling and testing and the cost of an additional ELISA test alone. "Thus, the overall national cost estimate for HIV counseling and testing of seronegative women was $19.50 per person. For seropositive women, the cost of HIV counseling and testing was $103, which included additional costs for post-test counseling and confirmatory tests (ELISA and Western Blot)" (Gorsky et al. 1996, 337).

Costs for the ZDV intervention were based on the average duration of treatment for women in the randomized, controlled trial, ACTG Protocol 076. The researchers contacted five principal investigators in the original trial to obtain wholesale costs of the recommended preparations of ZDV used in their pharmacies. These costs were $551 for maternal treatment during pregnancy, $46 for maternal treatment during labor and delivery, and $17 for newborn treatment (Gorsky et al. 1996). The cost of standard laboratory testing was also included in the overall cost of the intervention.

It was necessary to calculate the medical care treatment costs for infants infected with HIV, since these costs would be saved for any cases prevented by the intervention. Only data on the annual costs of treating HIV-infected children were available (Hsia et al. 1995). Thus, the researchers had to incorporate other data on disease progression in children to develop a profile for a child infected at birth—"no symptoms in the first 9 months of life followed by mild HIV symptoms in months 10 to 13, moderate symptoms in months 14 to 57, and AIDS development at months 58 to 113 (average life span, 113 months)" (Gorsky et al. 1996, 337). The cost data were then applied to these disease stages to derive an average cost for each year of life for an HIV-infected child. These costs are shown in the third column of Table 1 of the chapter 6 case study. However, since these costs would be incurred over slightly more than 9 years, given the life expectancy of an HIV-infected infant, the costs had to be discounted to account for this time pattern, as discussed earlier in the chapter. The fourth column in Table 1 in the case study shows the pattern of costs discounted at 5 percent. The present value of the lifetime medical treatment costs for an infant infected at birth and, thus, the medical care costs saved from preventing one pediatric HIV infection were estimated to be $161,137 (Gorsky et al. 1996).

The results of the cost-effectiveness analysis of the perinatal intervention are presented in Tables 2 and 3 in the chapter 6 case study. If there was no intervention, the model shows that there would be 1,750 HIV-infected infants resulting from 7,000 births annually to HIV-infected women and a 25 percent HIV transmission rate. The cost of treating these children was estimated to be $282 million, given the $161,137 per infant estimate of the present value of lifetime medical treatment costs. In the baseline model, the researchers estimated that 1,094 cases of HIV infection would still result with the intervention, given the proportion of mothers not tested, the small number of false negative results, the lack of completion of the ZDV intervention, and the 8 percent transmission rate even with the complete intervention. Thus, 656 infections would be prevented by the perinatal intervention, resulting in a medical care cost savings of $105.6 million ($282 million without the intervention minus $176.4 million with the intervention). The cost of the intervention was estimated to be $67.6 million ($65.1 million for the HIV counseling and testing and $2.5 million for the complete ZDV regimen). Thus, the net cost of the intervention is –$38.0 million ($67.6 million minus $105.6 million) and the intervention is cost saving.

Tables 2 and 3 in the case study also present the results for the two alternative models examined. For the "no partial effect" model, the cost of the intervention is the same as in the baseline model, but only 574 infections were estimated to be prevented by the intervention, given the assumed lack of effectiveness if the entire ZDV intervention was not completed. This resulted in a smaller cost savings of $24.9 million. The "complete treatment" model had the same counseling and testing costs as the baseline model but higher ZDV treatment costs, since all eligible HIV-infected women and HIV-exposed infants received the complete ZDV treatment regimen. In this model there were a larger number of infections prevented (1,007), a greater medical care cost savings ($162.3 million), and a net cost savings of $93.5 million.

The researchers performed sensitivity analyses on four key variables in the baseline model: maternal HIV seroprevalence, the proportion of women accepting HIV counseling and testing, the proportion of women receiving ZDV treatment, and the lifetime cost of medical treatment for an HIV-infected infant. The net cost of the intervention ranged from an additional $58.6 million with a maternal seroprevalence rate of 0.1 per 1,000 to a cost savings of $235.6 million at a seroprevalence rate of 5 per 1,000, with the intervention becoming cost saving at a rate of 1.1 per 1,000. Increasing the proportion of women receiving HIV counseling and testing had only a modest effect on the overall net cost of the intervention, while increasing the proportion of HIV-infected women receiving the ZDV treatment resulted in a substantial increase in the cost savings of the intervention. Changes in the estimated lifetime cost of treating an HIV-infected child also had a large impact on the net cost of the intervention. The intervention remained cost saving under all values of the parameters examined except when maternal seroprevalence was lowered below 1.1 per 1,000 (Gorsky et al. 1996). The fact that these results were robust in the sensitivity analysis led the researchers to conclude that the findings "strongly support implementation

of the PHS recommendations for the prevention of perinatal HIV infection"
(Gorsky et al. 1996, 340).

Use of Quality-Adjusted Outcome Measures in HIV Prevention

The Panel on Cost-Effectiveness in Health and Medicine has recommended
the use of QALYs as the preferred outcome measure in health care cost-effectiveness studies (Gold et al. 1996). Although this approach was not adopted
in the case for this chapter, researchers have undertaken numerous studies
of quality-adjusted outcome measures for HIV prevention interventions.
Much of this research has already been summarized (Holtgrave and Qualls
1995; Holtgrave, Qualls, and Graham 1996; and Holtgrave and Pinkerton
1997). Given the development of new drug therapies and the rapidly changing nature of treating HIV infection, estimates of these quality-adjusted outcomes have changed considerably in just a few years.

David Holtgrave and Steven Pinkerton (1997) frame their analysis in
terms of a simplified cost-utility ratio for comparing a new HIV counseling
and testing program with a "do nothing" option or leaving the program
unfunded. Thus, the cost-utility ratio would be $[C - (A)\ (T)]\ /\ [(A)\ (Q)]$,
where C is the cost of the intervention relative to no program, A is the number of HIV infections averted by the program, T is the present value of the
medical costs saved by preventing an HIV infection, and Q is the number of
QALYs saved by preventing an infection. Although their study focuses on
updating estimates of both T and Q, the discussion here will be only on the
outcome measure.

Measuring QALYs involves both developing a framework for the stages
of disease and attaching weights for the quality of life associated with each
stage. In an earlier study, David Holtgrave and Noreen Qualls (1995) adopted a disease progression framework from an earlier work (Guinan, Farnham,
and Holtgrave 1994) with an additional assumption that the average age at
the time of HIV infection was twenty-six years. Holtgrave and Qualls then
reviewed the available literature on the quality of life for HIV-infected persons to develop the following weights for different disease stages: (1) full
health or a value of 1.0 for persons unaware of their HIV infection status; (2)
0.90 of full health for persons aware of their HIV infection but with a moderate disease stage; (3) 0.65 for persons with symptoms and in a more
advanced disease stage; and (4) 0.40 of full health for persons with AIDS as
defined by clinical conditions, the most advanced disease stage. Assuming

that non-HIV-infected individuals enjoy full health, Holtgrave and Qualls (1995) calculated the average number of QALYs saved (before age 65) by preventing an HIV infection as 28.85. This result represents the difference between the number of years between age 26 and age 65 in perfect health, valued at 1.00 per year, and the number of years in each disease stage valued with the above weights. Since it was argued above that health outcomes should be discounted to make them comparable to monetary costs, the undiscounted number of 28.85 QALYs is reduced to 9.26 QALYs when a discount rate of 5 percent is used (Holtgrave and Pinkerton 1997). These calculations are shown in Table 6.2.

Given the development of new combination drug therapies that have had an impact on both treatment costs and length and quality of life, David Holtgrave and Steven Pinkerton (1997) updated the estimates presented above. They developed a new stage of disease progression that incorporated increased monitoring of HIV in the body and the use of both two- and three-drug therapies. These researchers also surveyed recently developed literature on quality of life for persons with HIV: most of this literature was based on quality of life estimates by persons living with HIV. This literature did not fully meet the recommendations of the Panel on Cost-Effectiveness in Health and Medicine that quality adjustments be made on the basis of community-wide surveys of persons not necessarily living with the particular

Table 6.2: Calculating the Number of Quality-Adjusted Life Years (QALYs) for Preventing a Case of HIV Infection

DISEASE STATE	NUMBER OF YEARS	UTILITY WEIGHT	QALYs
Perfect health (age 26–65)	39	1.00	39.00
HIV/AIDS			
Infected, unaware	6	1.00	6.00
Aware, asymptomatic	3	0.90	2.70
Aware, symptomatic	1	0.65	0.65
AIDS-affected	2	0.40	0.80
Sum for HIV/AIDS			10.15

QALYs saved by preventing one infection (undiscounted) = 39 – 10.15 = 28.85

QALYs saved by preventing one infection (discounted at 5%) = 9.26

disease in question (Gold et al. 1996). However, those types of data were not available for HIV infection. Holtgrave and Pinkerton found fewer differences in the quality of life estimates for advanced stages of HIV infection and AIDS compared with earlier disease stages than had existed in previous literature. They argued that this might have resulted from "patients learning to cope with HIV disease and using these coping strategies to improve or maintain their quality of life even as health problems mount" (Holtgrave and Pinkerton 1997, 57). These authors noted that community-wide surveys of both infected and noninfected individuals might result in quite different quality weights for advanced disease stages than those derived only from HIV-infected individuals. Holtgrave and Pinkerton also had to make several arbitrary estimates for the weights pertaining to the less severe disease stages, given the lack of empirical estimates for these variables.

Holtgrave and Pinkerton (1997) estimate the number of QALYs saved by preventing an HIV infection to be 11.23, when discounting at the rate of 3 percent recommended by the Panel on Cost-Effectiveness in Health and Medicine. This estimate is higher than the 9.26 estimate from the Holtgrave and Qualls study (1995), largely due to the use of a 3 percent rather than a 5 percent discount rate employed in the earlier study. This increase occurred even though several factors would have lowered the more recent estimate: "First, the new quality of life estimates employed in our calculations of Q are higher than previous estimates of quality of life weights; this tends to decrease Q. Second, our assumption of increased survival from new treatments also tends to decrease the parameter Q. Both of these downward tendencies, however, are more than offset by the change in the discount rate" (Holtgrave and Pinkerton 1997, 60).

These changes in QALYs saved can have an impact on the economic evaluation of HIV prevention programs. Since Holtgrave and Pinkerton estimated a larger value for both the costs of treating an HIV infection and the QALYs saved by preventing an infection, their results make HIV prevention programs appear more cost-effective. Some HIV prevention programs that might not have appeared cost-effective using the earlier estimates may be considered cost-effective with the new estimates. This example shows how the empirical data drawn from many studies and the assumptions made to incorporate this data in economic evaluations can have an impact on policy judgments about different prevention interventions. It also illustrates how a technical factor, the choice of a discount rate to calculate the present value of costs and outcomes, can have a substantial influence on the results of the evaluation.

Summary

In this chapter we discussed both the general issues in undertaking a cost-effectiveness analysis and the specific case of preventing transmission of HIV infection from mothers to newborns. We first described the conceptual problems involved with estimating both the costs and outcomes of various public policies. We noted that cost and outcome measurement may differ when the perspective is economic evaluation rather than program implementation and control, topics which were presented in earlier chapters of this book. We also showed how the time pattern of costs and outcomes and the discount rate selected to calculate the present value of these variables can impact the results of the analysis.

We then applied these economic evaluation principles to the specific case of the cost-effectiveness of the CDC guidelines for preventing HIV transmission from mothers to their infants. Numerous examples were given of how the authors of that cost-effectiveness study handled the various technical issues of cost-effectiveness analysis. We also described the implications of these technical problems for the use of cost-effectiveness analysis as a policymaking tool. Many of the issues discussed in this chapter will arise in the application of cost-benefit analysis to environmental problems, which is described in the following chapter. Readers should integrate the concepts from each chapter, since these chapters summarize the major components of economic evaluation for public policy analysis.

References

Arno, Peter S. (1986). "The Nonprofit Sector's Response to the AIDS Epidemic: Community-based Services in San Francisco," *American Journal of Public Health* 76, 11, pp. 1325–30.

Baumol, William J. (1970). "On the Discount Rate for Public Projects," in Robert H. Haveman and Julius Margolis (eds.). *Public Expenditures and Policy Analysis* (Chicago: Markham Publishing Company), pp. 273–90.

Brandeau, M. L., D. K. Owens, C. H. Sox, and R. M. Wachter. (1993). "Screening Women of Childbearing Age for Human Immunodeficiency Virus: A Model-Based Policy Analysis," *Management Science* 39, pp. 72–92.

Brandeau, M. L., D. K. Owens, C. H. Sox, and R. M. Wachter. (1992). "Screening Women of Childbearing Age for Human Immunodeficiency Virus: A Cost-Benefit Analysis," *Archives of Internal Medicine* 152, pp. 2229–37.

Brown, Kaye and Collin Burrows. (1990). "The Sixth Stool Guaiac Test: $47 Million That Never Was," *Journal of Health Economics* 9, pp. 429–45.

Connor, E. M., R. S. Sperling, R. Gelber, P. Kiselev, G. Scott, M. J. O'Sullivan, R. VanDyke, M. Bey, W. Shearer, R. L. Jacobson, E. Jimenez, E. O'Neill, B. Bazin, J. F. Delfraissy, M. Culnane, R. Coombs, M. Elkins, J. Moye, P. Stratton, and J.

Balsley for the Pediatric AIDS Clinical Trials Group Protocol 076 Study Group. (1994). "Reduction of Maternal-Infant Transmission of Human Immunodeficiency Virus Type 1 with Zidovudine Treatment," *New England Journal of Medicine* 331, pp. 1173–80.

Davis, S. F., R. H. Byers, M. L. Lindegren, M. B. Caldwell, J. M. Karon, and M. Gwinn. (1995). "Prevalence and Incidence of Vertically Acquired HIV Infection in the United States," *Journal of the American Medical Association* 274, pp. 952–55.

Drummond, Michael F., Bernie O'Brien, Greg L. Stoddart, and George W. Torrance. (1997). *Methods for the Economic Evaluation of Health Care Programmes* (New York: Oxford University Press).

Farnham, Paul G. (1998). "Economic Evaluation of HIV Counseling and Testing Programs: The Influence of Program Goals on Evaluation," in David R. Holtgrave (ed.) *Handbook of Economic Evaluation of HIV Prevention Programs* (New York: Plenum Press), pp. 63–79.

Farnham, Paul G. and Robin D. Gorsky. (1994). "Cost to Business for an HIV-Infected Worker," *Inquiry* (Spring) 31, pp. 76–88.

Farnham, Paul G., Robin D. Gorsky, David R. Holtgrave, Wanda K. Jones, and Mary E. Guinan. (1996). "Counseling and Testing for HIV Prevention: Costs, Effects, and Cost-Effectiveness of More Rapid Screening Tests," *Public Health Reports* 111 (January/February), pp. 44–53.

Farnham, Paul G., Robert J. Simonds, and Mary E. Guinan. (1999). "Alternative Perinatal HIV Prevention Policies in the United States: Cost-Effectiveness of Voluntary Versus Mandatory Screening and the Rapid HIV Test" (working paper).

Finkler, S. A. (1982). "The Distinction Between Costs and Charges," *Annals of Internal Medicine* 96, pp. 102–09.

Folland, Sherman, Allen C. Goodman, and Miron Stano. (1997). *The Economics of Health and Health Care*, 2d ed. (Englewood Cliffs, N.J.: Prentice Hall).

Gastonis, Constantine. (1990). "The Long Debate on the Sixth Guaiac Test: Time to Move on to New Grounds," *Journal of Health Economics* 9, pp. 495–97.

George, J. Richard and Gerald Schochetman. (1994). "Detection of HIV Infection Using Serologic Techniques," in Gerald Schochetman and J. Richard George (eds.), *AIDS Testing*, 2d ed. (New York: Springer-Verlag), pp. 62–102.

Gold, Marthe R., Joanna E. Siegel, Louise B. Russell, and Milton C. Weinstein (eds.) (1996). *Cost-Effectiveness in Health and Medicine* (New York: Oxford University Press).

Gorsky, Robin D., Paul G. Farnham, Walter L. Straus, B. Caldwell, David R. Holtgrave, Martha F. Rogers, and Mary E. Guinan. (1996). "Preventing Perinatal Transmission of HIV—Costs and Effectiveness of a Recommended Intervention," *Public Health Reports* 111 (July/August), pp. 335–41.

Gramlich, Edward M. (1990). *A Guide to Benefit-Cost Analysis*, 2d ed. (Englewood Cliffs, N.J.: Prentice Hall).

Gramlich, Edward M. (1981). *Benefit-Cost Analysis of Government Programs* (Englewood Cliffs, N.J.: Prentice Hall).

Grosse, Robert N. (1970). "Problems of Resource Allocation in Health," in Robert H. Haveman and Julius Margolis (eds.) *Public Expenditure and Policy Analysis* (Chicago: Markham Publishing Company), pp. 518–48.

Guinan, Mary E., Paul G. Farnham, and David R. Holtgrave. (1994). "Estimating the Value of Preventing a Human Immunodeficiency Virus Infection," *American Journal of Preventive Medicine* 10, 1, pp. 1–4.

Haddix, Anne C., Steven M. Teutsch, Phaedra A. Shaffer, and Diane O. Dunet. (1996). *Prevention Effectiveness: A Guide to Decision Analysis and Economic Evaluation* (New York: Oxford University Press).

Haveman, Robert H. (1983). "Evaluating Public Expenditure Under Conditions of Unemployment," in Robert H. Haveman and Julius Margolis (eds.). *Public Expenditure and Policy Analysis*, 3d ed. (Boston: Houghton Mifflin), pp. 167–82.

Healton, C., P. Messeri, D. Abramson, J. Howard, M. D. Sorin, and R. Bayer. (1996). "A Balancing Act: The Tension Between Case-Finding and Primary Prevention Strategies in New York State's Voluntary HIV Counseling and Testing Program in Women's Health Care Settings," *American Journal of Preventive Medicine* 12 (suppl. 1), pp. 53–60.

Hellinger, Fred J. (1993). "The Lifetime Cost of Treating a Person with HIV," *Journal of the American Medical Association* 270, pp. 474–78.

Holtgrave, David R. and Steven D. Pinkerton. (1997). "Updates of Cost of Illness and Quality of Life Estimates for Use in Economic Evaluations of HIV Prevention Programs," *Journal of Acquired Immune Deficiency Syndromes and Human Retrovirology* 16, pp. 54–62.

Holtgrave, David R. and Noreen L. Qualls. (1995). "Threshold Analysis and Programs for Prevention of HIV Infection," *Medical Decision Making* 15, pp. 311–17.

Holtgrave, David R., Noreen L. Qualls, and John D. Graham. (1996). "Economic Evaluation of HIV Prevention Programs," *Annual Review of Public Health* 17, pp. 467–88.

Hsia C. D., J. A. Fleishman, J. A. East, and F. J. Hellinger. (1995). "Pediatric HIV Infection: Recent Evidence on the Use and Costs of Health Services," *Archives of Pediatric and Adolescent Medicine* 149, pp. 489–96.

Krahn, M. and A. Gafni. (1993). "Discounting in the Economic Evaluation of Health Care Interventions," *Medical Care* 31, pp. 403–18.

Lesser, J.A. and R. O. Zerbe. (1994). "Discounting Procedures for Environmental (and Other) Projects: A Comment on Kolbe and Scheraga," *Journal of Policy Analysis and Management* 13, pp. 140–56.

Lind, Robert C. (1982). "A Primer on the Major Issues Relating to the Discount Rate for Evaluating National Energy Options," in Robert C., Lind, K. J. Arrow, G. R. Corey, and others, *Discounting for Time and Risk in Energy Policy* (Baltimore: Johns Hopkins University Press), pp. 21–94

Morbidity and Mortality Weekly Reports (1995). 44 (No. RR-7). "Public Health Service Recommendations for Human Immunodeficiency Virus Counseling and Voluntary Testing for Pregnant Women."

Morbidity and Mortality Weekly Reports (1994). 43 (No. RR-11). "Recommendations of the Public Health Service Task Force on the Use of Zidovudine to Reduce Perinatal Transmission of Human Immunodeficiency Virus."

Neuhauser, Duncan and Ann M. Lewicki. (1975). "What do we Gain From the Sixth Stool Guaiac?" *New England Journal of Medicine* 293, pp. 226–28.

Oster, G. and A. M. Epstein. (1987). "Cost-effectiveness of Antihyperlipidemic Therapy in the Prevention of Coronary Heart Disease: The Case of Cholestyramine," *Journal of the American Medical Association* 258, pp. 2381–87.

Parsonage M. and H. Neuburger. (1992). "Discounting and Health Benefits," *Health Economics* 1, pp. 71–76.

Phelps, Charles E. (1997). *Health Economics,* 2d ed. (Reading, Mass.: Addison Wesley).

Rice, Thomas. (1998). *The Economics of Health Reconsidered* (Chicago: Health Administration Press).

Rossi, Peter H. and Howard E. Freeman. (1993). *Evaluation: A Systematic Approach,* 5th ed. (Newbury Park, Calif.: Sage Publications).

Russell, Louise B. (1994). *Educated Guesses: Making Policy About Medical Screening Tests* (Berkeley: University of California Press).

Russell, Louise B. (1993). "The Role of Prevention in Health Reform," *New England Journal of Medicine* 329, 5, pp. 352–54.

Russell, Louise B. (1986). *Is Prevention Better Than Cure?* (Washington, D.C.: The Brookings Institution).

Shepard, D. S. and M. S. Thompson. (1979). "First Principles of Cost-Effectiveness Analysis in Health," *Public Health Reports* 94, pp. 535–43.

Simonds, R. J. and M. F. Rogers. (1996). "Preventing Perinatal HIV Infection. How Far Have We Come?" *Journal of the American Medical Association* 275, pp. 1514–15.

U.S. Department of Health, Education, and Welfare. (1979). *Healthy People: The Surgeon General's Report on Health Promotion and Disease Prevention* (Washington, D.C.: U.S. Government Printing Office).

Weinstein, M. C. and W. B. Stason. (1977). "Foundations of Cost-Effectiveness Analysis for Health and Medical Practices," *New England Journal of Medicine* 296, pp. 716–21.

Weisbrod, Burton A. (1983). "Benefit-Cost Analysis of a Controlled Experiment: Treating the Mentally Ill," in Robert H. Haveman and Julius Margolis (eds.) *Public Expenditure and Policy Analysis,* 3d ed. (Boston: Houghton Mifflin), pp. 230–59

World Bank. (1993). *World Health Development Report* (Washington, D.C.: World Bank).

Wright-DeAguero, Linda, Robin D. Gorsky, and G. M. Seeman. (1996). "Cost of Outreach for HIV Prevention Among Drug Users and Youth at Risk," *Drugs and Society* 9, pp. 185–97.

CHAPTER 7

Cost-Benefit Analysis
The Case of Environmental Air Quality Standards

Cost-benefit analysis is a policy evaluation tool closely related to cost-effectiveness analysis. All of the problems in measuring the costs of public programs discussed in chapter 6 apply to this evaluation technique also. The major differences between cost-effectiveness and cost-benefit analysis relate to the measurement of the outcomes of the programs. We noted in chapter 6 that program outcomes or consequences are measured in the most appropriate natural effects or physical units in cost-effectiveness analysis. These basic measures can simply be counted to determine the effectiveness of the intervention and then compared with its costs. Thus, cost-effectiveness results are expressed in terms such as cost per HIV infection prevented or cost per life-year saved from a cholesterol reduction program.

Cost-benefit analysis attempts to place a dollar valuation on the outcomes of a program or intervention and to answer the question: How much is society willing to pay for the output of this program or what are the benefits to society of having this output? The dollar valuation of this output or the benefits are then compared with the costs of producing it. If the benefits exceed the costs, the program is considered to be an efficient use of society's resources. With cost-benefit analysis, the policy analyst must confront the question of what it is worth to society to prevent an HIV infection or what is the value to society of a life saved by a cholesterol reduction program. In this chapter, we will focus on the approaches used to answer these difficult questions.

The case for chapter 7 involves the updated air quality standards for ozone and particulate matter (smog and soot) issued by the Environmental Protection Agency (EPA) on 19 July 1997 and announced in a *New York Times* article on 26 June 1997. This article, which is the case study appended to this chapter, discusses the policy debate over the increased air quality standards and raises most of the issues relevant to any cost-benefit analysis, including the role of cost-benefit analysis in a decisionmaking process. Issues regarding the efficacy of the regulations, the measurement of the benefits and costs, the role of the various stakeholders in the policy process, and the distributional impacts of the regulations are all discussed in the case study.

We will begin this chapter by describing the components of cost-benefit analysis and the problems involved in measuring the benefits of a program or set of regulations. We will pay particular attention to the question of how to place a monetary benefit on any lives saved by an environmental regulation. Cost measurement issues will be given less attention since they were discussed in the previous chapter. The role of cost-benefit analysis in decisionmaking and the limitations often placed on this role will also be discussed. We will then describe the policy issues in the debate over the tougher environmental air quality standards announced in June 1997 and relate these issues to the discussion of cost-benefit analysis methodology. We will discuss the specific benefit measurement issues in the case and how the uncertainty surrounding these issues has contributed to the policy debate.

An Overview of Cost-Benefit Analysis

Cost-benefit analysis has long been used by various government agencies to evaluate different public programs. The U.S. Army Corps of Engineers was one of the earliest users of the tool to evaluate such physical investment projects as the dredging of harbors, construction of canals and waterways, and flood control. Indeed, the U.S. Flood Control Act of 1939 specified the standard that "the benefits to whomever they accrue [be] in excess of the estimated costs" (Gramlich 1981, 7). In the 1960s cost-benefit analysis began to be applied to a much wider range of projects involving investment in human beings (human capital) as well as physical investment programs. This was related to President Lyndon Johnson's "Great Society" efforts to get the federal government actively involved in fighting poverty, creating jobs, and providing education and training. As the government moved into these new areas of activity, concern arose about which type of program provided the greatest return for the dollars invested. The use of cost-benefit analysis was also related to the formal installation of the planning, programming, and budgeting system (PPBS) in federal government agencies during the 1960s. Although the formal use of the PPBS system had died out by the mid-1970s, the use of such evaluation techniques as cost-benefit and cost-effectiveness analysis survived. Indeed, in the areas of health care and environmental policy, there has been a greater emphasis on these techniques, given the concern over rising health care expenditures and the impact of environmental regulations (Warner and Luce 1982; Tolley, Kenkel, and Fabian 1994).

Both benefits and costs have very specific meanings derived from economic theory. They are related to the basic economic concept of efficiency in resource allocation—making the best use of society's limited resources by comparing how people value different outputs with the cost of producing them. A program is said to be efficient if its benefits, that is, the total amount of money people are willing to pay for the output of the program, are greater than program costs, (i.e., the real opportunity costs reflecting what is sacrificed to produce the output).

This definition of efficiency is not without controversy, because it focuses on measuring willingness to pay and program costs without regard to who benefits and who pays the costs. The underlying theory is derived from welfare economics, the branch of economics that attempts to make value judgments about different policies, allocations of resources, and states of the world (Gramlich 1990; Hyman 1996). According to this theory, based on the work of the Italian social scientist Vilfredo Pareto, a policy improves the welfare of society if it makes at least one person better off without making anyone worse off. A state of the world is considered to be *Pareto-efficient* if it is *not* possible to make someone better off without making someone else worse off. Since most policies and policy changes result in both gainers and losers, this strict Pareto rule is not very useful for evaluating real-world policy changes. The rule has been modified by the British economists Nicholas Kaldor and John Hicks to state that a policy improves welfare if the gainers from the policy *could* compensate the losers from the policy and still be better off or at least no worse off. This rule has become known as a *potential compensation policy* because it does not require that the compensation from the gainers to the losers actually be paid (Gramlich 1990). Cost-benefit analysis is an application of this compensation rule because it states that a policy is efficient if society's benefits or willingness to pay for the program output (the gainers' gains) are greater than the costs of providing the output (the losers' losses).

This efficiency concept behind cost-benefit analysis has been criticized particularly regarding policies having an impact on health and human life, where societal values about differential access to health care resulting from inequalities in the distribution of income are important and controversial. An economic or Pareto-efficient allocation of resources can be consistent with any distribution of income or resources among the citizens in a given society (Hyman 1996). This has led health economists Uwe Reinhardt (1992) and Thomas Rice (1998) to argue that economic efficiency may not be a very relevant criterion for evaluating alternative health care policies. Reinhardt (1992, 312–13) is particularly critical of the potential compensation concept:

> Suppose, for example, that I feel very aggressive today and therefore would like to punch you in the nose. An honest referee (an economist) asks me what I would be willing to pay for that privilege. Suppose the maximum I'd be willing to pay were $1,000. Next, the honest referee asks you how much you would have to be paid to receive that punch in the nose without hitting me back. Because you are strapped for cash, you might accept the punch for $600. The referee (our economist) is ecstatic, for (s)he perceives here the opportunity to enhance *social welfare*. Consequently, the deal is struck, you kindly present your precious nose,

I punch, you bleed and hold out your hand in anticipation of my payment of $1,000. Alas, I walk happily away, along with my $1,000, which I refuse to surrender. Not to worry. The honest referee (our economist) will soothe you with the expert assurance that, according to Nicholas Kaldor, and in principle, we have just witnessed a major enhancement in *social welfare*, to the tune of $400, even though the expected $1,000 bribe is not actually paid.

These issues should be kept in mind when examining the use of cost-benefit analysis as a tool for policy evaluation. Economists often briefly mention that the use of these tools for public policy analysis either assumes that the underlying distribution of income is satisfactory or that problems with the distribution of income can be handled with a separate set of policies (the separation of resource allocation from income distribution problems). Neither of these situations is likely to exist. The vast number of government policies designed to influence individuals' ability to purchase food, shelter, and medical services clearly demonstrate society's concern with the existing distribution of income. Many of these policies change the prices people pay for various goods and services, thus having efficiency effects. Equity and efficiency issues are intertwined in most policy situations, and these problems will affect the use of cost-benefit analysis as noted throughout this chapter. Cost-benefit analysis is a tool to assist a public policy decisionmaking process, where all of society's values—legal, ethical, moral, and distributional—must be considered (Haddix et al. 1996; Freeman 1993). Cost-benefit analysis is not the decision itself and should not be considered a simple, mechanistic, quantitative tool for reaching the decision.

Since the benefits and costs in an economic evaluation are added up over all the individuals receiving and paying them, there can be a decision-making problem if some of these benefits and/or costs flow to individuals other than those undertaking the analysis. Dale Whittington and Duncan MacRae (1986) call this the problem of "standing" in cost-benefit analysis: Whose preferences are to count when summing benefits and costs? These issues have been discussed more recently by Richard Zerbe (1998). A given agency may want to count only the benefits to itself or its constituency. This may result in an underestimation of the total benefits of the project. For example, the benefits of a water pollution control project may flow to individuals across an entire metropolitan region. However, the agency financing the project may be concerned only with the benefits accruing to its taxpayers. Not counting the benefits or costs to other parties may significantly bias the resulting cost-benefit calculation. Whittington and MacRae (1986) raise questions about whether benefits should include those flowing to illegal aliens or criminals. They also cite a case in which the U.S. Nuclear

Regulatory Commission (NRC) concluded that approximately one-third of the benefits of controlling radon gas emissions would accrue to individuals outside the United States. In its analysis, the NRC included the effects on Canadians and Mexicans but ignored the benefits to the rest of the world. Subsequently, EPA assigned a zero weight to everyone outside the borders of the country (Whittington and MacRae 1986, 675).

The benefits of a project may bear no particular relationship to the flow of revenues or tax receipts to the agency undertaking the project. For many government projects there are no direct revenues to the agency. However, this does not mean that there are zero benefits from the project. The financing issues focus on the *distribution* of the benefits and costs, namely, who receives the benefits and who pays the costs. These issues may be very important from a decisionmaking point of view—indeed, they may determine whether a project is funded or not. In the 1970s during the controversy over Westway, the proposed West Side highway in New York City, construction options with less favorable cost-benefit ratios were favored over more efficient projects because the federal government was willing to finance a larger share of the total costs of the former. Therefore, the costs to New York City taxpayers were lower (Herzlinger 1979).

Distributional issues are typically not incorporated in the formal estimation of benefits and costs. Sometimes separate data are presented on how the benefits or costs are distributed by income group or region of the country, so that decisionmakers can see how different groups of people will be affected by the project. It has also been argued that distributional weights might be applied when the total benefits are being summed (Gramlich 1981; 1990). This approach directly incorporates the distributional or equity issues with the efficiency calculations. However, it is not clear what weights should be applied. Should benefits to low-income groups be weighted twice, five times, or one-half as heavily as benefits to high-income groups? This approach makes the estimation of program costs directly dependent on the method of financing the project. Many have argued that these issues should remain separate.

As with cost-effectiveness analysis discussed in the previous chapter, cost-benefit analysis involves a "with and without" comparison as opposed to a "before and after" comparison (Haveman and Weisbrod 1983). The attempt is made to calculate the benefits and costs of having the program compared with what would have happened without the program (the counterfactual). Thus, if a program provides job skills and training to teenagers, the increased wages these individuals will earn over their lifetime in contrast to what they would have earned otherwise may be considered one of the benefits of the program. This calculation is more complex than simply examining wages before and after the program. This example also illustrates the fact that the benefits and costs of a program may extend many years into the future. A teenager's working life may be forty years or more, while the life of a physical investment project may exceed 100 years. Thus, cost-benefit analysis, as well as cost-effectiveness analysis, involves not only the technical details of benefit and cost estimation but also the projection and comparison of dollar values over time. We discussed issues regarding the use of a discount rate to calculate the present value of a stream of benefits or costs in the previous chapter.

An advantage of cost-benefit analysis, compared with cost-effectiveness and cost-utility analysis, discussed in the previous chapter, is that cost-benefit analysis allows for comparison among a broader range of alternatives, since both outcomes and costs are measured in dollar terms. Cost-benefit analysis attempts to measure the value of all program outcomes. In cost-effectiveness and cost-utility analysis, costs are compared with one outcome at a time (i.e., cost per infection prevented or cost per quality-adjusted life year gained).

It may, however, be extremely difficult if not impossible to place dollar values on some of the benefits and costs of particular projects. The alternative methods for evaluating a program that reduces the risk of death (discussed below) will differ in their comprehensiveness of the benefits estimated. Some benefit-cost analyses include unmeasured or intangible benefits and costs along with those measured in dollar terms. Burton Weisbrod's (1983) study of inpatient versus outpatient treatment of the mentally ill, discussed in the previous chapter, used this procedure. External costs caused by patients' illnesses were measured as the number of families reporting physical illness and the percentage of family members experiencing emotional strain due to patient behavior. Improved consumer decisionmaking by patients was measured by the amount of insurance expenditures and by the percentage of the groups having savings accounts (Weisbrod 1983). These intangible costs and benefits were included because they were considered to be important, but they were not measured in dollar terms.

Methods for Estimating Benefits

As noted above, the benefits of a project are defined as the total amount of money individuals are willing to pay for the output of the project. *Benefit analysis* attempts to use an approach similar to that used in the market place to evaluate private goods and services. We noted in chapter 5 that prices

Figure 7.1: The Demand Curve for a Particular Good

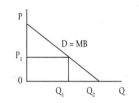

perform an allocating and rationing function in a market economy: if an individual is willing to buy a particular good at a certain price, that action gives us an estimate of how the person values the good. The goal of benefit analysis is to use that same approach in the valuation of public-sector, health-related, or environmental goods and services that may not be sold in the market or have any prices directly associated with them.

Figure 7.1 shows a demand curve for a particular good. Suppose that P_1 is the price of the good and Q_1 is the quantity demanded at that price. The amount of money spent on the good is price times quantity, or the area of the rectangle. However, this area does *not* represent the total amount that consumers would be willing to pay for the good rather than go without it. That total willingness to pay is represented by the area underneath the demand curve up to quantity Q_1. This results from the fact that the prices measured along a demand curve represent consumers' marginal benefit or valuation, the dollar value they attach to each additional unit of the product.

Table 7.1 shows a hypothetical demand schedule for oranges. If I observe you buying four oranges when the price of oranges is $0.25, I can infer that you did not buy the fifth orange because it was worth less than $0.25 to you. If the price of oranges is $0.50 per orange and you buy only three oranges, I can infer that the third orange is worth $0.50, but the

Table 7.1: Individual Demand for Oranges (Hypothetical)

PRICE	QUANTITY DEMANDED
$0.25	4
$0.50	3
$0.75	2
$1.00	1

fourth orange is worth only $0.25. Likewise, the second orange is worth $0.75, and the first orange is worth $1.00. Thus, a market price reflects a consumer's marginal valuation or benefit, the amount of money he or she is willing to pay for the last or marginal unit consumed.

If we add up all these valuations for each of the units, we obtain the total valuation or the amount consumers are willing to pay for all the units. This dollar amount, represented by the total area underneath the demand curve up to quantity Q_1 in Figure 7.1, is the total willingness to pay or the total benefit to consumers of that amount of output. If we look only at the actual consumer expenditure (the area of the rectangle in Figure 7.1), we would typically underestimate the total willingness to pay or the benefits to society of producing that output. In the numerical example of Table 7.1, the total willingness to pay for four oranges rather than do without is the marginal benefit of the first orange ($1.00) plus the marginal benefit of the second ($0.75) plus that of the third ($0.50) and fourth ($0.25), for a total of $2.50. If the price of oranges was $0.25, the amount actually spent on oranges would be only $1.00. Furthermore, if a decision had been made to have the government provide the good free of charge, that is, vaccinations by a public health clinic, there would be no consumer expenditure to measure. In this case, the quantity demanded in Figure 7.1 would be Q_2 at the zero price, and the total willingness to pay would be the monetary value of the entire area underneath the demand curve up to quantity Q_2.

This equality of price and marginal benefit and the resulting efficiency arguments have been questioned in the area of health care policy. Thomas Rice (1992; 1997; 1998) argues that the demand curve for health care goods and services may not reflect consumers' marginal benefits, given the lack of information and the inability of consumers to analyze and understand relevant information regarding the purchase of these goods and services. This is still a controversial argument (Pauly 1997; Gaynor and Vogt 1997), but it does raise questions about the use of the demand and efficiency criterion for health care policy.

Although *willingness to pay* is the term used in the cost-benefit literature, it must also be remembered, as noted in chapter 5, that income is one of the factors influencing the position of a demand curve. Oranges were chosen in the above example to illustrate the marginal benefit concept since income, for most people, is not a constraining factor influencing their demand for oranges. It can be safely argued that the reason the consumer did not purchase the fifth orange when oranges were priced at $0.25 per orange is that the consumer did not value the fifth orange at $0.25, *not* that the individual did not have the income to purchase the fifth orange. For many other goods and services, both private and public, income does play a major role in influencing demand. Indeed, demand is often defined as the willingness and ability to purchase a good or service. Thus, a demand curve for a city recreation project could be further from the origin, and the total benefits larger, for a high-income neighborhood than for a low-income neighborhood simply because the high-income residents have a greater ability to pay for the recreation output. This is an example of the income distribution problem discussed above. The variety of government programs, such as Medicare and Medicaid, which are designed to improve access to health care, demonstrate society's concern about income distribution problems in this policy area. Thus, even though cost-benefit analysis primarily focuses on efficiency issues, the distributional questions are never far away.

This discussion shows that benefit estimation is directly connected to the economic concept of demand. The goal of benefit measurement is to estimate the demand and, thus, the willingness to pay for the output of the project. Therefore, all the empirical demand estimation issues discussed in chapter 5 are relevant here. These include the problems of incorporating all relevant variables influencing demand and holding their effects constant while examining the relationship between price and quantity demanded.

Willingness to pay issues become more complicated in cost-benefit analysis, however, because many of the project outcomes being evaluated, such as good health or a clean environment, are not bought and sold in markets. Furthermore, prices may not be charged for many government-provided goods and services either because it is impossible to do so (the public goods problem) or because society has made a conscious decision not to do so (the income distribution or equity problem). Therefore, willingness to pay in these cases must be estimated either through observation of behavior in hypothetical or contingent markets or through inference from indirect methods on behavior in markets related to the project outcome in question. Thus, the choice is between methodologies that focus on how individuals answer questions about how they would behave in certain situations rather than inferring willingness to pay from the observed behavior of individuals in markets affected by the relevant project outcome. These methods will be catalogued and summarized under several broad headings below. More detailed descriptions of all of these methods, particularly in the health and environmental areas of interest in this chapter, can be found in Mishan (1976), Warner and Luce (1982), Cummings, Brookshire, and Schulze (1986), Gramlich (1981; 1990), Freeman (1993), Tolley, Kenkel, and Fabian (1994), Portney (1994), Hanemann (1994), Diamond and Hausman (1994), Bjornstad and Kahn (1996), and Haddix et al. (1996).

Estimation of willingness to pay from surveys and other hypothetical situations is known as the *contingent valuation method*. This is the method most directly related to the direct estimation of a market demand curve except that the market is hypothetical. Contingent valuation methods ask individuals to reveal their personal valuations of increases or decreases in unpriced goods through surveys or in experimental situations. Individuals are given information on the good in question, the institutional structure under which it will be provided, the method of payment, and the decision rule for determining the level of the provision of the good. Contingent markets are highly structured with scenarios designed to elicit contingent valuation: If this happens, what would you be willing to pay? This is a different process from determining peoples' attitudes or opinions about a subject (Cummings, Brookshire, and Schulze 1986; Bjornstad and Kahn 1996).

Economists have traditionally preferred to rely on the direct observation of individuals' behavior rather than responses to hypothetical questions about that behavior. However, the contingent valuation method has been widely used in the environmental area, particularly to evaluate willingness to pay for nonuse or existence values of environmental goods (Cummings, Brookshire, and Schulze 1986; Mitchell and Carson 1989; Carson 1991; Portney 1994; Hanemann 1994). Environmental economists argue that people may value the preservation of natural assets such as the Grand Canyon even if they never plan to visit or directly use it (Freeman 1993). This is called an existence value.

Contingent valuation methods have been subject to much professional debate about their accuracy, validity, and reliability (Cummings, Brookshire, and Schulze 1986; Diamond and Hausman 1994; Bjornstad and Kahn 1996). Although the results of a conference of experts evaluating contingent valuation methods are "generally positive" (Cummings, Brookshire, and Schulze 1986), the controversy over the use of these methods continues. Much current research is focused on validating contingent value estimates (i.e., comparing stated willingness to pay with actual willingness to pay). David Bjornstad and James Kahn (1996, 273) note that current contingent valuation methodologies "are not universally accepted as valid, reliable, and unbiased," but that ongoing issues in environmental policy "provide an immediate and pressing need to develop stronger estimates of the value of changes in the quantity and quality of environmental resources, particularly those associated with passive use values."

One indirect approach to benefit estimation can be termed the discounted future earnings approach. This has also been called the "capital values" (Gramlich 1990) or "hedonic price" approach (Freeman 1993). It focuses on the increased stream of future earnings from either individuals or land as a result of a public-sector investment project. Thus, a health, education, or job training program may make an individual more productive and increase his or her wages above what they would have been in the absence of the project. Land values may increase as a result of urban development, recreation, transportation, or environmental improvements. This increased earning stream is a proxy for the valuation of the increased output to society by the more productive individuals. Thus, the increased earnings of inpatients compared with outpatients were one of the benefits measured by Weisbrod (1983) in his study of alternative means of treating the mentally ill. A similar approach was taken by Peter Kemper, David Long, and Craig Thornton (1983) in their study of the Supported Work Experiment, a program providing work experience for individuals with severe employment problems, such as ex-drug addicts, ex-offenders released from prison, young school dropouts, and long-term recipients of Aid to Families with Dependent Children. Discounted future earnings are also related to the valuation of life problems to be discussed in the next section of this chapter.

Another indirect approach to benefit estimation focuses on the costs to society that are saved as a result of public-sector investment projects. This approach has been used in evaluating transportation, pollution control, and disease control projects. The costs to society that would have been incurred in the absence of a project are considered to be the benefits of the investment project. For transportation projects the emphasis is on time-cost savings: the goal of a transportation project (e.g., bus, rapid rail system) is to move people from one point to another. Since the "final" good or output is having passengers arrive at their desired destination, the transportation investment lowers the "price" of this final output. Thus, cost-savings are related to the basic willingness to pay concept of cost-benefit analysis. Transportation improvements would provide cost-saving benefits to those individuals who are currently using the system and they would attract additional users to the system. Both of these gains must be measured, and they involve questions of the valuation of time saved.

Benefit estimation has also been done through the *associated cost approach,* which has been widely used in the evaluation of the benefits of wilderness recreation areas. Early studies were done by Marion Clawson (1959) and Marion Clawson and Jack Knetsch (1966), while more recent research has been summarized by Myrick Freeman (1993). For many state and national parks, either direct prices are not charged or these prices are not high enough to influence consumer decisionmaking. Therefore, it is not possible to directly estimate demand curves for these projects; however, individuals do incur significant costs associated with reaching these recreation areas, including the money and time costs of traveling to these areas. These costs may be used as proxies for differences in "prices" faced by different groups of consumers. It would be expected that consumers facing higher associated costs would demand smaller quantities or have fewer visits to these recreation sites, and thus, differences in these associated costs could be used to derive an indirect measure of willingness to pay. Use of this method would involve defining the areas from which visitors attend the facility and then collecting data on visits, distance, time costs of travel, size of the population, income, and other variables affecting the number of visits. The demand function is then estimated under the assumption that people would react to increases in the entrance fee as they react to increases in travel costs. The relevant area underneath the demand curve is thus the estimate of recreation benefits.

Many studies use a combination of these methods to try to capture different types of benefits. For example, in addition to measuring the increased wages of the mentally ill in the experimental and control programs, Weisbrod (1983) also attempted to measure increased work stability and improved consumer decisionmaking. Data on absenteeism and on the number of "beneficial" and "detrimental" job changes were incorporated in the analysis. The subjects' expenditures on insurance and the percentage of the groups having savings accounts were included as a measure of forward thinking. In the analysis of the Supported Work Experiment, Kemper and colleagues (1983) focused on the participants' earning streams, the reduction in criminal activity (e.g., reduced property damage and injury, stolen property and justice system costs), the reduction in drug treatment costs, and the reduced use of alternative services.

Estimating Benefits Related to Health and the Value of Life

Environmental, health, disease control, and safety programs can all result in reductions in mortality (death) or morbidity (illness) that would have existed without the interventions. Placing a value on these reductions is a major problem in benefit estimation for these programs. We will discuss the conceptual problems involved with the different approaches to these questions and examine some of the numerical results of these analyses.

In an early discussion of the issues, Thomas Schelling (1968) pointed out that the question is not the worth of human life but the value of life saving or preventing death. The question should really be stated not as "what is the value of human life" but "what is society willing to pay (WTP) to reduce the probability of death by a certain amount." The concern in this policy area is not with a particular death but with a statistical death. When a situation arises involving particular individuals (e.g., the collapse of a building, a liver transplant for a sick child) hundreds of thousands of dollars may be voluntarily collected in response to media attention. However, there may be quite different responses when the issues involve a bill in Congress to increase construction safety standards or to devote more resources to medical research. Thus, the issue is the valuation of unidentified, statistical lives in public programs. "For example, if each of 100,000 persons is willing to pay $20 for a reduction in risk from 3 deaths per 100,000 people to 1 death per 100,000 people, the total WTP is $2 million and the value per statistical life is $1 million (with 2 lives saved)" (Fisher, Chestnut, and Violette 1989, 89).

There have been two major approaches to the problem of valuing reductions in the risk of death in the cost-benefit analysis literature. The first is termed the *discounted future earnings* or the *human capital* approach (Rhoads 1978; Gramlich 1981, 1990; Warner and Luce 1982; Landefeld and Seskin 1982; Freeman 1993; Tolley, Kenkel, and Fabian 1994; Haddix et al. 1996). Under this approach, researchers take the average age at which death occurs and then compute the expected future income individuals would have received if they had lived a normal term. This calculation is based on assumptions about labor force participation rates and average earning streams. Since much of this income would have been received at some point in the future, the flow of income is discounted using the procedures discussed in the previous chapter. This approach is based on the idea of maximizing society's present and future consumption. The value of preventing an individual's death is reflected in his or her contribution to the gross national product. Sometimes an individual's earnings net of consumption have been utilized. This approach is based on the concept that death results both in the loss of future production and consumption. Labor earnings are usually evaluated before taxes, reflecting society's viewpoint, instead of after taxes, which would be most relevant to the individual. Nonlabor income is generally excluded because capital holdings are not affected by an individual's continued existence (Landefeld and Seskin 1982).

This approach appears to place a market value on lives saved. However, as Edward Gramlich (1990) notes, it is the wrong market: the labor market focuses only on the productive activities of the individual and cannot value how much the individual actually enjoys life. The approach also implies that a low valuation should be placed on those individuals who have low market wages. This means that there will be different valuations for children versus adults, the working versus the retired, men versus women, those with high education and training versus others, and so on. Any differences in wages resulting from labor market discrimination and other institutional factors will be transmitted into the valuation of lives saved under this approach. Nonmarket activities are typically not included. If the discounted future earnings represent the decedent's utility loss from death, there are also losses to the individual's spouse, family, and friends. Some estimate of these losses would need to be made. This approach also ignores all costs of the fear of the risk of death and of nonmonetary suffering (Rhoads 1978; Freeman 1993; Tolley, Kenkel, and Fabian 1994).

The choice of a discount rate for computing the present value of these income streams can have a major impact on the analysis, given that life expectancies up to seventy-five years may be involved. Haddix et al. (1996, 192, Table I.2) show the present value of expected future lifetime earnings and housekeeping services according to age and a weighted average for all ages calculated with discount rates ranging from 0 percent (no discounting) to 10 percent. These data represent those in the labor force with earnings and those not in the labor force keeping house with the assumptions of a 1 percent annual growth in productivity and a seventy-five-year life expectancy. The weighted average for all ages is $1.7 million undiscounted, $790,400 with a 3 percent discount rate, $544,200 with a 5 percent rate, and $287,700 with a 10 percent rate. Despite the conceptual difficulties of this method and the sensitivity to the choice of a discount rate, this approach has been widely used, given the relative ease of gathering the data necessary for the calculations, most of which are available from standard government sources.

The second approach focuses on estimating society's willingness to pay to reduce the probability of a statistical death. This approach follows directly from the methodology discussed earlier in this chapter. The problem is how to apply the willingness to pay concept to these valuation questions. Three major approaches have been used in the literature: required compensation or wage-risk studies, consumer market studies, and contingent valuation studies (Fisher, Chestnut, and Violette 1989; Viscusi 1992; 1993; Freeman 1993; Tolley, Kenkel, and Fabian 1994; Haddix et al. 1996). The first two approaches examine choices individuals make in labor or product markets to infer values of reducing the risk of death, while the third method attempts to directly estimate these values using survey instruments.

Suppose there are two jobs that are alike in every respect except that there is no risk of death in one job but there is a positive risk in the other job. In a competitive labor market with a large number of available jobs and full information about the risks associated with each job, the only way companies with risky jobs could attract workers would be to pay them higher wages. Thus, these compensating wage differentials could be used as a measure of an individual's willingness to pay to reduce the risk of death. These differentials would have to be measured after controlling for education, race, experience, unionization, region, and all other factors that also contribute to differences in wage rates. The problems with this approach are obvious. Workers may not have freedom of choice among jobs, or they may be forced to take a particular job regardless of the risks involved if the only alternative is unemployment. Further, workers may not have accurate information on the magnitude of the risks involved. Moreover, as in the case of certain chemicals, no one in society may have adequate knowledge of the risks to human life in working with these products. Workers may also have different attitudes or preferences toward risk: those in risky jobs, for instance, may exhibit less risk aversion than the population as a whole. Even with good data, estimates based on wage differentials would typically omit the willingness to pay of most white-collar workers and of all nonworkers. Society's willingness to pay may also depend upon how painful the predeath stages of a disease are, whether the program is preventive or curative, and whether risks are "involuntary," such as those from nuclear power accidents or air pollution exposure (Fisher, Chestnut, and Violette 1989; Viscusi 1992, 1993; Tolley, Kenkel, and Fabian 1994).

Consumer market studies focus on the choices people make between risks and benefits in their consumption decisions, such as the purchase of smoke detectors, the use of automobile seat belts, speeding behavior by drivers, and the use of information about the risks of smoking. These studies are similar to the labor market studies since they analyze individuals' observed behavior, but this literature is much smaller than the literature on wage-risk trade-offs. Since many of these consumption decisions are discrete decisions (e.g., the purchase of a smoke detector), these studies will not provide information about the consumer's total willingness to pay for safety "because with such discrete decisions consumers are not pushed to the point where the marginal cost of greater safety equals its marginal valuation" (Viscusi 1993, 1936).

As discussed previously, contingent valuation studies are surveys of individuals conducted in the context of a hypothetical market situation where the participants are asked about their willingness to pay for alternative *
levels of safety. These studies are based on what people say they would do, not on actual revealed behavior. It is unclear whether individuals can understand and give consistent answers to these types of questions, particularly

when very small risks are involved. The literature in both psychology and economics shows that individuals tend to overestimate the size of very low-probability events, particularly those called to one's attention (Viscusi 1993). An individual's answer may also depend on the wording of the question.

Although these different WTP methods have numerous conceptual and empirical problems, they do give "value of life" estimates that are in relatively the same range. The estimates summarized by Fisher and colleagues (1989) range from $1.6 million to $8.5 million in 1986 dollars. The wage-risk studies surveyed by W. Kip Viscusi (1993) fall in the range of $3 million to $7 million in 1990 dollars. The contingent market estimates fall in approximately the same range, while the consumer market studies results are somewhat lower, falling between $800,000 and $2 million. Most important, the results of these willingness to pay studies are typically higher than those of the discounted future earnings or human capital approach, which fall in the range of $300,000 to $800,000. This is to be expected, given that the WTP approach attempts to encompass more factors that would relate to the value of reducing the risk of death.

CHAPTER 7 CASE STUDY

Clinton Sharply Tightens Air Pollution Regulations Despite Concern Over Costs

By John H. Cushman, Jr.

In one of the most important environmental decisions of the decade, President Clinton today approved significantly tighter pollution limits on deadly soot and choking smog, while offering states and cities substantial flexibility in deciding how to reach the new goals over the next ten years and beyond.

Ending a fierce behind the scenes battle, Mr. Clinton sided with the head of the Environmental Protection Agency, Carol M. Browner, against the concerns of his economic advisers, who had balked in the face of industry complaints that the rules would cost far more then they were worth.

The While House put aside many of those economic concerns once Vice President Al Gore jumped into the fray last week, after lobbying by environmental groups, Administration officials said today.

In the end, Ms. Browner made relatively modest changes to the rule her agency proposed last November.

Announcing his decision in a speech in Tennessee, the President cast it as an initiative to protect children, a favorite theme for the Administration. In this case, he cited especially the asthmatics who are most at risk from exposure to ozone and small particles of soot, two common pollutants caused by burning fossil fuels.

"I approved some very strong new regulations today that will be somewhat controversial, but I think kids ought to be healthy," Mr. Clinton said at a conference on families at which Mr. Gore was the host.

The rules are expected to have wide-ranging practical effects. For example, old power plants in the Midwest may have to install the kind of expensive pollution-control equipment that is already commonly used in much of the Northeast, where the air is dirtier. Also, states will probably have to put more money into mass transit and other measures to reduce pollution from automobiles.

In addition, some factories like steel plants that burn lots of coal may be required to adapt their equipment to cleaner-burning fuels to avoid emissions of soot. And even the United States Forest Service may have to change the way it sets controlled fires on public lands to avoid sending too much smoke into the air.

The air pollution regulation is one of two major environmental issues on the President's agenda this week, both of them intensely debated and each of them dividing one of the Administration core constituencies, environmentalists from business groups that the Administration does not want to alienate. On Thursday, he is to outline the Administration's policies on global warming to a United Nations conference in New York, where the United States has been criticized by European states for not moving swiftly enough to control emissions of carbon dioxide.

Although the pollutants are different and the problems they cause are not directly related, both global warming and the soot and smog issues addressed today stem largely from the combustion of fossil fuels.

Like the efforts to negotiate a binding treaty to limit emissions of gases that cause global warming, the Administration's decision on air quality rules faced an enormous campaign of opposition by industry and equally determined efforts by environmentalists who supported it.

"The final product, I am delighted to say, is a major step forward for protecting the public health of the people of this county," said Ms. Browner, whose adamant defense of the proposals was described by her backers as courageous and principled, but by her detractors as stubborn and close-minded. "These new standards will provide new health protections to 125 million Americans, including 35 million children."

She spoke at a White House briefing that included several officials who for weeks have argued over the rules.

Those millions of people, E.P.A. officials said, live in hundreds of counties that will eventually have to impose new pollution control measures to meet the new standards. The agency has claimed, based on epidemiological studies, that 15,000 people die every year from exposure to these pollutants, especially the fine sooty particles. And the agency expects that hundreds of thousands of acute asthma attacks can be avoided each year, since smog often triggers breathing difficulties in children with that disease.

By putting the new controls into place, states with relatively clean air will also be helping to clean the air in New York and other downwind states where the air is generally dirtier. Across most of the Northeast, a significant fraction of the chronic air pollution blows in from the Midwest.

Under the Clean Air Act, the E.P.A. must set health-based standards for air quality without regard to potential expense. States where the air violates these standards must then impose pollution controls that can cost industries billions of dollars and inconvenience motorists. The drive to tighten the standards touched off a huge lobbying campaign over the past two years, led by auto makers, electric utilities, fuel suppliers and manufacturers.

Although the final rules are not quite as aggressive as the version that was the first proposed, they are nonetheless a significant milestone in the long struggle against unhealthy air. The last time the ozone standard was changed, nearly 20 years ago, it was weakened. The tiniest particles of sooty chemicals, so small that they lodge deep in the lungs, have never been controlled before under the Clean Air Act.

Some of the expected health benefits from the new regulations will not be felt until at least 2003 in the case of smog and 2008 in the case of soot, officials said. In the meantime, steps that are already under way to control pollution should continue to provide more modest gains.

A coalition of powerful industry groups denounced the decision as "crushing blow" to the economy, and urged Congress to overturn it.

"The Administration lacked the courage to do what is right," said Charles J. DiBona of the American Petroleum Institute, a leader of the coalition. "Those who worked hard to bring reason to the debate, including some 250 members of Congress, 27 governors and more than a thousand mayors and other state, county, and local officials, were simply ignored."

Environmental groups highly praised the new standards and raised no objections to the flexible approach the Administration is offering to put the rules in place.

"They really stood up to the worst that industry could throw at them," said Philip Clapp, the head of the Environmental Information Center, who had lobbied hard on the issue and criticized Mr. Gore last week for not intervening strongly enough.

Mr. Clapp and other environmentalists said they believed that when the President and the Vice President focused on the rule in the past week or so, they acted decisively to favor the green faction in the Administration.

"They were extremely mindful of the fact that they had campaigned extensively on the environment, and the leaders of the Administration made their decision based on the promises they had made," Mr. Clapp said.

At the White House today, Mr. Clinton's advisers sought to describe the intense interagency fight over the rules as a normal process in writing regulations, and said all sides agreed that protecting the public health was a top priority all along.

But privately, Administration officials said there was a definite dispute between economic agencies and health agencies. The Treasury Department, for example, fought Ms. Browner's proposals, while the Department of Health and Human Services supported her.

Although the fight within the Administration over the proposals is now over, the new standards continue to face opposition in Congress and in the courts.

Industry opponents are making several claims. They contend that the scientific evidence linking air pollution to illness and death is not solid enough, and the predicted health benefits not great enough, to justify such large expenditures. And they maintain that the E.P.A. failed to adequately assess the economic effects of tighter controls on small businesses, as required by a new law that gives Congress 60 days to overturn any major Federal regulation.

The new standards for ozone, which is a compound of oxygen in a form that corrodes tissues, call for concentrations in the air not to exceed 80 parts per billion over an eight-hour period. Places where smog exceeds that standard more than four times a year averaged over three years would have to adopt corrective measures. The existing standard is 120 parts per billion over a one-hour peak period, a measure that the agency considers flawed because brief spikes of smog show up as violations, while persistent smog at lower but still damaging levels goes unprevented.

The new standards for fine particles of 2.5 microns in diameter call for daily averages not to exceed 65 micrograms per cubic meter of air, and for annual averages not to exceed 15 micrograms per cubic meter.

To provide more flexibility as states try to comply with the fine particle rule, the E.P.A. loosened its earlier proposal for the daily standard, which was to have been 50 micrograms per cubic meter. But it maintained its initial proposal for the annual standard, which is a better indicator of chronic air pollution.

The E.P.A. agreed to allow five years for constructing monitors to detect the fine particles, since they have not been regulated before, and a few years more will pass before states must actually control emissions. During that time, more scientific studies of the health effects will be conducted.

Tightening Air Quality Standards: The Policy Debate

In July 1997 EPA issued updated air quality standards for ozone and particulate matter, commonly known as smog and soot. The debate leading to this policy change, termed "one of the most important environmental decisions of the decade," is described in the case study for this chapter. "Ending a fierce behind-the-scenes battle, Mr. Clinton sided with the head of the Environmental Protection Agency, Carol M. Browner, against the concerns of his economic advisors, who had balked in the face of industry complaints that the rules would cost far more than they were worth." Thus, the case clearly states that the policy debate focused on the benefits and costs of the new regulations. President Clinton framed the debate in terms of protecting the health of children, particularly those with asthma: "I approved some very strong new regulations today that will be somewhat controversial, but I think kids ought to be healthy." The Clinton administration claims that 15,000 people die each year from exposure to these pollutants, especially the fine particles, and that hundreds of thousands of acute asthma attacks can be avoided each year as a result of the regulations. Carol Browner claimed that the revised standards "will provide new health protections to 125 million Americans, including 35 million children."

The new standards for ozone limit concentrations in the air to eighty parts per billion over an eight-hour period compared with the existing standard of 120 parts per billion over a one-hour period. EPA proposed the change to control lower, but persistent and still damaging, levels of ozone, rather than concentrate on sharp increases lasting only a short period of time. Small particles have never been controlled previously under the Clean Air Act. The new standards focus on fine particles of 2.5 microns in diameter and limit daily averages to 65 micrograms per cubic meter of air and annual averages to 15 micrograms per cubic meter. EPA did provide more flexibility for compliance by the states in loosening its earlier proposed daily standard of 50 micrograms per cubic meter. The agency is also allowing five years to construct monitors to detect the fine particles and several more years before states must actually control emissions.

These revised air quality standards were hotly debated both within and outside the Clinton administration. Administration officials acknowledged the dispute between the Treasury Department, which fought the EPA proposals, and the Department of Health and Human Services, which supported them. Vice-president Al Gore joined the debate on the side of the environmentalists, a group that had provided major support for the Clinton-Gore reelection campaign. The policy changes were announced at a conference on families that Gore hosted. Industry officials denounced the new policy as a "crushing blow" to the economy and urged Congress to overturn it. Opponents claimed that there is no solid evidence linking air pollution to illness and death and that any health benefits are not large enough compared with the expenditures that will be required under the program. Opponents also argue that the economic effects of the regulations on small businesses were not adequately assessed.

Carol Browner has noted that the Clean Air Act of 1970 does not allow EPA to consider costs at the standard-setting stage of the process. Pollution limits must be based solely "on health, risk, exposure, and damage to the environment, as determined by the best available science" (Browner 1997, 367). She also argued that the costs of the regulations were always raised by opponents of any regulations and that these costs were often overstated. "Why? Because industry ultimately rises to the challenge, finding cheaper, more innovative ways of meeting the standards and lowering pollution" (Browner 1997, 367). Browner stated that compliance costs could be considered at the implementation stage of the process and that the administration would be flexible in enforcing the regulations. "We will work with all who are affected—state governments, local governments, communities, and businesses large and small—to find the best strategies for reducing pollution, providing the public health protections, and, at the same time, doing everything we can to prevent adverse economic impact" (Browner 1997, 367).

Legislation governing air quality originated with the Air Pollution Control Act of 1955. This law was amended in 1970 by the Clean Air Act, which also created the Environmental Protection Agency. More than 300 pages of amendments were added to the Clean Air Act in 1990, including giving EPA authority to control particulate matter precursors. EPA has set National Ambient Air Quality Standards (NAAQS) for six key pollutants—lead, sulfur dioxide, nitrous oxide, particulates (soot), carbon monoxide, and ozone (smog), all of which are byproducts of industrialization and have a negative impact on public health and the economy (Hoffnagle 1997; Romani 1998). The changes in the NAAQS regulations regarding ozone and particulates discussed in the case were originally proposed by EPA in December 1996 and then revised when released in July 1997.

Concern over the costs and benefits of these regulations has also led to further actions in Congress. Senator James Inhofe (R-Okla) proposed a bill, the Ozone and Particulate Matter Research Act of 1997, to overturn the EPA rules. This proposal would restore the previously existing air quality standards and put off any decision on setting new standards for at least five years, which would allow further scientific research. The bill authorized $100 million for these purposes, with one-quarter of that directed for ozone research. According to Senator Inhofe, the proposal was supported by twenty-one cosponsors in the Senate and over thirty organizations, thereby reflecting the strong opposition to the new EPA rules by governors, mayors, and local and state officials across the nation. Inhofe also argued that his proposal followed the advice of three of the last four Clean Air Scientific Advisory Committee chairs and thus allowed for continuity (*Chemical Market Reporter* 1997a).

On 6 November 1997 Senator Inhofe led a bid to nullify the proposed EPA regulations. He attached his proposal to the fast-track trade legislation that was already on the Senate floor instead of moving through the usual committee process due to the reluctance of Senator John Chafee (R-R.I.) to support the move to block the new EPA mandates. Senator Chafee, chairman of the Environment and Public Works Committee, had suggested that states find the most cost-effective way to implement the tougher regulations. The amendment was attached to the trade legislation without objection because only two other senators were in attendance. When Democrats and other supporters of the EPA regulations learned of the amendment, protest ensued, the amendment was struck from the bill, and, in exchange, it was agreed that similar legislation on the EPA issue would be debated as a separate bill at some time in the future (*Chemical Market Reporter* 1997b).

In early 1998 Congress settled the dispute over EPA air quality standards for ozone and particulates. This represented a compromise between Senator Inhofe and EPA. "The provision codifies into law the extended implementation plan for the fine particulate standard and ensures that EPA will absorb the full cost of setting up a nationwide monitoring system" to ensure compliance with the new rule by December 1999 (Hess 1998). Codification ensures that the agency will gather three years of data on particulate matter before identifying which regions fail to comply with the tightened standards (Foster 1998). In addition, no state may be penalized for noncompliance for at least six years for ozone and at least nine years for particulate matter. Nothing in the compromise affected any pending lawsuits challenging the validity of the EPA rules (*Chemical Market Reporter* 1998).

Benefits and Costs of Tightened Air Quality Standards

We stated in the preceding section of this chapter that the debates over the new air quality standards for ozone and particulates center on different estimates of the policy's benefits and costs. Several observers have noted that even the estimates of these benefits and costs done by EPA have shown that further efforts to attain the *current* air quality standards for ozone have costs that exceed the benefits ($1.2 billion compared with $0.1 to $0.8 billion). Therefore, the proposed more stringent standards would also fail the benefit-cost test ($0.1 to $1.5 billion for benefits and $2.5 billion for costs) (Lave 1997). "Compliance with a tighter ozone standard will mitigate the threat of reduced pulmonary function, primarily to people exercising or working outside on warm summer days when smog forms. This reduction in lung function is reversible and not serious in most Americans, though for a few with severe respiratory problems it may be more important and may even put them in the hospital" (Crandall 1997). These researchers argue that the primary benefits of the new standards are to be derived from the regulation of particulates. Some argue that particulate regulation has benefits ten times greater than the costs ($58 to $110 billion in benefits versus $6 billion in costs) (Lave 1997). Yet even here there is controversy. "Clearly, the proposal to tighten air quality standards hangs on the fine particulate proposal. And that proposal is even more controversial than the ozone standard because of difficulties involved in translating epidemiological data into sound, health-based policy" (Crandall 1997, 43).

This last quote highlights the difficulties in undertaking an economic evaluation of any pollution abatement regulation. "Challenging an environmental proposal on the basis that its benefits do not outweigh its costs is almost as difficult as challenging the method for indexing Social Security benefit levels. Still, it is essential that we try, if only to lay the groundwork for a more rational approach to such problems in the millennium ahead"

(Crandall 1997, 40). All economic evaluations of pollution abatement programs require the following steps:

1. Estimate the changes in environmental quality resulting from the changes in the emissions.
2. Estimate the effects (damages) from the degradation in environmental quality.
3. Estimate the change in behavior occurring due to the degraded environment.
4. Value the damages to the environment.

"Each of these steps is difficult, requiring extensive data and analysis" (Cifuentes and Lave 1993, 322).

Damages to the environment are typically evaluated through the cost-savings approach and the contingent market approach, both of which were discussed previously. The cost-savings approach requires an estimate of the damages to the environment caused by the particular type of pollution in question: these damages represent the costs to be saved if pollution is prevented by such interventions as the tightening of the air quality standards discussed in this chapter. "Uncertainties come into play in translating emissions into ambient air quality; in estimating the adverse effects on health, agriculture, and the environment more generally; in translating the adverse effects of air pollution into dollars; and in estimating the costs of complying with the standards. The uncertainties for the effects of small particles are much greater than those for ozone" (Lave 1997, 42).

Some of these uncertainties result from problems in measuring the effects of the air pollution, which is typically measured for outdoor air at a few points in a city or metropolitan area. Since most people only spend a small amount of time outdoors (and not in vehicles), these measurements may not truly reflect the quality of the air that people breathe most of the time. If data are derived from clinical studies of a sample of volunteers, these studies are usually done under very controlled conditions, and they do not allow for the fact that people in real-world situations will probably take actions to avert or at least mitigate the air pollution (Cifuentes and Lave 1993). EPA notes that two types of data are used to monitor air quality: ambient concentrations and emissions estimates. Ambient concentrations are "measurements of pollutant concentrations in the ambient air from monitoring sites across the country," while emissions estimates "are based largely on engineering calculations of the amounts and kinds of pollutants emitted by automobiles, factories, and other sources over a given period" (U.S. Environmental Protection Agency 1998, 8). Changes in ambient concentrations do not always match changes in emissions estimates for several reasons. Air quality monitors are usually in urban areas, so they measure urban emissions from mobile sources more accurately than they do rural emissions from large stationary sources. The amount of pollution measured at the monitoring stations is also influenced by any chemical reactions in the atmosphere and other meteorological conditions (U.S. Environmental Protection Agency 1998).

In trying to measure "premature deaths due to air pollution," researchers must try to sort out what deaths are actually caused by the air pollution from those deaths that would have occurred in any case. It is often said that air pollution is simply "harvesting" deaths that would likely have occurred within a few days even without the pollution. This is another example of the problem of the counterfactual that was first discussed in the previous chapter. Studies that were done in the past may not reflect the changes in outcomes that have occurred over time as other environmental regulations were put into effect. Clinical studies of the morbidity effects of air pollution may use either very precise measures of pulmonary functions and other symptoms, such as eye or throat irritation or shortness of breath, or more comprehensive measures such as restricted activity days, which include days spent in bed, days missed from work, and other days when normal activities are restricted due to illness (Cifuentes and Lave 1993).

Ozone is formed by the "oxidation of nitrogen oxides in the presence of sunlight and reactive volatile organic compounds" (Cifuentes and Lave 1993, 333). It can cause significant respiratory problems when found in high concentrations. Although both clinical and epidemiologic studies have found health effects from ozone, how many people would benefit from tightening the air quality standards is uncertain. "The EPA's 1996 estimate of the number of beneficiaries has changed. For example, the number of asthmatics benefitting has been decreased by as much as a factor of 3. Projected numbers of beneficiaries in other impaired groups have also been reduced substantially" (Abelson 1997, 15).

The health effects of small particulates are more uncertain. Although several studies have confirmed associations between particulate matter and morbidity and mortality effects, these associations are weak. "The physiological mechanisms of these impairments are relatively unknown . . . such studies are plagued by confounders such as previous exposure to cigarette smoke; the coincidental presence of high levels of toxic gases, such as CO, NO, and SO; and extreme weather" (Abelson 1997, 15). Studies may also be based on levels of particulate matter greater than those faced by most individuals. In its 1998 air quality report on the new particulate standards, EPA notes that "there are not enough monitors in place at this time to portray an accurate national trend of urban air quality. The network of monitors for the new $PM_{2.5}$ standard will be phased in over the new few years" (U.S. Environmental Protection Agency 1998, 42).

Given these uncertainties, some researchers still interpret the data as favoring the tighter air quality standards. "In my judgment, it is highly unlikely that the benefits of the tightened particle standard would be less than the costs despite the uncertainty involved" (Lave 1997, 45). Others interpret the data more cautiously and note the disagreements among EPA's own experts:

> Even EPA's own Clean Air Scientific Advisory Committee, an outside board of advisers, split badly on whether EPA should set a fine particle standard given the available evidence. Two of the twenty-two members found the evidence insufficient to support any fine particle standard. Eight others declined to select a range for the standard, presumably because they felt the evidence was not sufficiently robust to do so. Seven others supported setting the standard at the upper end of EPA's recommended range—that is, the less stringent end. Only four of the twenty-two were willing to sign on to a standard in the more stringent range of EPA's proposal (Crandall 1997, 45).

The valuation placed on the lives saved from the increased air quality standards has also been criticized. Use of a value for a healthy, working-age adult who may have thirty to fifty more years to live may not be appropriate for this analysis.

> But surely someone who dies from temporarily elevated levels of fine particulates must be measuring his or her life expectancy in weeks or months, not years. Thus EPA's calculation that the potential benefits of a tighter particulate standard range from $22 billion to $192 billion a year is wildly exaggerated. A reasonable value for the weeks or months of additional life might reduce this estimate to one-tenth of EPA's estimate or even less (Crandall 1997, 46).

In addition to the discussion and debate on the overall benefits and costs of the tighter regulations, there have been a wide variety of charges and countercharges about the impacts of the regulation on specific industries. Thus, as noted in the conceptual discussion earlier in this chapter, issues about the distribution of benefits and costs are always an important part of the policy debate. A 600-member industry coalition has argued that the impacts on health used by EPA are based on limited science and has noted the disagreement among EPA's own researchers. The industry coalition also disputed EPA's analysis that the particulate matter rule would cost about $6 billion a year by citing a further analysis by one of EPA's own contractors that estimated costs as high as $19.6 billion for the Midwest and Northeast alone. The American Petroleum Institute's health and environmental affairs department has concluded that approximately 789 counties in forty-eight states would fall under the "nonattainment" status and would not be able to comply with the new standards. EPA estimates conclude that 335 counties would fail to meet the ozone standards, while 167 counties would fail to meet the particulate matter standards (Hess 1997). Motor carrier groups worry that truck fleets may have to make major changes in their fleet specifications to comply with the standards. The American Trucking Association, along with the U.S. Chamber of Commerce and several for-hire motor carriers, filed suit against the new rules arguing that EPA ignored laws governing small-business regulation by placing too heavy a burden on small business (Harrington 1997). Power plant operators will need to devote substantial attention and resources to developing modified operating procedures and applying unique emission control strategies due to concentrated point-source emissions of various ozone and particulate matter precursors from electric generating plants (Hoffnagle 1997).

Summary

The issues discussed here show the problems in undertaking any cost-benefit analysis and how that analysis is used in a decisionmaking process. Both the underlying impacts of many programs and regulations as well as the valuation of these impacts have large amounts of uncertainty involved. Some of this uncertainty can be dealt with through the sensitivity analysis procedures discussed in the previous chapter. The existence of multiple studies can also support the effectiveness of a program, even if all the studies have some methodological problems. In recent years there has been an increased use of meta-analysis, a procedure that "integrates findings from numerous studies through quantitative means, using many methods of measurement and statistical analysis" (Haddix et al. 1996, 204). This is a systematic review of the literature on a given subject to determine what conclusions can be drawn from this body of research. Principles of meta-analysis are outlined by Haddix et al. (1996).

There is a need for economic evaluation studies using cost-effectiveness, cost-utility, and cost-benefit analysis, even given their weaknesses. "Unless mechanisms exist for placing bounds on our risk reduction efforts, we can end up pursuing policies of diminishing marginal impact and diverting resources from more productive uses" (Viscusi 1996, 120). In the federal government, the Office of Management and Budget is the organization responsible for regulatory oversight. In recent administrations, the mandate to compare benefits and costs of regulatory policies has resulted from a series of executive orders, and the latter may conflict with the agency's legislative mandate, as noted above for EPA. Using an implicit value of life of $5 million as the cutoff for an efficient regulation, Viscusi (1996) has categorized a variety of government regulations as passing or not passing a benefit-cost test. He found wide variations both within and among government agencies in regulations that would pass this benefit-cost test. Many of the programs that would not pass this benefit-cost test are found in EPA, which is not surprising, given the legislation prohibiting the comparison of costs and benefits for many of these programs. Viscusi's analysis points out the need for more comprehensive and uniform analyses of government regulations and investment programs. This decisionmaking problem is the greatest challenge in the future for the economic evaluation of public sector programs, regulations, and interventions.

References

Abelson, Philip H. (1997). "Proposed Air Pollutant Standards," *Science* 277, 5322, p. 15.

Bjornstad, David J. and James R. Kahn (eds.) (1996). *The Contingent Valuation of Environmental Resources.* (Cheltenham, U.K.: Edward Elgar).

Browner, Carol M. (1997). "Smog and Soot: Updating Air Quality Standards," *Public Health Reports* 112, 5, pp. 366–67.

Carson, Richard T. (1991). "Constructed Markets," in John Braden and Charles Kolstad (eds.), *Measuring the Demand for Environmental Quality* (Amsterdam: Elsevier).

Chemical Market Reporter. (1998). 253, 10, p. 5.

———. (1997a). 252, 20, p. 5.

———. (1997b). 252, 18, pp. 7, 22.

Cifuentes, Luis A. and Lester B. Lave. (1993). "Economic Valuation of Air Pollution Abatement: Benefits From Health Effects," *Annual Review of Energy and the Environment* 18, pp. 319–42.

Clawson, Marion. (1959). *Methods for Measuring the Demand for and the Value of Outdoor Recreation.* (Washington, D.C.: Resources for the Future).

Clawson, Marion and Jack L. Knetsch. (1966). *Economics of Outdoor Recreation.* (Baltimore: Johns Hopkins University Press).

Crandall, Robert W. (1997). "The Costly Pursuit of the Impossible: EPA's Proposed Air Quality Standards," *Brookings Review* 15, 3, pp. 40–47.

Cummings, Ronald G., David S. Brookshire, and William D. Schulze. (1986). *Valuing Environmental Goods: An Assessment of the Contingent Valuation Method.* (Savage, Md.: Rowman & Littlefield Publishers, Inc.).

Diamond, Peter A. and Jerry A. Hausman. (1994). "Contingent Valuation: Is Some Number Better Than No Number?" *Journal of Economic Perspectives* 8, 4, pp. 45–64.

Fisher, Ann, Lauraine G. Chestnut, and Daniel M. Violette. (1989). "The Value of Reducing the Risks of Death: A Note on New Evidence," *Journal of Policy Analysis and Management* 8, 1, pp. 88–100.

Foster, A. (1998). "Road Bill Studded with Green Riders," *Chemical Week* (3 June), 160, 21, p. 41.

Freeman, A. Myrick, III. (1993). *The Measurement of Environmental and Resource Values: Theory and Methods* (Washington, D.C.: Resources for the Future).

Gaynor, Martin and William B. Vogt. (1997). "What Does Economics Have to Say About Health Policy Anyway? A Comment and Correction on Evans and Rice," *Journal of Health Politics, Policy and Law* 22, 2, pp. 476–96.

Gramlich, Edward M. (1990). *A Guide to Benefit-Cost Analysis,* 2d ed. (Englewood Cliffs, N.J.: Prentice Hall).

———. (1981). *Benefit-Cost Analysis of Government Programs.* (Englewood Cliffs, N.J.: Prentice Hall).

Haddix, Anne C., Steven M. Teutsch, Phaedra A. Shaffer, and Diane O. Dunet. (1996). *Prevention Effectiveness: A Guide to Decision Analysis and Economic Evaluation* (New York: Oxford University Press).

Hanemann, W. Michael. (1994). "Valuing the Environment Through Contingent Valuation," *Journal of Economic Perspectives* 8, 4, pp. 19–43.

Harrington, Lisa H. (1997). "Two Motor Issues Draw Attention," *Transportation and Distribution* 38, 9, p. 104.

Haveman, Robert H. and Burton A. Weisbrod. (1983). "Defining Benefits of Public Programs: Some Guidance for Policy Analysts," in Robert H. Haveman and Julius Margolis (eds.), *Public Expenditure and Policy Analysis,* 3d ed. (Boston: Houghton Mifflin), pp. 80–104.

Herzlinger, Regina. (1979). "Costs, Benefits, and the West Side Highway," *The Public Interest* (Spring) pp. 77–98.

Hess, Glenn. (1998). "Broad Transportation Bill Extends Ethanol Tax, Settles Air Standards," *Chemical Market Reporter* 253, 22, pp. 1, 12.

———. (1997). "A Battle Over Air Standards," *Chemical Market Reporter* 251, 11, p. SR17.

Hoffnagle, Gale F. (1997). "New NAAQS Demand Reductions," *Power Engineering* 101, 13, pp. 41–45.

Hyman, David N. (1996). *Public Finance: A Contemporary Application of Theory to Policy,* 5th ed. (Fort Worth, Tex.: The Dryden Press).

Kemper, Peter, David A. Long, and Craig Thornton. (1983). "A Benefit-Cost Analysis of the Supported Work Experiment," in Robert H. Haveman and Julius Margolis (eds.) *Public Expenditure and Policy Analysis,* 3d ed. (Boston: Houghton Mifflin), pp. 260–300.

Landefeld, J. Steven and Eugene P. Seskin. (1982). "The Economic Value of Life: Linking Theory to Practice," *American Journal of Public Health* 72, pp. 555–66.

Lave, Lester B. (1997). "EPA's Proposed Air Quality Standards: Clean Air Sense," *Brookings Review* 15, 3, pp. 40–47.

Mishan, Edward J. (1976). *Cost-Benefit Analysis, New and Expanded Edition* (New York: Praeger Publishers).

Mitchell, Robert C. and Richard T. Carson. (1989). *Using Surveys to Value Public Goods: The Contingent Valuation Method* (Washington, D.C.: Resources for the Future).

Pauly, Mark V. (1997). "Who Was That Straw Man Anyway? A Comment on Evans and Rice," *Journal of Health Politics, Policy and Law* 22, 2, pp. 467–73.

Portney, Paul R. (1994). "The Contingent Valuation Debate: Why Economists Should Care," *Journal of Economic Perspectives* 8, 4, pp. 3–17.

Reinhardt, Uwe E. (1992). "Reflections on the Meaning of Efficiency: Can Efficiency Be Separated From Equity?" *Yale Law & Policy Review* 10, pp. 302–15.

Rhoads, Steven E. (1978). "How Much Should We Spend to Save a Life?" *The Public Interest* (Spring) pp. 74–92.

Rice, Thomas. (1998). *The Economics of Health Reconsidered* (Chicago: Health Administration Press).

———. (1997). "Can Markets Give Us the Health System We Want?" *Journal of Health Politics, Policy and Law* 22, 2, pp. 383–426.

———. (1992). "An Alternative Framework for Evaluating Welfare Losses in the Health Care Market," *Journal of Health Economics* 11, 1, pp. 88–92.

Romani, Paul N. (1998). "Environmentally Responsible Business," *Supervision* 59, 2, pp. 6–9.

Schelling, Thomas C. (1968). "The Life You Save May Be Your Own," in Samuel B. Chase, Jr. (ed.) *Problems in Public Expenditure Analysis* (Washington, D.C.: The Brookings Institution), pp. 127–76.

Tolley, George, Donald Kenkel, and Robert Fabian. (1994). *Valuing Health for Policy* (Chicago: The University of Chicago Press).

U.S. Environmental Protection Agency. (1998). *National Air Quality and Emissions Trend Report, 1997* (Research Triangle Park, N.C.: U.S. Environmental Protection Agency).

Viscusi, W. Kip. (1996). "Economic Foundations of the Current Regulatory Reform Efforts," *Journal of Economic Perspectives* 10, 3, pp. 119–34.

———. (1993). "The Value of Risks to Life and Health," *Journal of Economic Literature* 31, 4, pp. 1912–46.

———. (1992). *Fatal Tradeoffs: Public & Private Responsibilities for Risk* (New York: Oxford University Press).

Warner, Kenneth E. and Bryan R. Luce. (1982). *Cost-Benefit and Cost-Effectiveness Analysis in Health Care* (Ann Arbor, Mich.: Health Administration Press).

Weisbrod, Burton A. (1983). "Benefit-Cost Analysis of a Controlled Experiment: Treating the Mentally Ill," in Robert H. Haveman and Julius Margolis (eds.) *Public Expenditure and Policy Analysis,* 3d ed. (Boston: Houghton Mifflin), pp. 230–59.

Whittington, Dale and Duncan MacRae, Jr. (1986). "The Issue of Standing in Cost-Benefit Analysis," *Journal of Policy Analysis and Management* 5, 4, pp. 665–82.

Zerbe, Richard O., Jr. (1998). "Is Cost-Benefit Analysis Legal? Three Rules," *Journal of Policy Analysis and Management* 17, 3, pp. 419–56.

CHAPTER 8

Summary and Conclusions

In this chapter, we summarize the issues developed earlier in this book and discuss practical lessons from the case applications. The aim in the previous chapters was to present generic analytic tools and indicate how adaptable they are to particular cases. In that sense, there is no one tool for "problem definition" or "forecasting policy options" but, rather, many variants. The sophisticated policy analyst will have to use values and exercise judgment on how to analyze policies with these tools. Policy analysis is part art and part science.

Decisionmakers need to sort good from bad or incomplete analysis before deciding on policies. Knowledge of the analyst's tools can also help policymakers trust such analysis, thus increasing its relevance. This was in part the rationale for the creation of such in-house policy analysis bodies as the Congressional Research Service, which aids individual House and Senate members in their policy choices, and the Congressional Budget Office, which assists the members in economic policymaking. The data and information produced independently by these bodies were considered more trustworthy than that produced for the executive branch of government.

Analytic Frameworks and Decision Values Revisited

As discussed in chapter 1, the issue of values is inherent in policy analysis. Many analysts would prefer to eliminate value problems with more helpings of quantitative data and methods. But that is neither possible nor desirable, since values must be recognized and weighed in even the most technical engineering analyses of, for example, roads and other infrastructure choices. Analytic tools can narrow the range of the values problem but cannot eliminate them because values are built into many of the tools. For example, with cost-benefit analysis, decisionmakers attempt to compare the "value" of policy A (an education program) with policy B (an irrigation program). Yet, as discussed in chapter 7, the criterion of economic efficiency, which underlies the cost-benefit analysis tool, is based on value judgments about what improves social welfare (the potential compensation policy). There are also conflicts between equity and efficiency issues in the application of cost-benefit analysis, and the conflicts are not resolved simply by adding more data and quantitative tools.

We noted in chapter 1 that the emphasis of the book would be on three of the four phases of the policy process (Figure 1.1), excluding the "Deciding" phase. Given the linkage of values, analytic tools, and frameworks, we conclude with a word on decisionmaking. Analysts should be skeptical of one-size-fits-all methods when deciding on policies, given the underlying subjectivity of broader frameworks. Proponents of the planning, programming, and budgeting system (PPBS) "program structure" of the 1960s claimed it was a new tool that would facilitate analysis by comparing means and ends and integrating institutional and budgetary questions in the analysis of proposed public policies (Axelrod 1995). Rather than facilitate analysis, the new framework posed many unanswerable questions and generated quantities of data that did not contribute to better policy analysis. By bringing in multiple actors and analysts with their own political agendas, the structure actually deepened the level of conflict. Paradoxically, the new policy analysis framework often impeded analysis.

The major problem with such overarching frameworks is that they are too general to serve as a guide. They cannot point to the right questions or provide criteria to evaluate the answers. For example, "program structures" could not point to the core issues or criteria for institutional analysis. Although some observers such as Carlson believed them absolutely essential to program analysis, others such as Wildavsky found them to be vehicles to pile up meaningless data (cited in Axelrod 1995). A major problem is that program structures ignored the political costs of the structural changes to institutions that were often needed to rationalize budget allocations (e.g., consolidation and elimination of departments and bureaus).

In addition, many policy analysis tools and frameworks may lead the analyst to presume that institutional life is simple. The tools may seem most appropriate for comparing single programs or policies that deal with only one institution. In fact, most real problems deal with trade-offs between multiple policies in an environment of multiple institutional responsibilities—often for the same program (e.g., the Departments of Defense, State, Commerce, and Treasury, as well as USAID, are all involved in the foreign aid program). Analysts using the tools need to recognize these conflicting values, which may involve trade-offs as well as policy and program rankings in a complex environment.

The difficulty of deciding which policies to fund and implement requires decision tools to simplify reality. This takes place in the third phase of the policy process described in chapter 1 (see Figure 1.1). Policy tools are needed to narrow the range of disagreement over technical issues. Many of these tools were discussed in chapters 6 and 7. However, technical disagreements often turn on fundamental value differences. One remedy for this problem is the "weighting-and-scoring model." Weighting and scoring models serve the overt purpose of structuring choices where stakeholders have multiple values and argue about multiple criteria (Lehan 1984).

These models are derived from methods used to select capital projects but they can feasibly be applied to current programs and policies. Moreover, "investment" programs include not only physical assets such as buildings but human capital (health and education), as well as research and development. In any of these cases, policymakers often do not have access to quantitative economic studies on relative rates of return before allocating funds to programs (Posner, Lewis, and Laufe 1998, 17). For this practical reason, providing more criteria for decisionmaking can increase the chances that a program will be effective. A weighting-and-scoring model uses multiple criteria that allow the ranking and trading of policy options based on stakeholder values. It serves as a summary framework to structure choice once problems have been defined and analytic tools utilized to isolate potentially beneficial programs and policies.

Whatever method of policy selection is used, it should incorporate elements of intangible values (e.g., social benefits, health risk if deferred, availability of central transfers) and quantitative cost-benefit criteria. There are many possibilities here and analysts should develop a system that utilizes the values from assessments (e.g., health clinic facility conditions) to produce a separate and overall summary score for decisionmaking. The goal of this system is not to replace judgment or exclude political considerations. Rather, a ranking system is needed to make issues and trade-offs explicit.

For example, using a combination of existing and recommended criteria, health project planners could assign scores of 0, 1, or 2 for each category. The weighting-and-scoring model then produces rankings based on these combined scores (see Table 8.1). To determine timing of implementation, the scores can be added and projects classified according to six categories of urgency (e.g., 14–16 = urgent). For example, the World Bank uses an ascending scale of project rehabilitation (1–3) to program needed renovations: (1) minimal level, (2) increased level of services, and (3) higher level of services. These criteria are in the "Needs" column below. Since the interest is typically to bring health and education facilities up to minimal levels of service, a 2 should be assigned for "minimal" existing levels of service, a 1 for "increased levels," and a 0 for "higher levels" of service. The Table 8.1 matrix could be used for ranking health or education projects.

Based on the total score in the last column from use of the weighting-and-scoring model, policymakers could classify programs or projects according to such values as (1) urgent (cannot be postponed for safety reasons), (2) essential, (3) necessary, (4) desirable, (5) acceptable (meaning adequately planned but deferrable), or (6) deferrable (policies that are not only deferrable but that do not meet cost-benefit or timing criteria).

Table 8.1: Sample Weighting-and-Scoring Matrix for Health Investment Projects

CAPITAL REPAIR PROJECT	COST SHARING: OR ALTERNATIVE FUNDING 2-HIGH/ 1-SOME/ 0-LOW	BENEFITS: OR FORECAST DEMAND 2-HIGH/ 1-SOME/ 0-LOW	CONDITION: 2-BAD/ 1-FAIR/ 0-GOOD	NEEDS: 2-MINIMAL/ 1-INCREASED LEVEL/ 0-HIGHER LEVEL OF SERVICE	LOCATION: 2-RURAL/ 1-SEMIRURAL/ 0-URBAN	INVESTMENT: 3-2-REPAIR/ 1-REPLACE/ 0-COMPLETE CONSTRUCTION	COST: 2-LESS THAN $850,000/ 1-$850,000– $1 MILLION/ 0-GREATER THAN $1 MILLION	OCCUPANCY: 2-75–100%/ 1-50–74%/ 0-LESS THAN 50%	SCORE
A									
B									
C									

In short, useful policy tools need to provide guidance in ranking and trading off proposed public expenditures. To the extent that guidance is general, policymakers are relatively free to select on the basis of subjective, often political preferences. When cost-benefit, efficiency, and effectiveness data have been properly assembled, the weighting-and-scoring model can help the decisionmaking process.

Lessons from the Case Study Analyses

We hope that our survey from the stages of problem identification to the use of analytic methods will provide students and practitioners with useful tools and insights on their application to real-world policy problems.

STRUCTURING POLICY PROBLEMS

In chapter 2, we learned that policy problems are unrealized values that produce dissatisfaction over issues (Dunn 1981). To be actionable later, problems should have an empirical basis, meaning that data should exist on the scope and intensity of the proposed problem. We learned that some policy problems are well structured, involving few decisionmakers and a small number of options, such as sanitation removal, rat control, or scheduling of facilities maintenance. Moderately well-structured problems involve more decisionmakers and options. Such problems often contain both a well- and ill-structured component, such as current demographic changes and social insurance liabilities for future generations. Ill-structured or messy problems are the most common policy issues. They have multiple, overlapping decisionmakers and many options, such as the regulation of tobacco use and its widely varying implications for numerous stakeholders in the economy.

We have indicated that there are many methods of structuring problems, including brainstorming, as well as boundary, classification, causal, and assumptional analyses. Some or all of these methods should be applied when decisionmakers are faced with an obvious messy problem such as jail overcrowding. The following lessons can be reached in applying these methods to the cases.

- Do not define the problem so narrowly as to exclude related problems. To do so invites major unintended consequences at the implementation stage of policymaking. Jail overcrowding is related to drug use and apprehension of offenders.

- Include all relevant stakeholders to avoid a narrow mechanical definition of the problem. Failure to include all relevant stakeholders may allow the problem to be defined by powerful industry interest groups, such as prison construction and engineering.
- To avoid being overwhelmed with conflicting data and studies, isolate and study the major explanatory arguments and data trends. Current studies on the effects of racial preference systems in university student selection, for example, are largely contradictory and need to be sorted out before the problem-structuring process can begin.
- Examine the remote as well as the immediate, actionable causes. Problems must be defined in actionable terms. Obviously, a college dean in Priština, Kosovo, cannot contain a conflict caused by long-term deep-seated ethnic and religious conflict. Definition of an ethnic-nationalistic local autonomy problem as one of classroom space would be both reductionist and oblivious to the more remote causes.
- Isolate controlling variables. Three-strikes legislation and similar types of punitive statutes are major determinants of jail overcrowding.
- Brainstorm for alternatives to develop counterintuitive causal links and problem definitions. For example, it might be stated that the problem of jail overcrowding results from the lack of sufficient judicial discretion to define crimes as misdemeanors. This approach suggests that the problem is of a single dimension. Defining a multidimensional problem leads to more innovative solutions, such as hybrid policies that legalize certain drugs, provide treatment, and strengthen enforcement and regulation of drugs.

FORECASTING PROBLEMS: INSTITUTIONAL EFFECTS

To structure and define actionable policy problems, we learned that institutions are very much part of the problem as well as the solution. As noted in chapter 2, the U.S. Department of Justice has its own preferences on the allocation of funds for enforcement instead of treatment of drug abuse, and this powerfully contributes to persistence of the jail overcrowding problem. Whether this is as important to problem causation as existing legislation is a matter for further analysis. Similarly, during the policy design stage, decision-makers could have foreseen and examined the defective accounting and payments systems of the Department of the Interior, which have hindered American Indian trusteeship policy implementation. Institutions clearly matter to problem definition and policy design. Policies are not simply rules consisting of language that can be modified by legislatures or administrative agencies. Policies operate in institutional contexts that must be analyzed. The question is where to start and what to use. How can we narrow the analysis to make such work feasible within the context of calendar deadlines?

Chapter 3 proposed two dimensions of analysis: organizational structure and institutional functions, particularly financial management. There is no "one best way" to perform this analysis, and jurisdictions must improvise and develop their own methods that are then transferred and adopted elsewhere. Textbooks typically offer little help here except to report existing innovative practices by the public sector.

Thus, analysis of policy options should include available data on the performance of existing organizational structures. Specifically, the analyst should review data on the following:

- Are there too many layers of management (using such data as management-to-staff ratios)?
- Is the span of control inappropriate to existing tasks and staff technical capacities (review of task appropriateness and feasible levels of reporting requirements being consistent with task performance)?
- Is the method of service delivery appropriate (comparative staffing ratios for similar services in other jurisdictions; analysis of the relation between service and outcome, such as fire services focusing on prevention versus cure and resultant number of accidents or deaths)?
- Are costs of service delivery by a public department compared with full costs of contractor use?

With these data, the analyst can make a reasonable assessment of the contribution of structural problems to policy problems.

The second level of analysis focuses on institutional functions, particularly administrative and financial management. The analyst should probe repetitive processes, such as licensing, contracting, and permit issuing, which are major tasks of many government agencies. The efficiency and effectiveness of these processes will have an important effect on how legislated policies actually perform. Thus, the analyst can apply workflow processing techniques to inventory the number of required steps and the clearances and time required for each. Elimination of licensing and permit-granting steps can streamline government and increase the productivity of private investments in a particular jurisdiction.

The analyst should also examine how well financial management functions are performed and their relationships to each other. Are budgeting and accounting performed separately? Is procurement or payroll linked to budgeting and cash management? If not, how does this affect the results of particular public policies? Analysts can examine obvious candidates in payroll that are unlinked to budget codes and accounting systems. For example, purchasing commitments or obligations (i.e., purchase orders) are often not recorded; this then affects the ability of the finance department to manage cash effectively. With cash shortfalls, policy implementation will be profoundly affected in many cases. Thus, the capacity to perform each function, as well as enforcement of procedures to ensure that information flows between functions in an integrated system, is critical for detection of potential issues in policy implementation.

In chapter 3, we used the case of Washington, D.C., as an excellent example of dysfunctional organizational structures, administrative practices, and financial management systems. These conditions persisted from the 1970s through the 1990s and affected the capacity of the city to translate policies into viable services and programs. In this period, a rich analytic literature developed that permits us to see many of the subtle institutional issues and to indicate why it is critical to analyze them along with other dimensions of policy problems. Beginning in the late 1990s, Mayor Anthony A. Williams took control and has been applying many of the techniques and tools suggested here to improve the implementation of city programs and services.

Some lessons of the case applications can be drawn:

- For apparent cases of bureaucratic bloat, develop staffing ratios by service and function. This should include costs and revenue per employee and ratios of management to staff members. Wage and nonwage costs per unit of workload should also be examined.
- For the glacial-bureaucracy problem, review legal constraints to reasonable action. For example, if the law requires multiple steps for clearance, recommend analysis of the statute and its potential impact on such variables as opportunities for abuse of power with public resources for a private purpose (e.g., corruption).
- Where fragmented financial management information exists, perform a "transaction analysis" of the most common public-sector processes, such as paying civil servants and contracting for equipment and services. There are often "islands of information" that are unlinked, usually not from stupidity or lack of technical capacity, but often precisely the opposite. Officials perceive opportunities to short-circuit reporting for personal gain. Payroll systems may not be linked to accounting and budgeting, permitting "ghost workers" to

be hired and paid without appearing on the personnel rosters. This is as true in the Third World (e.g., Nepal) as it has been in Washington, D.C. The only difference is that in the latter case, the transactions have been relatively obvious—though not enough to become an "actionable policy problem" for at least a decade.

- Design internal controls with a balance in mind. They should not stifle administrative initiative by requiring second-guessing of every decision by generalist accountants and contracts people. Reporting requirements should not be so severe that goal displacement takes place (e.g., from lack of trust, the process of reporting displaces the focus of the program on service delivery). More resources may be used for reporting transactions to serve auditors and accountants than for service delivery. This is clearly a displacement of institutional purpose that needs to be defined and remedied by new control systems that prevent corrupt practices and abuse of power by requiring periodic reporting on a sample of transactions. This discourages corruption without damaging incentives to deliver services efficiently and effectively. Regular reporting on interfund transfers and payments of funds should continue, but controls should be exercised after the fact to speed processing while discouraging opportunism.

FORECASTING POLICY OPTIONS: REVENUES

Policy analysts also need to know how to forecast future trends of policy problems. Using available trend data, analysts will apply a combination of statistical and common-sense techniques to develop reasonable forecasts for their clients. The purposes of the forecast are not always the same. The analysts may need to forecast the impact of several macropolicy or "high"-policy options in energy. Or, the assignment may be to forecast the effects of new spending programs on an existing base that assumes no changes in policies. Finally, the analyst may have to forecast the exogenous effects of new policies on stakeholders, such as country political risks for new investors.

In chapter 4, we reviewed several approaches to forecasting and indicated the problems with each method. Judgmental forecasting examines hard data trends and uses judgments to assess future patterns. Problems here include the identification of turning points at which trends shift directions and the possibility of within-year data variations. Time-series or trend extrapolation is a common technique that assumes past observed patterns will continue into the future. Since this is a big "if," analysts have to assume that this will happen at least for the short term. The proportionate change method of analyzing time-series data is frequently used to project tax receipts. In our analysis of MARTA forecasts of sales tax receipts, we determined that in some cases, the less elegant method may be the most accurate. Causal or regression analysis is the most sophisticated method and can employ single- or multiequation techniques. Regressions and correlations alone cannot prove causation. Hence, the analyst must revert to judgment to fashion a comprehensive framework of problem causation. Only with a clear picture of causation can forecasts be accurate over time. One can get lucky for a year or two, perhaps with countervailing errors canceling each other out. But over time, the analyst must understand the causation of each variable that affects the problem at hand.

Using the case of MARTA sales tax forecasting, we concluded that the analyst must answer two major questions before presenting a forecast. First, which variables determine sales tax receipts? Answering this question requires testing variables against the dependent variable of sales tax receipts in the past, recognizing that some of the variables are correlated with each other. Similarly, missing income and employment data mean that the analyst has to forecast from incomplete data. This is not uncommon, and often the problem of missing data is quite severe. Second, the analyst needs to know which statistical technique(s) to apply to the data. This often depends on data quantity and quality, that is, whether we have nominal-, ordinal-, or interval-level data.

In the MARTA case, we used different methods to try to approximate the forecasts of the professional forecasters that have produced accurate results for the transit authority in the past. Comparing simple-regression, multiple-regression, and trend analysis techniques, it was concluded that, in this case, the better forecast could be provided by using the less elegant trend analysis (proportionate change) method.

THE ROLE OF PRICING

In chapter 5 we combined the issues of problem definition, institutional performance, and quantitative techniques, which were discussed in the earlier chapters, to analyze the use of pricing as a tool to achieve public policy objectives. Changing prices through taxation, subsidization, and regulation is a key element of many public policies. Both consumers and producers respond to changes in the prices of goods and services purchased or the inputs or factors of production sold. Influencing prices though public policy is, therefore, an effective means of changing behavior. We illustrated the role of prices in several different policy contexts and then through the specific case in chapter 5, using cigarette taxes to reduce smoking, particularly among teenagers. The efficacy of this tool has been noted by both those in the tobacco industry and by antismoking advocates.

Since economics is the primary discipline that focuses on the role of pricing, this chapter drew more heavily on basic economic analysis than did the previous chapters. We reviewed the elements of demand, supply, and price determination. We then discussed the important concept of price elasticity, which is used to measure consumer responsiveness to changes in prices. This was followed by a description of the statistical tools, many of which had already been presented in chapter 4, that are used to provide empirical estimates of different elasticities. Although many readers of this book may not ever undertake such empirical studies, the readers need to be able to interpret the results of these studies and be aware of their strengths and limitations. In the case of cigarette taxes, as with most policy issues, the key task is to separate the influence of one variable, price, from that of all other variables that affect cigarette consumption. Multiple-regression analysis is the major empirical tool used to perform this task. The reader can contrast how this tool is used to estimate the parameters influencing cigarette demand in chapter 5 with its use in forecasting sales tax receipts in chapter 4.

We also noted in chapter 5 that much public policy analysis draws on different disciplines and methodologies. To analyze the role of taxes and pricing on cigarette consumption, analysts rely heavily on the economic theory of consumer behavior and the statistical technique of multiple-regression analysis to estimate cigarette demand functions. Since pricing policies will likely be combined with other approaches to prevent smoking, analysts must also draw on the literature from psychology, public health, and other behavioral sciences that attempts to directly measure the impact of these interventions. The evaluation of these programs often raises questions regarding their impacts on the population and the costs of achieving these outcomes. These are issues in the economic evaluation of public policies, topics in chapters 6 and 7 of this casebook.

COST-EFFECTIVENESS ANALYSIS

In chapter 6 we illustrated an important technique for the economic evaluation of public policies: cost-effectiveness analysis. This is one of several tools, including cost-utility analysis and cost-benefit analysis, that are used to compare the outcomes or impacts of public programs and regulations with the costs of achieving these outcomes. We illustrated the use of cost-effectiveness analysis primarily in the health care sector, given recent developments in the use of economic evaluation techniques in this area and the rapid increase in the number of health care cost-effectiveness studies. The specific case for this chapter was the analysis of the current guidelines from CDC for preventing transmission of HIV from mothers to infants.

We first outlined the major steps that must be undertaken in any cost-effectiveness analysis:

1. Framing the problem and identifying the options to be analyzed.
2. Identifying the appropriate outcome measures.
3. Measuring intervention and outcome costs.
4. Constructing a decision tree to evaluate the alternatives being considered.
5. Gathering the input data needed to analyze the decision tree.
6. Determining the results of the model and performing sensitivity analysis on the key parameters.

We noted how steps 1, 2, and 4 relate directly back to the problem structuring issues which were discussed in chapter 2 of this book. We also described how the timing of program benefits and costs is an important issue in both cost-effectiveness and cost-benefit analysis. The budgetary and implementation aspects of multiyear costs and revenues were discussed previously in chapter 3. There are both similarities and differences in viewing costs from the perspective of accounting and control and from the perspective of economic evaluation.

We also discussed the role of cost-utility analysis in chapter 5. This is an economic evaluation technique that lies between cost-effectiveness and cost-benefit analysis. Cost-utility analysis attempts to provide a weighting to program outcomes, although that weighting is not done in monetary terms as in cost-benefit analysis. Thus, cost-effectiveness analysis would measure a program outcome as the number of life-years saved by a health care intervention, while cost-utility analysis would use the number of quality-adjusted life years. In using cost-benefit analysis, we would try to place a monetary valuation on the number of lives or life-years saved by an intervention.

COST-BENEFIT ANALYSIS

In chapter 7 we focused on the key aspect of cost-benefit analysis that distinguishes it from the other tools for the economic evaluation of public policies. This is the goal of valuing all outcomes of the policy in monetary terms and of deriving society's willingness to pay for those outcomes. The case for this chapter was the updated air quality standards regarding ozone and particulate matter that EPA announced in July 1997.

In this chapter we discussed the alternative approaches for deriving estimates of society's willingness to pay for program outcomes. We paid particular attention to the "value of life" questions or what society is willing to pay to reduce the probability of death by a certain amount. We illustrated the strengths and weaknesses of different approaches to this issue. In analyzing the policy debate over the increased air quality standards, we saw that most of the arguments centered on different estimates of program costs and benefits. These estimates could be influenced by stakeholder positions in the debate, but also by scientific disagreement or uncertainty about program effects and how they should be valued.

DECISIONMAKING

We concluded that economic evaluation is an important dimension of public policy analysis because it forces decisionmakers to logically consider program outcomes and costs and the alternative uses of resources. However, none of the techniques discussed in chapters 5, 6, and 7 are a substitute for the decisionmaking process itself. There are always values and criteria, presented in the earlier chapters, that must be considered in that process and that cannot be adequately incorporated in any quantitative tool.

In this book we demonstrated that policy analysis is a sequence of logical steps in which messy data and conflicting information are used to structure alternatives to complex problems. We restricted our discussion to problem identification and definition methods in the diagnostic phase, and institutional capacity, pricing, and economic evaluation tools in the forecasting phase. It is our view that the analyst who masters many of the techniques learned in these case applications will be capable of monitoring policy performance problems and resolving them during the actual implementation and evaluation phases.

References

Axelrod, Donald. (1995). *Budgeting for Modern Government,* 2d ed. (New York: St. Martin's).

Dunn, William N. (1981). *Public Policy Analysis: An Introduction* (Englewood Cliffs, N.J.: Prentice Hall).

Lehan, Edward. (1984). *Budgetmaking: A Workbook of Public Budgeting Theory and Practice* (New York: St. Martin's).

Posner, Paul, Trina Lewis, and Hannah Laufe. (1998). "Budgeting for Capital," *Public Budgeting and Finance* 18, 13 (Fall), pp. 11–24.

GLOSSARY

Accrual Accounting System: Captures the cost of programs in resources consumed and obligations to pay. To prevent overestimation of revenues, governments often use "modified accrual" systems—cash-based revenues and accrued expenditures.

Associated Cost Approach: An indirect method of estimating the benefits of a program or public policy that focuses on the costs associated with the outcomes of the program. Differences in travel costs could be used to value the benefits of a wilderness recreation area.

Audit: A systematic examination of resource use to determine legality and accuracy of financial transactions and whether financial statements represent the actual financial position and operations of the government entity.

Budget Classification: Breakdown of a budget into mutually exclusive categories for such purposes as control (e.g., objects of expense like salaries and supplies); organizational responsibility (e.g., departments); sectoral planning and allocations (e.g., agriculture, education); activity measurement (e.g., workload in passenger miles of bus service); efficiency measurement (e.g., units costs in operating costs per passenger mile of bus service); and effectiveness (i.e., attainment of policy objectives—percentage of the population with adequate health care coverage or access).

Budget Outlays: Actual payments of budget obligations through checks issued or interest accrued on public debt.

Budgetary Obligations: Commitments made by government through such recorded transactions as orders placed, contracts awarded, or services rendered.

Capital Budgeting: Planning and allocation for durable assets that provide longer-term benefits (e.g., highways, health care, and educational facilities).

Cash-Accounting System: Captures flow of funds into and out of budgetary accounts based on actual receipts and outlays.

Cash Management System: System to prevent running out of cash during the fiscal year, failure to collect bills and deposit receipts, and failure to invest idle funds. Cash management systems rely on timely reporting by the accounting system of expenditures, revenues and cash flow (e.g., daily cash reports, operating balances). Such data enable finance departments to manage cash effectively in order to fund agency programs and policy implementation.

Ceteris Paribus: Latin phrase for "all else held constant"; used when defining the concepts of demand and supply in economic analysis.

Change in Demand: Represents a shift in a demand curve that results from a change in one or more of the factors held constant when defining the demand curve (e.g., income, tastes, and preferences).

Change in Quantity Demanded: Represents a movement along a demand curve for a good or service that results from a change in the price of that good or service.

Complementary Good: A good that is consumed together with another good. Complementary goods have a negative cross-elasticity of demand.

Contingent Valuation Method: A method for evaluating benefits or willingness to pay that asks individuals to reveal their personal valuations of increases or decreases in unpriced goods through surveys or in experimental situations.

Cost-Accounting System: Budgets do not usually reflect the full costs of programs and policies. Among the missing costs by agency are allocated portions of agency overhead, fringe benefits, depreciation of equipment, allocation of personnel time to specific programs and activities, and operating costs of capital assets. Cost-accounting systems attempt to measure not just agency expenditures but actual resources consumed.

Cost-Benefit Analysis: An economic evaluation tool that places a monetary valuation on the outcomes of a program representing society's benefits or willingness to pay for those outcomes. Benefits are then compared with the costs of the program.

Cost Centers: "Buckets" into which an organization's costs are classified and accumulated for purposes of cost analysis. Often, an organization's departments serve as cost centers (e.g., a hospital department of radiology). Cost centers can also be functions, programs, or even objects of expense.

Cost-Effectiveness Analysis: An economic evaluation tool that compares the costs of a program with its outcomes measured in the most appropriate natural effects or physical units (e.g., the number of infections prevented or the number of life-years saved).

Cost-Savings Approach: An approach to estimating the benefits of a program that measures the costs saved as a result of the program. Often used in evaluating transportation, pollution control, and disease control programs.

Cost-to-Charge Ratio: A tool for making adjustments between the economic costs of providing health care services and the amounts of money charged for those services.

Cost-Utility Analysis: An economic evaluation tool that uses a quality-adjusted measure of the outcome of the program (such as a quality-adjusted life year) to compare with the program costs.

Counterfactual: What would have happened if a given event had not occurred; used as a comparison case in economic evaluation.

Cross-Elasticity of Demand: A number that measures the percent change in the quantity of one good relative to the percent change in the price of another good; used to distinguish between substitute and complementary goods.

Demand: An economic concept defined as the relationship between the price of a good and the quantity demanded of that good, all else held constant *(ceteris paribus).*

Discount Rate: An interest rate chosen to calculate the present value of a flow of costs or benefits; used to make comparable a flow of expenditures at different points in time.

Discounted Future Earnings Approach: A method of estimating the benefits of a program that measures the increased stream of future earnings from individuals or land resulting from a public-sector investment project. The flow of earnings is discounted to account for the time pattern of the earnings.

Economic Evaluation: A set of techniques that focus on relating some measure of the output, outcomes, or consequences of a program with the costs of the inputs used to provide those outcomes.

Encumbrance/Obligation Accounting System: Captures cash flow together with commitments of government in the form of salaries, other bills, and purchase orders. This form of accounting prevents overexpenditure and ensures coverage of future commitments.

Equilibrium Price: The price that exists in a competitive market that is determined by the forces of supply and demand.

Ex-Parte Contacts: During the notice-and-comment period of administrative rulemaking, contacts between agency commissioners and interested participants are prohibited apart from the record. If contacts occur, they must be made part of the rulemaking record so that interested parties may comment on them. Failure to place such contacts on record (ex-parte contacts) contaminates the process, and the rule may be challenged as arbitrary and capricious.

Explicit Cost: A cost that is actually paid out to another party and that usually is recorded in an accounting or budgetary system.

Extensive Margin: Applying a screening procedure to a different group of people, such as extending mammography screening from women over 50 years old to women between 40 and 50 or between 30 and 40 years old.

Fixed Cost: A cost that does not increase or decrease with corresponding changes in the amount of service provided (e.g., rent).

Forecast: A single projection chosen from a series of possible projections.

Implicit Cost: A cost that may have to be imputed for economic evaluation since it is not actually paid out to someone. The value of a volunteer's or a patient's time would be an implicit cost.

Income Elasticity of Demand: A number that measures the percent change in quantity demanded of a good relative to the percent change in consumers' income; used to distinguish between normal and inferior goods.

Inferior Good: A good whose quantity demanded decreases as income increases. Inferior goods have a negative income elasticity of demand.

Informal Rulemaking: Development of administrative rules by a process akin to legislative lawmaking until the end of a formal notice-and-comment period.

Integrated Financial Management Systems (IFMS): A single database from which endusers look from different points of view (e.g., budget reports, budget execution analysis, revenue collections, and cash management). The core IFMS typically consists of budgeting and accounting functions. The more advanced or noncore system includes purchasing, payroll, and capital budgeting.

Intensive Margin: Applying a screening procedure to a given group of individuals at different time intervals. Screening for cervical cancer could be done every five years, every three years, or even annually.

Internal Controls: Review of financial sufficiency and legal authority for expenditures primarily by agency auditors and accountants. Reviews by agencies have broadened to include analysis of resource utilization (value for money or performance audits). Internal control systems also subdivide official duties so that no single employee handles a financial transaction from beginning to end.

Iron Triangles: Continuing coalitions of congressional representatives and staff members, executive officials, and interest groups that influence the shape and content of public policies (e.g., agriculture). Iron triangles are considered closed policymaking subsystems.

Issue Networks: Shared-knowledge groups with mutual interests in maximizing influence over particular aspects of public policies (e.g., health policy through U.S. Public Health Service officials, insurance companies, and medical professional organizations). These are temporary, impermanent groups that contribute to policymaking fragmentation in the United States.

Marginal Benefit: The valuation a consumer places on an additional unit of a good or service. The price of a good measures this marginal benefit.

Meta-Analysis: A systematic review of a body of literature on a given subject to determine what conclusions can be drawn from that literature; often used to evaluate different medical or health care interventions.

Normal Good: A good whose quantity demanded increases as income increases. Normal goods have a positive income elasticity of demand.

Notice-and-Comment Period: A formal period established for administrative rulemaking during which notice of proposed rulemaking is published and formal written and oral comments on the proposed rule are invited (e.g., seat belt rules by the National Highway Traffic Safety Administration).

Opportunity Cost: The cost of using society's resources in one activity in terms of the opportunities foregone or the activities not undertaken; includes both explicit and implicit costs.

Pareto-Efficient: A concept for evaluating alternative policies or states of the world. A state of the world is Pareto-efficient if it is not possible to make someone better off without making someone else worse off.

Performance Audit: A type of "value-for-money" audit that consists of three elements: (1) program results review—whether the entity is doing the right thing, (2) economy and efficiency review—whether the entity is doing things right, and (3) the compliance review—whether in doing the right thing in the right way, the entity observes rules imposed on it in the form of laws, regulations, and policies.

Performance Budget: A budget that bases expenditures primarily on measurable performance of activities and workloads.

Planning, Programming, Budgeting System, or PPBS: A budgeting system instituted in the federal government in the 1960s that attempted to identify and examine goals and objectives in each area of government activity, analyze program output in terms of its objectives, measure program costs over several years, and analyze alternatives to find the most effective means of reaching program objectives and at the least cost.

Policy: Common rules, standards, or norms guiding or directing government activities that are promulgated by such rulemaking bodies as parliaments and administrative regulatory agencies.

Potential Compensation Policy: A rule that modifies the Pareto-efficiency concept for evaluating alternative states of the world. A policy improves social welfare if the gainers from the policy could compensate the losers and still be better off or at least no worse off. This rule forms the basis for cost-benefit analysis.

Price Elasticity of Demand: A number that measures the percent change in the quantity demanded of a good relative to the percent change in the price of that good.

Pricing: The use of prices to allocate and ration goods and services; often used as a tool of public policy.

Program: A group of related activities performed by one or more organizational units for the purpose of accomplishing measurable goals and objectives. The measurable goals and activities are often part of a function for which the government is responsible.

Program Budget: A budget that allocates money to the functions or activities of a government rather than to specific objects of expenditure or departments.

Project: A set of microactivities that implement all or part of a program. For example, training and technical assistance projects implement financial management programs.

Projection: A range of forecasts based on extrapolation of data.

Quality-Adjusted Life Year, or QALY: An outcome measurement in cost-utility analysis in which the number of life-years gained by an intervention has been adjusted for factors relating to the quality of those life-years.

Randomized Controlled Trials: A method for evaluating medical procedures in which subjects are randomly assigned to an experimental and a control group to test the efficacy of the procedure. These are usually "double-blind" so that neither the participants nor the evaluators know who is in which group.

Reprogramming of Funds: Shifting funds within appropriations accounts (e.g., supplies to maintenance). Reprogramming agreements between appropriations committees and an agency typically establish thresholds below which the agency can reprogram funds without congressional approval.

Step-Function Cost: A cost that is added in lumps as volume of service increases (e.g., staff salaries, additional faculty members added to cover increased full-time student enrollments).

Substitute Good: A good that can be used instead of another. Substitute goods have a positive cross-elasticity of demand.

Supplemental Appropriations: Additional budget authority provided during the fiscal year by Congress to cover urgent needs for programs and activities.

Supply: An economic concept defined as the relation between the price of a good and the quantity producers are willing to supply, all else held constant *(ceteris paribus)*.

Transfer of Funds: Shifting funds between appropriations accounts requiring congressional approval. In the classic example, President Nixon transferred foreign assistance account funds to the U.S. Defense Department to bomb Cambodia.

Variable Cost: A cost that increases/decreases with increases/decreases in the amount of service provided (e.g., supplies).

Willingness to Pay: The amount of money society will pay for a good or service. Used as a measure of the benefits of a program in a cost-benefit analysis.

Zero-Based Budgeting: An alternative budgeting system that encourages analysis of the incremental inputs and outputs at marginally different levels of expenditure. This was first used in the public sector by the state of Georgia in the early 1970s and later applied to the federal government in 1977.

INDEX

Tables are indicated with *t*

linear model, in demand function estimation, 222–23
linear thinking, in problem definition, 24, 25t, 50–51
Liner, Charles, 164
log-linear model, in demand function estimation, 223–24
Long, David, 313
Loraine, Donna, 128–29n2
Los Alamos National Laboratory, 136
Los Angeles Superior Court, 55
Lusk, Rufus S., III, 115, 116

Maastricht Treaty, euro qualification, 137–38
Maine, cigarette taxes, 226
Mallett, Robert L., 103
management layers, analysis purpose, 15–16, 73–74, 341
mandatory sentencing, relation to prison population characteristics, 49–50, 55–56
marijuana law, enforcement effects, 38
MARTA forecast: data sources, 172–73, 177; modeling assumptions, 174–76, 181–82, 191, 193; overview of economic conditions, 173–74, 176–81; policy importance, 140, 189–91, 205; sales projections, 182–89; tax collection trends, 171–72, 173–74, 190
MARTA forecast, accuracy analysis: averaging method, 195–96, 204, 344; causal modeling, 196–204; technique selection decisions, 194–95; variable/tax receipt relationships, 192–94
Maryland: cigarette taxes, 226, 227; Montgomery County's services, 33, 72–73
Mason, Hilda H.M., 111
Massachusetts, 227, 241
mass transit: analogy approach to problem structuring, 45–46; as ill-structured problem, 36; importance of forecasting accuracy, 140, 152. See also MARTA forecast; MARTA forecast, accuracy analysis
McClendon, Samuel, 116
McRae, Duncan, 306
Medicare program, 80, 95
Mendota Mental Health Institute (MMHI), Weisbrod's study, 264–65, 308, 314, 318
Merryman, Walker, 227, 228
messy problems. See ill-structured problems
meta-analysis approach, 224–25, 241–42, 328
methodologies, problem definition. See structuring techniques

Metropolitan Atlanta Rapid Transit Authority. See MARTA forecast; MARTA forecast, accuracy analysis
Miami, mass transit policy, 46
Milošević, Slobodan, 29–30
Milwaukee, Wisconsin, 32–33, 120
mining policy, 6
mission conflicts, analysis purpose, 77–78
Mobile, Alabama, sales receipts forecasting, 168–69
models, economic, purpose, 250–51
moderately structured problems, characterized, 34–35, 339
modified accrual accounting, 91, 93
Montgomery County, Maryland: institutional reviews, 72–73; recycling problem, 33
Morales, Wanda, 228
morbidity/mortality reduction, valuation: in analysis of air pollution regulations, 326–27; human capital approach, 315–16, 318; statistical definition, 314–15; willingness to pay methods, 316–18
multiple-equation models, causal forecasting: described, 169–70; MARTA forecast, 201–4
Murphy, Kevin (cigarette demand studies), 232, 236, 238

Nachmias, David, 162, 163, 194
Nagel, Stuart, 55
Narcotics Treatment Administration, 59
National Ambient Air Quality Standards (NAAQS), 323
National Bureau of Economic Research, 227
National Health Service (Britain), 35, 269
National Highway Traffic Safety Administration (NHTSA), 10
National Railroad Passenger Corporation (Amtrak), 10–11
National Regulatory Commission (NRC), 306–7
National Weather Service, 138–39
Native American policy. See Indian trusteeship policy
needle exchange programs, 26
Neef, Marian G., 55
Nelson, Ray D., 151
Neuhauser, Duncan, 253, 254
New England Journal of Medicine, 155
New Hampshire, cigarette taxes, 226
New Jersey, cigarette taxes, 226, 239–40
New York, 53, 84, 228, 261
New York City: crime reduction approach, 45; rat problem, 28, 34; Westway project, 307